# China and East Africa

# China and East Africa

## Ancient Ties, Contemporary Flows

Edited by
Chapurukha M. Kusimba, Tiequan Zhu,
and Purity Wakabari Kiura

LEXINGTON BOOKS
*Lanham • Boulder • New York • London*

Published by Lexington Books
An imprint of The Rowman & Littlefield Publishing Group, Inc.
4501 Forbes Boulevard, Suite 200, Lanham, Maryland 20706
www.rowman.com

6 Tinworth Street, London SE11 5AL, United Kingdom

Copyright © 2020 by The Rowman & Littlefield Publishing Group, Inc.

*All rights reserved.* No part of this book may be reproduced in any form or by any electronic or mechanical means, including information storage and retrieval systems, without written permission from the publisher, except by a reviewer who may quote passages in a review.

British Library Cataloguing in Publication Information Available

**Library of Congress Cataloging-in-Publication Data Available**

Library of Congress Control Number: 2019952979
ISBN 978-1-4985-7614-7 (cloth)
ISBN 978-1-4985-7615-4 (electronic)

*We dedicate this book to Ms. Wang Youlin and
Mr. Lu Chung Chun for their commitment to African civilizations
and promotion of the African Studies in East Asia.*

# Contents

List of Figures and Tables ... ix

Preface: China and East Africa: Ancient Ties, Contemporary Flows ... xi
*Chapurukha M. Kusimba*

**PART I: ANCIENT TIES** ... 1

1. The Emergence of Stone Tool Technology: A Comparative Study between Some Early Stone Age Assemblages in East Africa and China ... 3
   *Louis De Weyer*

2. Tracing Prehistoric Trade and Economic Links between the East African Coast and East Asia ... 23
   *Emmanuel K. Ndiema*

3. Ancient Connections between China and East Africa ... 35
   *Chapurukha M. Kusimba*

4. Life, Death, and Identity of the Early Swahili Peoples of the Kenyan Coast ... 65
   *Janet Monge, Allan Morris, Sloan Williams, and Chapurukha M. Kusimba*

5. China, East Africa, and Incipient Globalization in the First Millennium CE ... 79
   *Herman Kiriama*

6. Siyu Intertwined Exchange Networks from the Early Beginnings to the Fifteenth Century ... 89
   *Ibrahim Busolo Namunaba*

| | | |
|---|---|---|
| **7** | Unraveling the Links between the Tanzania's Coast and Ancient China<br>*Elgidius Ichumbaki* | 105 |
| **8** | Chinese Porcelain as Proxy for Understanding Early Globalization between China and Eastern Africa<br>*Tiequan Zhu and Chapurukha M. Kusimba* | 121 |
| **9** | The Sources of East African Chinese Longquan Celadon and Imitation Celadon<br>*Min Wang, Tiequan Zhu, Khalfan Bini Ahmed, and Chapurukha M. Kusimba* | 135 |
| **10** | The Consumption of Glass Beads in Ancient Swahili East Africa<br>*Gilbert Oteyo and Chapurukha M. Kusimba* | 147 |
| **PART II: CONTEMPORARY FLOWS** | | **165** |
| **11** | Six Hundred Years of Harmony: Comparing Zheng He's West Ocean Navigation with China's African Policy<br>*Xinfeng Li* | 167 |
| **12** | Impacts of Chinese Influence in Contemporary East Africa<br>*Angela Kabiru* | 187 |
| **13** | Becoming Mitumba: Transnational Secondhand Clothing Trade between China and Kenya<br>*Boyang Ma* | 215 |
| **14** | The Potentials, Opportunities, and Challenges of Underwater Cultural Heritage for Understanding Early Global Networks<br>*Caesar Bita* | 235 |
| **15** | Opportunities and Challenges of Preserving Cultural Relics in a Globalized World<br>*Zhan Changfa* | 251 |
| **16** | China and East Africa Ancient Ties and Contemporary Flows: A Critical Appraisal<br>*Augustin F. C. Holl* | 259 |
| Index | | 269 |
| About the Editors and Contributors | | 275 |

# List of Figures and Tables

## FIGURES

| | | |
|---|---|---|
| Figure 2.1 | Map of Eastern and Southern Africa Showing All the Sites Mentioned in the Book. | 24 |
| Figure 3.1 | Mrs. Baraka Badi Shee, Her Son Badi Sharif, and Her Grandson Saidi Are the Residents of Siyu Whose DNA Revealed Paternal Ties to East Africa. | 55 |
| Figure 9.1 | Chondrite-Normalized Rare Earth Elements Patterns Spider Diagram Showing Comparison of the African (a), Longquan (b) and Dapu (c) Samples and the $La_N$–$Yb_N$ Scatter-Plot (d) For Various Samples. Chondrite Elemental Values. | 137 |
| Figure 12.1 | How Did a $12 Million Chinese Built Bridge in Kenya Collapse Days after Been Officially Inaugurated? | 197 |

## TABLES

| | | |
|---|---|---|
| Table 3.1 | Renaissance in Asia and Africa during the Tang-Sung Dynasties 618–1279 CE | 40 |
| Table 3.2 | Chronological Context of Long-Distance Trade | 41 |
| Table 3.3 | Commodities Exchanged Between China and East Africa | 44 |
| Table 4.1 | Sex Distribution | 69 |
| Table 4.2 | Distribution by Age. Skeletons Not Aged Were too Fragmentary and/or without Skeletal Elements for Aging | 70 |
| Table 8.1 | Macro Description of Mtwapa Samples | 129 |

| | | |
|---|---|---|
| Table 9.1 | Analytic Results of Manda Samples by EDXRF (wt.%) | 140 |
| Table 10.1 | Kenyan Sites with v-Na-Al Glass Beads | 152 |
| Table 10.2 | Other Sites on the Eastern Coast of Africa and around with M-Na-Al 2 and M-Na-Al 6 Glass Beads | 154 |
| Table 12.1 | The Number of Chinese Tourists Visiting Kenya Has Been Rising Steadily Since 2009 | 193 |
| Table 15.1 | Investment in Antiquities and Monuments by Province in 2016/17 Final Year | 256 |

# Preface

## China and East Africa: Ancient Ties, Contemporary Flows

Chapurukha M. Kusimba

Ancient trade between East Africa and Asia was a complex affair that involved many communities and took several routes (Casson 1990; Mitchell 2005; Pearson 2003). For over two millennia, African commodities have been highly desirable in the world. During the same period, Africans have imported and consumed commodities from the rest of the world. Regular bidirectional consumption of African and Chinese products begun during the Tang period has continued to the contemporary times. From the Tang (616–907) through the Yuan Dynasties (1271–1368), the volume of trade between East Africa and China was lower compared to that from Southwest Asia and South Asia largely due to distance factors. Initially, trade between the two regions was predominantly indirectly through the agency of Muslim and Hindu merchants from Southwest and South Asia. There were two principle routes of trade: first, the overland caravan through Central Asia and Southwest Asia via the Persian Gulf and India Ocean (Hansen 2012; Liu and Luo 2004), and second, a direct maritime route through the South China Sea and Indian Ocean via Sri Lanka along the West Indian Seaboard to East Africa via Aden (Jacq-Hergoualc'h 2002; Miksic 2013).

The destruction of Guangzhou in 878 CE provided an opportunity for expansion and extension of maritime trade (Cho 2009). The growth of settlements like Mantai and Galle in Sri Lanka and Chaul, Khambat, and Gujarat along the west coast of India into major ports of trade illustrates the expansion of maritime trade and the growing economic and political power of Chinese, Hindu, and Muslim merchants. Along with Chinese ceramics and silks reaching Africa were also Indo-Pacific beads, pottery, cloth, jewelry, and foodstuffs (Kusimba 2017, 2018a, 2018b). Chinese artifacts in Syria, India, and East Africa show the reach of these indirect trade routes. These artifacts include whitewares made in Fujian, mainly Ding, qingbai, and molded whitewares, the use of Chinese and Indian coins, and the close similarity of Chinese greenwares.

This book explores Sino–Africa connections in the contexts of globalism and globalization around the following key questions. What do we know about globalism and globalization based on material remains and historical records? How were local communities, such as inland huntergatherers, nomadic pastoralists, and swidden farmers, entangled with regional sociopolitical groups, and trading communities around the world? What power dynamics can be detected and how did these change over time? What were the costs and benefits of participating in globalized social, economic, and political networks? What was the role of ancient chiefly, state, and imperial governments in initiating interregional exchange, integration, and isolation? More broadly, what impacts, if any, did local rivalries and competition have on international trade in the region? Are these detectable and/or even testable in the archaeological record and how do they complement and/or contradict historical records?

Multiple authors in this volume address specific questions such as (a) how and in what ways did political tensions during the Ming Dynasty (1368–1644 CE) affect China's balance and trade with Africa? (b) To what extent did the imperial policy to abolish international engagement affect global trade? and (c) How do we explain the presence of Chinese exports including ceramics, jewelry, and cloth, especially silk, outside China despite the official imperial policy of disengagement with foreign lands?

Archaeologists have documented a sharp decline in the proportion of Chinese ceramics found in shipwrecks and terrestrial sites from that period in Southeast Asia, (Junker 1990, 2008; Niziolek 2011, Niziolek and Junker 2010). In contrast to East Africa, such documentation has yet to be verified. What role did smuggling, black marketeering, and corruption play in redirecting trade between China and the rest of the world? One of our goals of the book is to explore possible avenues through which trade may have continued, especially overland trade between China and West Asia. Does the presence of imperial ceramics in East Africa suggest that diplomatic relationships continued despite the official policy to the contrary? Were there specific ports and kilns in China that were involved in clandestine international maritime trade?

## SIGNIFICANCE OF THE BOOK

Globalization theories and discussions as a research topic gained prominence in economics, business, and international relations in the 1990s (Beynon and Dunkerly 2014; Berger and Huntington 2003; Eriksen 2014; Kusimba 2017;

McLuhan et al 1989; Stiglitz 2003). However, the process of globalization is deeply rooted in history (Chaudhuri 1985; Curtin 1984). Despite not being formally named until the latter part of the twentieth century, globalization is a central concern of anthropology and other disciplines focused on understanding cross-cultural interactions and survival strategies developed through cooperation and competition as well as isolation and integration (Hodos 2017). Research on early forms of globalization and globalism incorporates multiple lines of evidence including archaeology, history, epigraphy, and art. Using the China-Africa connection, we move away from paradigms that have traditionally privileged Western perspectives, unintentionally creating an "East" versus "West" dichotomy (e.g., Ferguson 2011) and excluding Africa (e.g., Abu-Lughod 1989; Millward 2012) from the conversation. Economists, historians, and cultural anthropologists have tackled the modern manifestation of globalism (e.g., Acemoglu and Johnson 2012; Berger and Huntington 2003; Ferguson 2011). But as globalism and globalization can now be detected in the archaeological record (Hodos 2017), it presses a broader conversation about the relationship between these early interaction spheres and later connections assumed to be driven by European capitalist expansion (O'Rourke and Williams 2012). This volume contributes new knowledge about the vastness of early global connections and African actors involvement in these interactions.

This book engages globalization from an archaeological and long-term perspectives and deals with pressing issues facing the modern world. Will greater connectivity that has emerged from globalization lead to homogenization of culture, or the creation of a monoculture (Marsella, 2005)? What are the benefits and weaknesses of globalization with respect to environmental sustainability and social inequality (e.g., Diaz, Schneider, and Mantal 2012; Nieuwenhuys 2006)? What challenges does globalization pose to Western ideologies of power and prestige (Wallerstein 1976, Wallerstein 2004)? Is the new globalization and re-emergence of the East a new form of globalization? How different is it from a previous one? (Abu-Lughod 1989; Chaudhuri 1985; Frank 1998 Maalouf 2009; Ray and Salles 2012; Wong 1997).

Globalization connected the world and contributed to its current complexity. As such its careful study must integrate the disciplines—from biological, earth, and social sciences to the humanities. Integrated research that employs complementary approaches leads to more successful and richer perspectives for making sense of the complexities of early globalisms. The multiscalar, interdisciplinary approach taken by the contributors lead to better and much richer understanding of broad significance by early globalism anticipated modern globalization.

The contributions in this book were originally presented at an international conference that brought Chinese and Kenyan scholars for the first time to discuss and place in context the nearly 1,400 year history of relationship between China and East Africa. Although the conference was broadly conceived, participants were tasked to speak to the nature, scale, and impact of both preindustrial and contemporary relationships. Where applicable, participants were asked to discuss archaeological and historical evidence that illustrated the long-term connections, contributions, and consequences of Chinese and African relationship and deep history. The conference provided an opportunity for African-based scholars to share and exchange ideas on building long-term collaborative programs in research, conservation, and exhibition with their Chinese colleagues. All the chapters are based on original research by academics, conservators, museum experts, and students from several institutions and organizations from the Republic of Kenya the People's Republic of China, and the United States.

Archaeological evidence of stone tool making from the end of the Pliocene to the beginning of the Pleistocene has exponentially increased. Early stone tool technologies appear in East Africa between 3.3 and 2.6 million years ago (Harmand et al. 2015). This phenomenon also spread later in Eastern Asia, especially in China from 2.2 million years ago until 1 million years ago (e.g., Schick and Zhuan 1993; Yamei et al. 2000). The data base on early hominin regional behaviors is credible enough for comparative analyses on the inner variability of African and Asian Early Stone Age assemblages. In chapter 1, Louis De Weyer presents several clues about the stone tool-making appearance, discusses the geographical constraints, environment, and behavioral or technical traditions that may explain the differences between those two major rising regions for hominin evolution. His discussion on stone tool technological addresses the environmental constraints versus cultural choices, which are often used as a proxy for understanding human mobility/territory interactions. He compares the stone tool technologies employed at lower Paleolithic sites of Fejej (Ethiopia), Koobi Fora (Kenya), and Olduvai (Tanzania) assemblages in East Africa and Longgupo (Chongqing), Majuanggou and Donggutuo (Nihewan Basin) assemblages in China to address questions around hominid behavior, procurement strategies, flaking and shaping techniques, and links between toolkit and raw material, and knappers' choices.

In chapter 2, Emmanuel Ndiema explores the potential of local archaeologies and histories for serving as models for understanding larger transregional networks between the East African coastal and hinterland communities. He reviews published data and contextualizes the impact of millennial old trade and the economic, relationships between East Africa and Southwest Asia and concludes that trade along the East African coast was intimately integrated with inland communities and served to stimulate extra regional trade with during the early globalized world. In chapter 3 Janet Monge, Allan Morris, Sloan Williams, and Chapurukha M. Kusimba provide the first comprehensive report on biological and cultural identities of early Swahili peoples based on a series of over one hundred human skeletons excavated from the sites of Manda Island and Mtwapa on the Kenya Coast. The sample constitutes the largest collection of systematically excavated human remains of the Swahili peoples. This skeletal series samples both sexes equally and range in age from ten to eighteen months to extreme old age (fifty plus). Although all the skeletons were interred in a traditional Islamic pattern and thus show near identical mortuary context, analysis of the bones themselves reveals a very complex individual biological life history. Metric and nonmetric traits indicate a very heterogeneous skeletal sampling from these sites with affinities to hinterland neighbors, Middle Eastern and East Asian populations. This result is supported by preliminary genetic evidence. Thus, a very complex population structure has begun to emerge of the inhabitants of the Swahili Coast. A comprehensive analysis of the dentition reveals cultural patterns of dental modification reinforcing identity. In addition, dental wear, calculus formation, the pattern of caries, and periodontal disease indicate both age and sex-related differences in diet and masticatory and para-masticatory function. Finally, the distribution and extent of skeletal trauma, including healed and peri-mortem bone fractures, shows a pattern of the hazards of everyday life among the early Swahili urban residents.

Trade between China and East Africa started in a limited period during the Tang Dynasty (616–907 CE) but increased considerably during the subsequent Song period (960–1279 CE). Large quantities of Chinese ceramics and other items from this period are found on the Kenyan coast especially in the areas between Lamu and Mombasa. During the Ming dynasty (1368–1644 CE) direct contacts were initiated for the first time between China and Kenya. In 1418, a Chinese fleet commanded by a Muslim Chinese Admiral Zheng He reached the East African coast followed by subsequent visits in 1421–1422 CE and 1431–1433 CE. It is during these travels that commercial and diplomatic contacts were established. In chapter 5, Herman Kiriama reviews the integration of East Africa into the globalized ancient world began during the Tang Dynasty.

In chapter 6, Ibrahim Busolo examines the factors that influenced the settlement and growth of the Swahili city state of Siyu. He employs a variety of approaches including site survey, excavation, and analysis of excavated materials to understand and reconstruct the evolution of Siyu city-state. The evidence recovered shows that Siyu first served as seasonal camp for hunters, fishermen, and mangrove cutters subsistence and economic activities. The town was accessible by a navigable creek to its neighbors across Pate island, the immediate hinterland, and other communities beyond. His analysis of the materials leads him to conclude that like other urban centers, Siyu was not completely self-sufficient and it's political economy, relied upon strong exchange networks of with neighboring urban and rural regions and across the Indian Ocean.

In chapter 7, Elgidius Ichumbaki presents further archaeological evidence showing the linkages between East Asia and Tanzania. He engages the copious artifacts from East Asia that have been excavated at Tanzania sites to offer critical insights into the growth of African communities and fluctuations in Africa-Indian Ocean networks. Items from China and broader Eastern Asia appear among the finds from the middle AD second millennium. He further engages the implications of these finds for developing a more complete and nuanced understanding of East Africa, its communities, and Africa-China relations from antiquity to the present. In chapters 8 and 9, Tiequan Zhu, Chapurukha M. Kusimba, Min Wang, and Khalfan Bini employ a variety of analytical methods of archaeological classification, micro X-ray fluorescence spectroscopy, and optical microscopy in the analysis of Chinese porcelain samples from Manda (ca. 600–1600 CE) Mtwapa (1000–1750 CE) to determine the provenance of the porcelain. Their analysis reveal that trade ceramics consumed at Manda and Mtwapa and other settlements in East Africa originated from multiple and diverse kiln complexes in China, including in Jingdezhen, Zhejiang, Guangdong, and Changsha. These serve as a proxy for evaluating the nature, organization, and scale of export trade between China and Africa from the late Tang to early Qing Dynasties. In chapter 10, Gilbert Oteyo and Chapurukha M. Kusimba, and discuss the distribution, consumption, and significance of glass beads in understanding African-Asian connections.

Turning to contemporary flows, Li Xinfeng of the Chinese Academy of Social Sciences provides an official vision of scientific collaboration in chapter 11. His chapter emphasizes equal partnership but depoliticizes the context of these relationships and global inequalities. It is included here as evidence of the Chinese point of view. It contrasts with the following chapter 12 in which Angela Kabiru explores the impacts of Chinese influence in Kenya. She evaluates the nature of Kenya's collaboration with China, impacts of this relationship, and Kenyans' perception of the Chinese. She discusses the major investments, in particular, infrastructural projects that have been made in Africa using loans acquired from China. The relationship between Africa and China is neocolonial. China has a huge appetite for African raw materials, markets, and consumers. This leads to an uncomfortable question: Given the enduring nature of these inequities, and the emerging Asian and entrenched Western interests competing over African resources and markets through development and aid, how should African societies and their leaders neutralize these empires of extraction, whether Western or Eastern, in both ongoing and future interactions? Will the current perception that China is only interested in enriching itself at the expense of its African partners, slow down south-south economic and political integration? What can be done to circumvent the inevitable recolonization of Africa?

The used clothing economy has flourished in sub-Saharan Africa countries since the early twentieth century and for many epitomizes the global north and global south relationships. However, in chapter 13 Boyanga Ma shows that Chinese used clothing industry not only joined but is taking over the task of clothing Africans. The market share of Chinese used clothing accounted for 66 percent used clothing exports to Africa in 2015. Through careful ethnographic research, he shows how Chinese merchants have built up the transnational supply chain of used garments in African countries, the interaction between Chinese wholesalers and local communities. He concludes by cautioning that the narratives arising from this transnational network will offer us new perspectives to examine the increasing China's influence in Africa.

Caesar Bita picks up the question of ongoing collaborations between China and Kenya with a discussion on the potential opportunities that joint underwater archaeological investigations might bring in chapter 14. Arguing that millennial maritime interactions have left tangible heritage in the form of shipwrecks, structures, cannons, and anchors and intangible ones such as religious practices, traditional boat building styles, and food ways. Through exploration of the maritime cultural heritage of the East African coast, he addresses the opportunities and challenges of managing and proposes development of a maritime museum, underwater archaeology and underwater cultural heritage training institute that will serve the entire region and East and Central Africa. Finally, in chapter 15, Zhan Changfa uses specific examples of conservation and preservation that he has been engaged in to discuss the opportunities and challenges of preserving cultural relics in a globalized world.

This book will play a crucial role in resetting the lens not only on globalization before capitalism but also on another world system, that of the Indian Ocean. Long-distance trade, industrialization, and mass consumption have their roots in early interactions that arose in Asia beginning from the Tang Dynasty. Famously referred to as the Silk Road trade, interregional trade connected all of Asia, Europe, and Africa into a web of interactions that shaped early globalism. This book discusses the impact of these early, noncapitalist globalizations on the current moment of globalization. It also examines the relationship between Asian globalization and contemporary economic relationships and flows. China's growing influence in Africa today has reignited a debate on the history of these relationships in the premodern Indian Ocean. The contradictions between official institutional view setting forth the hope that China-Africa interactions are mutually beneficial as articulated by Li Xinfeng and on ground realities discussed by Kabiru and Ma underscore the contrasts in the approaches among the volumes contributors and foreshadow the perils that may emerge from these collaborations. Augustin Holl's appraisal of the book in the final chapter 16 contextualizes this ongoing debate in the academy and in the public arena.

# REFERENCES

Abu-Lughod, J.L, 1989. *Before European Hegemony. The World System AD 1250–1350*. Oxford: Oxford University Press.

Abu-Lughod, J.L. 2008. The World Systems in the Thirteenth Century: Dead-end or Precursor?' *In* S. Khagram and P. Levitt (ed.), *The Transnational Studies Reader*, pp. 184–195. New York: Routledge.

Acemoglu, D and J.A. Robinson. 2013. *Why Nations Fail: The Origins of Power, Prosperity, And Poverty*. New York: Crown Business

Berger, P.L and S.P. Huntington. Editors. 2003. *Many Globalizations: Cultural Diversity in the Contemporary World*. Oxford: Oxford University Press.

Beynon, J and D. Dunkerley. 2002. *Globalization: The Reader*. New York: Routledge.

Chaudhuri, K.N. 1985. T*rade and Civilisation in the Indian Ocean: An Economic History From the Rise of Islam to 1750*. Cambridge: Cambridge University Press.

Curtin, P. D. 1984. *Cross-cultural Trade in World History*. Cambridge: Cambridge University Press.

Deng, G. 1997. "Chinese Maritime Activities and Socioeconomic Development, c. 2100 B.C.-1900 A.D." Vol. 188. Contributions in Economics and Economic History. Westport, CT: Greenwood Press.

Diaz, J., R. Schneider, and P. S. Mantal. 2012. "Globalization as Re-traumatization: Rebuilding Haiti from the Spirit Up." *Journal of Social Issues* 68:493–513.

Eriksen, T.H. 2014. *Globalization: The Key Concepts*. London: Bloomsbury.

Ferguson, N. 2011. *Civilization: The West and the Rest*. New York: Penguin Press.

Frank, A. G. 1998. *Re-Orient: Global Economy in the Asian Age*. Berkeley: University of California Press.

Harmand, S., Lewis, J. E., Feibel, C. S., Lepre, C. J., Boës, X., Prat, S., *et al.* (*2015*). "3.3 Million-Year-Old Stone Tools from Lomekwi 3, West Turkana, Kenya." *Nature*, 521, 310–316.

Hansen, V. 2012. *The Silk Road: A New History*. Oxford: Oxford University Press.

Hodos, T. Editor. 2017. *The Routledge Handbook of Archaeology and Globalization*. New York: Routledge.

Jacq-Hergoualc'h, M. 2002. *The Malay Peninsular: Crossroads of the Maritime Silk Road (100BC-1300AD*. Boston: Brill.

Junker, L. L. 1999. *Raiding, Trading, and Feasting: The Political Economy of Philippine Chiefdoms*. Honolulu, HI: University of Hawaii Press.

Junker, L. L.. 2008. "The Impact of Captured Women on Cultural Transmission in Contact-Period Philippine Slave-Raiding Chiefdoms," in *Invisible Citizens: Captives and Their Consequences, Foundations of Archaeological Inquiry*. Edited by C. M. Cameron. Salt Lake City, UT: The University of Utah Press.

Kusimba, C.M., 2017. "The Swahili and Globalization in the Indian Ocean." pp.104–122. In Tamar Hodos (ed.) *The Routledge Handbook of Archaeology and Globalization*. London: Routledge Handbooks.

Kusimba, C.M. 2018a. "(Re) Introducing the State on the Medieval Swahili Coast." In John L. Brook, J.C Strauss, and G. Anderson (eds.), *State Formations: Global Histories and Cultures of Statehood,* pp 90–107. Cambridge: Cambridge University Press.

Kusimba, C. M. 2018b. "Trade and Civilization in Medieval East Africa: Socioeconomic Networks." In K. Kristiansen, T. Lindkvist, and J. Myrdal (eds.), *Ancient Trade and Civilization*, pp 320–353. Cambridge: Cambridge University Press.
Liu, Y. and H. Luo 2004. "Impact of Globalization on International Trade between ASEAN-5 and China: Opportunities and Challenges." *Global Economy Journal* 4(1):6–6
Maalouf, A., 2012. *Samarkand*. London: Hachette UK.
Marsella, A. J. 2005. "Hegemonic" Globalization and Cultural Diversity: The Risks of Global Monoculturalism." *Australian Mosaic* 12:15–22.
McLuhan, Marshall and Bruce R. Powers. 1989. *The Global Village: Transformations in World Life and Media in the 21st Century*. Oxford: Oxford University Press.
Miksic, J.N. 2013. *Singapore and the Silk Road of the Sea, 1300–1800*. Singapore: National University of Singapore Press.
Millward, J.A. 2012. *The Silk Road: A Very Short Introduction*. Oxford: Oxford University Press.
Morris, Ian. 2010. *Why the West Rules for Now: The Patterns of History and what they Reveal about the Future*. New York: Farar. Strauss and Giroux
Nieuwenhuys, E. C. 2006. *Neo-liberal Globalism and Social Sustainable Globalisation*. Boston: Brill Academic Publishers.
Niziolek, L. C. 2011. Ceramic Production and Craft Specialization in the Prehispanic Philippines, A.D. 500 to 1600. Doctoral, University of Illinois at Chicago.
Niziolek, L. C., and L. L. Junker. 2010. "Food Preparation and Feasting in the Household and Political Economy of Prehispanic Philippine Chiefdoms," in *Inside Ancient Kitchens: New Directions in the Study of Daily Meals and Feasts*. Edited by E. Klarich, pp. 17–53. Boulder: University Press of Colorado.
Ray, H. P., and J.-F. Salles. Editors. 2012. *Tradition and Archaeology: Early Maritime Contacts in the Indian Ocean*. New Delhi: Manohar.
Schick, K.D and D. Zhuan. 1993. "Early paleolithic of China and eastern Asia." *Evolutionary Anthropology* 2(1):22–35.
Stearns, P. N. 2010. *Globalization in World History. Themes in World History*. London: Routledge.
Stiglitz, J. 2003. *Globalization and Its Discontents*. New York: WW Norton and Company.
Wallerstein, I. 1976. "A World-System Perspective on the Social Sciences." *The British Journal of Sociology* 27:343–352.
Wallerstein, I. 2004. *World-Systems Analysis: An Introduction*. Durham: Duke University Press.
Wong, R. B. 1997. *China Transformed: Historical Change and the Limits of European Experience*. Ithaca: Cornell University Press.
Yamei, H., R. Potts, Y. Baoyin, G. Zhengtang, A. Deino, W. Wei, J. Clark, X. Guangmao, H. Weiwen. 2000. "Mid-Pleistocene Acheulean-like Stone Technology of the Bose Basin, South China." *Science* 287:1622–1626.

*Part I*

# ANCIENT TIES

*Chapter 1*

# The Emergence of Stone Tool Technology

## *A Comparative Study between Some Early Stone Age Assemblages in East Africa and China*

Louis De Weyer

### INTRODUCTION

The development of the human lineage is undeniably traced to the African continent. All current data of the evolutionary branch of hominids are in Africa, from Sahelanthropus, Orrorin, Ardipithecus, Australopithecus, Kenyanthopus, Paranthropus to Homo. Ancient fossils found outside Africa are rare during the Lower Pleistocene.[1] The oldest are dated around 1.9–1.8 million years ago, MYA, and attributed to *Homo ergaster* or *erectus*. In Dmanisi (Georgia) in the Caucasus, five fossil skulls dating back to 1.8 million years, have been discovered and represent the largest number of individuals found at the same archaeological level. Originally named *Homo georgicus* (Lumley and Lordkipanidze 2006), the authors initially considered these fossils to be "descendants of early African Homo" (Lumley and Lordkipanidze 2006, 8), that is to say of a *Homo habilis* or *rudolfensis* at an evolutionary stage close to that of *H. ergaster*. Other authors prefer, instead, on the basis of anatomical and dimensional characters, to use the name *Homo erectus* (Rightmire et al. 2006). The analysis of a new complete skull made it possible to go in the direction of the second hypothesis, and the fossils of Dmanisi are today integrated at the initial stage of the *H. erectus* branch, denominated *H. erectus ergaster georgicus* (Lordkipanidze et al. 2013).

On the Asian side, data before 1.5 million years are rare but exist, nonetheless. Hominid remains have been identified in Longgupo, dated to more than 2 million years. However, the bones are limited to mandibula fragments and their interpretation is much debated. Some authors attribute the fossils to a *Homo taxon* (Huang et al. 1995), while others prefer to consider it as a great ape (Ciochon 2009; Schwartz and Tattersall 1996; Wu 2000). Without any fossil record as old to compare in the region, the question cannot be solved by paleoanthropology. It is interesting to notice that these fossils are associated with a significant lithic material. More recent fossils have been found in Indonesia, at 1.9 million years at Mojokerto (Anton 1997; Huffman et al. 2005) and 1.6 Ma at Sangiran (Sartano 1961, 1982; Swisher et al. 1994) attributed to *H. erectus* sensu lato. Yuanmou site in Yunnan, Southern China, two incisors attributed to *Homo* sp. were discovered and dated around 1.7 million years (Qian and Zhou 1991; Worm 1997; Zhu et al. 2003).

However, older indirect evidence of the presence of hominines exists in China. The ancient deposits of Majuangou III in the Nihewan Basin in Northern China (Wei 1994; Xie et al. 2006; Zhu et al. 2004) dated around 1.7 million years are regularly cited as representing the oldest continental Asian sites. Several sites also compose an Early Stone Age record in the Nihewan Basin, with especially Xiaochangliang, at 14 million years (Zhu et al. 2001; Li et al. 2008; Ao et al. 2011), and Donggutuo at 11 million years (Singer et al. 1999; Hilgen et al. 2012). But two very old sites, well dated and rich in archaeological material, are also known.

A large collection of lithic artifacts associated with well-preserved fauna has been discovered in Renzidong sinkhole (Jin et al. 2000; Gao et al. 2005). The site was recently dated between 2.4 and 2 million years (Jin and Liu 2009; Wang et al. 2012). The stratigraphic unit CIII of Longgupo site, where the fossil remains presented above have been discovered, has yielded a fauna, and a consequent lithic industry (Boëda and Hou 2011). The dating has also been done very recently and confirms a very ancient age, between 2.5 and 2.2 million years (Han et al. 2017). Those assemblages are debated though, as no hominin remain was associated with the lithics so far. Although these sites have been known for a long time, summaries about the peopling of Eurasia hardly ever refer to them.

The oldest current data are therefore not paleoanthropological but lithic. This is also the case for the majority of information in Eurasia for the Lower Pleistocene, since very few hominin remains have been found in comparison with the archaeological sites discovered. The question of the first dispersal out of Africa remains open, and it is likely that a hominin older than *H. ergaster* or *H. erectus* may be discovered in Eastern Asia. The question of the first hominin incursion out of Africa is not an archaeological problem in itself. The dates are destined to go back in time as discoveries come up. The recent publication of the Lomekwi 3 site, dated at 3.39 million years (Harmand et al. 2015), shows that the history of techniques is much longer than we perceive at present.

## LITHIC ASSEMBLAGES

Apart from Lomekwi 3 at 3.39 million years, considered by the authors by preceding the Oldowan and named lomekwian (Harmand et al. 2015; Hovers 2015), the earliest evidence of the technical phenomenon appears at Gona, northern Ethiopia at 2.6 million years (Semaw 2000).

From 2.6 until 2.2 million years, early evidences of stone tool production appear in several geological formations of northern Ethiopia and the border between southern Ethiopia and Northern Kenya.

In the north, Gona EG-10 and EG-12 delivered an early evidence of stone tool production, at 2.6 Ma (Semaw 2000). The localities A.L. 666 and A.L. 894, Hadar Formation, Afar Depression, also delivered stone artifact at 2.5 million years (Roche et Tiercelin 1980; Hovers et al. 2002). In the Hata Member of the Bouri Formation, in the Middle Awash Valley, dated at 2.5 million years, bones with cut marks were found, but no stone tools (Asfaw et al. 1999; de Heinzelin et al. 1999).

The Turkana Basin, at the border of Ethiopia and Kenya, also provided numerous occurrences. In the lower Omo Valley, the Members E and F of the Shungura Formation provided several localities dated around 2.3 Ma where stone tools were found (Chavaillon 1976; Delagnes et al. 2011). In the Lokalelei Member of the Nachukui Formation, in West Turkana, northern Kenya, three sites provided stone artifacts, at Lokalalei 1 1α and 2C, dated at 2.34 Ma (Roche et al. 1999; Delagnes et Roche 2005).

Fejej Fj-1, in southern Ethiopia (de Lumley et Beyene 2004), dated around 1,9 Ma (Chapon et al. 2011) delivered a numerous quartz assemblage. The KBS Member of the Koobi Fora Formation, East Turkana, northern Kenya, provided numerous sites (Isaac 1997), as well as KS-1 to 3, Kanjera South Formation, in southwestern Kenya (Plummer et al. 1999; Braun et al. 2008, 2009). Several sites from the Bed I of Olduvai Gorge in Tanzania (Leakey 1971; Mora and de la Torre 2005) are also emblematic from this period. Oldowan evidences are also documented in Gauteng, South Africa, at Swartkrans (Kuman 2007; Kuman and Field 2009) and Sterkfontein around 2.2–2 million years (Clarke 1994; Kuman and Clarke 2000).

In Northern Africa the site complex of Ain Hanech (Setif region, Algeria) delivered three Oldowan sites dated at 1.8 million years: Ain Hanech, Ain Boucherit, and El Kherba (Sahnouni et al. 1997; Sahnouni et al. 2002). The site of Ounjougou in Mali is the only Oldowan site known in stratigraphy. An Oldowan-like industry has been discovered in the lower levels, very similar to Ain Hanech and Olduvai Bed II assemblages (De Weyer 2017). Unfortunately, it is impossible to date the sediments older than 150 ka (Tribolo et al. 2015), so the age of this assemblage is unknown.

Outside of Africa, the evidence is divided between Western Europe and Eastern Asia, with only one site in between. In Caucasus, Dmanisi, Georgia, dated at 1.81 million years, delivered an important lithic assemblage associated with five individuals of *H. erectus ergaster georgicus* (de Lumley et al. 2005; Mgeladze et al. 2011; Lordkipanidze et al. 2013). In Western Europe, the earliest evidence for lithic industries are dated at 1.4 Ma in Pirro Nord, southern Italy (Arzarello et al. 2009, 2016), and between 1.4 and 1.2 Ma in Barranco León and Fuente Nueva 3, Orce, southern Spain (Toro et al. 2003, 2010).

The earliest lithic assemblages in Eastern Asia are all located in China. They were discovered in three areas: the Yangtze River Beds in Chongqing region, the sinkhole of Renzidong in Anhui province, Central China, and the Nihewan Basin in Northern China, West of Beijing. Longgupo and Renzidong are the earliest evidence of hominin activities outside Africa to date, at around 2.2 million years (Huang et al. 2015; Gao et al. 2005). The Nihewan Basin is a very rich area for Lower Pleistocene deposits, and several key sites were discovered for the Mode 1. Majuangou III at 1.7 million years, Xiaochangliang at 1.4 million years and Donggutuo at 1.1 million years are the most representative examples, with large assemblages to study.

The Oldowan/Mode 1 technical complex is not homogeneous. An important variability is hidden under this name, and several hypotheses were proposed to explain this diversity. In this chapter, we will provide an overview of the different hypotheses and compare the African Oldowan with the Mode 1 in China to highlight the technical universals and local specificities involved in the history of techniques.

## OLDOWAN/MODE 1 STONE TOOL TECHNOLOGY

The Early Stone Age industries are composed of "low-elaborated" flakes and artifacts such as pebbles or blocks made by one-sided or two-sided removals that produce a continuous cutting edge (typically called choppers and chopping-tools), as well as polyhedrons, subspheroids, and spheroids. This set refers to the assemblages prior to the appearance of the bifaces and cleavers, tools that characterize the Acheulean. Nevertheless, this type of industry continues during the following periods, associated with the new tools.

Flake production is said to be "undeveloped" or "low-elaborated" because it has simple characteristics in terms of knowledge and know-how (Pelegrin 1991), is not standardized, and is almost always made from the raw material available locally, whatever its quality for knapping. Nevertheless, this type of debitage involves an understanding of the principles of hard rock fracturing, which involve the mass of the hammerstone and the percussion angle necessary for the production of a conchoidal fracture.

The cores are pebbles or blocks of raw material, which are knapped on one or more faces in short series of flakes. The most common knapping technique is freehand hammer percussion. The use of bipolar percussion on anvil is attested in many deposits, often used to cut pebbles of small dimensions, or presenting specific reactions to size, such as quartz, for example. (de Lumley and Beyene 2004; Mgeladze et al. 2011; de la Torre et al. 2004).

## HYPOTHESES CONCERNING THE VARIABILITY

Mary Leakey (1971) proposed a chronological division based on Beds I and II of the Olduvai sequence: the classical Oldowan dated between 1.85 and 1.65 million years, composed of cobbles, flakes, and hammering and grinding tools; the Developed Oldowan A (DOA), which sees an increase in the intensity of flake debitage and the proportion of spheroids, dated between 1.65 and 1.53 million years; the Developed Oldowan B (DOB), between 1.53 and 1.2 million years, with a regression of the number flakes per core, and especially the appearance of shaped tools, as well as the proportion of spheroids that remains important.

Glynn Isaac (1976) considered both Oldowan and Developed Oldowan as a single entity called Oldowan Industrial Complex. Some authors also argue that Developed Oldowan sites should be included as part of the Early Acheulian (de la Torre et al. 2005). Braun and Harris (2003, 2009) highlighted a variability depending on the occupation context of several sites of KBS and Okote Member of Koobi Fora. Other researchers have also proposed to group the sites older than 1.9 million under the term Pre-Oldowan, by pointing out the smaller number of sites and the less-diversified nature of the tools, notably the absence of large percussion tools (Roche 1996, 1999; Lumley and Beyene 2004; Lumley et al. 2009).

The analysis of Lokalalei 2C sites in West Turkana, Kenya, dated at 2.34 million years (Delagnes and Roche 2005) and Kanjera South, near Lake Victoria, Kenya, between 2.3 and 1.9 million years (Braun et al. 2008, 2009; Plummer and Bishop 2016) has shown that a significant level of technical knowledge is present even in the oldest sites, and today, we speak more generally of Oldowan technocomplex, as proposed by Isaac (1976).

## COGNITIVE ABILITIES AND TECHNICAL SKILLS

The variability of the industries is the result of many factors, the most frequently cited of which are the site occupation context and the availability and quality of raw material resources near archaeological sites. Studying the Koobi Fora KBS industry (1.8–1.65 million years), authors have proposed the "Least effort strategy" model (Toth 1982, 1985, 1987; Schick 1994), with reference to raw material savings (use of local raw material, whatever its quality) and debitage ("opportunistic" debitage with the sole search for a cutting edge, without control of the debitage). The theory of the least effort strategy is based on the idea that Mode 1 technologies cannot be regarded as traditions comprising a set of defined rules and tool design, since they consist only of applying simple principles of percussion. (Schick 1994).

Some authors contest this interpretation (Reti 2016; De Weyer 2016). Joseph Reti (2016) proposed an experimental study of this hypothesis by studying the DK site at Olduvai Gorge. Taking the least effort strategy as a null hypothesis, he found that the results obtained by experimentation did not correspond to the reduction strategies observed on the DK site. His study shows a planning of the debitage from the stage of selection of the blocks of raw materials, and a management of the nucleus during the phase of reduction.

Hominin techno-economic behaviors have also been studied in West Turkana, particularly at the Lokalelei 2C site (Harmand 2005, 2009). Lokalelei 2C is dated at about 2.34 million years. The raw material used is a phonolite of good quality for knapping, found in the form of pebbles at about 50 m from the site with other raw materials of lower quality, as rhyolite, for example. On some phonolite pebbles, more than fifty flakes per core have sometimes been knapped. The authors conclude that hominines of Lokalelei 2C were probable awareness of the different knapping qualities of the rocks and predominantly utilized phonolite to produce their tools (Delagnes and Roche 2005; Harmand 2009).

The question of raw material availability is presented as the main factor in the variability of the Oldowan assemblages. On most sites, the selected raw materials are local, and sometimes of poor quality. However, several authors have demonstrated a selection of the best raw materials available in the surrounding space, such as in Hadar (Hovers 2012). In Kanjera South, the groups brought back a substantial portion of the raw materials of more than 10 km (Braun et al. 2008, 2009). Some of the quartz materials used on Olduvai Gorge DK site also come from at least 8 km (Blumenschine et al. 2003). In order to understand and describe how raw material quality influences tool production, De Weyer (2016) compared production systems and tools produced at three sites with different raw material choices. Fejej, with an assemblage composed almost exclusively of quartz, Koobi Fora with a use of the local basalt, and DK, composed of quartzite and basalt, and also some pieces in quartz.

At Koobi Fora, knapping methods are said to be single-flake oriented, with the research of a suitable angle to produce flakes, without predetermination of large series of flakes. The cores are quickly exhausted as the angles disappear.

At Fejej, the selection of pebbles with a large flat surface makes it possible to produce series of flakes on the same core, and long continuous series are observed from the natural striking platform created by the plane surface. At Olduvai, the methods change according to the raw material worked. Quartzite pebbles are produced using the same recurrence methods as in Fejej, while flake-by-flake strategy is used on basalt pebbles.

From this work, the variability observed within the Oldowan Industrial Complex appears more complex, and not only the fact of geographical constraints. We may conclude that hominin groups were able to adapt to their environment for raw material procurement, and that they performed a strong selection based on their knowledge and specific choices that may be different from one site to another. Then, lithic assemblages may be considered as significant cultural traits, or at least witness different technical traditions (De Weyer 2016). This diversity should also be investigated in Chinese Early Stone Age assemblages. Indeed, many Lower Pleistocene sites are located in China, and the different context gives a good opportunity to question the technical variability in other contexts than Eastern Africa.

## EARLY STONE AGE IN CHINA

### Longgupo

The site of Longgupo was discovered in 1984 (Huang 1986). It is located at Wushan, Chongqing Municipality, south of the crossing of the Three Gorges of the Yangtze, in the Miaoyu Basin. Three excavation campaigns have been led, directed by Pr. Huang W.B. for the first and second (Huang and Fang 1991; Huang et al. 1995; Huang and Zheng 1999), and Pr. Boëda E. and Pr. Hou Y.M. for the third one (Hou et al. 2006; Boëda and Hou 2011).

This site delivered mandibula fragments first attributed to a hominid (Huang et al. 1995), but the attribution has been debated (Schwartz and Tattersall 1996; Ciochon 2009). Some remains of Gigantopithecus blacki contributed to spread doubt, and it is still impossible today to know which species made the stone tools (Wei et al. 2014).

The stone-tools modification, though debated at the beginning, has been clearly established and constitutes the earliest record of the hominid presence in Eastern Asia. The sequence has been recently dated to 2.5–2.2 million years for the Lowest Member and 1.8–1.5 million years for the Upper Member (Han et al. 2015; Huang et al. 2015). Although no hominin species has been clearly identified in Longgupo, the site represents the earliest evidence of human presence in China and in Eastern Asia in general. The richness of its very detailed sequence makes of this site a key one to study earliest Chinese hominin behaviors.

Longgupo site was originally a cave formed in a classic karst system in the Miaoyu Basin. The sedimentation is mostly attributed to alluvial deposits coming from the Miaoyu He, as demonstrated by the rounded gravels and cobbles deposited in the cave. Some karst infiltration deposits may also have occurred occasionally, as some speleothems indicate (Rasse et al. 2011).

More than 1,500 artifacts were uncovered from the different field seasons led by several teams (Huang et al 1995; Hou et al. 2006; Boeda and Hou 2011). The authors highlighted a short stone tool modification strategy. The hominins selected their raw materials on purpose and only modified the cutting edge. On the other hand, a huge techno-functional variability is suggested, meaning that unless a short and effective reduction sequence, the tool diversity was large (Boëda and Hou 2011).

The main raw material used is local limestone, collected in the form of pebbles or fragmented blocks. However, 10 percent of the tools are produced on exogenous materials (lava, chert) absent from the vicinity of the site. Their provenience has not been identified. These tools arrived on the site already knapped. It is made of pebbles tools and large retouched flakes.

The production methods in Longgupo are based on the shaping of cutting edges on pebbles. The material consists mainly of pebbles with transverse or lateral cutting edge. Some products from bipolar percussion on anvil have also been identified and can be retouched. The particularity of the site of Longgupo is to include a lithic industry almost entirely oriented on the shaping of pebbles. While these objects are known in Africa, their proportions are always anecdotal, and these tools come in addition to a tool-kit mainly consisting of flakes from the debitage. In addition, this technical system is observed continuously on forty-one archaeological levels. These data make this site a unique case, hardly comparable with other Chinese sites but also with African assemblages. The raw material can be invoked as a factor of this technical otherness. The selected limestone pebbles are indeed very hard at knapping, and the choice of shaping can be considered as a cultural response to this natural constraint (Boëda and Hou 2011).

## Renzidong

The site of Renzidong (Anhui, Central China) seems most conducive to comparison, because of its chronological proximity to Longgupo (Gao et al. 2005). This is a sinkhole that seems to have trapped animals that hominins would come to recover, or at least consume. The site has yielded numerous faunal remains and an important lithic industry (Jin et al. 2000, 2009).

Although the data still needs to be published in detail, Boëda and Hou (2011) were able to make some observation on the assemblage. The lithic industry seems to be composed of shards debited on local raw materials, with a preferential use of blocks of pyrite, but one also finds chalcedony, chert, and limestone. Some pebble tools are also mentioned. The Renzidong industry may have characteristics common to Oldowan sites in Africa, particularly in the proportions of flake tools compared to cobbles, but more detailed publications will be required to carry out systematic comparison work.

## The Nihewan Basin

The Nihewan Basin is located in northern China, 300 km west of Beijing. These are the highest latitudes in which lower Pleistocene hominin occupations were found, the same as Dmanisi in Georgia (Gabunia et al. 2000). Many sites were discovered between 1.7 and 1 million years, indicating a recurrent presence of hominin groups in the region, though the area was under high climatic variations. Denell and colleagues (2013) studied the climatic data from the Lower Pleistocene record and concluded that those occupations may have been short and seasonal due to very cold temperature during glacial episodes. Nonetheless, many sites have yielded numerous assemblages, both with fauna and lithics. Liu and colleagues (2013) summarized the technological data of eight major sites, Majuangou (Li and Xie 1998; Xie and Li 2002a,b), Xiaochangliang (You et al. 1979; Huang 1985; Chen et al. 1998, 2002; Li 1999; Zhu et al. 2001), Dachangliang (Pei 2002; Deng et al. 2006), Banshan (Wei,1994; Zhu et al. 2004), Donggutuo (Li and Wang 1985;Wei 1985; Hou et al. 1999), Feiliang (Xie et al. 1998; Zhu et al. 2007), Huojiadi (Feng and Hou 1998) and Xujiapo (Wei et al. 1999).

According to the authors (Liu et al. 2013), for those localities, the raw material exploitation is quite similar. The main raw material used is chert, distributed along the basin through failures and cracks along a Brescia fault. The chert is only available under small fragments though, so the cores are small. Although the authors argue that Majuangou III site is composed of at least 90 percent of this chert, other researchers have noticed a larger raw material diversity in this site especially, with the use of other materials collected in alluvial accumulations close to the site, leading to select bigger pebbles than on the other sites (Boëda and Hou 2011). Apart from this site, most of raw material procurement is focused on the selection of small chert fragments from the fracture belts close to the sites (Pei and Hou 2001). Raw material procurement in the Nihewan Basin is then almost exclusively local.

Concerning the technology, Liu and colleagues (2013) sorted out three "degrees of sophistication" in the Lower Pleistocene assemblages. First corresponds to a free-hand hammer percussion debitage system leading to produce few tool types, with very retouched pieces and almost no pebble tools. The site of Majuangou III is representing this category. Second degree still involves hard hammer flaking, and also bipolar debitage. Small tools were produced on flakes, with a diversity of tool types and retouch pieces. Xiaochangliang is the most relevant site for this category. Third stage is composed of the same characteristics than the previous category, and also more prepared cores such as the Donggutuo core described by Hou (2000), a prismatic core prepared to produce series of small elongated flakes. This site is naturally representing this category.

## Majuangou III

The Majuangou III site is the oldest known to date in the Nihewan Basin. Dated at 1.66 Ma (Zhu et al. 2004), it is an open-air site, one level of which has yielded several hundred artifacts. A full analysis of the Majuangou lithic industry is difficult as the detailed data are not published. According to a quick study, Boëda and Hou (2011) describe an industry consisting mostly of flakes made from a variety of raw materials from alluvial pebbles and small blocks of chert.

The core reduction process consists in producing small series of flakes from a natural convex surface selected on the blocks. The flakes are used as produced and sometimes slightly retouched. The authors emphasize the very different production systems between Longgupo and Majuangou, and conclude that they are different evolutionary lineages, proposing the hypothesis of two distinct technical traditions during the Early Stone Age in China.

## Xiaochangliang

The site of Xiaochangliang, dated at 1.4 million years (Zhu et al. 2001; Li et al. 2008; Ao et al. 2011), has yielded nearly 2,000 artifacts after several excavation campaigns between the 1990s (Chen et al. 1999). The vast majority of the material is produced on nodules or small blocks of chert (96, 7%). Chert artifacts have two possible sources, one from a nodular or stratified outcrop and the other from pyroclastic rocks, mainly with asymmetric and sub-angular breccias of chert, dolomite, limestone, and quartzite (Yang et al. 2016).

The technological study carried out on the materials revealed two debitage methods to produce small flakes. First, a classic debitage by small series of removals, to obtain flakes with regular characters. When the cores are too small to be knapped by free-hand hammer percussion, bipolar debitage is observed, in significant proportions (30% of the cores, Yang et al. 2016). The authors attribute this use of the bipolar debitage as an adaptation to the morphologies of chert block fragments, of small dimensions and sometimes difficult to knap freehand. The retouched pieces are not numerous ($n = 45$), but they give useful information. A total of 38 percent are made on whole or broken flakes 13.3 percent are on bipolar cores or splinters, and others are on angular fragments. Scrapers compose the majority of the toolkit, but notches and other pieces without regular patterns were observed (Yang et al. 2016).

The retouch tools indicate that the blanks were not produced to be standardized, and that the confection phase is the more important stage of tool making. This pattern is very similar to small tool industries in Eastern Europe during the Mid Pleistocene transition, described in Bilzingsleben in Germany or Vertesszolos in Hungary, for example (Rocca 2016). The diversity of flaking methods and the use of uncontrolled methods like bipolar percussion make sense here, as the main objective is to get small pieces without special technical criteria. Those criteria will be created by the retouch phase.

## Donggutuo

The site of Donggutuo was discovered in 1981 and has been excavated through several campaigns during the 1990s. It has yielded thousands of artifacts and is one of the richest assemblages in the Nihewn Basin. Dated to 1.1 million years (Singer et al. 1999; Hilgen et al. 2012). The material has been described by several authors (Wei et al. 1985; Hou 2008; Yuan et al. 2011; Wei 2014), and a debate emerged on the degree of conceptualization and technical skills on the site. Free-hand hammer percussion was identified, as well as bipolar percussion. Authors also described finely retouched flakes (Wei et al. 1985; Schick et al. 1991).

Besides to this classical technical set for the region, Hou (1999) noticed and described prepared cores at Donggutuo, which consist in a preparation of a wedge-shaped debitage surface to obtain series of small elongated flakes (Hou 2000, 2003). This interpretation has been contested by other researchers, claiming they could be a variant of the classic cores found in the site (Chen 2003; Xie et al. 2006). Other proposed that they could be the result of bipolar reduction (Wei 2014). Though still debated, the wedge-shaped cores show a preparation that was not observed earlier in the Nihewan Basin. The elongated flakes can be retouched to get pointed pieces. Notched pieces and borers are also documented. The retouch pieces are all made on flake blanks (Yang et al. 2017).

The Donggutuo lithic assemblage is displaying another kind of knapping strategy to take advantage of the raw material constraints. Though in Xiaochangliang the knappers produced any possible blanks and then used retouch to make their tools, in Donggutuo the cores show steps for the preparation of technical criteria that are determining the morphology and the shape of the flakes produced. The core preparation to obtain elongated flakes is unique to Donggutuo in the Nihewan Basin at this period.

## DISCUSSION AND CONCLUSION

The Early Stone Age in China gives a new perspective on the notion of variability of the lithic industries. In Africa, the raw material selected plays an important role in the debitage methods employed. From a good knowledge of the raw material knapping reactions, the hominins selected the type of raw material and adopt a method adapted to produce the flakes they wanted. Although the retouch rate is not very high, the technical criteria defined by the debitage make it possible to obtain a diverse range of flakes, which offers the possibility to use these flakes directly as tools, and sometimes to retouch them to obtain specific cutting edges. If the raw material determines how to produce these tools, the common toolkit remains relatively the same in all sites. The presence of heavy-duty tools to use the mass comes in addition to a toolkit based on small flakes with fine cutting edges. Thus, in East Africa, the raw material constraints are balanced by an understanding of the reactions to knapping of each material, and the choices of raw material constitute a cultural act, or at least a technical tradition.

This idea can also work on several Chinese sites, including Longgupo and Majuangou. The lithic industry of Longgupo, based on the creation of a cutting edge by shaping pebbles is unique and persists on forty-one archaeological levels, between 2.5–2.2 and 1.8–1.6 million years. The choice of shaping can be considered as a technical solution to the hardness of the limestone used. This choice of shaping is not found in other assemblages and echoes bifacial shaping systems that will develop in East Africa from 1.7 million years (Lepre et al. 2011; Beyene et al. 2013). The Longgupo industry is not bifacial at all, but the choice of the "all-shaped-strategy" is the same type of technical option that will prevail during the Acheulean, especially in the Bose Basin in southern China (Xie and Bodin 2007).

The characteristics of the lithic assemblage of Majuangou III seem similar to the technical systems of the African Oldowan. The choice of alluvial pebbles to obtain large flakes, and chunks of chert to make the small ones correspond to the same management of the constraints related to the raw materials as on the Oldowan sites, as for example DK at Olduvai (de la Torre and Mora 2005; De Weyer 2016).

However, a different phenomenon is observed when comparing the technical choices of Xiaochangliang and Donggutuo. Indeed, on these two sites, the almost exclusive use of the same blocks of chert highlights the differences in raw material management. In Xiaochangliang, the recurrent use of bipolar percussion allows to obtain numerous small flakes and fragments, without controlling the products obtained. The retouching phase is thus preponderant in the tool confection and can greatly vary. In Donggutuo, the technical option is different, since we observe a control of the flake morphology by a preparation of the core, leading to produce standardized blanks for future tools.

Then, how to define the variability of Early Stone Age lithic industries? What is the inherent part of natural constraints, and what is that of culture, of tradition? Though it is impossible to choose a point of view in a categorical way, it is important to consider the diversity of possible technical options in a given context and to observe the response of human groups to the constraints of their environment. By multiplying detailed analyses and looking for the technical criteria, taking into account the phase of selection, production and retouch, we highlight both recurrences and otherness, that is to say technical universals and cultural specificities.

By considering the technical fact by an anthropological approach based on the analysis of hominin stone tool assemblages, it is possible to highlight a diversity that is too often hidden by reductive and general descriptions of the lithic industries. The comparison between two rich areas such as East Africa and China gives new key for understanding cultural diversity at the very beginning of the history of techniques.

## NOTE

1. I am grateful to Chapurukha M. Kusimba and Zhu Tiequan for the invitation to contribute to this volume. Yang Shixia invite me to visit the Nihewan basin Lower Pleistocene sites and have a look at Xiaochangliang materials, I sincerely thank her.

## REFERENCES

Antón S.C. 1997. "Developmental Age and Taxonomic Affinity of the Mojokerto Child, Java, Indonesia." *American Journal of Physical Anthropology* 102: 497–514.

Ao H, Deng C L, Dekkers M J, Liu Q S, Qin L, Xiao G Q et al. 2010. "Astronomical Dating of the Xiantai, Donggutuo and Maliang Paleolithic Sites in the Nihewan Basin (North China) and Implications for Early Human Evolution in East Asia." *Palaeogeography Palaeoclimatology Palaeoecology* 297: 129–137.

Arzarello M., De Weyer L. and Peretto C. 2016. "The First European Peopling and the Italian Case: Peculiarities and "opportunism." *Quaternary International* 393: 41–50.

Arzarello M., Marcolini F., Pavia G., Pavia M., Petronio C., Petrucci M., Rook L. and Sardella R. 2009. "L'industrie Lithique du Site Pléistocène Inférieur de Pirro Nord (Apricena, Italie du Sud) : Une Occupation Humaine Entre 1,3 et 1,7 Ma." *L'Anthropologie* 113: 47–58.

Asfaw B., White T., Lovejoy O., Latimer B. and Simpson S. 1999. "*Australopithecus garhi*: A New Species of Early Hominid from Ethiopia." *Science* 284:629–634.

Beyene Y., Katoh S., WoldeGabriel G., Hart W., Uto K. Sudo M., Kondo M., Renne P.R., Suwa G. and Asfaw B. 2013. "The Characteristics and Chronology of the Earliest Acheulean at Konso, Ethiopia." *Proceedings of the National Academy of Sciences* 110 (5): 1584–1591.

Blumenschine R.J., Peters C.R., Masao F.T., Clarke R.L., Deino A.L., Hay R.L., Swisher C.C., Stanistreet I.G., Ashley G.M., McHenry L.J., Sikes N.E., van der Merwe N.J., Tactikos J.C., Cushing A.E., Deocampo D.M., Njau J.K. and Ebert J.I. 2003. "Late Pliocene Homo and Hominid Land Use from Western Olduvai Gorge, Tanzania." *Science* 299:1217–1221.

Boëda E. and Hou Y.M. 2011. "Étude du site de Longgupo—Synthèse." *L'Anthropologie* 115 (1): 176–196.

Braun D.R., Plummer T., Ditchfield P., Ferraro J.V., Maina D., Bishop L.C. and Potts R. 2008. "Oldowan Behavior and Raw Material Transport: Perspectives from the Kanjera Formation." *Journal of Archaeological Science* 35: 2329–2345.

Braun D.R., Plummer T.W., Ditchfield P.W., Bishop L.C. and Ferraro J.V. 2009. "Oldowan Technology and Raw Material Variability at Kanjera South." In Hovers E., Braun D.R. (eds.), *Interdisciplinary Approaches to the Oldowan*, pp. 99–110. Dordecht: Springer.

Chavaillon J. 1976. "Evidence for the Technical Practices of Early Pleistocene Hominids, Shungura Formation, Lower Omo Valley, Ethiopia." In: Coppens Y., Howell F.C. Isaac G.L. and Leakey R.E.F. (eds.), *Earliest Man and Environment in the Lake Rudolf Basin*, pp. 565–573. Chicago: University of Chicago Press.

Chen C. 2003. *The Early Pleistocene Lithic Assemblage and Human Behaviors in Nihewan Basin.* Shanghai:Xuelin Press.

Chen C., Shen C., Chen W.Y. and Tang Y.J. 1998. "Excavation of the Xiaochangliang site at Yangyuan, Heibei." *Acta Anthropologica Sinica* 18 (3): 225–239.

Chen C., Shen C., Chen W.Y. and Tang Y.J. 2002. "Lithic analysis of the Xiaochangliang industry." *Acta Anthropologica Sinica* 21 (1): 23–40.

Ciochon, R. 2009. "The Mystery Ape of Pleistocene Asia." *Nature* 459: 910–911.

Clarke R.J. 1994. "The Significance of the Swartkrans *Homo* to the *Homo erectus* Problem." *Courier Forschungs-Institut Senckenberg* 171: 185–193.

de Heinzelin J., Clark J.D., White T.D., Hart W.K., Renne P.R., WoldeGabriel G., Beyene Y. and Vrba E.S. 1999. "Environment and behavior of 2.5-million-year-old Bouri hominids." *Science* 284: 625–629.

de la Torre I. 2004. "Omo Revisited: Evaluating the Technological Skills of Pliocene Hominids." *Current Anthropology* 45: 439–465.

de la Torre I. and Mora R. 2005. Technological Strategies in the Lower Pleistocene at Olduvai Beds I and II, Liège, ERAUL.

de Lumley H. and Beyene Y. (eds.). 2004. *Les sites Préhistoriques de la Région de Fejej, Sud-Omo, Ethiopie, dans leur Contexte Stratigraphique et Paléontologique.* Paris: Editions Recherche sur les Civilisations.

de Lumley H., Barsky D. and Cauche D. 2009. "Les Premières étapes de la Colonisation de l'Europe et L'arrivée de l'Homme sur les Rives de la Méditerranée, *L'Anthropologie* 113: 1–46.

de Lumley H., Nioradzé M., Barsky D., Cauche D., Celiberti V., Nioradzé G., Notter O., Zvania D. and Lordkipanidze D. 2005. "Les industries Lithiques

Préoldowayennes du début du Pléistocène inférieur du Site de Dmanissi en Géorgie, *L'Anthropologie* 109: 1–182.
de Lumley M.-A. and Lordkipanidze D. 2006. "L'Homme de Dmanisi (*Homo georgicus*), il y a 1 810 000 ans." *Comptes Rendus Palevol* 5: 273–281.
De Weyer 2016. *Systèmes Techniques et Analyse Techno-fonctionnelle des Industries Lithiques Anciennes. Universaux et variabilité en Afrique de l'Est et en Europe.* PhD Dissertation. Université Paris Ouest Nanterre La Défense.
De Weyer L. 2017. "An Early Stone Age in Western Africa? Spheroids and polyhedrons at Ounjougou, Mali." *Journal of Lithic Studies*, 4 (1).
Delagnes A. and Roche H. 2005. "Late Pliocene Hominid Knapping Skills: The case of Lokalalei 2C, West Turkana, Kenya." *Journal of Human Evolution* 48: 435–472.
Delagnes A., Boisserie J.-R., Beyene Y., Chuniaud K., Guillemot C. and Schuster M. 2011. "Archaeological Investigations in the Lower Omo Valley (Shungura Formation, Ethiopia): New Data and Perspectives." *Journal of Human Evolution* 61 (2): 215–222.
Dennell R.W. 2013. "The Nihewan Basin of North China in the Early Pleistocene: Continuous and Flourishing, or Discontinuous, Infrequent and Ephemeral Occupation." *Quaternary International* 295 (438): 223–236.
Feng X.W. and Hou, Y.M. 1998. Huojiadi e a New Palaeolithic Site Found in NihewanBasin. *Acta Anthropologica Sinica* 17 (4): 310–316.
Gabunia L.K., Vekua A.B., Lordkipanidze D., Swisher C.C., Ferring R., Justus A., Nioradze M., Tvalcrelidze M., Antón S.C., Bosinski G., Jöris O., de Lumley M.-A., Maisuradze G. and Mouskhelishvili A. 2000. "Earliest Pleistocene Hominid Cranial Remains from Dmanisi, Republic of Georgia: Taxonomy, Geological Setting, and Age." *Science* 288: 1019–1025.
Gao X., Wei Q., Shen C. and Keates S. 2005. "New Light on the Earliest Hominid Occupation in East Asia." *Current Anthropology* 46: 115–120.
Han F., Bahain J.-J., Deng C., Boëda E., Hou Y., Wei G., Huang W., Garcia T., Shao Q., He C., Falguères C., Voinchet P. and Yin G. 2017. "The Earliest Evidence of Hominid Settlement in China: Combined Electron Spin Resonance and Uranium Series (ESR/U-series) Dating of Mammalian Fossil Teeth from Longgupo Cave." *Quaternary International* 434 A, 75–83.
Harmand S. 2005. *Matières Premières Lithiques et Comportements Technoéconomiques des Homininés Plio-Pléistocènes du Turkana Occidental, Kenya.* Thèse de Doctorat de l'Université de Paris X-Nanterre.
Harmand S. 2009. "Raw material and Economic Behaviours at Oldowan and Acheulean in the West Turkana region, Kenya." In Adams B. and Blades B. (eds.), *Lithic Materials and Paleolithic Societies*, pp. 3–14. Oxford: Blackwell Publishing,
Harmand S., Lewis J.E., Feibel C.S., Lepre C.J., Prat S., Lenoble A., Boës X., Quinn R.L., Brenet M., Arroyo A., Taylor N., Clément S., Daver G., Brugal J.-P., Leakey L., Mortlock R.A., Wright J.D., Lokorodi S., Kirwa C., Kent D.V. and Roche H. 2015. "3.3-Million-Year-Old Stones Tools from Lomekwi 3, West Turkana, Kenya." *Nature* 521: 310–315.
Hou Y.M. 1999. "Expecting Two-Million-Year-Old Human Remains in the Nihewan Basin, North China." *Quaternary Sciences* 1: 95.

Hou Y.M. 2000. *Donggutuo Lithic Industry of the Nihewan Basin, North China*. PhD Dissertation of the Institute of Vertebrate Paleontology and Paleoanthropology, Beijing: Chinese Academy of Sciences.

Hou Y.M. 2003. "Naming and Preliminary Study on the Category of the "Donggutuo Core." *Acta Anthropologica Sinica* 22 (4): 279–292.

Hou Y.M. 2008. "The 'Donggutuo core' from Donggutuo Industry of Lower Pleistocene in the Nihewan Basin, North China and Its Indication." *L'Anthropologie* 112 (3): 457–471.

Hou Y.M., Li Y.H., Huang W.B., Xu Z.Q. and Lu N. 2006. "New Lithic Materials from Level 7 of Longgupo Site." *Quaternary Sciences* 26, 555–561 (in Chinese with English abstract).

Hou Y.M., Wei Q., Feng X.W. and Lin, S.L. 1999. "Re-Excavation at Donggutuo in the Nihewan Basin, North China." *Quaternary Sciences* 19 (2): 139–147.

Hovers E., Schollmeyer K., Goldman T., Eck G.G., Reed K.E., Johanson D.C. and Kimbel W.H. 2002. "Late Pliocene Archaeological Sites in Hadar, Ethiopia." *Paleoanthropology Society Abstracts, Journal of Human Evolution* 42 (3): A17.

Hovers E. 2015. "Archaeology: Tools Go Back in Time." *Nature* 521: 294–295.

Huang W.B., Ciochon R., Gu Y., Larick R., Fang Q., Schwarcz H.P., Yonge C., de Vos J. and Rink W.J. 1995. "Early *Homo* and Associated Artifacts from Asia." *Nature* 378: 275–278.

Huang W.B. 1986. "An Analysis of the Karst Cave and Mammalian Fauna in Three Gorges, Changjiang River." *Geographical Research* 5 (4).

Huang W.B. and Fang Q.R. 1991. *Wushan Hominid Site*. Beijing: Ocean Press (in Chinese with English abstract).

Huang W.B. and Zheng S.H. 1999. "Résumé de l'analyse des Fossiles vertébrés." In Huang W.W. and Fang Q.R. (eds.), *Wushan Hominid Site*, pp. 135–149. Beijing: Ocean Press (in Chinese

Huang W.W. 1985. "On the Stone Industry of Xiaochangliang." *Acta Anthropologica Sinica* 4 (4): 301–307.

Huffman F., Shipman P., Hertler C., de Vos J. and Aziz F. 2005. "Mojokerto skull discovery, East Java." *Journal of Human Evolution* 48: 321–363.

Isaac G.L. 1976. Plio-Pleistocene Artifacts Assemblages from East Rudolf, Kenya." In Coppens Y., Howell F.C., Isaac G.L. and Leakey R.E. (eds.), *Earliest Man and Environments in the Lake Rudolf Basin: Stratigraphy, Paleoecology and Evolution*, pp. 552–564. Chicago: University of Chicago Press.

Jin C.Z. and Liu J.Y. 2009. *Paleolithic Site—The Renzidong Cave, Fanchang, Anhui, China*, Beijing: Science Press.

Jin C.Z., Dong W., Liu J.Y., Wei G., Xu Q. and Zheng J. 2000. "A Preliminary Study on the Early Pleistocene Deposits and the Mammalian Fauna from the Renzi Cave, Fanchang, Anhui, China." *Acta Anthropologica Sinica* 19 (Suppl.): 235–246.

Kuman K. 2007. "The Earlier Stone Age in South Africa: Site Context and the Influence of Cave Studies." In Pickering T.R., Schick K. and Toth N. (eds.), *Breathing Life Into Fossils: Taphonomic Studies in Honor of C.K. (Bob) Brain*, pp. 181–198. Bloomington (Indiana): Stone Age Institute Press.

Kuman K. and Clarke R.J. 2000. "Stratigraphy, Artifact Industries and Hominid Associations for Sterkfontein, Member 5." *Journal of Human Evolution* 38: 827–847.

Kuman K. and Field A.S. 2009. "The Oldowan Industry from Sterkfontein Caves, South Africa." In Schick K. and Toth N (eds.), *The Cutting Edge, New Approaches to the Archaeology of Human Origins*, pp. 151–169. Bloomington (Indiana): Stone Age Institute Publication Series.

Leakey M.D. 1971. *Olduvai Gorge, Volume 3: Excavations in Beds I and II, 1960–1963*. Cambridge: Cambridge University Press.

Lepre C.J., Roche H., Kent D.V., Harmand S., Quinn R.L., Brugal J.-P., Texier P.-J., Lenoble A. and Feibel, C.S. 2011. "An Earlier Origin for the Acheulian." *Nature* 477: 82–85.

Li H., Yang X., Heller F. and Li H. 2008. "High Resolution Magnetostratigraphy and Deposition Cycles in the Nihewan Basin (North China) and Their Significance for Stone Artifact Dating." *Quaternary Research* 69: 250–262.

Li Y.X. 1999. "On the Progress of the Stone Artifacts from the Xiaochangliang Site at Yangyuan, Hebei." *Acta Anthropol Sinica* 18(4): 241–254.

Li J. and Xie, F. 1998. "Excavation Report of a Lower Palaeolithic Site at Majuangou." In Hebei Province Institute of Cultural Relics (ed.), *Archaeological Corpus of Hebei*. pp. 30–45. Beijing: Oriental Press.

Liu Y., Hou Y.M. and Ao H. 2013. "Analysis of Lithic Technology of Lower Pleistocene Sites and Environmental Information in the Nihewan Basin, North China." *Quaternary International* 295: 215–222.

Lordkipanidze D., Ponce de León M.S., Margvelashvili A., Rak Y., Rightmire P., Vekua A. and Zollikofer C.P.E. 2013. "A Complete Skull from Dmanisi, Georgia, and the Evolutionary Biology of Early *Homo*." *Science* 342: 326–331.

Mgeladze A., Lordkipanidze D., Moncel M.-H., Despriée J., Chagelishvili R., Nioradze M. and Nioradze G. 2011. "Hominin Occupations at the Dmanisi Site, Southern Caucasus: Raw Materials and Technical Behaviours of Europe's First Hominins." *Journal of Human Evolution* 60 (5): 571–596.

Mora R. and de la Torre I. 2005. "Percussion Tools in Olduvai Beds I and II (Tanzania): Implications for Early Human Activities." *Journal of Anthropological Archaeology* 24 (2): 179–192.

Pei S.W. and Hou Y.M. 2001. "Preliminary Study on Raw Materials Exploitation at Donggutuo Site, Nihewan Basin, North China." *Acta Anthropologica Sinica* 20 (4): 271–281.

Pelegrin J. 1991. "Les Savoir-faire: Une très Longue Histoire." *Terrains* 16: 106–113.

Plummer T., Bishop L., Ditchfield P. and Hicks J. 1999. "Research on Late Pliocene Oldowan Sites at Kanjera South, Kenya." *Journal of Human Evolution* 36: 151–170.

Plummer, T. and Bishop, L.C. 2016. "Oldowan Hominin Behavior and Ecology at Kanjera South, Kenya." *Journal of Anthropological Science* 94: 29–40.

Qian F. and Zhou G.X. 1991. *Quaternary Geology and Paleoanthropology of Yuanmou, Yunnan, China*, Beijing, Sciences Press.

Rasse M., Huang W.B. and Boëda E. 2011. "The Site of Longgupo in His Geological and Geomorphological Environment." *L'Anthropologie* 115: 23–39.

Reti J. 2016. "Quantifying Oldowan Stone Tool Production at Olduvai Gorge, Tanzania." *PLoS ONE* 11 (1): 0147352.

Rightmire G.P., Lordkipanidze D. and Vekua A. 2006. "Anatomical Descriptions, Comparative Studies and Evolutionary Significance of the Hominin Skulls from Dmanisi, Republic of Georgia." *Journal of Human Evolution* 50: 115–141.

Rocca R. 2016. "Depuis l'Est ? Nouvelles Perspectives sur les premières dynamiques de peuplement en Europe." *L'Anthropologie* 120 (3): 209–236.

Roche H. 1996. "Remarques sur les Plus anciennes Industries en Afrique et en Europe." *XIIIème Congrès UISPP, Colloquia* 4, Forlí, Italie, 53–63.

Roche H. and Tiercelin J.-J. 1980. "Industries lithiques de la Formation pliopléistocène d'Hadar, Ethiopie (campagne 1976)." In Leakey R.E. and Ogot B.A. (eds.), *Pre-Acheulean and Acheulean Cultures in Africa. Proceedings of the 8th Panafrican Congress of Prehistory and Quaternary Studies*, pp. 194–199. Nairobi: National Museums of Kenya.

Roche H., Delagnes A., Brugal J.-P., Feibel C., Kibunjia M., Mourre V. and Texier P.-J. 1999. "Early Hominid Stone Tool Production and Technological Skill 2.34 Myr Ago in West Turkana, Kenya." *Nature* 399: 57–60.

Sahnouni M., Hadjouis D., van der Made J., Derradji A.-e.-K., Canals A., Medig M. and Belahrech H. 2002. "Further Research at the Oldowan Site of Ain Hanech, North-Eastern Algeria." *Journal of Human Evolution* 43: 925–937.

Sahnouni, M., Schick, K., and Toth, N. 1997. "An Experimental Investigation Into the Nature of Faceted Limestone 'Spheroids' in the Early Palaeolithic." *Journal of Archaeological Science* 24: 701–713.

Sartano S. 1961. "Notes on a New Find of a *Pithecanthropus* Mandible." *Publikasi Teknik Seri Paleontologi* 2: 1–51.

Sartano S. 1982. "Characteristics and Chronology of Early Man in Java." In de Lumley H. (ed.), *L'Homo erectus et la place de l'Homme de Tautavel parmi les Hominidés fossiles. 1er Congrès International de Paléontologie Humaine*, pp. 491–533. Nice.

Schick K.D. 1994. "The Movius Line Reconsidered." In Corruccini R.S. and Ciochon R.L. (eds.), *Integrative Paths to the Past*, pp. 569–596. New Jersey: Prentice-Hall.

Schick K., Toth N., Wei Q., Clark J., Desmond Etler and Denis A.1991. "Archaeological Perspectives in the Nihewan Basin, China." *Journal of Human Evolution* 21: 13–26.

Schwartz J.H. and Tattersall I. 1996. "Whose Teeth?" *Nature* 381: 201–202.

Semaw S. 2000. The World's Oldest Stone Artefacts from Gona, Ethiopia: Their Implications or Understanding Stone Technology and Patterns of Human Evolution Between 2.6–1.5 Million Years Ago." *Journal of Archaeological Science* 27: 1197–1214.

Swisher C.C., Curtis G.H., Jacob T., Getty A.G., Suprijo A. and Widiasmoro A.S. 1994. "Age of the Earliest Known Hominids in Java, Indonesia." *Science* 263:1118–1121.

Toro I., de Lumley H., Barsky D., Celiberti V., Cauche D., Moncel, M.-H., Fajardo B. and Toro M. 2003. "Las industrias líticas de Barranco Leon y Fuente Nueva 3 de Orce. Estudio Técnico y Tipologico. Las Cadenas Operativas. Analisis Traceologico. Resultados Preliminares." In Toro I., Agusti J. and Martinez-Navarro B. (eds.), *El Pleistoceno inferior de Barranco Leon y Fuente Nueva 3, Orce (Granada), Memoria scientifica campañas 1999–2002*. Junta de Andalucia, Consejeria de Cultura, Arqueologia.

Toro-Moyano I., de Lumley H., Barrier P., Barsky D., Cauche D., Celiberti V., Grégoire S., Lebègue F., Mestour B. and Moncel M.-H. 2010. *Les industries lithiques archaïques de Barranco León et de Fuente Nueva 3, Orce Guadiz-Baza, Andalousie*. Paris: CNRS Editions.

Toth N. 1982. The Stone Technologies of Early Hominids at Koobi Fora, Kenya: An Experimental Approach, Ph. D. Dissertation, University of California at Berkeley.

Toth N. 1985. "The Oldowan Reassessed: A Close Look at Early Stones Artifacts." *Journal of Archaeological Science* 12 (2): 101–120.

Toth N. 1987. "Behavioral Inferences from Early Stone Age Artifact Assemblages: An Experimental Model." *Journal of Human Evolution* 16: 763–787.

Tribolo C., Rasse M., Soriano S. and Huysecom E. 2015. Defining a Chronological Framework for the Middle Stone Age in West Africa: OSL Ages at Ounjougou (Mali)." *Quaternary Geochronology* 29: 80–96.

Wei G.B., Huang W.B., Chen S.K., He C.D., Pang L.B. and Wu Y. 2014. "Paleolithic Culture of Longgupo and Its Creators." *Quaternary International* 354: 154–161.

Wei Q. 1994. "Banshan Paleolithic Site from the Lower Pleistocene in the Nihewan Basin in Northern China." *Acta Anthropologica Sinica* 13: 223–238.

Wei Q. 1985. "Palaeolithics from the Lower Pleistocene of Nihewan Basin in the North China " *Acta Anthropologica Sinica* 4 (4): 289e300.

- Wei Q., Hou Y.M. and Feng X.W. 1999. "Stone Artifacts from Xujiapo in the Nihewan Basin." *Longgupo Prehistoric Culture* 1: 119–127.

Worm H.U. 1997. "A Link Between Geomagnetic Reversals and Events and Glaciations." *Earth and Planetary Science Letters* 147: 55–67.

Wu X.Z. 2000. "Longgupo Mandible Belongs to Ape." *Acta Anthropologica Sinica* 19: 1–10.

Xie F., Li J. and Liu L. 2006. *The Nihewan Paleolithic Culture*. Shijiazhuang: Huashan Literature Publishing House.

Xie G.M. and Bodin E. 2007. "The Lithic Assemblages of Xiaochangliang, Nihewan Basin: Implications for Early Pleistocene Hominin Behaviour in North China." *PLoS ONE* 11(5): e0155793.

Xie F. and Li J. 2002a. "Nihewan Majuangou Site." In *State Administration of Cultural Heritage Major Archaeological Discoveries in China in 2001*. Beijing: Culture Relics Publishing House.

Xie F. and Li J. 2002b. "Characteristics of the Stoneware in Majuangou Site." *Wenwuchunqiu* 15 (3): 19.

Xie F., Li J. and Cheng, S.Q. 1998. "Excavation Report of the Feiliang Site." In Hebei Province Institute of Cultural Relics (ed.), *Archaeological Corpus of Hebei*, pp. 1–29. Beijing: Oriental Press.

Yang S-X., Petraglia M.D., Hou Y-M., Yue J-P., Deng C-L. and Zhu R-X. 2017. "The Lithic Assemblages of Donggutuo, Nihewan Basin: Knapping Skills of Early Pleistocene Hominins in North China." *PLoS ONE* 12 (9): 0185101.

You Y.Z., Tang Y.J. and Li Y. 1979. "The Discovery of Xiaochangliang Site and Its Significance.' *Chinese Science Bulletin* 24 (8): 365–367.

Yuan B.Y., Xia Z.K. and Niu P.S. 2011. *Nihewan Rift and Early Man*. Beijing: Geology Publishing House.

Zhu R.X., Potts R., Xie F., Hoffman K.A., Deng C.L., Shi C.D., Pan Y.X., Wang H.Q., Shi R.P., Wang Y.C., Shi G.H. and Wu N.Q. 2004. "New Evidence on the Earliest Human Presence at High Northern Latitudes in Northeast Asia." *Nature* 431: 559–562.

Zhu R.X., Zhisheng A., Potts R. and, Hoffman K.A. 2003. "Magnetostratigraphic Dating of Early Humans in China." *Earth Sciences Reviews* 61: 341–359.

Zhu R., Hoffman K., Potts R., Deng C., Pan Y., Guo B., Guo Z., Yuan B., Hou Y. and Huang, W. 2001. "Earliest Presence of Humans in Northeast Asia." *Nature* 413: 413–417.

Zhu R.X., Deng C.L. and Pan, Y.X. 2007. "Magnetochronology of the Fluvio-Lacustrine Sequences in the Nihewan Basin and its Implications for Early Human Colonization of Northeast Asia." *Quaternary Sciences* 27 (6): 922–943.

*Chapter 2*

# Tracing Prehistoric Trade and Economic Links between the East African Coast and East Asia

Emmanuel K. Ndiema

## INTRODUCTION

The past 3,000 years in Eastern Africa are characterized by social, technological, and political transformations (figure 2.1). These transformations are visible in region wide innovations in food acquisition strategies. The universal making and use of metals, primarily iron and the interregional trade networks that linked all East African peoples—from foragers to pastoralists to emergent agrarian communities—into an economic mosaic that has persisted into modern times (Ambrose 1982; Kusimba and Kusimba 2005, 2018). The emergence of farming simultaneously increased sedentism and intensified trade among the interacting forager, pastoral, and farming communities such that the mid-first millennium, distinct local, regional, and extraregional exchange network were in operation (Pawlowicz 2012). The first was the maritime trade network along the East African littoral that incorporated coastal, inland, and Indian Ocean actors (Abungu and Mutoro 1998; Dussubieux et al. 2008; Kusimba et al. 2013a, 2017; Pwiti 2005; Walz 2010). The second was inland economic networks that connected into a regional interaction spheres across subsistence and ecological zones. These networks created opportunities for the movement of goods, information, and people across that East African landscape that has made East Africans the most genetically diverse group of people that are united by shared deep histories and ways of life making (Wood et al. 2005; Tishkoff 2009). Although these interaction spheres have local origins, the wide circulation and distribution of different products point to the interdependence between different communities through trade and exchange. Regional trade connected interacting partners, created opportunity for making a living through cooperation,

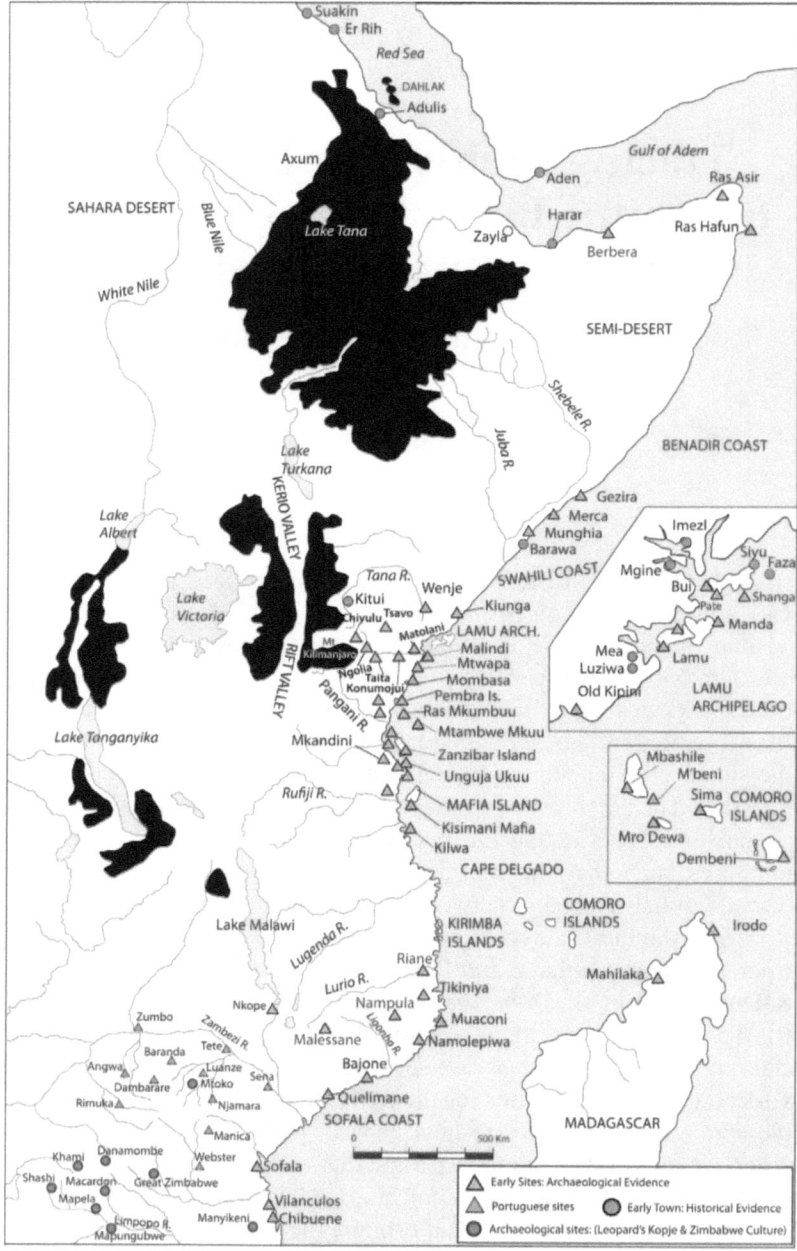

**Figure 2.1 Map of Eastern and Southern Africa Showing All the Sites Mentioned in the Book.** *Source*: Chapurukha M. Kusimba/Foreman Bandama.

collective action, and interdependence that for the first time did not require seasonal group mobility. It was these regional trading networks that were later to make East Africa an attractive trading partner for the emergent global economics in the wider Mediterranean and Indian Ocean world (Casson 1990; Seland 2014).

The archaeological context of trade and exchange networks between the East Africa and East Asia remains poorly understood and, consequently the impact and significance of this millennial old transregional trade between East Africa and East is underexplored. This chapter reviews diverse lines of archaeological evidence that could be employed to document regional and extraregional trade and exchange networks to understand the impact of millennial relationships between Africa and East Asia that have persisted to contemporary times.

The archaeological heritage of East African coast bears witness to a complex mosaic of human and cultural influences that are traceable to many regions of inland Africa and the wider Indian Ocean (Allen 1993; Batai et al. 2013; Chami 1998; Kusimba et al. 2013b; Raaum et al. 2018; Tishkoff et al. 2009). Traditionally, archaeological research on the coast concentrated on the stone walled towns with a goal of unveiling the emergence of the Swahili city-states (Kirkman 1964; Horton 1996). In contrast to this site approach, this chapter proposes a landscape approach that incorporates the region into the narrative since many products that were part of the maritime network between the East African Coast and East Asia were derived from inland trade networks and many from East were also consumed beyond the coast itself, incorporated into the larger African food ways (Hanotte et al. 2002, MacHugh et al. 2002, Pillay 2001). I will focus on the methodological transformation, over time and space, discuss how advance in scientific characterization might be used to answer the type of questions at transcontinental scale. I argue that the relationship between Asian and the Indian Ocean cannot be fully understood without incorporating that role of the interior. It is only through examination of different facets of archaeological evidence from inland East Africa that we can begin to build a complete assessment of the contributions of East Africans to premodern global economies that gave rise to Swahili urbanism and the African involvement in the maritime silk road trade.

## LOCAL ARCHAEOLOGIES TRANS-REGIONAL NETWORKS: WHAT WE KNOW AND HOW WE KNOW IT

Archaeological evidence indicates that long-distance exchange networks in East Africa predate the establishment of settled farming some 3,000 years ago. Late Stone Age sites show that trade in obsidian and chert cores and artifacts from the central Rift Valley to other regions was widespread (Ambrose and Lorenz 1990; Barut 1999; Brown and Merrick 1984; Ndiema et al. 2011). The emergence of food production thus interlocks on already preexisting regional trade and exchange networks. The same argument is extended to the later maritime trade along the East African littoral that extended to lands bordering the Indian Ocean connected the two regions: inland East Africa, the coast, and the Indian Ocean (Kusimba et al. 2013a, 2018; Mutoro 1998). Although each regional network had its own locus, it is the networks that tied them together that are of great anthropological relevance for understanding the evolution and sustenance of these premodern interactions.

Archaeological investigations carried out by Robert Soper in (1966) and Richard Helm (2000) at inland coastal sites shed light on the importance of integrating the inland coastal archaeological heritage into the wider narrative of coastal archaeology. Robert Soper excavations of a rock a shelter along the Dzitsoni Uplands near Malindi, Kilifi County, located 15 km inland from the coastal littoral recovered an assortment of well-preserved Later Stone Age (LSA) assemblages including lithic and Early Iron Age (EIA) and Middle Iron Age/Late Iron Age (MIA/LIA) pottery, as well as terrestrial and marine and carbonized material. He also reported the presence of a 'polished stone axe,' a fragment of iron blade, a worked bone/ivory tool, and shell/bone beads (Soper 1975). The site was latter revisited by Helm (2000), who recovered more LSA lithic and MIA/LIA pottery.

More recently, the Sealinks project retuned to the area with aim of identifying new data for recognizing interactions between communities occupying the region during the LSA and EIA transition. The Sealinks project also sought to recover evidence that might elicit the introduction of Asian domesticates into Africa. These data would enable the establishment of broader models for understanding how early East African coastal societies transformed and were impacted through the wider Indian Ocean world interactions, which included the bidirectional transfer, adoption, and adaptation of African domesticates in Asia and Asian domesticates in Africa (Bovin et al. 2013). Further research has been carried out at Panga Ya Sidi (PYS)—also previously investigated by Robert Soper—in which MIA/LIA ceramics were recovered. At Mgombani, Helm (2000), recovered evidence for a transitional EIA to MIA settlement. A single radiocarbon date gave a calibrated date range of 1300 ± 50 BP (Pta-7957), though occupation is likely to have started somewhat earlier. Despite the diversity of archaeological lithic and other varieties dating to the LSA there, the ceramic artifacts that were recovered were mainly characterized by different designs and decorative motifs. The diversity and decorative motifs depicted by the ceramics point at the existence of trade ceramics, including nonlocal materials. The disparities could also be indicative of disparities and special differences in the distribution of power and differential tastes, preferences, and networks with the region

In the early phases of its development, trade between the coast and the interior predominantly took the form of a series of loosely organized networks along the main river valleys and other suitable routes. Movement of people was over relatively short distances to barter for goods from neighboring communities. The goods themselves passed from one market to another, thereby moving steadily further away from their point of production. This "down-the-line" exchange accounts for the finds of limited numbers of exotic items, such as cowrie shells and trade wind beads, on Iron Age and earlier sites in the interior (Oka and Kusimba 2008).

Although Helms and colleagues have not recovered trade ceramics and porcelain in hinterland sites they have investigated to date (e.g., Abungu 1989; Chami 1994; Helm 2000), there is evidence for trade ceramics in other regions of the inland East Africa, including the Tanzania about 200 km inland (Kusimba and Walz 2018; Walz 2010). The scarcity of multiproxy archaeological data and their poorly constrained radiometric dating, together with modest paleoenvironmental evidence of increasing agricultural activity from that period onward was still lacking in the previous research.

While previous researchers would have characterized East Africa's coastal links and the East Asia in terms of the Paleolithic population dispersals, the same sentiment might apply to later periods like the Neolithic, when livestock and crops were also being spread by people to new regions and continents (Marshall and Hildebrand 2002). Interesting but more Infor needed here. Further inland at Turkana Basin and Lukenya Hill, assemblages show the lowest occurrence and the simplification of the material expression of the ceramic and funerary traditions. It is fair to ask to what extent this apparent simplification reflects a broader simplification of social and economic organization, including participation in long distance exchange networks have been reported that show connection with the coastal population (Kusimba 1998). Although the evidence is scanty, once established, pastoral exchange networks endured and were available for development as trading ports emerged along the trading routes in the interior and the coast of Eastern Africa. However, a great deal more work needs to be done to determine to what extent, and how, such early pastoral networks were used. It's likely that such exchange needs mechanism could have developed through gift-giving practices as a way for social insurance for risk minimization or some other social cultural mechanism (Schrire 2009).

The question of how precisely African crops reached East Asia as early as 2000 BCE has attracted the attention of archaeologists and botanists for decades (e.g. Allchin 1969; Hutchinson 1976; Boivin and Fuller 2009; Fuller 2003a). Less discussion has been devoted to African domesticates such as millet, sorghum, and the donkey that were adopted in and Asian crops that became incorporated into the Africa food culture such as banana (Mbida et al. 2006).

One Asian domesticate, the Zebu has received attention (e.g., Gifford-Gonzales 1998 2000; Marshall 1989; Grigson 1996; Magnavita 2006). Recent studies suggest no major influx of zebu, but rather occasional occurrences in Africa, based mainly on evidence from rock art rather than osteological evidence, and probably indicating rare imports. As demonstrated by skull fragments, Bos indicus was present in Kenya by 2000 BCE–CE 100 (Marshall 1989). While this could represent overland diffusion via northeast Africa, it is also possible that this relates to the later era of mid-Indian Ocean exchanges. As Marshall (1989) notes, the many advantages of *Bos indicus* (or hybrids thereof) may have been important for the emergence of a more intensive and specialized pastoralism in East Africa at the time. The role of animal of burden such as donkey also needs to be investigated as they must have served as "vehicle" for to facilitate trade and exchange.

## LOOKING FORWARD: INTEGRATING FIELD AND LABORATORY APPROACHES IN THE STUDY OF EAST AFRICA AND EAST ASIAN DEEP HISTORY OF INTERACTIONS

The complementary use of scientific characterization at all scales of analysis has transformed archaeology enabling the investigation of questions that previously fell outside the domain the knowable past. Traditional field and typological studies influenced interpretation that had largely been driven by research questions that assumed *a priori* that Africans lack agency to innovate. The coastal archaeological tradition-inherent bias toward the monumental remains of urban centers and expansive states has militated against the incorporation of the small-scale communities from inland East Africa that not only pioneered long-distance communication and transport but were also the sources of the bulk of African products destined for the Asian markets during the maritime silk road trade (Kusimba and Kusimba 2018; Kusimba and Walz 2018). More archaeological research is needed to understand the organization of overland long-distance exchange networks and the nature of interaction between the three regions that were involved in this millennial exchange. In particular, the changing relationship between the emerging urban centers of the coast and the diverse rural hinterland that is stull home to agrarian, pastoral, and foraging East African need to be integrated into this narrative (Kassam and Bashuna 2004).

This chapter hopefully has demonstrated the critical role that the archaeological sciences will undoubtedly play in meeting this challenge. Thus, a turn toward using different lines of proxies and cutting-edge analytical techniques, for example, genetic diversity and similarities reflected a vision of coastal towns within a broader landscape, as well as providing data to back up that vision. As its results become more prevalent, archaeologists and historians of the coast will need to adapt other frames of reference to accommodate these types of data. The insights from a DNA analysis, on human and faunal remains (Batai et al. 2013, Monge et al., this volume) can evoke transcontinental contacts through trade or networks. Especially in what was brought to East Africa, and what East Africa on the other hand was able to offer. Adapting our view of coastal society to pull these diverse narratives into an understanding of the big picture will be a challenge for the future.

At the other end of the scale, scientific techniques have also expanded our understandings of the Eastern African coast by pointing to a series of connections beyond those visible in the record of imported ceramics and glass (e.g., Dussubieux et al. 2008; Dussubieux and Kusimba, this volume)). Studies of plant and animal translocations around the Indian Ocean have extended the range of connections visible to archaeological study (Walshaw 2010, 2018). In some cases, these studies have simply refined our understandings of existing sites and chronologies, as at sites such as Unguja Ukuu and Fukuchani on Zanzibar, where recent paleobotanical analyses have provided precise dates of the introduction of crops at sites known to have been connected to early networks of trade.

The significance and transfers of livestock and plants remain largely unstudied, though it has the potential to reveal new body of evidence for early human contacts across at transcontinental scale. Excavations at coastal sites are now routinely accompanied by sampling for archaeobotanical remains and this is accompanied by sampling for phytoliths that is beginning to yield more information regarding the significance of plant remains as a potential line of evidence (Walshaw and Stoetzel 2018).

Analytical techniques that investigates the exploration of craft-working and enhanced by metallurgical studies that illuminate aspects of ancient technology (Kusimba et al. 1994; Kusimba and Killick 2003) and by isotopic analyses of trade beads (Wood 2011) and XRF characterization of metals used for objects such as coins (Perkins 2014) should also be pursued further. Each of these points to a landscape of resource use and technology that was previously unknown but can be used to shed on the cultural connection between the East Africa's mainland, the coast and far East states.

## CONCLUSION

The focus of this chapter was to review the archaeological data in the context of production, exchange, and trade networks for understanding the integration of East Africa in the premodern globalized world. I have also emphasized that whereas the coastal Swahili states and urban polities were important in promoting East Africa's contribution to early trade and globalization, it is incumbent upon archaeologists to study the trading networks in relation to inland settlements especially those that were further inland since they the main source of trade goods critical at the coast for foreign exchange (Kusimba and Kusimba 2018; Kusimba et al. 2013, Kusimba and Walz 2018). Analyzing the balance sheet of this trade, it is concluded that prehistoric societies in inland East Africa have been engaged in long-distance exchanged for several millennia, and they cannot be erased for the LIA transformations that occurred in Coastal East Africa. Trade between the coast and the inland took the form of a series of loosely organized networks along the main river valleys and other suitable spaces across the landscape (Oka and Kusimba 2008; Wakefield 1873). Movement of goods and people were like over relatively short distances to barter for goods from neighboring communities. The goods themselves could easily have passed from one market to the next, thereby moving steadily further away from their point of production. This of "down-the-line" exchange needs to be investigated more intensively.

To conclude, trade and exchange is an important human institution that promotes friendship, knowledge-transfer, and fosters interdependence, and tolerance but also the opposite, rivalry—greed, violence, and wars. A clear understanding of the mechanisms of cultural contact, influence, and change through time and space is very relevant for thinking about the how these contacts and interactions influenced and were influenced by one another across time and space. These mechanisms are as relevant today as they were in the past and will contribute to the well-being of an increasingly multicultural and globally connected society.

## REFERENCES

Abungu, G. 1989. *Communities on the River Tana. Kenya: An Archaeological Study of Relations*. PhD Thesis. Cambridge: University of Cambridge.

Abungu, G. 1996. "Pate: A Swahili Town Revisited." *Kenya Past and Present 28* (1): 50–60.

Abungu, G. H. 1998. "City States of the East African Coast and Their Maritime Contacts." In G. Connah (ed.), *Transformations in Africa: Essays on Africa's Later Past,* pp. 204–218. Leicester: Leicester University Press.

Allchin, F. R. 1969. "Early Cultivated Plants in India and Pakistan." *Archaeologies: Journal of the World Archaeological Congress 4* (1): 24–49.

Ambrose, S. H. 1982. "Archaeology and Linguistic Reconstructions of History in East Africa." In C. Ehret and M. Posnansky (eds.), *The Archaeological and Linguistic Reconstruction of African History*, pp. 104–157. Los Angeles: University of California Press.

Ambrose, S. H. and Lorenz, K. G. 1990. "Social and Ecological Models for the Middle Stone Age in Southern Africa." *The Emergence of Modern Humans: An Archaeological Perspective*: 3–33.

Batai, K., Babrowski, K. B., Arroyo, J. P., Kusimba, C. M., and Williams, S. R. 2013. "Mitochondrial DNA Diversity in Two Ethnic Groups in Southeastern Kenya: Perspectives from the North-Eastern Periphery of the Bantu Expansion." *American journal of physical anthropology 150* (3): 482–491.

Blench, R. 2003. "The Movement of Cultivated Plants Between Africa and India in Prehistory." In K. Neumann, A. Butler, and S. Kahlheber (eds.), *Food, Fuel and Fields: Progress in African Archaeobotany*, pp. 273–292. Köln: Heinrich-Barth-Institut.

Boivin, N. and Fuller, D. Q. 2009. "Shell Middens, Ships and Seeds: Exploring Coastal Subsistence, Maritime Trade and the Dispersal of Domesticates In and Around the Ancient Arabian Peninsula." *Journal of World Prehistory 22* (2): 113–180.

Boivin, N., Crowther, A., Helm, R., and Fuller, D. Q. 2013. "East Africa and Madagascar in the Indian Ocean World." *Journal of World Prehistory 26* (3): 213–281.

Chami, F. 1994. *The Tanzanian Coast in the First Millennium AD: An Archaeology of the Iron-Working, Farming Communities* (Vol. 7). Upsalla: Societas Archaeological Upsaliensis.

Chami, F. A. 1998. "A Review of Swahili Archaeology." *African Archaeological Review 15* (3): 199–218.

Chami, F. A. 1999. "Graeco-Roman Trade Link and the Bantu Migration Theory." *Anthropos 94*: 205–215.

Dussubieux, L., Kusimba, C. M., Gogte, V., Kusimba, S. B., Gratuze, B., and Oka, R. 2008. "The Trading of Ancient Glass Beads: New Analytical Data from South Asian and East African Soda–Alumina Glass Beads." *Archaeometry 50* (5): 797–821.

Fleisher, J. 2010. "Rituals of Consumption and the Politics of Feasting on the Eastern African Coast, AD 700–1500." *Journal of World Prehistory 23* (4): 195–217.

Frahm, E., Goldstein, S. T., and Tryon, C. A. 2017. "Late Holocene Forager-Fisher and Pastoralist Interactions Along the Lake Victoria Shores, Kenya: Perspectives from Portable XRF of Obsidian Artifacts." *Journal of Archaeological Science: Reports 11*: 717–742.

Fuller, D. Q. 2003. "African Crops in Prehistoric South Asia: A Critical Review." In K. Neumann, A. Butler and S. Kahlheber (eds.), *Food, Fuel and Fields: Progress in African Archaeobotany*, pp. 239–27. Köln: Heinrich-Barth Institut.

Grigson, C. 1996. "Early Cattle Around in the Indian Ocean." In J. E. Reade (ed.), *The Indian Ocean in Antiquity*, pp. 66–74. London: The British Museum.

Haaland, R. 1999. "The Puzzle of the Late Emergence of Domesticated Sorghum in the Nile Valley." In C. Gosden and J.G. Hather (eds.), *The Prehistory of Food: Appetites for Change*, pp. 397–418. London: Routledge.

Hanotte, O., Bradley, D. G., Ochieng, J. W., Verjee, Y., Hill, E. W., and Rege, J. E. O. 2002. "African Pastoralism: Genetic Imprints of Origins and Migrations." *Science 296* (5566): 336–339.

Harlan, J. R. and Stemler, A. B. L. 1976. "The Races of Sorghum in Africa." In J. R. Harlan, J. M. J. De Wet and A. B. M. Stemler (eds.), *Origins of African Plant Domestication*, pp. 465–478. The Hague: Mouton Publishers.

Helm, R. M. 2000. *Conflicting Histories: the Archaeology of the Iron-working, Farming Communities in the Central and Southern Coast Region of Kenya* (Doctoral dissertation, University of Bristol).

Horton, M. and Middleton, J. 2000. *The Swahili. The Social Landscape of a Mercantile Society.* Oxford: Blackwell Publishers.

Hutchinson, E. P. 1976. *Immigrants and Their Children, 1850–1950.* New York: Russell and Russell Publishers.

Junker, L. L. 1990. "The Organization of Intra-Regional and Long-Distance Trade in Prehispanic Philippine Complex Societies." *Asian Perspectives* 29 (2): 167–209.

Kassam, A. and Bashuna, A. B. 2004. "Marginalisation of the Waata Oromo Hunter–Gatherers of Kenya: Insider and Outsider Perspectives." *Africa* 74 (2): 194–216.

Kusimba, C. M. and Killick, D. 2003. "Iron Working on the Swahili Coast of Kenya." In C. M. Kusimba and S. B. Kusimba (eds.), *East African Archaeology: Foragers, Potters, Smiths, and Traders.* Philadelphia: University of Pennsylvania Press.

Kusimba, C. M., Kusimba, S. B., and Dussubieux, L. 2013. "Beyond the Coastalscapes: Preindustrial Social and Political Networks in East Africa." *African Archaeological Review* 30 (4): 399–426.

Kusimba, C. M., Kusimba, S. B., and Wright, D. K. 2005. "The Development and Collapse of Precolonial Ethnic Mosaics in Tsavo, Kenya." *Journal of African Archaeology* 3(2): 243–265.

Kusimba, C. M. 1999. *The Rise and Fall of Swahili States.* Walnut Creek (CA): Alta Mira Press.

Kusimba, S. B. 1999. "Hunter–Gatherer Land Use Patterns in Later Stone Age East Africa." *Journal of Anthropological Archaeology* 18(2): 165–200.

LaViolette, A. 2008. "Swahili Cosmopolitanism in Africa and the Indian Ocean World, A.D. 600–1500." *Archaeologies: Journal of the World Archaeological Congress* 4 (1): 24–49.

MacHugh, D. E., Shriver, M. D., Loftus, R. T., Cunningham, P., and Bradley, D. G. 1997. "Microsatellite DNA Variation and the Evolution, Domestication and Phylogeography of Taurine and Zebu Cattle (Bos Taurus and Bos Indicus)." *Genetics* 146 (3): 1071–1086.

Magnavita, S. 2013. "Initial Encounters: Seeking Traces of Ancient Trade Connections Between West Africa and The Wider World." *Afriques. Débats, Méthodes Et Terrains D'histoire*, 4: 79–104.

Marshall, F. and Hildebrand, E. 2002. "Cattle Before Crops: The Beginnings of Food Production in Africa." *Journal of World Prehistory* 16 (2): 99–143.

Mbida, C. H., De Langhe, E., Vrydaghs, L., Doutrelepont, H., Swennen, R., Van Neer, W., and de Maret, P. 2006. "Phytolith Evidence for the Early Presence of Domesticated Banana (Musa) in Africa." In M. A. Zeder, D. G. Bradley, and E. Emschwiller (eds.), *Documenting Domestication: New Genetic and Archaeological Paradigms*, pp. 68–81. Berkeley: University of California Press.

Merrick, H. V. and Brown, F. H. 1984. "Obsidian Sources and Patterns of Source Utilization in Kenya and Northern Tanzania: Some Initial Findings." *African Archaeological Review* 1 (1):129–152.

Merrick, H. V., Brown, F. H., and Nash, W. P. 1994. "Use and Movement of Obsidian in The Early and Middle Stone Ages of Kenya and Northern Tanzania." *Society, Culture, and Technology in Africa* 11(6): 29–44.

Misra, V.N and Kajale, M (eds.), *Introduction of African Crops into South Asia*, 23–48. Pune: Indian Society for Prehistoric and Quaternary Studies.

Mutoro, H. W. 1998. "Precolonial Trading Systems of the East African Interior." In G. Connah (ed.), *Transformations in Africa: Essays on Africa's Later Past*, pp. 186–203. Leicester: Leicester University Press.

Ndiema, K. E., Dillian, C. D., Braun, D. R., Harris, J. W. K., and Kiura, P. W. 2011. "Transport and Subsistence Patterns at the Transition to Pastoralism, Koobi Fora, Kenya." *Archaeometry 53* (6): 1085–1098.

Oka, R. and Kusimba, C. M. 2008. "The Archaeology of Trading Systems, Part 1: Towards a New Trade Synthesis." *Journal of Archaeological Research 16* (4):339–395.

Pawlowicz, M. 2012. "Modelling the Swahili Past: the Archaeology of Mikindani in southern Coastal Tanzania." *Azania: Archaeological Research in Africa 47* (4): 488–508.

Perkins, P. 2014. "Processes of Urban Development in Northern and Central Etruria in the Orientalizing and Archaic Periods." *Journal of Roman Archaeology 97*: 62–80.

Pillay, M., Ogundiwin, E., Nwakanma, D. C., Ude, G., and Tenkouano, A. 2001. "Analysis of Genetic Diversity and Relationships in East African Banana Germplasm." *Theoretical and Applied Genetics 102* (6): 965–970.

Possehl, G. L. 1986. *Kulli: An Exploration of Ancient Civilization in Asia* (Vol. 1). Carolina Academic Press.

Pwiti, G. 2005. "Southern Africa and the East African Coast." In A. B. Stahl (ed.), *African Archaeology: A Critical Introduction*, pp. 378–391. Cambridge: Blackwell.

Robertshaw, P., Wood, M., Melchiorre, E., Popelka-Filcoff, R. S., and Glascock, M. D. 2010. "Southern African Glass Beads: Chemistry, Glass Sources and Patterns of Trade." *Journal of Archaeological Science 37* (8): 1898–1912.

Schrire, C. (ed.). 2009. *Past and Present in Hunter Gatherer Studies*. Walnut Creek: Left Coast Press.

Shipton, C., Helm, R., Boivin, N., Crowther, A., Austin, P., and Fuller, D. Q. 2013. "Intersections, networks and the Genesis of Social Complexity on the Nyali Coast of East Africa." *African Archaeological Review 30* (4): 427–453.

Soper, R. 1976. "Archaeological Sites in the Chyulu Hills, Kenya." *Azania: Journal of the British Institute in Eastern Africa 11* (1): 83–116.

Soper, R. C. 1966. "Archaeological Sites in Tsavo East National Park." Unpublished manuscript, Nairobi.

Stahl, A. B. 2004. Political Economic Mosaics: Archaeology of the Last Two Millennia in Tropical Sub-Saharan Africa." *Annual. Review of Anthropology 33*: 145–172.

Tishkoff, S. A., Reed, F. A., Friedlaender, F. R., Ehret, C., Ranciaro, A., Froment, A and Ibrahim, M. 2009. "The Genetic Structure and History of Africans and African Americans." *Science 324* (5930): 1035–1044.

Walz, J. R. 2010. *Route to a Regional Past: An Archaeology of the Lower Pangani (Ruvu) Basin, Tanzania, 500–1900 CE.* Doctoral dissertation, University of Florida.

Wood, E. T., Stover, D. A., Ehret, C., Destro-Bisol, G., Spedini, G., McLeod, H., and Hammer, M. F. 2005. "Contrasting Patterns of Y Chromosome and MtDNA Variation in Africa: Evidence for Sex-biased Demographic Processes." *European Journal of Human Genetics 13* (7): 867–876.

Wood, M. (2000). *Making Connections: Relationships Between International Trade and Glass Beads from the Shashe-Limpopo Area. Goodwin Series*, pp. 78–90.

## Chapter 3

# Ancient Connections between China and East Africa

Chapurukha M. Kusimba

### EAST AFRICA AND THE INDIAN OCEAN TRADE

Over the past five decades, investigations from archaeological as well as historical sources have revealed that the cultural growth on the eastern coast of Africa is closely linked to the development of complexly organized merchant towns, receiving ship borne goods from the far corners of the world and sending forth the produce of the interior of Africa (Kusimba 1999, 2, figure 2.1). The coastal region of East Africa played a prominent part in world history from the very beginnings of recorded time. In prehistoric times, it was the bridge from which the first Africans left the continent to venture east and colonized the world. In historic times, the north, the Somali coast, offered entrepots to the caravan routes leading to the Nile Valley through such legendary towns as the forbidden city of Harar. Its central reaches in Kenya and Tanzania linked the people and produce of the Great Lakes region on the Highlands with the markets on Zanzibar and the island archipelagos. In the south, ports along the Mozambique Strait trafficked inland with the plateaus of Zambezia and the mineral riches controlled by the Shona kingdoms ruled from monumental towns like Great Zimbabwe (Kusimba 1999, 1; Kusimba et al. 2017; Pikirayi 2001; Pwiti 2005; Mitchell 2005; Sinclair et al. 2012).

Up to the 1980s, the East African coast was strewn with the remnants of this ancient culture: the ruins of once flourishing towns with their elite mansions and mosques built in coral rag.[1] These prominent remains were built by ancestors of modern coastal peoples about 500 to 1,200 years ago. Their culture was nominally Islamic, and they interacted with and were influenced by centuries of economic contact with and colonization from southern Arabia, western India, and Portugal (Hourani 1995; Pearson 1999, 2003). Direct and indirect connections with communities as far as Indonesia and China was likely established early following the successful settlement of Austronesians in Madagascar (Dewar and Wright 1993; Dewar et al. 2013). Yet despite this welter of external contacts, it was a culture that remained essentially African in nature (Mathew 1956).

Archaeological and anthropological research specifically aimed at understanding ancient transcontinental communication between Africa and Eurasia are still in their infancy. Subaltern scholarship attempts to fill the void has callously engaged in silencing Africa from the conversation (Abu-Lughod 2008, 186–89; Chaudhury 1985, 1990). Fortunately, this is beginning to change (e.g., Hawley 2008; Pearson 1999, 2003). Africa and Asia have shared in cultural, economic, and technological innovations for millennia. Many of the food crops that are now staple foods in much of sub-Saharan Africa were first experimented with and domesticated in Asia. Some of the African domesticates including sorghum, millet, and coffee are widely consumed by contemporary Asians as staples (Crowther, et al. 2014, 2016; Fuller et al. 2011; Prendergast et al. 2016; Shipton et al. 2013).

Ancient connections between Africa and Asia, including China are exhibited in the numerous archaeological remains that have been recovered at many sites across the continent (e.g., Chami 1998; Chittick 1984, 65–71; Horton and Middleton 2000; Pikirayi 2001). Artifacts including Indo-Pacific beads, glass, Middle-East glazed pottery and jewelry, Chinese stoneware and porcelain, among others have been recovered at nearly all medium-to-large settlements along the Eastern and Southern African subcontinent from the Tang Dynasty to the present (Wilson 2016). These non-African materiality bears witness to the global connections, contributions, and complexity of the Africa's past and systematically dismantles the long-held narrative that Africa was isolated from Eurasia and, apart from North Africa, contributed precious little to global civilization (Abu-Lughod 2008, 188).

Recent and ongoing collaborative research investigation across Africa and Eurasia are unveiling new data sets that enable us to move beyond traditional uses archaeologists and historians have made of exotic artifacts. In Africa, nonlocal pottery, including Islamic and Chinese porcelain, have been employed in the (1) determination of settlement chronologies (2) establishment of Islam and Islamization, a code word for Arabian immigration; and (3) establishment of commercial and political colonies in Africa by Asians. Much of this way of interpreting ancient connections, contributions, and complexities of cultural interactions has been thoroughly discredited (Kusimba and Walz 2018; Wynne-Jones and LaViolette 2018).

## GLOBAL CONNECTIONS: CHINA AND AFRICA

Trade played an important role in the development of cultures throughout ancient times. Trade linked diverse peoples and communities in a network on interactions that had a huge impact in advancement of the daily life. Archaeologists and historians have documented evidence of biological, cultural, linguistic, commercial, and technical communication between East Africa and the Middle East beginning from the early first millennium CE (e.g., Beaujard 2012; Seland 2014). The *Periplus of the Erythrean Sea*, a third-century mariner's guide presumably written in Alexandria, mentions that iron lances, hatchets, daggers, and awls made at Muza, east of Aden constituted trade items consigned for African markets (Casson 1989). Trade items from the East African coast consigned for foreign markets in India, the Middle East, and China included marine products—tortoise shells and ambergris; animal products ivory, rhinoceros' horns and cat skins; and vegetable products—mangrove poles, wood, and timber. Turtle shells and ambergris were in high demand in India and China. (Horton 1996, 414). Ivory, rhinoceros' horns and leopard skins were exported to India, China, and Persian Gulf. (Yulvisaker 1982). Timber for building and aromatic products were needed in the Persian Gulf until relatively recently. Demand for African timber in the Gulf was high enough to be reported by Ibn Hawqal c. 960 CE who wrote that houses in Siraf were built of wood from the country of the Zinjs (Martin and Martin 1978).

Textiles including silk and cotton were spurn in Mogadishu, Pate, Manda, Zanzibar, Kilwa, Mahilaka, and other major towns and their products widely traded in Eastern Africa reaching as far as Egypt. Upon their visit to Pate, the Portuguese were sufficiently impressed by the high-quality silk manufactured there. Mining and working of iron was an important industrial activity at Malindi and other Swahili towns. The superior quality of iron products made in East Africa was impressive enough to be added on the list of African exports to India by Indian merchants who regularly visited the coast with the aid of annual monsoon winds (Horton 1996, 418). Noted Arab scholar Al Masudi who visited East Africa in 912 CE left one of the most cogent descriptions of the iron industry on the coast in his *The Meadows of Gold and the Mines of Gems*. Commenting on the ongoing transoceanic trade between East Africa and Asia, he wrote:

> The Zanj exported gold, silver, iron, ivory, tortoise shell, and slaves. Iron was probably the source of the largest profits. Indian merchants came to buy iron and took it back to their own country where they resold it to the manufactures of iron weapons. The Zanj of Malindi owned and worked iron mines, as did other towns, but Malindi must have been the most important. East African iron

was much valued in India, partly because there was no lack of supply and partly because it was of good quality yet easy to fashion and they became masters of the skill of working. The Indians were said to make better swords than anyone else, and weapons made of the iron of Zanj were used throughout the Middle East and countries of the Indian Ocean. (Freeman-Grenville 1962, 20; Shinnie 1965, 107)

Long-distance trade was a crucial factor in the development of complex African chiefdom, states, and urban polities that emerged during the latter half of the first millennium of our era to the sixteenth century CE. Autonomous urban polities emerged along the East African coast, from Somalia to Mozambique. The residents who were drawn largely from the region pursued diverse but complementary vocations, which ranged hunting, agrarian, fishing, and trading. Available records indicate connections with countries to the north extending in Eurasia. The locals' engagement in local, region, and transoceanic trade appear to have served as the main catalyst for building communal and personal wealth which witnessed a steady transformation of the villages and hamlets into small towns, cities, and ultimately to city-states that increasing boasted large and diverse citizenry. As these cities transformed into states that hosted an economic and political elite that vied for managerial control of sources of wealth, they attracted attention and strove to forge and maintain relationships and build alliances with their transoceanic and hinterland partners (Kusimba and Kusimba 2005, 2018; Kusimba et al. 2005). The cities' prosperity was affirmed and fostered by social and political stability across the region. Evidence for relational and political stabilities is found in, bonds, pacts, and treaties, usually, called blood brotherhoods in East Africa (Herlehy 1984). Within the cities themselves, alliances sanctified through opportunistic intermarriages among the political and economic elite, who included foreign residents were the norm. These relationships bound the city's residents to their neighbors in the rural hinterland and strangers across the sea were the kernel upon which African connections, contributions, and complexity depended. Continued regional and intercontinental prosperity depended upon forging and maintaining commercial and cultural dialogue among interacting partners (Middleton 2004).

It is now apparent from genetic studies that the residents of early coastal towns and city-states were initially drawn from different linguistic and ethnic groups but in time, one language, Kiswahili, became the dominant language of choice (Nurse and Spear 1985; Walsh 2018). Thus, economic and social interaction among diverse groups who made their living from hunting, herding, farming, and trading must be credited with laying the foundation from which international trade exchange systems interlocked. Toward the last quarter of the first millennium, ca. 750 CE, Islam was introduced and gradually expanded to become the primary religion and means of elite cultural expression by the time of European contact in early 1500 CE and into the present day.

At the beginning of the second millennium CE, Eastern and Southern Africa, indeed the much of Africa had become a regular partner in the millennial old long-distance exchanges that reached as far as the Arabian Peninsula, India, Sri Lanka, and China (Walmsey 1970; Warmington 1974; Wilkinson 2003). By the thirteenth century, there had emerged a local African urban elite that financed, managed, and controlled local, regional, and transoceanic trade and communications along the East African seaboard. Innovations were made in ironworking-aided agricultural intensification and specialization in hunting, fishing, and herding. These changes improved the quality of life and precipitated population growth, and economic prosperity for some two hundred years.

In the late fifteenth century, however, Europe began to control and benefit from the millennial old trade in the Indian Ocean (Acemoglu and Robinson 2012; Kusimba 1999). The rivalry for control of Indian Ocean commerce was economically crippling for Africa and Asia and beneficial for Europe. The consequences of competition for control of transoceanic trade led to warfare that favored Europeans due to their superior naval and military power. The post-sixteenth century ushered in an era of decline and dependence while paving way for Europe's colonization of Asia in the seventeenth century and Africa in the nineteenth (Oka 2018a 2018b; Oka et al. 2009).

Economic decline and the ceding of sociopolitical power to European nations was a region-wide phenomenon that affected Asian and African political economies. Legitimate and mutualistic regional and transoceanic trade gave way to the now-infamous ivory and slave caravans, financed by overseas merchant groups. Coastal slave raiding expeditions weakened long-standing alliances among peoples, cut off traditions of herding and farming and decimated populations. Today, the ruined walled towns of the east African coast and in the African interior suggest the magnificence of Africa's achievements and contributions to world history.

## THE ROLE OF ISLAM IN LINKING CHINA AND EAST AFRICA

The statement attributed to Prophet Mohamed, "seek knowledge even unto China" lays the basis for understanding the importance of China in global trade in the Western Indian Ocean and Southwestern Asia in ancient times. The Memorial Mosque in Guangzhou is the first mosque in China. Build on orders of Emperor Yong Hui in 651 CE, the mosque, which still stands today, provides the earliest evidence of formalization of Islam in China. Historically, and in ancient times, there were two routes that linked China to the western Asia and Africa: an overland route through central Asia and western Asia and the sea through South China Sea and the Indian Ocean by way of Indonesia, Sri Lanka, the Persian Gulf (Horton 1996, 307).

The Tang through Song Dynasties (618–1279 CE) six centuries of unprecedented technological, scientific, and sociopolitical advances in Asia, called the period of Asian renaissance (Abu-Lughod 2008 187; Gordon 2007). The rise of Islam and imperial unification and consolidation of power in China, Central Asia, Western Asia, and North Africa under the Caliphates based in Baghdad and Cairo, and the rise of large states and kingdoms in South Asia fostered social and political stability.

Advances in science and technology were accompanied by investment in large industrial complexes that manufactured silk, ceramics, beads, jewelry, cloth, spices, and other items for the global market heralded the first truly global economy since the fall of the Roman Empire (Wilkinson 2003). Local traders and merchants, encouraged and quite possibly financed by the political elite, felt more emboldened to invest in long distance more risky business enterprises. Networks of trade created conditions for free movement of traders, merchants, scholars, and adventurers leading to bidirectional transfer of knowledge, culture, and people (table 3.1).

Islam and its cultural norms were transmitted to China, Central Asia, and Africa during this period. There was also a simultaneous transmission of cultural values in the opposite direction. Relations between China, Central Asia, Western Asia, Southeast Asia, and South Asia during the Tang Dynasty through the Sung, until the Ming Revolt, were a combination of commerce, diplomacy, and gift exchange. The political elite played a crucial role in the establishment of trade agreements. For example, between 651 to 798 CE, nearly forty diplomats visited China. Increased trade missions Arabian and

Table 3.1 Renaissance in Asia and Africa during the Tang-Sung Dynasties 618–1279 CE

| Region | Science | Technology | Economy | Politics |
|---|---|---|---|---|
| China | Chinese medical systems | Porcelains, Stonewares | Global Trade | Tang, Sung, Yuan Dynastic rule |
| Southeast Asia | ?? | Porcelains, Stonewares | Global Trade | Srivijaya Empire |
| Southwest Asia | Unani | Lustre wares, Green Glazed wares | Global Trade | Abbasid in Baghdad and Mamluks in Cairo |
| South Asia | Ayurveda | Crucible steel | Global Trade | Chola, Rashtrakuta, Chalukya |
| Africa | ?? | Crucible steel | Global Trade | Swahili, Great Zimbabwe |

Ancient Connections between China and East Africa    41

**Table 3.2    Chronological Context of Long-Distance Trade**

| Period | Time | Archaeological Finds | Transoceanic Trade |
|---|---|---|---|
| Period V | 1750–1950 CE | Indo-Pacific beads, glass bangles, Chinese blue on white, Japanese Karatzu ware, European Floral ware Islamic monochrome pottery, iron and iron slag, | Frequent regional and international trade—Persian Gulf, India, China (decline) and Europe, Americas (expand) |
| Period IV | 1500–1750 CE | Stylistically diverse local pottery, Indian pottery, European peasant floral wares | Regular regional and international trade-Persian Gulf, India, China, Indonesia |
| Period IIIb | 1250–1500 CE | Stylistically diverse local pottery, spindle whorls, coins, portable stoves and lamps, chlorite schist, Islamic monochromes, Chinese Longquan and Tongan ware, Indonesian Sawankholok or Sisatchanalai jars, Indo-Pacific beads and Egyptian glass, | Regular regional and international trade with China, Southeast Asia, India, Persian Gulf |
| Period IIIa | 1000–1250 CE | Stylistically diverse local pottery, rock crystal, spindle whorls, copper and silver coins, Islamic Sgraffiato, Chinese Qing Bai, Cizhou ware, Bronze mirrors, Indo-Pacific beads, | Regular regional and international trade with Persian Gulf, Egypt, India, and possibly China |
| Period IIb | 600–1000 CE | Zanjian Pottery: red burnished and hagshaped cooking pots, graphite finish and trellis patterns; Partho-Sassanian Islamic, white-glazed, Chinese green glazed stone ware, grey-green "Yue" ware, Guangdong Coastal Green, white porcelain, white stone ware, and Egyptian glass, carnelian beads, iron and iron slag | Egypt, Persian Gulf and Indian Subcontinent |
| Period IIa | 300–600 CE | Azanian pottery: triangular oblique, and double zigzag patterns predominate; Sassanian Islamic, glass, and carnelian beads and Roman Amphora | Some trade |
| Period I | 100BCE–300 CE | Local Early Iron Age pottery, iron and Iron slag | No Evidence |

Persian traders. The convergence of politics and commerce benefited from the peaceful climate that was fostered between the two empires.

Seen from a strictly anthropological lens, the Eastern and Southern Africa subcontinent was an integral component of a large network of ancient maritime trade in the Indian Ocean frequently mentioned in early travel accounts by Chinese, Arab, Indian mariners and scholars. The Periplus of the Erythraen Sea published in the first century CE is a standard volume describing the expansive interaction spheres and the agents of this universe (Casson 1984). Much of the interactions appear to have been indirect through the agency of South Asia or Southwest Asian merchants, primarily Persian, Arabian, Indian, and quite possibly Indonesian. Although there is ample archaeological evidence of Chinese material culture in Africa, there does not seem to have been regular direct evidence during the Roman colonization of North Africa. The earliest known evidence for direct contact dates between 202 BCE and 220 CE. The first mention of Africa in Chinese sources has been attributed to Tuan Ch'eng-Shi (died 863 CE), in the land of Po-pa-li, the fabled the land of Punt to Greeks or the Cinnamon Coast to Romans (Duyvendak 1949).

Bulk trade consisted of foodstuff and food crops including rice, honey, millet, and bananas. Other products exchanged included textiles—silk and cotton cloth, spices and aromatics, precious stones, construction materials. These include mace, nutmeg, cinnamon cloves, ambergris, rubies, diamonds, sapphires, emeralds, pearls, porcelain, beads, gold, silver, cowry shells (Cyraea moneta), animal skins, leather, and slaves[2] among others (Pearson 2003, 84, 86). These much sought after items are not preserved in the archaeological record and are not easy to account for where literary records have not survived. Instead, the most archaeologically frequently recovered remains have included jewelry, ceramics—stoneware and porcelain, glass, beads, and coinage. For instance, Chinese trade ceramics have been recovered at virtually all urban settlement in East Africa. Most appear from the Tang-Sung transition to modern times.

The recovery of Chinese coinage from several East African settlements, including Mogadishu, Kilwa, and recently at Mambrui and Manda dating from Song through Ming Dynasties (960–1644), provides critical evidence for interactions between China and East Africa (Kusimba et al. 2018; Pankhurst 1961, 268). Such evidence, especially that of coinage, points to possible diplomatic missions between China and Africa. The issuance and circulation of gold coinage was highly restricted and when issued, often pointed to direct diplomatic gestures from the Emperor to his counterpart. Therefore, the presence of imperial Chinese coins might provide the most direct archaeological evidence for direct contact.

Archaeological investigations on the African subcontinent and on the Western Indian Ocean, at sites such as Chaul, Palshet, Sanjan, and Kelshi (Gogte

2002) have yielded material remains that point to nearly 2,000 years of continuous interaction of East Africa and India at least from the eighth century up to eighteenth century. Islamic and Chinese pottery as well as Islam and its cultural norms were transmitted to China, Central Asia, and Africa during this period. There was also a simultaneous transmission of cultural values in the opposite direction. Relations between China, Central Asia, Western Asia, and South Asia during the Tang Dynasty were a combination of commerce, diplomacy, and gift exchange (Wilkinson 2003). Chinese records show that nearly forty diplomats visited China between 651 and 798 CE. Trade missions by Arabian and Persian traders who primarily used the overland trade route via the Black Sea and Indian merchants who sailed through the port of Malacca exponentially increased.

China had become the fulcrum upon which global trade in Asia, Africa, and Europe hinged (Mitchell 2005). The convergence of politics and commerce benefited from the peaceful climate that was fostered between the two major empires—the Abbasids and China. The presence of Indo-Pacific beads produced in India (Dussubieux et al. 2008; Wood 2011), the occurrence of typical Indian pottery, and to some extent, portable cooking stoves in archaeological contexts on the East African Coast indicates locational and relational stability that encourages immigration between India, Western Asia, and the East Africa. The region and especially the main ports of trade had become cosmopolitan centers of commerce and hosted diverse Diaspora residences and quarters (Datoo 1970: Laviolette 2008, Oka 2018a).

Today, the great majority of East Africans who identify themselves Swahili still live on the coast or within a few miles of it. They are Muslims and speak an Eastern Bantu language, Swahili, which has over the years borrowed and adapted Arabic, Hindi, Urdu, Portuguese, and more recently English words into its vocabulary. This is testimony to the transnational character of the world of the Indian Ocean nurtured by the "peaceful coexistence" fostered between 700 and 1500 CE when a power shift in favor of Europe destroyed the millennial old global trade (Curtin 1984, 34). Swahili social structure, domestic, and religious architecture provide testament to the cultural fusion of indigenous and Diaspora value systems (Mazrui and Shariff 1994; Knappert 1979; Middleton 2004). Nevertheless, these Diaspora influences did not change African peoples' identities as some scholars have vigorously argued. Rather as Swahili scholar Mohamed Abdulaziz (1979, 8) reminds us:

> The Arab-Islamic component . . . acted as a strong cultural stimulus to the development of this urban form of African culture. Past historians have often failed to acknowledge the African initiative in the formation of Swahili culture. To them, it would appear, every aspect of urban living represented remnants of direct Arab presence. In any given period, the Arab population element must have been very small, compared to the population of the local inhabitants. Indeed, the

Table 3.3  Commodities Exchanged Between China and East Africa

| Dynasty | Chinese Exports | African Exports | Sites |
|---|---|---|---|
| Han Dynasty (206 BCE–220 CE) | Sugar, wine, wheat flour, paper, silk, ceramics, ironware | Rhinoceros horn, elephant tasks, tortoise shell, Pearls | Nanyue Kingdom (Guangzhou) |
| Six Dynasties (220–589 CE) | | | |
| Sui Dynasty (581–618 CE) | | African ambergris | |
| Tang Dynasty (618–907 CE) | Sugar, wine, wheat flour, paper, silk, ironware, ceramics: Tongguan and Qionglai Wares (Changsha Painted Wares) (Hunan); Grey-green ware of Yue type; Green-glazed stoneware (Guangdong); Nn white glazed stoneware-Fanchang kiln (Anhui); White Stoneware (Ding Ware) | Rhinoceros horns, ambergris, elephant tusks, incense and ebony, *Aloe vulgraris*, bloom, | Manda, Shanga, Dembeni, Unguja Ukuu  *Fujian and Guangzhou ports were principal gateways |
| Song Dynasty (960–1279 CE) | Monochrome stonewares, Sn Chinese qingbai, green glazed stonewares (Zhejiang, Guangdong, Fujian); green glazed stoneware (Yaozhou kilns (Shaanxi); Ding style white ivory glazed porcelain (Hebei) | Rhinoceros horn, elephant tusks; ambergris, incense, pearl, and so forth | *Qingbai stone ware and porcelain were the most popular exports to East Africa |
| Yuan Dynasty (1279–1368 CE) | Silk, ceramics: Green-glazed stoneware Longquan (Fujian coastal kilns); blue-on-white, copper-red, white-ivory glazed, Qingbai porcelain, green-grey glazed stoneware | Rhinoceros horn, elephant tasks, tortoise shell, pearls  *Iran sgraffiato | Mapungubwe, Great Zimbabwe, Manda, Mtwapa, Gede, Mogadishu, Mombasa, Songo Mnara, and so forth |
| Ming Dynasty (1368–1644 CE) | Blue-and-white (Jingdezhen); Longquan green-glazed stoneware declines | *Blue-and white porcelain and green glazed stoneware from southeast Asia—Vietnam, Thailand, and Myanmar | Mapungubwe, Great Zimbabwe, Manda, Mtwapa, Gede, Mnarani, Mombasa, Songo Mnara, and so forth |
| Qing Dynasty (1644–1912 CE) | | | |
| Republic (1912 CE) | | Rhinoceros horns, ambergris, elephant tusks, Incense and ebony, *Aloe vulgraris*, bloom, | |

trend on the Coast has always been the Swahilization of Arabs rather than the Arabization of the African Muslim inhabitants, in such facets of culture, and the mode of living in general. This trend has been so forceful that most Arabs on the Coast, who have settled here within the last two centuries or so, have lost their original culture and language and completely adopted Swahili culture. (Cited from Askew 1999, 72)

Contrary to scholarship that has sought to diminish East Africa's role in international trade, tangible archaeological evidence for regular connections is traced as far back as third century CE, when cultural artifacts including Roman era beads and ceramics Arab, Persian, Chinese and Indian jewelry, beads, cloth, and porcelain by the eighth century. These artifacts show East Africa's involvement and connection to the global trade networks of the Mediterranean Sea, Persian, Gulf, and Indian Ocean without whose participation the sought-after African products, including gold from Zimbabwe would not have been possible (Curtin 1984, 34; Pearson 2003, 76).

## CHINESE TRADE CERAMICS FOUND IN EAST AFRICA

The ubiquity of Chinese porcelain and other precious stones recovered in archaeological contexts has shaped a narrowly focused narrative for archaeology, leading them to assume that porcelain was the most important item from China. Porcelain and other items are overrepresented because of their survivability. In reality, they constitute a very small percentage, perhaps as low as 5 percent of the entire bulk trade carried out between China and the western Indian Ocean (see Pearson 2003, 85). Spices, cloth precious metals, and enslaved persons were among the principal products exchanged.

Trade ceramics, including Chinese porcelain excavated from the East African coastal sites constitutes 0.04 percent of the entire pottery assemblage. In other words, 4 out of every 10,000 ceramic shards recovered are trade ceramics (Mutoro 1978). Trade ceramics recovered in East Africa usually include Islamic stoneware and glazed ceramics, Chinese stoneware and porcelain, Indonesian and Thai porcelain, and Indian unglazed pottery (e.g., Chittick 1984; Horton 1996; Sassoon 1975). Trade ceramics have been reported from fifth century contexts at Swahili sites such as Chibuene, Unguja Ukuu, Kilwa, Shanga, Manda, Mogadishu, and Ungwana. Interestingly, nearly 50 percent of trade ceramics are of Chinese origin (Oka 2008). The volume of transoceanic trade appears to have increased between the tenth and fourteenth centuries in favor of Chinese ceramic products. The preference for Chinese porcelain over Islamic and Indian glazed pottery speaks to the superior quality of Chinese products (Oka et al. 2009). Contact between East Africa and China from the Tang to Sung to Yuan Dynasties was primarily indirect through Persian and Arab merchants using the overland trade routes through central Asian across the Black Sea and through the South China Sea via Malacca, around the Coromandel coast, Aden, and onward to East Africa through the agency of Chinese, Indian, and Arab merchants. Another equally plausible reason for trade expansion by the Yuan Dynasty beginning from the thirteenth century encouraged Chinese merchants to invest in long-distance trade with other regions (Pearson 2003, 89).

The technical and aesthetic superiority of Chinese ceramics over their potential competitors ensured their high value among the emerging local economic and political elite (Montella 2017). Chinese ceramics, unlike African and Islamic pottery, were made from a wide range of clay raw materials available throughout China (Vainker 1991 218). Qualitatively, Chinese clay was nonvitreous such that when fired it matured at about 1200°C, forming nonporous vessels with a long-use life. In addition, the design, form, and decorative motifs employed by Chinese designers--ranging from naturalistic to landscape—had universal appeal for use in both sacred and profane contexts—in the home entertaining and impressing one's guests and as décor in temples and mosques. These attributes, including transportability and durability ensured the global high demand and near monopoly for Chinese trade ceramics.

As already noted above, import trade in East Africa included many items from China. However, the popularity of trade ceramics to East Africa continued from the ninth to the nineteenth century (Chittick 1986: 65; Horton 1996, 303). This importation declined when Europeans took control of Indian Ocean trade. The Taiping rebellion destroyed the famous Jingdezhen kilns and disrupted overland trade in China (Abu-Lughod 2008 191).

## CHINESE TRADE CERAMICS FOUND IN EAST AFRICA

Chinese trade ceramic excavated in East Africa date from the Han to Qing Dynasty, from 206 BCE to 1912 CE (Zhao and Qin 2018). I provide brief descriptions, below.

### Tongguan and Qionglai Wares (Changsha Painted Wares)

Tongguan wares are thickly potted bowls with freely painted abstract and floral motifs in green and green and brown under a yellowish or greenish-olive glaze. They are known to have been made at Tongguan kilns near Changsha in Hunan Province, some considerable distance from the coast (Hughes-Stanton and Kerr 1981, 57–9). The glaze was lead-free glaze of amber and brown color. The decoration was executed in underglaze color painted onto the body. Qionglai wares made from the Qionglai kilns in Sichuan are also painted wares Many Qionglai wares were covered with a whiter slip and glazed light green, yellow, or brown. The painting was underglaze usually in brown. Both wares, primarily in the form of bowls were excavated at Manda and Shanga in ninth century contexts (Chittick 1984, 66; Horton 1996, 303). Elsewhere, Tongguan and Qionglai painted pottery has been reported at Laem Pho and Ko Kho Khao on the Kra Isthmus in Thailand, at Prambanan in central Java, at Mantai in Sri Lanka, and Brahminabad and Bambore, in Pakistan, and Samarra in Iraq and Aqaba in Jordan (Ho 1994; Vainker 1991, 82; Whitcomb 1989 182). The wide distribution of Changsha painted ware is a very reliable indicator of the international appeal and increasing trade between China and the rest of the world, including Africa as early as the Tang Dynasty (Horton 1996, 303; Whitehouse and Williams 1975).

## Grey-Green Ware of Yue Type

Yue ware occurred in different colors from a matte/gray-green glaze on a grayish-white body. Color variation ranging from yellow-green to gray green to the rare jade may be attributed to different sources of clay, firing conditions, and kilns. Although the precise regions of production are not reliably known, the diversity in color points to multiple kilns involvement, primarily those in Fujian, Guangdong, and Zhejiang (Horton 1996, 303; Tregear 1976, 47). The Chinese regarded green porcelain, which resembled jade, as being superior to whiter porcelain, which was popular abroad. Natural forms including plants and clouds, typify the decorative motifs of early Yue ware and were incised by hand under the glaze. Later Yue wares have bird designs added to their repertoire. The popularity of Yue ware both in China and overseas is apparent in the second part of the Tang Dynasty (618–907 CE) and through the period of the Five Dynasties (906–960 CE). Yue ware, primarily bowls, have been found at Manda and Shanga and dated to ca. 750–920 CE (Chittick 1984, 66; Horton 1988, 311 1996, 303). Elsewhere outside China, these wares have been reported in Indonesia, Sri Lanka, Brahminabad in Pakistan, Siraf in Iran, Samarra in Iraq, and Fustat in Egypt (Tampoe 1989, 64; Vainker 1991, 72).

## White Stoneware (Ding Ware)

Usually associated with Dingyao and Fujian kiln industrial complexes, white stonewares are dated to the after 900 CE (Horton 1986 209 1996, 309; Hughes and Kerr 1981, 72). They are composed of cream-colored paste with a white glaze similar to white porcelain, above, but more thickly potted

(Chittick 1984, 67). Decorations consist of faint vertical ribs on the body of the vessel. The forms are all open bowls with foot rings, which are slightly outward flaring (Horton 1996, 309). They appear at Shanga and Manda in tenth-century contexts and are used "beyond the twelfth century—at the time when the Ding kilns had converted to the production of true white porcelain" (Horton 1996, 309; Chittick 1984, 67).

## White Wares (Qingbai Glazed Ware)

White porcelain or Qingbai are characterized by the absence of slip between the body and the glaze. Traditionally, the slip is widely used by potters to mask imperfections in the body and to provide a smooth surface for glazing. Typical white porcelain vessels were primarily made from the exceptionally pure clays of Gongxian and Xing famous for their unusually low iron and titanium content. This accounted for the whiteness and their popularity both in China and abroad. However, like all other vessels Qingbai glazed white wares were produced at different industrial complexes including those in Fujian, Jiangxi, Jingdezhen, and Dehua. Qingbai vessels have been recovered at Manda in unstratified contexts and assigned to 850–950 CE contexts (Chittick 1984, 66) and at Shanga in the period spanning the twelfth and mid-thirteenth century (Horton 1996, 309). White porcelain has also been reported at several other sites and was imported into East Africa until the thirteenth century (e.g., Abungu 1990; Wilding 1980). Elsewhere large quantities of Gongxian and Xing wares have been found at Siraf in the Persian Gulf and Samarra in Iraq (Vainker 1991, 67; Whitehouse 1968 17).

## Longquan Greenware (Celadons)

Longquan greenwares, also known as celadon, are characterized by light gray paste, very hard, with air bubbles, and slightly granular texture. The bowls usually have a pale gray "sugary" fabric. The glazes range through shades of greens and grays to pure dark while the fabric thickness ranges from 3 to 12 mm. Most Longquan vessels tend to be single colored and were decorated with impressed or incised lines or molded forms. Although production at Longquan kilns in Southern Zhejiang began in the Five Dynasty period (906–960AD) and intensified during the Song period (960–1279 CE), it was only during the Yuan period that Longquan wares became wildly popular outside China (Ho 1994, ix-x). In fact, once established, demand for Longquan products rivaled and outcompeted local Islamic, Indian, and African ceramics (Ho 1994; Miksic 1994; Tampoe 1989, 65). The earliest examples in East Africa date only to the eleventh to early twelfth century (Horton 1996, 307). The ubiquity of Longquan at archaeological sites in late thirteenth to early fourteenth century contexts attests to their popularity as export ware and points to incontrovertible evidence for mass production (Kamei 1994). James Kirkman recovered large amounts of Longquan wares from Ungwana, Gede, Ishakani, Kilepwa, and Mnarani (Kirkman 1954, 1963, 1966).

Two groups of these wares have been identified in East Africa. The first group consists of a white body, green glaze, and incised decorative motifs. The second group is the coarse type with a dark grayish body with a light greenish glaze. The foot-ring of coarse celadon is usually unglazed (Chittick 1974, 309). Their popularity often transcended their beauty and utility both to their consumers. To the Chinese, the celadon impressed with a lotus signified purity since the lotus is the seat of Buddha. To the Muslim Arabs and Swahili, celadons were highly valued because of their presumed ability to crack if they came in contact with poison (Sassoon 1975). This characteristic made them especially popular with the economic and political elite who often feared that once in their life, a close member of the family would attempt to end their life prematurely in order to inherit their wealth or political office (Phillips 1967).

## Blue-on-White Porcelain

Blue-on-white porcelains were developed during the Yuan Dynasty (ca. 1279–1368 CE) at the Jiangxi kilns (Hughes-Stanton and Kerr 1981 242–7). This porcelain was a high-fired porcelain with an underglaze decoration in blue on a white background. This decorative style was achieved by first painting blue designs using cobalt directly on the unfired clay then blowing a transparent glaze on the piece and firing it in the kiln at temperatures in the range of 1350°C. Blue-on-white wares were so popular because any design could be painted on them. The Chinese Blue-on-white wares were the commonest imported wares after the fourteenth century during the Ming Dynasty (Horton 1996, 310; Kusimba 1993). The Chinese potters were very flexible and opportunistically made designs in response to market demands. Some of the common designs were dragons, primarily three-clawed dragons, rhinoceros horn cups (for happiness), feather fans (zhong-li-quan's emblem— a Taoist god and discoverer of the secret of immortality), sacred incense burners, flaming pearls (for faith), the endless knot (a Buddhist symbol for long life), classic scrolls, diaper or diamond patterns, lotus panels (or false gadroons), vertical leaf patterns, chrysanthemums, a variety of unidentifiable flowers, and others. The list of possible designs was endless. Once the Chinese potters mastered the technique of achieving cobalt blue locally the demand for these wares soared. Before 1300 CE, the Chinese imported pure cobalt from the Middle East, hence the name cobalt blue (Zhu et al. 2015).

Not surprisingly, both Muslim and European potters made imitations of blue-on-white and after the destruction of the pottery factories of Jingdezhen,

European, Arab, Persian, Indian, Japanese, and Thai potters had mastered the technique well enough to establish pottery factors that made Chinese imitation porcelain to satisfy the global demand of Chinese porcelain (Chittick 1974, 310; Oka et al. 2009).

## Transitional Pottery

Transitional pottery was made between 1673 and 1683 from the time of Emperor Wanli (1573–1620) to the early days of Kangxi (Vainker 1991, 226). Transitional bowls with the yin-yang symbols first appeared during the Transitional Period. The yin-yang symbols represent the duality of nature and the balance between male and female. They are recognized by the eight horizontal lines between the yin-yang representing natural forces—heaven, wind, earth, fire, water, vapor, thunder, and mountains (Sassoon 1975). Designs with dancing boys as well as naturalistic representations of the Three Friends, the pine, prunes, and bamboo, were added to the traditional trade ceramics out of China during the Ming (1368–1644 CE) and Qing Dynasties (1644–1912 CE). Transitional pottery recovered at Swahili coast sites has included bowls and dishes with formal floral patterns in blue and white on the inside and single-colored glazes outside.

## Dehua Wares

Dehua wares are a creamy white ware commonly referred to as blanc-de-chine or Chinese white ware made in Dehua, in Fujian Province. Blanc-de-chine were made during the Qing Dynasty following the reopening of porcelain factories in the reign of Kangxi in 1683. Artifacts recovered in contexts have mostly been small objects and figurines (Sassoon 1975).

## Yang-Ts'ai, the Foreign Colors: Rose Porcelains of the Qing Dynasty

Yang-ts'ai or foreign colors is often regarded by many authorities as one of the finest porcelain made during the Qing Dynasty. The French were impressed by this fine porcelain and christened it famille rose, or the pink family. This was successfully achieved by combining fine particles of gold with tin to produce a dull-pink enamel polychrome. Yang-Ts'ai, wares appear in East African during the reigns of Yongzheng (1723–1735) and Qianlong (1736–1795) (Ho and Bronson 2004). Plain white wares, quite similar to the celadons, in blue borders patterned with under glaze-incised lines were also imported to East African during this period. Many were recovered at Fort Jesus (Kirkman 1974).

## USES OF IMPORTED CERAMICS IN EAST AFRICA

Archaeologists in East Africa traditionally use Chinese trade ceramics to (1) characterize the nature and intensity of Indian Ocean trade and China's role in this commerce; (2) determine regional relative site chronologies, settlement patterns, and class and wealth distinctions; and (3) understand technology transfer and influence on cultural practice. Due to their nondestructive character, Chinese trade ceramics constitute the clearest archaeological evidence for contact between East Asia and Africa. Trade ceramics has enabled archaeologists to determine relative site chronologies as well as dates of early contacts and connections (Kirkman 1974, 87). As noted above, international trade in East Africa included many items from China, especially silk (Zhijuan 2006). Trade in the Indian Ocean declined following the Taiping Rebellion, which ended with the destruction of the Jingdezhen kilns, impacted both overland and Oceanic trade. However, the popularity of trade ceramics and other Chinese products in Africa has continued up to the present day.

Data drawn from ethnography and archaeology continues to reveal the relatively early engagement of coastal communities including hunter-gatherers, pastoralists, farmers, and townsfolk in regional trade, which included transoceanic trade (Kusimba 2008; Kusimba et al 2013, 2018; Oka 2018a, 2018b; Walz 2010). Chinese trade ceramics was among the principle imports and were universally popular and in high demand in the region. Trade ceramics were displayed in elite homes, in Mosques, and on tombs to memorialize ancestors (Wilson 1982). Thus, in addition to serving utilitarian functions, trade ceramics were symbols of prestige and status among the coast East African peoples.

## TRADE CERAMICS AS SYMBOLS OF POWER, STATUS, AND PRESTIGE

The Swahili elite home was sometimes built with niches, called vidaka, in which valued family objects were displayed. Vidaka were usually located in the inner sections of the home. These objects included expensive Chinese plates, bowls, and jars, Islamic bronze jars, plates, and other exotic items. Like other communities, the Swahili regarded the success and status of a family in the size of its household and stone house, the beauty of the home, and the value of the contents. Since the Swahili were predominantly matrilocal, daughters often inherited their parent's homes. Families used their daughter's wedding ceremony to publicly display wealth through gift exchange. Public display of wealth in the form of Chinese trade ceramics, silk, jewelry, and other expensive items served to enhance family status, prestige, and standing

## Use in Water Cisterns

Water shortage was a perennial concern for urban residents in East Africa. The Swahili constructed large water cisterns to collect rain water. Communal as well as extended family wells supplied water to the resident populations. Cisterns helped increase the humidity in the houses during the hot and dry seasons. Although the cisterns were a partial solution to the water shortage their construction provided a health risk. Because of their nonporous and non-corrosive qualities, the Swahili found Chinese porcelains to be finely suited for placing under the water cisterns primarily to monitor the cleanliness of water and to provide shelter for the small fishes or cichlids so that when the cisterns were drained to be cleaned, the fishes would collect on the plates or bowls to avoid suffocation. Cichlids consumed mosquito larva keeping their numbers manageable. The white and blue-and-white porcelains made it easier to detect dirty water, even in the usually poorly lit windowless interior rooms of the Swahili homes.

## Use to Memorialize Ancestors

Chinese porcelain was placed on tombs to memorialize ancestors on the East African coast. The Swahili high regard for Chinese porcelain transcended its durability, beauty, and function. Among the Swahili also, tombs memorialized ancestors to ensure continuity of the bond with their descendants (Fleisher and Wynne-Jones 2012; Wilson 1982). Well-constructed and maintained tombs symbolized family or clan success and good standing in the community. Two general tombs' styles coexisted: with pillars and without pillars. According to Ahmed Sheikh Nabhany, pillar tombs were built for men, while those without belonged to women. Only women's tombs were decorated with Chinese porcelain to display the identity of the deceased and family's wealth. Thus, although Islam forbade burial with property, the Swahili seem to have found a way of connecting with and honoring ancestors without dishonoring the Holy Qur'an. Swahili tombs are uniquely local and African. Pillar tombs do not occur in Arabia, Iran, or Iraq.

# DISCUSSION AND CONCLUSION: TRADE CERAMICS AS EVIDENCE FOR EARLY CONTACT WITH CHINA

The available archaeological evidence shows little evidence for direct contact between China and Africa before the Ming Dynasty (1368–1644 CE). However, as the pre-Ming records show, both regions maintained indirect contact (e.g., Duyvendak 1949). Chinese imperial voyages increased during the Yuan Dynasty as trade with Central and Western Asia increased (Zhujian 2006). However, historians hail expeditions led by Admiral Zheng He (his fifth voyage) through the South China Sea to the Indian Ocean and East Africa in 1417 and 1419 as the standard. During this East African voyage, the admiral visited the East African coast cities of Malindi in Kenya and Barawa and Muqdishu in Somalia. In an earlier visit to China, the ambassador of Malindi had presented to Emperor Yongle (1403–1425), the third Ming emperor, among other gifts a tsu-la (giraffe in Chinese?). Impeccable records regarding the voyages undertaken by Zheng He and his lieutenants were kept. They were however destroyed following the palace coup following the death of the Yongle emperor (Kusimba 1999, 1).

Despite this unfortunate turn of events, some records of Zheng He's voyages are preserved in books written by his lieutenants who recount the ports, towns, cities, peoples, cultures, and products of places they visited. For example, Kung Chen published *Record of the Barbarian Countries in the Western Ocean* (1434), Fei Hsin wrote *Triumphant Visions of the Starry Raft* (1436), Ma Huan wrote *The Triumphant Visions of the Boundless Oceans* (1451). The fourth book was *The Record of Tribute-Paying Western Countries* (1520) was a compendium of compass directions and mariners chart incorporating the maritime knowledge acquired by Zheng He's expeditions (see Xinfeng, this volume). Fei Hsing's description of the east coast of Africa is instructive:

> The country is situated in a remote corner of the west. The inhabitants live in solitary and dispersed villages. The walls are piled-up bricks and the houses are masoned in high blocks. The customs are very simple. They grow neither herbs nor trees. Men and women wear their hair in rolls; when they go out they wear a linen hood. The mountains are uncultivated, and the land is wide; it rains very rarely. There are deep wells worked by means of cogwheels. Fish are caught in the sea with nets. The products of the country are lions, gold-spotted leopards, and camel birds [ostriches], which are six or seven feet tall. The dragon saliva [ambergris], incense, and golden amber. As merchandise are used vermilion, colored silks, gold, silver, porcelains, pepper, colored satins, rice, and other cereals. (Mirsky 1964, 256)

The golden era of East African coastal civilization was in the fourteenth century. Zheng He's visit to East Africa coincided with severe droughts which were followed by the devastating Little Ice Age (1450–1715 CE). Most Swahili settlements Shanga, Manda, Ungwana, Mwana, Gede, Mnarani, Kilepwa, Jumba la Mtwana, and Mtwapa among others declined and were abandoned during that period. Upon their visit to Mogadishu, the Chinese sailors found the cities citizens already dealing with the effects of drought. Intracommunity tensions and violent behavior were high. Lacking pastures, they fed fish to their camels, horses, cattle, and sheep (Mirsky 1964, 256).

According to the late Swahili scholar Ahmed Sheikh Nabhany, the relations between the East African coast and China during the preindustrial period transcends commercial contact through trade ceramics. In my interview with him in 1994, he told me of

> A Swahili legend that Washanga are descended from Chinese sailors who got wrecked along the coast of Shanga. The previous name for that village was Kwa Bakari. The story runs thus: On one of their voyages, a Chinese junk got wrecked along the coast of Shanga. The crew swam across and were rescued by the local inhabitants. Knowing that they would not be able to make the return voyage, these Chinese people asked for and were granted permission to settle on the island but outside the main village. For subsistence, these people used to fish and sell the fish to the town's people in exchange for rice, sorghum and other cereals. It so happened that one day when all the Chinese fishermen were at sea fishing, the village was attacked by some marauding forces [name not given] that killed everybody leaving very few women, children, and the elderly. When the Chinese fishermen returned in the evening not having any idea what had happened, they were very surprised to find the entire town in smoke with dead bodies strewn all over the place. The Chinese fishermen attended to the wounded and rebuilt the town. They also married some of the widowed women and raised families with them. The Swahili word for surprise is Kushangaa. I understand the name for Kwa Bakari changed to Shanga from that day on. (Nabhany interview August 12 1994)

Since our interview, Chinese geneticists have reportedly successfully identified Swahili residents who bear direct Chinese ancestry in the village of Siyu on Pate Island (Embassy of the People's Republic of China in the Republic of Kenya 2005; figure 3.1).

## A SUMMING UP

Ancient trade between East Africa and China was a complex affair that involved many communities and took several routes. One the one hand, some African commodities such as ivory, ambergris, gold, rhinoceros' horns, sandalwood were in high demand in Asia, including China (Freeman-Grenville 1962, 21). On the other hand, demand for Chinese porcelain and silk among African elites was high. The recovery of Chinese porcelain from early Swahili settlements place trade between Africa and China to the Tang Dynasty. Owing to distance, the volume of trade between East Africa and China was

Figure 3.1  Mrs. Baraka Badi Shee, Her Son Badi Sharif, and Her Grandson Saidi Are the Residents of Siyu Whose DNA Revealed Paternal Ties to East Africa. *Source*: Chapurukha M Kusimba.

comparatively lower than that from Southwest Asia and South Asia. There were two principle routes of trade; the overland caravan through Central Asia and Southwest Asia via the Persian Gulf and India Ocean and the direct maritime route through the South China Sea and Indian Ocean via Sri Lanka along the West Indian Seaboard to East Africa via Aden (Horton 1996, 418).

The expansion of maritime trade in the South China Sea and Indian Ocean saw settlements like Mantai and Galle in Sri Lanka and Chaul, Khambat, and Gujarat along the west coast of India, develop into major ports of trade (Carswell and Prickett 1980; Oka 2018a). Hindu, Muslim, and Jewish merchants were the primary agents of the western Indian Ocean commerce (Ghosh 1994). Thus, significant quantities of whitewares made in Fujian, mainly Ding, qingbai, and molded whitewares, the use of Chinese and Indian coins, the close similarity of Chinese greenwares recovered at ports like Homs, Syria; Chaul, India; Shanga, Manda, and Mtwapa, Unguja Ukuu, Kilwa, and Songo Mnara (Horton 1996, 418; Whitehouse 1976, 146), points to the major advances that China had made in technology and which, though indirect linked the two regions global commercial networks. Our ongoing research at Manda, Takwa, Shanga, and Siyu in the Lamu archipelago in Kenya has begun a multiyear interdisciplinary project that hope to address the nearly 2,000 history of interaction between China and Africa.

## NOTES

1. Hundreds of these ruins have been destroyed since the 1990s by developers, local communities, and neglect (Kusimba, 1996 see also Mturi, 2005, Pollard et al. 2012; Schmidt and McIntosh, 1996).
2. African slaves were first brought to China by Arab merchants during the Tang-Sung times (Pearson, 2003, 85).

## REFERENCES

Abdulaziz, M. 1979. *Muyaka: 19th Century Swahili Popular Verse*. Nairobi: Kenya Literature Bureau.
Abu-Lughod, J. L. 1989. *Before European Hegemony*. Oxford: Oxford University Press.
Abu-Lughod, J. L. 2008. "The World Systems in the Thirteenth Century: Dead-end or Precursor?" In S. Khagram and P. Levitt (eds.), *The Transnational Studies Reader*, pp. 184–195. New York: Routledge.
Abungu, G. H. O. 1990. *Communities on the River Tana, Kenya: An Archaeological Study of Relations Between the Delta and the River Basin, 700–1890 AD*. Unpublished Ph.D. Dissertation, Cambridge University.
Acemoglu, D. and Robinson, J. A. 2013. *Why Nations fail: The Origins of Power, Prosperity, and Poverty*. New York: Crown Business.
Allen, J. 1993. *Swahili Origins: Swahili Culture and the Shungwaya Phenomenon*. Athens: Ohio University Press.
Askew, K. M. 1999. "Female Circles and Male Lines: Gender Dynamics Along the Swahili Coast." *Africa Today* 46(3): 67–102.
Beaujard, P. 2018a. "The Progressive Integration of Eastern Africa into an Afro-Eurasian World-System, First-Fifteenth Centuries CE." In S. Wynne-Jones and A. LaViolette (eds.), *The Swahili World*, pp. 365–377. London: Routledge.
Beaujard, P. 2018b. Trade, Traders, and Trading Systems: Exchange, Trade, Commerce and the Rise/Demise of Civilization." In K. Kristiansen, T. Lindkvist, and J. Myrdal (eds.), *Ancient Trade and Civilization*, pp. 242–250. Cambridge: Cambridge University Press.
Carswell, J. and Prickett, M. 1980. "Mantai 1980: A Preliminary Investigation." *Ancient Ceylon* 5: 11–37.
Casson, L. 1984. *Ancient Trade and Society*. Detroit, MI: Wayne State University Press.
Casson, L. 1989. *Periplus Maris Erythraei*. Princeton, NJ: Princeton University Press.
Chami, F. 1998. "A Review of Swahili Archaeology." *African Archaeological Review* 15: 199–218.
Chaudhuri, K. N. 1985. *Trade and Civilization in the Indian Ocean: An Economic History from the Rise of Islam to 1750*. New York: Cambridge University Press.
Chaudhuri, K. N. 1990. *Asia Before Europe: Economy and Civilisation of the Indian Ocean From the Rise of Islam to 1750*. New York: Cambridge University Press.

China Daily. July 11, 2005. I"s this young Kenyan Chinese descendant?" *China Daily* [website]. Available at http://www.chinadaily.com.cn/english/doc/2005–07/11/content_459090.htm.

Chittick, H. N. 1974. *Kilwa: An Islamic Trading City on the East African Coast. Memoir – British Institute in Eastern Africa;* no. 5. Nairobi: British Institute in Eastern Africa.

Chittick, H. N. 1984. *Manda: Excavations at An Island Port on the Kenya Coast. Memoir British Institute in Eastern Africa*; no. 9. Nairobi, London: British Institute in Eastern Africa.

Crowther, A., Horton, M., Kotarba-Morley, A., Prendergast, M., Quintana Morales, E., Wood, M., Shipton, C., Fuller, D. Q., Tibesasa, R., Mills, W. and Boivin, N. 2014. "Iron Age Agriculture, Fishing and Trade in the Mafia Archipelago, Tanzania: New Evidence from Ukunju Cave." *Azania: Archaeological Research in Africa* 49(1): 21–44.

Curtin, P. D. 1984. *Cross-Cultural Trade in World History*. Cambridge: Cambridge University Press.

Datoo, B. 1970. "Rhapta. The Location and Importance of East Africa's First Port." *Azania* 5: 65–77.

Dewar, R. E. and Wright, H. 1993. "The culture history of Madagascar." *Journal of World Prehistory* 7(4): 417–466.

Dewar, R. E., Radimilahy, Chantal, Wright, Henry T., Jacobs, Zenobia, Kelly, Gwendolyn O. and Berna, Francesco. 1993. "Stone Tools and Foraging in Northern Madagascar Challenge Holocene Extinction Models." *Proceedings of the National Academy of Sciences* vol. 110(31): 12583–12588.

Dussubieux, L., Kusimba, C. M., Gogte, V., Kusimba, S. B., Gratuze, B. and Oka, R. 2008. "The Trading of Ancient Glass beads: New Analytical Data From South Asian and East African Soda–Alumina Glass Beads." *Archaeometry* 50(5): 797–821.

Duyvendak, J. J. L. 1949. *China's Discovery of Africa*. London: A. Probsthain.

Fleisher, Jeffrey B. 2003. *Viewing Stonetowns from the Countryside: An Archaeological Approach to Swahili Regions, AD 800–1500*. PhD. Dissertation, Department of Anthropology, University of Virginia.

Fleisher, J. 2010. "Rituals of Consumption and the Politics of Feasting on the Eastern African Coast, AD 700–1500." *Journal of World Prehistory* 23(4): 195–217.

Fleisher, J. and Wynne-Jones, S. 2012. "Finding Meaning in Ancient Swahili Spatial Practices." *African Archaeological Review* 29(2–3): 171–207.

Freeman-Grenville, G. S. P. 1962. *The East African Coast: Select Documents from the First to the Nineteenth Century*. Oxford: Clareton Press.

Ghosh, A. 2011. *In An Antique Land: History in the Guise of a Traveler's Tale*. New York: Vintage.

Gogte, V. D. 2002. "Ancient Maritime Trade in the Indian Ocean: Evaluation by Scientific Studies of Pottery." *Man and Environment* 27(1): 57–67.

Gordon, S. 2007. *When Asia Was the World: Traveling Merchants, Scholars, Warriors, and Monks Who Created the 'Riches of the 'East'?* Da Capo Press.

Hawley, J. C. ed. 2008. *India in Africa, Africa in India: Indian Ocean Cosmopolitanisms*. Bloomington: Indiana University Press.

Herlehy, T. J. 1984. "Ties That Bind: Palm Wine and Blood-Brotherhood at the Kenya Coast During the 19th Century." *The International Journal of African Historical Studies* 17(2): 285–308.

Ho, C. ed. 1994a. *New Light on Chinese Yue and Longquan Wares: Archaeological Ceramics Found in Eastern and Southern Asia, AD 800–1400.* Hong Kong: University of Hong Kong.

Ho, C. 1994b. "The Production and Distribution of Zhejiang Green Glazed Wares." In C. Ho (ed.), *New Light on Chinese Yue and Longquan Wares: Archaeological Ceramics Found in Eastern and Southern Asia, AD 800–1400,* pp. ix–xxvi. Hong Kong: University of Hong Kong.

Ho, C. and Bronson, B. 2004. *Splendors of China's Forbidden City: The Glorious Reign of Emperor Qianlong.* New York: Merrell.

Hodgson, M. G. 1993. *Rethinking World History: Essays on Europe, Islam and World History.* Cambridge: Cambridge University Press.

Horton, M. 1984. *The Early Settlement of the Northern Swahili Coast.* Ph.D. Dissertation, Cambridge University.

Horton, M. 1988. Early Muslim Trading Settlements on the East African Coast: New Evidence from Shanga. *The Antiquaries Journal* 68: 290–325.

Horton, M. 1996. *Shanga: The Archaeology of a Muslim Trading Community on the Coast of East Africa.* Memoirs of the British Institute in Eastern Africa; no. 14. London: The British Institute in Eastern Africa.

Horton, M. 2013. "Ibadis in East Africa: Archaeological and Historical Evidence. In M. Hoffman- Ruf and A. Al Salimi (eds.), *Oman and Overseas,* pp. 93–106. Heldesheim: Georg Olms. Verlag.

Horton, M. and Middleton, J. 2000. *The Swahili: The Social Landscape of a Mercantile Society.* Oxford: Blackwell Publishers.

Hourani, G. F. 1995. *Arab Seafaring in the Indian Ocean in Ancient and Early Medieval Times: revised and expanded by John Carswell.* Princeton: Princeton University Press.

Hughes-Stanton, P. and Kerr, R. 1981. *Kiln Sites in Ancient China: An Investigation Let by the People's Republic of China.* London: Oriental Ceramic Society.

Kamei, M. 1994. "Chronology of Longquan Wares of the Song and Yuan Periods." In C. Ho (ed.), *New Light on Chinese Yue and Longquan Wares: Archaeological Ceramics Found in Eastern and Southern Asia, AD 800–1400,* pp. 46–84. Hong Kong: University of Hong Kong.

Kirkman, J. S. 1954. *The Arab City of Gedi: Excavations at the Great Mosque: Architecture and Finds.* Oxford: Oxford University Press.

Kirkman, J. S. 1963. *Gedi: The Palace.* The Hague: Mouton and Company.

Kirkman, J. S. 1964. *Men and Monuments on the East African Coast.* London: Lutterworth Press.

Kirkman, J. S. 1966. *Ungwana on the Tana: Studies in African History, Anthropology and Ethnology.* The Hague: Mouton and Company.

Kirkman, J. S. 1974. *Fort Jesus: A Portuguese Fortress on the East African Coast.* Oxford: Clarendon Press.

Knappert, J. 1979. *Four Centuries of Swahili Verse.* London: Heinemann.

Kusimba, C. M. 1993. *The Archaeology and Ethnography of Iron Metallurgy of the Kenya Coast*. Ph.D. Dissertation, Bryn Mawr College.

Kusimba, C. M. 1994. "Chinese Ceramics in the Fort Jesus Museum Collection." *Kenya Past and Present* 26, 55–59.

Kusimba, C. M 1999. *The Rise and Fall of Swahili States*. Walnut Creek: AltaMira Press.

Kusimba, C. M. 2008. "Early African Cities: Their Role in Shaping Rural Urban Interaction Spheres." In J. Marcus and J. Sabloff (eds.), *The Ancient City: New Perspectives on Urbanism in the Old and New World*, pp. 229–246. Santa Fe: School of Advanced Research Press.

Kusimba, C. M. 2013. "African Perspectives." In M. Hoffman-Ruf and A. Al Salimi (eds.), *Oman and Overseas*, pp. 387–402. Heldessheim: Georg Olms. Verlag.

Kusimba, C. M. 2017. "The Swahili and Globalization in the Indian Ocean." In Tamar Hodos (ed.), *The Routledge Handbook of Archaeology and Globalization*, pp. 104–122. London: Routledge Handbooks.

Kusimba, C. M. 2018a. "(Re) Introducing the State on the Medieval Swahili Coast." In John L. Brook, J. C. Strauss and G. Anderson (eds.), *State Formations: Global Histories and Cultures of Statehood*, pp. 90–107. Cambridge: Cambridge University Press.

Kusimba, C. M. 2018b. "Trade and Civilization in Medieval East Africa: Socioeconomic Networks." In K. Kristiansen, T. Lindkvist and J. Myrdal (eds.), *Ancient Trade and Civilization*, pp. 320–353. Cambridge: Cambridge University Press.

Kusimba, C. M. and Oka, R. 2009. "Trade and Polity in East Africa: Re-Examining Elite Strategies for Acquiring Power." In T. Falola and Matt D. Childs (eds.), *The Changing Worlds of Atlantic Africa*. Durham: Carolina Academic Press.

Kusimba, C. M and Kusimba, S. B. 2005. "Mosaics and Interactions: East Africa, 2000 b.p. to the present." In A. B. Stahl (ed.), *African Archaeology*, pp. 392–419. Oxford: Blackwell Publishers.

Kusimba, C. M. and Kusimba, S. B. 2018. "Mosaics: Rethinking African Connections in Coastal and Hinterland Kenya." In S. Wynne-Jones and A. LaViolette (eds.), *The Swahili World*, pp. 403–418. London: Routledge.

Kusimba, C. M. and Walz, J. R. 2018. "When Did the Swahili Become Maritime?: A Reply to Fleisher et al. (2015), and to the Resurgence of Maritime Myopia in the Archaeology of the East African Coast." *American Anthropologist* 120(3): 429–443.

Kusimba, C. M., Kusimba, S. B. and Wright, D. K. 2005. The Development and Collapse of Precolonial Ethnic Mosaics in Tsavo, Kenya. *Journal of African Archaeology* 3(2): 243–265.

Kusimba, C. M., Kusimba, S. B. and Dussubieux, L. 2013. "Beyond the Coastalscapes: Preindustrial Social and Political Networks in East Africa. *African Archaeological Review* 30(4): 399–426.

Kusimba, C. M., Nam, K. and Kusimba, S. B. 2017. "Trade and State Formation on the Ancient East African and Southern Zambezia." In R. J. Chacon and R. G. Mendoza (eds.), *Feast, Famine or Fighting? Multiple Pathways to Social Complexity*. New York: Springer.

Kusimba, C. M.. Williams, Sloan R., Monge, Janet, Mchula, Mohamed, Oka, Rahul, Oteyo, Gilbert, Kusimba, Sibel and Dussubieux, Laure. 2018. "Mtwapa, Betwixt in Between Land and Sea: Foundings of an African City State." In Stephanie Wynne-Jones and Adria LaViolette (eds.), *The Swahili World*, pp. 226–230. London: Routledge.

LaViolette, A. 2008. "Swahili Cosmopolitanism in Africa and the Indian Ocean World, AD 600–1500." *Archaeologies* 4(1): 24–49.

LaViolette, A. and Fleischer. J. 2005. "The Swahili." In A. B. Stahl (ed.), *African Archaeology*, pp. 392–419. Oxford: Blackwell Publishers.

Liu, Z., Ji, H. and Gao, W. 2006. *The Story of Silk*. Beijing: Foreign Languages Press.

Martin, E. B. and Martin, C. P. 1978. *Cargoes of the East: The Ports, Trade and Culture of Arabian Seas and Western Indian Ocean*. Nairobi: Elm Tree Books.

Mathew, G. 1956. "The Culture of the East African Coast in the Seventeenth and Eighteenth Centuries in the Light of Recent Archaeological Discoveries." *Man* 56(5): 64–68.

Mazrui, A. M. and Shariff, I. N. 1994. *The Swahili: Idiom and Identity of an African People*. Trenton, NJ: Africa World Press.

Middleton, J. 1992. *The World of the Swahili: An African Mercantile Civilization*. New Haven: Yale University Press.

Middleton, J. 2001. "Merchants: An Essay in Historical Ethnography." *Journal of the Royal Anthropological Institute* 9: 509–526.

Middleton, J. 2004. *African Merchants of the Indian Ocean: Swahili of the East African Coast*. Long Grove: Waveland Press.

Miksic, J. 1994. "Recently discovered Yue and Longquan Green Glazed Wares in the Thirteenth and Fourteenth Centuries in Singapore and Riau Islands." In C. Ho (ed.), *New Light on Chinese Yue and Longquan Wares: Archaeological Ceramics Found in Eastern and Southern Asia, AD 800–1400*, pp. 229–250. Hong Kong: University of Hong Kong.

Mirsky. 1964. *The Great Chinese Travelers*. Chicago: University of Chicago Press.

Mitchell, Peter. 2005. *African Connections: Archaeological Perspectives on Africa and the Wider World*. Walnut Creek: Altamira.

Montella, A. 2017. "Chinese Porcelain as a Symbol of Power on the East African Coast from the 14th Century Onward." *Ming Qing Yanjiu* 20(1): 74–93.

Mutoro, H. W. 1978. *Takwa*. Masters Thesis. University of Nairobi.

Nabhany, Ahmed Sheikh. 1994. *Personal Interview*. Mombasa: Fort Jesus Museum.

Nurse, D. and Spear, T. 1985. *The Swahili: Reconstructing the History and Language of an African Society 800–1500*. Philadelphia: University of Pennsylvania Press.

Nurse, D., Hinnebusch, T. J. and Philippson, G. 1993. *Swahili and Sabaki: A Linguistic History* University of California Press.

Oka, R. 2008. *Resilience and Adaptation of Trade Networks in East African and South Asian Port Polities, 1500–1800 CE*. Ph.D. Thesis. University of Illinois at Chicago.

Oka, R. 2018a. "Global Commerce: South Asia and the Swahili Coast." In S. Wynne-Jones and A. LaViolette (eds.), *The Swahili World*, pp. 419–429. London: Routledge.

Oka, R. 2018b. "Trade, Traders, and Trading Systems: Macromodeling of Trade, Commerce and Civilization in the Indian Ocean." In K. Kristiansen, T. Lindkvist and J. Myrdal (eds.), pp. 279–319. Cambridge: Cambridge University Press.

Oka, R. and Kusimba, C. M. 2008. "Archaeology of Trading Systems 1: A Theoretical Survey." *Journal of Archaeological Research* 16: 339–395.

Oka, R., Dussubieux, L., Kusimba, C. M. and Gogte, V. D. 2009. "The Impact of Imitation Ceramic Industries and Internal Political Restrictions on Chinese Commercial Ceramic Exports in the Indian Ocean Maritime Exchange, ca. 1200–1700." In *Scientific Research on Historic Asian Ceramics: Proceedings of the Fourth Forbes Symposium at the Freer Gallery of Art* (pp. 175–185).

Pankhurst, R. 1961. "Introduction to the Economic History of Ethiopia. Ethiopia." *Observer* 5(3): 234–235.

Pearson, M. N. 1999. *Port Cities and Intruders: The Swahili Coast, India, and Portugal in the Early Modern Era.* Baltimore: Johns Hopkins University Press.

Pearson, M. N. 2003. *The Indian Ocean.* London, New York: Routledge.

Phillips, W. 1957. *Oman: A History.* Reynal.

Pikirayi, I. 2001. *The Zimbabwe Culture: Origins and Decline of Southern Zambezian States.* Walnut Creek: Altamira.

Pollard, E., Fleisher, J. and Wynne-Jones, S. 2012. "Beyond the Stone Town: Maritime Architecture at Fourteenth–Fifteenth Century Songo Mnara, Tanzania." *Journal of Maritime Archaeology* 7(1): 43–62.

Popelka, R. S., Glascock, M. D., Robertshaw, P. T., and Wood, M. 2003. "Chemical Analysis of Ancient African Glass Beads." In *68th Annual Meeting of the Society for American Archaeology.* Milwaukee, WI.

Possehl, G. L. 1986. "African Millets in South Asian Prehistory." In J. Jacobsen (ed.), *Studies in the Archaeology of India and Pakistan*, pp. 237–256. New Delhi: Oxford University Press.

Prendergast, M E., Rouby, H., Punnwong, P., Marchant, R., Crowther, A., Kourampas, N., Shipton, C., Walsh, M., Lambeck, K. and Boivin, N. L. 2016. "Continental island formation and the archaeology of defaunation on Zanzibar, Eastern Africa." *PloS One* 11(2): e0149565.

Pwiti, G. 2005. "Southern Africa and the East African Coast." In A. B. Stahl (ed.) *African Archaeology: A Critical Introduction*, pp. 378–391. Cambridge: Blackwell Publishers.

Raaum, R. L., Williams, S. R., Kusimba, C. M., Monge, J. M., Morris, A. and Mohamed, M. M., et al. 2018. "Decoding the Genetic Ancestry of the Swahili." In S. Wynne-Jones and A. Laviolette (eds.), *The Swahili World*, pp. 81–103. London: Routledge.

Ratnagar, S. 2004. *Trading Encounters from the Euphrates to the Indus in the Bronze Age.* New Delhi, IN: Oxford University Press.

Ray, H. P. 2003. *The Archaeology of Seafaring in Ancient South Asia.* Cambridge, UK: Cambridge University Press.

Rougeulle, A. 1998. "Medieval Trade Networks in the Western Indian Ocean (8th–14th Century): Some Reflections from the Distribution Pattern of Chinese Imports in the Islamic World." In H. P. Ray and J.-F. Salles (eds.), *Tradition and Archaeology: Early Maritime Contacts in the Indian Ocean.* New Delhi: Manohar.

Sarjeant, R. J. 2000. "The Hadrami Network in the Indian Ocean." In D. Lombard and G. Aubin (eds.), *Asian Merchants and Businessmen in the Indian Ocean and the China Sea*, pp. 145–153. Oxford; New Delhi, India: Oxford University Press.

Sassoon, C.1975. *Chinese Porcelain in Fort Jesus*. Mombasa: National Museums of Kenya.

Sassoon, C.1978. *Chinese Porcelain Marks from Coastal Sites in Kenya: Aspects of Trade in the Indian Ocean, XIV–XIX Centuries*. BAR International Series (Supplementary) 43.

Sedov, A. V. 1998. "Qana (Yemen) and the Indian Ocean: The Archaeological Evidence." In H. P. Ray and J.-F. Salles (eds.), *Tradition and Archaeology: Early Maritime Contacts in the Indian Ocean*, pp. 11–35. New Delhi: Manohar.

Seland, E. 2014. Archaeology of trade in the western Indian Ocean, 300 BC–AD 700. *Journal of Archaeological Research* 22(4): 367–402.

Shinnie, M.1965. *Ancient African Kingdoms*. London: Edward Arnold.

Sinclair, P. and Hakansson, T. 2000. "The Swahili City-State Culture." In M. Hansen (ed.) *Comparative Study of Thirty City-State Cultures*, pp. 461–482. Copenhagen: CA Reizels Forlog.

Sinclair, P., Ekblom, A. and Wood, M. 2012. "Trade and Society on the South-East African Coast in the Later First Millennium AD: The Case of Chibuene." *Antiquity* 86(333): 723–737.

Steensgard, N. 1987. "Indian Ocean Networks and Emerging World Economy." In S. Chandra (ed.), *Indian Ocean: Explorations in History, Commerce and Politics*, pp. 125–150. New Delhi: Munshiram Manoharlal Publishers Pvt. Ltd.

Tampoe, M. 1989. *Maritime Trade between China and the West: An Archaeological Study of the Ceramics from Siraf (Persian Gulf), 8th–15th Centuries AD*. Vol. 555. BAR International Series. London: British Archaeological Reports.

Tolmacheva, M., Stigand, C. H. and Weiler, D. 1993. *The Pate Chronicle: Edited and Translated from MSS 177, 321, 344, and 358 of the Library of the University of Dar es Salaam*. East Lansing: Michigan State University Press.

Tregear, M. 1976. "Chinese Ceramic Imports to Japan Between the Ninth and Fourteenth Centuries." *The Burlington Magazine* 118(885): 816–825.

Udovitch, A. L. 1970. *Partnership and Profit in Medieval Islam*. Princeton, NJ: Princeton University Press.

Vainker, S. J. 1991. *Chinese Pottery and Porcelain*. London: British Museum Press.

Vance, J. E. J. 1970. *The Merchant's World: The Geography of Wholesaling*. Englewood Cliffs, NJ: Prentice Hall.

Walmsey, A. 2000. "Production, Exchange and Regional Trade in the Islamic East Mediterranean: Old Structures, New Systems?" In I. L. Hansen and C. Wickham (eds.), *The Long Eighth Century*, pp. 265–343. Leiden: Brill.

Walsh, M. 2018. "The Swahili Language and Its Early History." In S. Wynne-Jones and A. LaViolette (eds.), *The Swahili World*, pp. 121–130. London: Routledge.

Walz, J. R. 2010. *Route to a Regional Past: An Archaeology of the Lower Pangani (Ruvu) Basin, Tanzania, 500–1900 CE*. PhD Dissertation, University of Florida.

Warmington, E. H. 1974. *The Commerce Between the Roman Empire and India*. New Delhi: Vikas Publishing House.

Whitcomb, D. 1989. "Coptic Glazed Ceramics from the Excavations at Aqaba, Jordan." *Journal of the American Research Center in Egypt* 26: 167–182.

Whitehouse, D. 1968. "Excavations at Siraf, first interim Report." *Iran* 6: 1–22.

Whitehouse, D. and Williamson, A. 1975. "Sassanian Maritime Trade." *Iran* 11: 29–49.

Wilding, R. F. 1980. *The Shorefolk*. Mombasa: Fort Jesus Museum.

Wilkinson, D. 2003. "Civilizations as Networks: Trade, War, Diplomacy, and Command-Control." *Complexity* 8: 82–86.

Wilson T. H. 1979. "Swahili Funerary Architecture of the North Kenya Coast." In J. de V. Allen and T. H. Wilson (eds.), *Swahili Houses and Tombs of the Coast of Kenya*, pp. 33–46. London: Art and Archaeology Research Papers.

Wood, M. 2011. "A Glass Bead Sequence for Southern Africa from the 8th to the 16th Century AD." *Journal of African Archaeology* 9(1): 67–84.

Wynne-Jones, S. and LaViolette, A. (eds.). 2018. *The Swahili World*. London: Routledge.

Xinhua. January 14, 2006. "More and More Kenyans Benefit from Chinese Scholarship, Assistance." *People's Daily Online*. Available at http://english.peopledaily.com.cn/200601/14/eng20060114_235401.html

Xinhua. June 30, 2005. "Kenyan Girl with Chinese Blood Steals Limelight." Embassy of the People's Republic of China in the Republic of Kenya [website]. Available at http://www.mfa.gov.cn/ce/ceke/eng/sbgx/ t202741.htm

Ylvisaker, M. 1982. *Lamu in the Nineteenth Century: Land, Trade, and Politics*. Boston: Boston University.

Zhao, B. 2012. "Global Trade and Swahili Cosmopolitan Material Culture: Chinese-style Ceramic Shards From Sanje ya Kati and Songo Mnara (Kilwa, Tanzania)." *Journal of World History* 23(1): 41–85.

Zhao, B and Qin, D. 2018. "Links with China." In S. Wynne-Jones and A. LaViolette (eds.), *The Swahili World*, pp. 430–444. London: Routledge.

Zhu, T., Ding, X., Kusimba, C. M. and Feng, Z. 2015. "Using Laser Ablation Inductively Coupled Plasma Mass Spectroscopy (LA-ICP-MS) to Determine the Provenance of the Cobalt Pigment of Qinghua porcelain from Jingdezhen in Yuan Dynasty of China (1271–1368AD)." *Ceramics International* 41(8): 9878–9884.

*Chapter 4*

# Life, Death, and Identity of the Early Swahili Peoples of the Kenyan Coast

Janet Monge, Allan Morris, Sloan Williams, and Chapurukha M. Kusimba

## THE MORTUARY CONTEXT OF SWAHILI PEOPLES OF THE KENYA COAST

One of the key areas in the archaeology and anthropology of the East African coast has been the identity of the people who founded the urban cities of the Swahili coast (figure 2.1). Up until this research, no systematic study had been taken on the human remains of the people who lived at these settlements to address and settle once and for all, the question of the identity of the people who founded the Swahili urban states. This chapter reports the results of our study.

Beginning in the late 1980s, with the inclusion of the Shanga individuals, human skeletal remains have been excavated from early Swahili graves along the Kenyan Coast. Over 100 skeletons are now available for study and assessment documenting the earliest inhabitants of the Kenyan Swahili coast. A subsample of this collection, excavated in the 1996–1997 field season from Mtwapa, was reported in Kusimba et al. 2014. In this chapter, we present a preliminary study of all 118 skeletons excavated from Mtwapa and Manda from 1996 to 2013. Archaeological, historic, and linguistic data have been used to address the complex issues associated with the origin of the Swahili (Horton and Chami 2018). The skeletal materials add a new dimension to these discussions with a special emphasis on the identity of these intrepid peoples who are by religious identity Islamic, by social identity African but biologically very heterogeneous.

There are a total of ninety-nine skeletons at various stages of preservation from Mtwapa excavated from 1996 to 2010 (Kusimba et al. 2018a). The Manda sample was excavated in one field season in 2012–2013 and yielded the remains of nineteen skeletons (Kusimba et al. 2018b). Immediately after exposure of the skeletons and excavations, bone/tooth samples were taken for aDNA, isotopic, and radiocarbon dating[1]. Observations were also made on the Shanga skeletal materials excavated by Horton (1996).

The burial practice at Swahili settlements conforms to the general tradition throughout the Islamic World: burial with the body close to perpendicular to the geographic position of Mecca with the head and body resting on the right side sometimes with a stone pedestal keeping the head in that position (Peterson 2013). Knees are slightly flexed with arms to the side and crossed near the area of the pelvis, either to the side of the body or directly into the pelvis cavity. Other Muslim practices, including shrouding with no coffin and lack of grave goods, is consistent with the Islamic tradition in many areas of the world[2]. In two cases, objects were found within the burial: a brass ring (finger) at Burial Unit 4J, Operation 7, and a chicken femur bone found inside the skeletal mouth of a young child (Burial Unit 4J, Operation 6). The symbolic meaning or accidental occurrence of these objects is not understood.

At Mtwapa during the 2010 field season, a tomb reduction (Burial Unit 4K) was exposed and excavated containing the commingled remains of at least three individuals. At Manda, fragmentary remains of several different individuals, all of very young children, were found throughout a single excavation unit. Except for these, all burials are similar in mortuary context. There appears to be no distinction between the burial practices associated with male/female or young/old. In several instances, the skeletons were preserved collapsed onto their ventral surface so that they appeared to be lying on their stomachs with the skull face down.

The state of preservation of the remains varies, but in general, Manda skeletons are better preserved than Mtwapa ones, although all the recovered material is fragile and fragmentary. At Mtwapa, the bones, and especially the skull, underwent plastic deformation. So, although the bones are intact, the position of the individual neurocranial bones were compressed and distorted. Thus, because of the fragmentary condition of the remains, we could not undertake metric analysis of the skeletal materials. When possible, long bones were measured and used for a determination of height.

Primary comparisons of the Swahili human skeletal remains were made to the Taita skull materials curated at the Duckworth Laboratory, Leverhulme Centre for Human Evolutionary Studies at the University of Cambridge and to the Dinka, Tepe, Hasanlu, and Tepe Hissar skeletal collections, all derived from archaeological contexts in Iran curated in the Physical Anthropology Section, University of Pennsylvania Museum of Archaeology and Anthropology in Philadelphia, Pennsylvania. The Taita peoples are the closest hinterland neighbors and trading partners of the Swahili peoples and possibly the closest African genetic and morphologically to the Mtwapa and Manda skeletal materials. These skulls were removed from rockshelter shines in the Taita Hills in the 1920s by Louis Leakey and moved to the University of Cambridge and are of recent origin (MacDonald 1996). The Iranian skeletal series derive from a Middle Eastern context, dated to the Bronze and Iron Age, and are used to test the hypothesis that the Swahili have close ties or biological origins in that part of the world.

## MATERIALS AND METHODS

We report a subsample of the Mtwapa materials, thirty-eight in total, and all of the Manda materials nineteen in total, in detail here. Age and sex assignations were performed during excavation and after removal of the skeletons for all of the Mtwapa skeletons. All skeletal materials were reburied after observation. No radiographs or CT scans were performed on the materials in the field. Height estimates were made either by measuring the skeletons in situ (head/trunk to acetabulum-femur length-lower limb segments to calcaneous) or by measurements performed on individual long bone of skeletally mature individuals (Trotter and Glesser 1952; Albanese et al. 2016).

### Determination of Sex

Morphological sex analysis, not to be confused with socially defined gender identification, was undertaken on each individual skeleton that was first aged as skeletally mature (epiphyseal closure on all long bones and at least eighteen to twenty years of age). When possible, the pelvis and skull were used in conjunction with each other using the criteria outlined in the Workshop of European Anthropologists (1980) and Walrath et al. 2004). Skeletal robusticity was used to confirm sex assignation (Uberlaker 1999). Thus, sex of children and juveniles was not determined. In addition, some of the adult skeletal materials could not be assigned to a morphological sex due to the state of preservation of the bones.

### Determination of Age at Death

No fetal remains were recovered among the skeletal remains at either Mtwapa or Manda. Age at death of immature individuals was determined using dental eruption and dental calcification when tooth crown and root formation could be assessed up to the time frame of beginning tooth calcification, eruption through apex formation of the M3s. When tooth calcification could be observed, Demirjian et al., (1973) stage scoring was applied and yielded developmental age at death. However, there is some disagreement as to whether the same age-assessed developmental standards can be applied across all populations (Monge et al. 2007; but see Liversidge 2003). Aging of immature individuals by tooth eruption is less precise and highly variable within individuals in the same population (Smith and Garn 1987). In addition, epiphyseal formation and the stage of union were observed and recorded on all individuals from the teens to the early twenties (Scheuer and Black 2004).

Aging the remains of adults is more challenging and thus are placed into three broad categories containing fifteen plus years of the life span. Aging as a process is more varied among individuals (Crews 2003), whereas growth and development, while still being variable is contained within a shorter time interval and is more predictable.

Aging adults was a multiprong process. First, dental wear based on an internal population assessment of the time frame of wear over the molar sequence using subadults and adult individuals (Miles 1962, 1963, 2001). This technique is considered the best technique for archaeological samples (Lovejoy 1985; Mays 1998; Walker et al. 1991). Second, although results of these analyses by themselves not specific to age categories, showing a very large range of variation, within the postcrania, two areas on the innominate were used to estimate age in adults: the pubic symphyseal face (Brooks and Suchey 1990) and the auricular surface (Buckberry and Chamberlain 2002). On the skull, cranial suture closure (ectocranial and endocranial when possible) and eventual obliteration was also assessed (Meindl and Lovejoy 1985). Third, changes to the bone structure that are primarily age related were also added to the assessments outlined above. Osteoarthritis is known to increase with age affecting multiple joints (Rogers and Waldron 1995; Rogers et al. 1987). Finally, age-related change in bone weight/mass was assessed (Lovejoy et al. 1985; Mays 2000).

## Determination of Ancestry

The skeletal collections from Manda and Mtwapa offer a unique opportunity to focus on the biological origins of the Swahili peoples. Since biological origins is a complex issue, a tiered approach was undertaken with both ancient DNA analysis (results were published in Raaum et al. 2018) and morphological analysis (Sauer 1992 and Ousley et al. 2009). Morphological analysis of the cranial material, along with bone sampling, was performed on skeletons at each of the sites.[3] Macro morphological features were identified on the ancient Swahili crania. These features were developed in the early part of the twentieth century and used as part of the identification of race in the United States in forensic case studies summarized by Brues (1990), Rhine (1990) and Krogman and Iscan (1986) and include features of Americans of

European and African descent. Codification of these features is presented in Hefner 2009. To test the efficacy of these features on crania not of origin in the Americas, comparisons were made to the Taita, Hasanlu, Dinka Tepe, and Tepe Hissar materials described above.

Dental characteristics described as "Afridonty" in living sub-Saharan African populations (Irish 1997, 2013) were also assessed but bearing in mind the critical assessment by Warren et al. 2013 when used on archaeological samples. Comparisons were made to other populations, most especially to the peoples of Asia, using Scott and Irish (2017).

## Determination of Trauma

Cranial trauma was assessed using the criteria outlined by Lovell (1997), Walker (1997), Berryman and Symes (1998), and Sauer (1998). All analyses were performed based on gross morphology with the aid of a hand magnifier (5× to 10×). Distinctions were made among recent/excavation related bone breaks and ante-, peri-, and postmortem fractures. In blunt force trauma, both healed and unhealed, were assessed using concentric and radiating fractures. It is likely that the number of sustained traumatic fractures are underestimated in the Swahili materials due to the state of preservation of the remains, for example, of burst or cranial base ring fractures or fractures of the small bones of the face.

## RESULTS

The sex distribution of the Mtwapa and Manda adult samples are listed in table 4.1. Because of the small sample size for both sites, it is difficult to draw any conclusion except that there is a clear bias to males within the Manda sample and a more equal male/female distribution within the larger Mtwapa sample. Average height of adult females is 1.55 m; adult males, 1.70 m.

Table 4.2 gives the age distribution of the samples. The age distribution of the Mtwapa sample is interesting and unique. Over half of the individuals died under the age of twenty years. This is in stark contrast to the Manda

**Table 4.1 Sex Distribution**

| Site | Male | Female |
| --- | --- | --- |
| Mtwapa | 25 | 21 |
| Manda | 8 | 3 |
| Total | 33 | 24 |

Table 4.2 Distribution by Age. Skeletons Not Aged Were too Fragmentary and/or without Skeletal Elements for Aging

| Age in years | Mtwapa | Manda |
|---|---|---|
| Birth–3 | 12 | 2 |
| 4–to 11 | 8 | 3 |
| 12–19 | 14 | 0 |
| 20–34 | 13 | 3 |
| 35–49 | 9 | 2 |
| 50+ | 7 | 5 |
| Skeletons not aged | 11 | 1 |

sample where mostly adults are represented. The preponderance of youngsters (children and juveniles) within the Mtwapa sample is consistent with a catastrophic event (Paine 2000). The youngest individual was aged based on erupted deciduous incisors and is estimated to have died between six to twelve months of age. The oldest individuals are equally distributed between male and female. Three of the reported individuals who were over fifty years old from Manda are probably best described as geriatric at died at over sixty-five years (Selinsky 2009. The small size of both samples precludes any further analysis of paleodemographic parameters.

Five individuals show evidence of traumatic injury to cranial bones. All are adult males in the categories of middle or late adulthood. Four are derived from Mtwapa, one from Manda. Three of cranial remains clearly show that the injury was antemortem with evidence of extensive healing from a blunt force trauma. All injuries are on the right central squama of the left parietal and all are above the "hat brim line." There is no evidence to suggest that these injuries are part of interpersonal violence, but it cannot be ruled out. More likely these injuries relate to occupation-based injuries with sustained damage from perhaps falling objects from some height. In other words, the location of the injuries is not consistent with a fall. Two individuals from Mtwapa show perimortem wounds with no evidence of healing. Both injuries are consistent with interpersonal violence and are associated with the death of these individuals and both show clear evidence of heaving with both concentric and radiating fractures. In one of these skeletal individuals, there is clear evidence of a cut wound that severed the orbital process of the right frontal bone.

Paleopathological description of the skeletal material were made on linear enamel hypoplasia, arthritic changes in the skeleton, mastoiditis, osteoporosis, long bone fractures with and without healing, markers of occupational stress to name a few. The overall picture emerges of a population facing life and lifestyle challenges leaving an impression on the hard tissues of the Swahili coastal communities both at the earlier Manda settlement site and in the urban environment of Mtwapa.

## THE DENTITION IN AGING, HEALTH, AND DISEASE

Detailed description of the dentition and oral health was recorded on a subset of the skeletons, fifty-seven skeletal individuals. These included carious lesions, periodontal disease, periapical assesses, tooth wear, tooth loss, and calculus formation were recorded. The patterning of these disease processes were consistent with a diet of stone-milled sorghum and millet, the occasional chewing of sugar cane stalks, and, perhaps, with the introduction of gritty sea-acquired animal resources including vegetation. This pattern was also reported by MacDonald (1993) on the Taita collection at the Duckworth Laboratory.

Tooth wear is extensive and angled to the plane of occlusion. The association of tooth wear extent and angle has been related to agricultural-based diets, but the evidence is not clear-cut with mixed results (see Smith 1984; Larsen 1995; Fiorenza et al. 2018). Tooth wear is probably operated synergistically to produce tooth loss in these skeletal individuals along with caries and periodontal disease related to calculus formation. Internal seriation of tooth wear was instrumental in the aging of adult individuals within the coastal Swahili sample (Lovejoy 1985).

Dental calculus formation is also extensively developed within the sample with all adults (young, middle, and old) showing some degree of encrusted formation. Following the classification by Sledzik and Moore-Jensen (1991) calculus was classified as: (1) none, (2) minimal (only effecting the area of the cemental enamel junction), (3) slight to moderate (extending at least 1/3rd up the tooth crown from the cemental enamel junction), (4) heavy (over half the tooth crown is covered in cementum). No individual within the Swahili series had calculus formation considered as "heavy." However, 90 percent of adults had minimal to moderate formation.

Age-related tooth loss and ensuing alveolar bone changes were common within the Swahili samples. Tooth loss most usually affected the lower M3 and M2, next in the sequence of loss were upper M3s and M2s. Least common was loss of both the upper and lower incisors and canines. Within the over fifty years age category, periodontal resorption reduced the depth of the mandible by over 50 percent.

About 1,102 teeth were assessed for position and extent of carious lesions (Hillson 2001); 13.9 percent of teeth have carious lesions ranging in extent from small demineralizations of enamel to penetration of dentin and pulp. Over 70 percent of carious lesions are present on the cemental enamel junction and between the teeth at the gingival line, a pattern that is probably associated with the raking of sugar cane fibers through the teeth. This is a unique pattern of caries formation and not within the classification framework of Larsen et al. 1991.

## POPULATION AFFINITIES: THE SKELETAL AND DENTAL EVIDENCE

Over the last two decades, technological developments in genetics, as well as in the extraction of ancient DNA from hard tissue from archaeological samples, has shown that the biological diversity within Africa is exceptionally high (Tishkoff et al. 2009). Simultaneously, various researchers collecting data on morphological variation of living populations within Africa and have begun the process of linking genetic and phenotypic variation to each other (e.g., Hubbard et al. 2015; Kimura et al. 2015; Park, et al. 2012; Rathmann et al. 2017). It is becoming clear that morphology is reflecting underlying genetic processes and that populations can be distinguished from each other using both lines of evidence. As archaeological materials are integrated into these studies, a picture has begun to emerge of even the time ordered changes encompassed within dynamic population structure (Warren et al. 2014).

The Kenya coast populations are exceptionally complex with circum Indian Ocean peoples probably trading and exchanging genetic materials long before the emergence of the Swahili complex (Raaum et al. 2013). The Mtwapa and Manda skeletal individuals reflect this complexity as shown in both the morphology and genetic structure of the population with the 118 skeletons giving us a unique view of early Swahili peoples and origins.

To begin testing of the biological affinities of the Mtwapa and Manda skeletal individuals, craniodental morphological data was collected along with bone samples for DNA testing. Comparisons of the morphological data was used in comparison to the Taita and Iranian skeletal collections. Because craniomorphological features used to assess identity in peoples of African American origin described in Hefner (2009), Hefner and Ousley (2014) and Pilloud et al. (2018), the Taita collection was studied to confirm the presence of these features in an African community located in the hinterland of the Swahili Coast. Kusimba et al. (2014) reviews this information and that for all of the features used to identify African affinity are present in the Taita peoples, there are some differences that describe unique features among the Taita, features that are also found in the Mtwapa and Manda crania (shallow maxillary notch, minimally excavated canine fossae). Similarly, the Iranian archaeological collections at the Penn Museum were compared to the morphological characteristics generally described for European Americans. These Iranian crania in morphological detail are similar to the ones that define European ancestry in forensic analysis.

A comparison of two Mtwapa crania (Operation #6) and (Operation #19) show strong African morphologies represented among the skeletal individuals at Mtwapa and Manda. This is confirmed by mtDNA analysis of ancestry

(Raaum et al 2018). The presence of Middle Eastern or European has not been confirmed from mtDNA analysis, but a portion of mtDNA lineages from Mtwapa have not as yet been identified to region and are not of African origin, leading the authors to propose a circum Indian Ocean origin of seven individual specimens including Operation #19.

Manda Operation #8 has strong evidence of both upper central and lateral incisor shoveling not observed in a significant frequency or extent as part of Afridonty (Irish 1997 and 2013; Scott and Irish 2017). Preliminary unpublished DNA analysis by Yu Dong at Sun Yet Sun University, China shows that in three out of ten samples from Manda, there are genetic connections to East Asia.

Finally, there are several cultural practices expressed in the dentitions of the Mtwapa and Manda individuals that are especially noteworthy. In both the Taita and Swahili Coast archaeological materials, there is evidence of ritual incisor tooth ablation (Pinchi et al. 2015). Additionally, the Mtwapa and Manda peoples practiced tooth filing and notching as well as polish and staining (probably by betel nut chewing) practices that are present in many regions within sub-Saharan Africa. As with cranial modification described by Tiesler (2014), dental modifications are a symbolic embodied representation of social identity. These practices appear to be central in the establishment of group African identity among the early Swahili Coast inhabitants as they are today.

## CONCLUSION

A rich and complex biological origin of the early Swahili peoples is beginning to emerge. Although clearly primarily African in ancestry, the Swahili culture accommodated elements of world culture even accepting and fully integrating outside peoples as witnessed by burial side by side with their indigenous African counterparts. While it is difficult to fully understand these relationships and how these maintained and structured, the associations are sustained over decades most likely reinforced by intermarriage and religious practice (Middleton 2004, 88). The physical remains give us a glimpse into the life-ways of the people. The skeletons indicate a physically challenging life style resulting in trauma, high mortality rates among children and juveniles, and occupation markers of a strenuous life. In addition, the combination of DNA and morphological analysis yields a powerful tool for understanding the ancestry of these peoples. Used with historic, archaeological, and linguistic data sources, the intricacies, complexities, and fine-grained analysis of the Swahili world are beginning to emerge.

## NOTES

1. These samples are now being analysis by David Reich of the Harvard medical School and will be reported when the results become available.
2. For an expanded discussion and alternative explanations of the burial practice within local Mijikenda burial traditions, see Kusimba et al. 2014.
3. Since the skeletal materials from each site were both fragmentary and pressure distorted, no metric analysis could be undertaken. Thus, the forensic anthropological tool FORDISC 3.1 (https://fac.utk.edu/fordisc-3-1-personal-computer-forensic-discriminant-functions/) could not be applied to this collection (for a critical assessment of metric tools and application to forensic case studies, see Konigsberg et al. 2009).

## REFERENCES

Albanese, J., Tuck, A., Gomes, J. and Cardoso, H.F.V. 2016. "An Alternative Approach for Estimating Stature from Long Bones That Is Not Population- or Group-Specific." *Forensic Science International* 259: 59–68.

Berryman, H.E. and Symes, S.A. 1998. "Recognizing gunshot and blunt cranial trauma through fracture interpretation." In Reichs, K.J. and Bass, W.M. (eds.), *Forensic Osteology: Advances in the Identification of Human Remains*, pp. 333–352. Springfield, IL: Charles C. Thomas.

Brooks, S.T. and Suchey, J.M. 1990. "Skeletal Age Determination Based on the Os Pubis: A Comparison of the Acsádi-Nemeskéri and Suchey-Brooks Methods." *Human Evolution* 5: 227–238.

Brues, A.M. 1990 "The once and future diagnosis of race." In Gill, G.W. and Rhine, S. (eds.), *Skeletal Attribution of Race: Methods for Forensic Anthropology*, pp. 1–9. Albuquerque, NM: Maxwell Museum of Anthropology.

Buckberry, J.L and Chamberlain A.T. 2002 "Age Estimation from the Auricular Surface of the Ilium: A Revised Method." *American Journal of Physical Anthropology* 119: 231–239.

Crews, D.E. 2003. *Human Senescence: Evolutionary and Biocultural Perspectives*. Cambridge, UK: Cambridge University Press.

Crummett, T.L. 1994. *The Evolution of Shovel Shaping: Regional and Temporal Variation in Human Incisor Morphology*. PhD Dissertation. Ann Arbor: University of Michigan.

Da-Gloria, P. and Larsen, C.S. 2014. "Oral Health of Paleoamericans of Lagos Santa, Central Brazil." *American Journal of Physical Anthropology* 154: 11–26.

Demirjian, A., Goldstein, H. and Tanner, J.M. 1973. "A New System of Dental Age Assessment." *Human Biology* 45: 211–227.

Edgar, H.J.H. 2017. *Dental Morphology for Anthropology*. New York: Routledge/Taylor and Francis.

Fiorenza, L., Benazzi, S., Oxilia G. and Kullmer, O. 2018. "Functional Relationship Between Dental Macro Wear and Diet in Late Pleistocene and Recent Modern Human Populations." *International Journal of Osteoarchaeology* 28 (2): 153–161.

Hanihara, T. 2008. "Morphological Variation of Major Human Populations Based on Non-metric Dental Traits." *American Journal of Physical Anthropology* 136: 169–182.

Hefner, J.T. 2009. "Cranial Non Metric Variation and Estimating Ancestry." *Journal of Forensic Science* 54: 985–995.

Hefner, J.T. and Ousley, S.D. 2014. "Statistical Classification Methods for Estimating Ancestry Using Morphoscopic Traits." *Journal of Forensic Science* 59: 883–890.

Hillson, S. 2001. "Recording Dental Caries in Archaeological Human Remains." International *Journal of Osteoarchaeology* 11: 249–289.

Horton, M. 1996. Shanga: *The Archaeology of a Muslim Trading Community on the Coast of East Africa*. London: British Institute of East Africa.

Hubbard, A.R., Guatelli-Steinberg, D. and Irish, J.D. 2015. "Do Nuclear DNA and Dental Non Metric Data Produce Similar Reconstructions of Regional Population History? An Example from Modern Coastal Kenya." *American Journal of Physical Anthropology* 157: 295–304.

Inoue, N., Sakashita, R., Inoue, M., Kamega, T., Ohashi, K. and Katsivo, M. 1995. "Ritual Ablation of Front Teeth in Modern and Recent Kenyans." *Anthropological Science* 3: 263–277.

Irish, J.D. 1997. "Characteristic High- and Low-Frequency Dental Traits in Sub-Saharan African Populations." *American Journal of Physical Anthropology* 102: 455–467.

Irish, J.D. 2013. "Afridonty: The 'Sub-Saharan African dental complex' Revisited." In Scott, G.R. and Irish, J.D (eds.), *Anthropological Perspectives on Tooth Morphology: Genetics, Evolution, Variation*, pp. 278–295. Cambridge: Cambridge University Press.

Kimura, R., Watanabe, C., Kawaguchi, A., Kim, Y.-I., Park, S.-B., Maki, Ki, Ishida, H. and Yamaguchi, T. 2015. "Common Polymorphisms in WNT10A Affect Tooth Morphology as well as Hair Shape." *Human Molecular Genetics* 24: 2673–2680.

Konigsberg. LW. Algee-Hewitt BFB, Steadman DW. 2009. "Estimation and Evidence in Forensic Anthropology: Sex and Race." *American Journal of Physical Anthropology* 139: 77–90.

Krogman, W.M. and Iscan, M.Y. 1986. *The Human Skeleton in Forensic Medicine*, 2nd ed. Springfield, IL: Charles C. Thomas.

Kusimba, C.M., Monge, J.M. and Kusimba, S.B. 2014. "The identity of early Kenyan coastal peoples: A comparative analysis of human remains from Shanga, Mtwapa, and the Taita Hills." In Gearhart, R. and Giles, L. (eds.), *Contested Identities, The Mijikenda and Their Neighbors in Kenyan Coastal Society*, pp. 3–24. Trenton, NJ: African World Press.

Kusimba, C.M., Williams, S.R., Monge, J.M., Mohamed, M.M., Oka, R., Oteyo, G., Kusimba, S.B. and Dussubieux, L. 2018a. "Mtwapa." In Wynne-Jones, S. and LaViolette, A. (eds.), *The Swahili World*, pp. 226–230. New York: Routledge/Taylor and Francis.

Kusimba, C.M., Williams, S.R., Oteyo, G., Monge, J.M., Cheong, K. and Mohamed, M.M. 2018b. "Manda." In Wynne-Jones, S. and LaViolette, A. (eds.), *The Swahili World*, pp. 156–162. New York: Routledge/Taylor and Francis.

Larsen, C.S., Shavit, R. and Griffin, M.C. 1991. "Dental caries evidence for dietary change: An archaeological context." In Kelley, M.A. and Larsen, C.S. (eds.), *Advances in Dental Anthropology*, pp. 179–202. New York: Wiley-Liss.

Larsen, C.S.1995. "Biological Changes in Human Populations with Agriculture." *Annual Review of Anthropology* 24: 185–213.

Liversidge, H.M.2003. "Variation in Modern Human Dental Development." In Thompson, J.T., Krovitz, G.E. and Nelson A.J. (eds.), *Patterns of Growth and Development in the Genus Homo*, pp. 73–113. Cambridge: Cambridge University Press.

Lovejoy, C.O. 1985. "Dental Wear in the Libben Population: Its Functional Pattern and Role in the Determination of Adult Skeletal Age at Death." *American Journal of Physical Anthropology* 68: 47–56.

Lovejoy, C.O., Meindl, R.S., Mensforth, R.P. and Barton T.J. 1985. "Multifactorial Determination of Skeletal Age at Aeath: A Method and Blind Tests of Its Accuracy." *American Journal of Physical Anthropology* 68: 1–14.

Lovell, N.C. 1997. "Trauma Analysis in Paleopathology." *Yearbook of Physical Anthropology* 40: 139–170.

MacDonald, R.H. 1993. "Teeth in pale-dietary reconstruction: Pastoralists versus agriculturalists." In Pwiti, G. and Soper, R. (eds.), *Aspects of African Archaeology*. Harare: University of Zimbabwe Publications.

Mays, S. 2000. "Age-Dependent Cortical Bone loss in Women from 18th and Early 19th Century London." *American Journal of Physical Anthropology* 112: 349–361.

Meindl, R.S. and Lovejoy, C.O. 1985. "Ectocranial Suture Closure: A Revised Method for the Determination of Skeletal age at Death Based on the Lateral-Anterior Sutures." *American Journal of Physical Anthropology* 68: 57–66.

Miles, A.E.W. 1962. "Assessment of the Ages of a Population of Anglo-Saxons from Their Dentitions." *Proceedings of the Royal Society of Medicine* 55: 881–886.

Miles, A.E.W. 2001. "The Miles Method of Assessing Age from Tooth Wear Revisited." *Journal of Archaeological Science* 28, 973–982.

Miles, A.E.W.1963. "The Dentition in the Assessment of Individual Age in Skeletal Material." In Brothwell, D.R. (ed.), *Dental Anthropology*, pp. 191–209. New York: Pergamon Press.

Monge, J.M., Mann, A., Stout, A., Roger, J. and Wadenya, R. 2007. "Dental calcification stages of the permanent M1 and M2 in U.S. children of African-American and European-American ancestry born in the 1990s." In Bailey, S.E. and Hublin, J-J. (eds.), *Dental Perspectives on Human Evolution,* pp. 263–274. New York: Springer.

Ousley, S., Jantz, R. and Freid, D. 2009. "Understanding Race and Human Variation: Why Forensic Anthropologists are Good at Identifying Race." *American Journal of Physical Anthropology* 139: 68–76.

Paine, R.R. 2000. "If a Population Crashes in Prehistory, and There Is no Paleodemographer There to Hear It, Does It Make a Sound?" *American Journal of Physical Anthropology*112: 181–190.

Park, J-H., Yamaguchi, T., Watanabe, C., Kawaguchi, A., Haneji, K., Takeda, M., Kim, Y-I., Tomoyasu, Y., Watanabe, M., Oota, H., Hanihara, T., Ishida, H., Maki,

K., Park, S-B. and Kimura, R. 2012. "Effects of an Asian-Specific Non Synonymous EDAR Variant on Multiple Dental Traits." *Journal of Human Genetics* 57: 508–514.

Petersen, A. 2013. "The archaeology of death and burial in the Islamic world." In Stutz, L.N. and Tarlow, S. (eds.), *Oxford Handbook of the Archaeology of Death and Burial*. Online: DOI: 10.1093/oxfordhb/9780199569069.013.0014.

Pilloud, M.A., Maier, C., Scott, G.R. and Hefner, J.T. 2018. "Advances in cranial macromorphoscopic trait and dental morphology analysis for ancestry estimation." In Latham, K.E., Bartelink, E.J. and Finnegan, M. (eds.), *New Perspectives in Forensic Human Skeletal Identification*, pp. 23–34. Cambridge, MA: Academic Press.

Pinchi, V., Barbieri, P., Pradella, F., Focardi, M., Bartolini, V. and Norelli, G.-A. 2015. "Dental Ritual Mutilations and Forensic Odontological Practice: A Review of the Literature." *Acta Stromatologica Croatica* 49: 3–13.

Raaum, R.L., Williams, S.R., Kusimba, C.M., Monge, J.M., Morris, A., Mohamed, M.M. 2018. "Decoding the Genetic Ancestry of the Swahili." In Wynne-Jones, S. and LaViolette, A. (eds.), *The Swahili World*, pp. 81–102. New York: Routledge/Taylor and Francis.

Rathmann, H., Reyes-Centeno, H., Ghirotto, S., Creanza, N., Hanihara, T. and Harvati, K. 2017. "Reconstructing Human Population History from Dental Phenotypes." *Nature Scientific Reports* 7: 12495. DOI:10.1038/s41598–017–12621-y.

Rogers, J. and Waldron, T. 1995. *A Field Guide to Joint Disease in Archaeology*. New York: Wiley.

Rogers, J., Waldron, T., Dieppe, P. and Watt, I. 1987. "Arthropathies in Palaeopathology: The Basis of Classification According to Most Probable Cause." *Journal of Archaeological Science* 14: 179–193.

Sauer, N.J. 1992. "Forensic Anthropology and the Concept of Race: If Races Don't Exist, Why are Forensic Anthropologists So Good at Identifying Them?" *Social Science and Medicine* 34: 107–111.

Sauer, N.J. 1998. "The timing of injuries and manner of death: Distinguishing among antemortem, perimortem and postmortem trauma." In Reichs, K.J. and Bass, W.M. (eds.), *Forensic Osteology: Advances in the Identification of Human Remains*, pp. 321–332. Springfield, IL: Charles C. Thomas.

Scheuer, L. and Black, S.M. 2004. *The Juvenile Skeleton*. New York: Academic Press.

Scott, G.H. and Turner, C.G. II. 1997. *The Anthropology of Modern Human Teeth*. New York: Cambridge University Press.

Scott, G.R. and Irish, J.D. 2017. *Human Tooth Crown and Root Morphology*. New York: Cambridge University Press.

Selinsky, P. 2009. "Dental Aging Using Multiple Tooth Wear Indicators in Conjunction with Antemortem Tooth Loss." *American Association of Physical Anthropologists*, 78th Annual Meeting, March 31 to April 4, Chicago, IL.

Sledzik, P.S. and Moore-Jensen, P.H. 1991. "Dental disease in nineteenth century military skeletal samples." In Kelley, M.A. and Larsen, C.S. (eds.), *Advance in Dental Anthropology*, pp. 215–224. New York: Wiley-Liss.

Smith, B.H. and Garn, S.M. 1987. "Polymorphisms in Eruption Sequence of Permanent Teeth in American children." *American Journal of Physical Anthropology* 74: 289–303.

Smith, B.H. 1984. "Patterns of Molar Wear in Hunter-Gatherers and Agriculturalists." *American Journal of Human Evolution* 63: 39–56.

Tayles, N. 1996. "Tooth Ablation in Prehistoric Southeast Asia." 1996. *International Journal of Osteoarchaeology* 6: 333–345.

Tiesler, V. 2014. "Chapter 2: Cultural Frameworks for Studying Artificial Cranial Modifications: Physical Embodiment, Identity, Age and Gender." *The Bioarchaeology of Artificial Cranial Modifications. Interdisciplinary Contributions to Archaeology* 7, 13–32.

Tishkoff, S.A., Reed, F.A., Friedlaender, F.R., Ehret, C., Ranciaro, A., Froment, A., Hibro, J.B., Awomoyi, A.A., Bodo, J-M., Doumbo, O., Ibrahim, M., Juma, A.T., Kotze, M.J., Lema, G., Moore, J.H., Mortensen, H., Nyambo, T.B., Omar, S.A., Powell, K., Pretorius, G.S., Smith, M.W., Thera, M.A, Wambebe, C., Weber, J.L. and Williams, S.M. 2009. "The Genetic Structure and History of Africans and African Americans." *Science* 324: 1035–1044.

Trotter, M. and Glesser, G.C. 1952. "Estimation of Stature from Long Bones of American Whites and Negroes." *American Journal of Physical Anthropology* 10(4):463–514.

Ubelaker, D.H.1999. *Human Skeletal Remains*. Taraxacum: Washington.

Walker, P.L.1997. "Wife beating, boxing, and broken noses: Skeletal evidence for the cultural patterning of violence." In Martin, D.L. and Frayer, D.W. (eds.), *Troubled Times: Violence and Warfare in the Past*, pp. 145–179. Gordon and Breach: Amsterdam, The Netherlands.

Walker, PL, Dean G, Shapiro P. 1991. "Estimating Age from Tooth Wear in Archaeological Populations." In Kelley, M.A. and Larsen, C.S. (eds.), *Advances in Dental Anthropology*, pp. 169–178. New York: Wiley-Liss.

Walrath, D.E., Turner, P. and Bruzek, J. 2004. "Reliability Test of the Visual Assessment of Cranial Traits for Sex Determination." *American Journal of Physical Anthropology* 125: 132–137.

Warren, K.A., Hall, S. and Ackermann, R.R. 2014. "Craniodental Continuity and Change Between Iron Age Peoples and Their Descendants." *South African Journal of Science* 110: 1–11.

Workshop of European Anthropologists (WEA).1980. "Recommendations for Age and Sex Diagnosis of Skeletons." *Journal of Human Evolution* 9: 517–549.

*Chapter 5*

# China, East Africa, and Incipient Globalization in the First Millennium CE

Herman Kiriama

Trade between China and East Africa started in a limited period before the ninth century but increased considerably during the subsequent Song Dynasty (960–1279). Large quantities of Chinese ceramics and other items from this period are found on the Kenyan coast especially in the areas between Lamu and Mombasa. It is however during the Ming Dynasty (1368–1644) that direct contacts were initiated for the first time between China and East Africa. In 1418, a Chinese fleet commanded by Admiral Zheng He reached the East African coast followed by subsequent visits in 1421–1422 and 1431–1433. It is during these travels that commercial and diplomatic contacts were established. This chapter states that it was in this period that regular interactions between China and African began. However, unlike the present globalization that is characterized by cut-throat competition, the nature and patterns of this incipient globalization appear to have been characterized by friendships and tributary relationships. This may be explained by the fact that the dominant social ideology in ancient China was Confucianism with the result that the elites in China saw business as immoral and corrupt. What lessons can we learn from this incipient globalization? This chapter attempts to answer this question.

The East African coast is that land that stretches over 3,000 km from the Somalia coast in the north to the Mozambican coast in the south. For the past two millennia, this coast has been characterized by a number of settlements ranging from small thatch and daub villages to large stone-built city states. Other than the stone-built settlements, the heritage of these coastal settlements is marked by sailing and fishing and exchange networks with both the interior and the Indian Ocean going back to at least the mid-first millennium CE (Kusimba 1999; Kusimba and Walz 2018; Pawlowicz 2017).

Various Chinese documents show that as early as the first millennium CE, the Chinese had some knowledge of the East African coast indicating that some form of interactions between Africa and China existed. For instance, Anshan (2012) and Xingliang (1977) argue that during the Han Dynasty (206 BCE–220 CE), China had indirect knowledge of Africa but that during the Tang (618–907) and Song (960–1279) dynasties this knowledge transformed from indirect to direct. During the Tang Dynasty, there are the Ching-hsing Chi (Record of Travels), and Yu-yang Tsa tsu (Assorted Dishes from Yu-yang), while in the Song Dynasty, most information is found in the Chu-fan-chih (gazetter of Foreigners) and Ling-wai-Tai-ta (Information from beyond the mountains). The records of the Ming Dynasty's naval expeditions into the western Indian Ocean is found in the Wu-pei-chih (Notes on military preparedness) (Anshan 2012). During the Tang Dynasty, the You Yang Za Zu Jing Yi written between 850 and 860 CE by Duan Chengshi, makes reference to the Bobali Kingdom, thought to be in modern-day Berbera in Somalia, while Jia Dan in the Xing Tang Shu Di Li Zhi identified seven of the major traffic routes used by the Chinese traders; two of these were sea routes, with one from Dengzhou to Korea and the other from Guangzhou to the Persian Gulf via East Africa (Anshan 2012, 25). These routes enabled both official and private contacts between China and Africa. This was particularly so as a result of the emphasis on foreign trade during the Zhao Song Period, and also the Yuan rulers' public policy to advance foreign trade (Anshan 2012).

Maritime contacts between Africa and China intensified during the Song and Yuan Dynasties. For example, in the Nan Song Dynasty, both Zhuo Qufei (1178 CE) in the Ling Wai Dai Da and Zhao Rushi (125CE) in Zhu Fang Zhi mention increased maritime contacts while the Yuan Dynasty writer, Wang Dayuan in his *Dao Yi Zhi Lue* reinforces what the other writers had written (Anshan 2012; Xiang 1987). Wang Dayuan is particularly important because his account is based on his own experiences during his two oceanic voyages made between 1330 and 1339 CE (Yongzhang 1993).

During the early Ming Dynasty increased contact between Africa and China comes from the writings of authors who accompanied Zheng He in his voyages. These include Fei Xing's *Xing Cha Sheng Lan*, *Yeng Yai Sheng Lan* by Ma Huan, and *Xi Yang Fang Guo Zhi* by Fang Zhen (Fuwei 1990; Junyan 1986; Hao 1983).

## ARCHAEOLOGICAL EVIDENCE OF CONTACT AND CONNECTIONS BETWEEN CHINA AND EAST AFRICA

Archaeological evidence provides some confirmation for these very early trade contacts between Han China and Africa. In 1993, while studying the hairs of a female corpse from the Egyptian Twenty-first Dynasty (1070–954 BC), Austrian scientists discovered remnants of silk fabric. At the time, China was the only known producer of silk. This suggests that Chinese goods had already arrived in Egypt. Also, in 1979, a stone that had several drawings of Kirins (Qilins) or giraffes, some of which were distinctly African, dating from the Don Han period (25–220 CE), was discovered in Xu Zhuo Jia Wang (Anshan 2012; Xu Zhou Museum 1980). Archaeological excavations along this coast started from the mid-twentieth century and even though focused on the large stone settlements, they led to the discovery of several objects such as local pottery, Islamic pottery and stoneware, Chinese porcelain and stoneware, coins, and other objects that help us understand the nature of these coastal communities in the years past (Kusimba 1999, 1).

## SINO-KENYA ARCHAEOLOGICAL PROJECT

Dotted along the various villages of the East African coast are fragments of Chinese ceramics dating to various periods. Despite the fact that archaeological excavations carried out since the 1950s to the present in coastal East Africa has unearthed several Chinese ceramics in stratigraphical contexts, there have however, been disputes that some of the ceramics assigned as Chinese porcelains may actually have been imitations from Indonesia and other parts of South East Asia (Zhao 2015). Therefore, in order to provide firm evidence that indeed these ceramics were actually Chinese, a team of Kenyan and Chinese archaeologists undertook both underwater and terrestrial excavations as well as reanalysis of excavated Chinese ceramics from sites in the Lamu archipelago, Malindi, and Mombasa and held at Gede and Fort Jesus Museums. This project was carried out from 2010 to 2013.

The terrestrial excavations were concentrated in the Malindi area, while the underwater excavations were done in the Lamu, Malindi, and Mombasa areas. The reanalysis was done in Gede and Mombasa and these included the reanalysis of the ceramics that were recovered from the excavations carried out in the late 1970s and early 1980s on the Portuguese frigate, the San Antonio, that sunk just outside Fort Jesus (Liu et al. 2012).

The excavations and reanalysis confirmed earlier conclusions that indicated that Chinese porcelain first appears in East Africa during the Tang Dynasty but becomes more prominent from 1300 CE (Kirkman 1963; Chittick 1974; Horton 1996). For example, the reanalysis of the Manda site porcelain found a series of Yue green-glazed stoneware sherds that dates to 800 CE and a tenth century white porcelain bowl fragment produced in the Fanchang kiln sites in Anhui Province (Qin 2015), while in Shanga a Changsha ware of the ninth–tenth century was identified. Juma (2004), on the other hand, reports excavating a green-glazed Yue stoneware sherd and an early Changsha ware sherd in a sequence preceding the Islamic period at the Unguja Ukuu site on Zanzibar Island. These findings show that it is probable that Chinese stoneware and porcelain may have occasionally reached Africa earlier than the ninth century. The Mambrui excavations have further shown that from around the end of the thirteenth century onward, the amount of Chinese green-glazed stoneware increases, overtaking Islamic ceramics, particularly the sgraffiato, which had been the major imported ceramic to East Africa between the tenth and thirteenth centuries CE. It has further been shown that the early Chinese export porcelains were mainly concentrated in the northern Kenya archipelago of Lamu and particularly in the sites of Pate, Shanga, and Manda (Chittick 1984; Horton 1996; Wilson and Omar 1997).

This work has further indicated that Chinese ceramics found on the coast of East Africa come from a number of kilns that include the Changsha kilns, Northern white porcelain kilns, Fanchang kilns, Jingdezhen kilns, kilns in Fujian as well as the Guangdong kilns (Liu et al. 2012; see also Kusimba; Namunaba; Ichumbaki; and Wang et al. this volume).

At the height of the Chinese porcelain trade into East Africa during the 1300s and 1400s, celadon was the most popular export ware; its plain glazes ranging through shades of greens and grays to pure dark green. Celadon was more valued because it was believed that it would reveal the presence of poison in any food served by cracking. The Mambrui excavations uncovered large Longquan green-glazed stoneware dishes of a quality equal to those sent to the Chinese imperial court in the late fourteenth and early fifteenth centuries (Kiriama and Qin 2015).

## COINAGE, CURRENCY, AND TRADE

Several Chinese coins dating back to the Tang and Song Dynasties have been recovered at various African sites. These include four coins made during the Tang Gao Zong period (649–683 CE) found in Kichwele, in Zanzibar, and one in Mogadishu, Somalia. Coins of the Song Dynasty have been found at the Kuumbi Cave in Zanzibar and in the ruins of the medieval village of Harla, near Dire Dawa. All three Song coins come from inner China, from the northern Song capital of Kaifeng, and are an indication that Chinese trade presence was perhaps more extensive than had previously been thought. Ming Dynasty coins have been found at Mambrui and in Manda, both in the Northern Kenya coast. Both coins bear the name "Yongle Tongbao"—the name of the reign that minted the coin sometime between 1403 and 1424 and since these coins were only carried by the envoys of the emperor, it can be surmised that these coins may have been brought to East Africa by

Admiral Zheng He who led a vast fleet between 200 and 300 ships across the Indian Ocean in 1418. Indeed, according to the Akhbār al-Ṣīn wa'l-Hind, *An account of India and China*, written in 851 CE, Chinese merchants used their own currency only for trade (Zhao 2015).

Some scholars have argued that despite the presence of all these imported ceramics and coins on the East African coast, East Africa was on the periphery of the Indiana Ocean (Chaudhuri 1990; Beaujard 2005, 2012). However, as Sheriff (1997, 2) has argued, the East African Swahili coast is not only part of the western rim of the Indian Ocean but is also the western part of its "bazaar nexus" that stretched from Zanzibar to Djakarta, from long before the arrival of the Portuguese well into the twentieth century. Indeed, the work of the Sino-Kenya Archaeological team has shown that the Chinese trade into East Africa goes earlier than the ninth century BCE, East Africa was firmly involved in this trade. It was the demand for African and Asian products that eventually lured Europeans, beginning with the Portuguese, into the Indian Ocean commerce. As history shows, the European entry into the Indian Ocean led to the marginalization of the region within this trade system (Kusimba 1999). As Kiriama and Qin (2014) have shown, the Chinese porcelain trade into East Africa had four peak periods, but we will be concerned with the first three periods that occurred before the arrival of the Portuguese in East Africa. The first peak started in the ninth century and lasted up to the tenth century. The ceramics exported during this period were the Yue ware, Changsha Ware, Canton Celadon and Northern whitewares. These ceramics are found mainly in the Lamu Archipelago. According to Zhao (2015), during this peak, the ports of the Persian Gulf, especially the port of Siraf, was an important conduit for East African products onto the long-distance trade market. The second peak period lasted from the second half of the thirteenth century to the beginning of the fifteenth century and this period witnessed the maximum output of the Yuan Dynasty. The ceramics exported during this period were the green porcelains and the Longquan kiln porcelain wares, Jingdezhen Qingbai wares, the Fujian Celadon, the Qingbai wares and the Jingdezhen blue and white and copper red wares. The third Peak occurred during the Ming period. There is an increasing amount of Chinese ceramics from middle Ming-Chenghua, Hongzhi, Zhengtong periods that has been found in Gede and Mambrui. During this period, high-quality ceramics make their appearance, and this may be attributed to the fact that the Ming court was actively involved in the trade business by actively sending envoys to various parts of the world.

More interesting is the fact that the analysis of the Chinese porcelain found in the sunken Portuguese Frigate, San Antonio, came from the kilns of Jingdezhen, Dehua, Fujian Zhangzhou, and Guangdong. It is noteworthy that during the second half of the sixteenth century, there was an increase of the Jingdezhen blue and white porcelain in the East African coast, and this may be an indication that the Portuguese, who now had occupied parts of the East African coast were able either to access the Jingdezhen Kilns or at least they had a way of getting the products of this kiln (Kiriama and Qin 2014). But then the Chinese ceramics found in the San Antonio is of lower quality compared to the ceramics that had been imported earlier into East Africa or compared to the Dutch East India Company's exquisite porcelain produced in Jingdezhen and exported by the Dutch to their Cape Colony in South Africa. It should be noted that during this period, East African sites witness a marked reduction of the green-glazed porcelain from Longquan kiln, while imitations probably produced at Jingdezhen in Jiangxi Province and at Chaozhou and Huizhou (both in Guangdong Province) may have been imported. Furthermore, it has been shown that between 1430/50 and 1500/10 CE the East African coast sees a growth in the volume of Southeast Asian ceramics, including Vietnamese blue-and-white and green-glazed stoneware from Thailand. From the 1470s, these ceramics were replaced by green-glazed stoneware and opaque white-glazed earthenware from the Twante and Bago regions in Burma (Zhao 2015). Could it be that the Portuguese, who had been cut off from accessing the high-quality Chinese porcelain market by the Dutch now turned to imitations from Southeast Asia to satisfy the East African demand? Whatever the case, one may argue that the decline in the number of Chinese ceramics as well as in their quality is an indication that the Portuguese may have either directly or indirectly, in fact stifled the exportation of Chinese ceramics to East Africa (Qin 2015; Kiriama and Qin 2014). This coupled with the fact that high-quality porcelain is found in East Africa before the coming of the Portuguese, indicate that incipient globalization between East Africa and East Asia had started prior to the coming of the Europeans to the waters of the Indian Ocean.

## EAST AFRICAN EXPORTS TO CHINA

What did Africa contribute to the Indian Ocean trade? Available evidence indicates that Swahili ships and merchants did indeed at times cross the ocean and go to Southeast Asia. For instance, Pires mentions among the foreign merchants that were in Malacca in 1515 included "people from Kilwa, Malindi, Mogadiscio and Mombasa." Also, Japanese historian Takano Terada (1988) argues that the wealth of the medieval Swahili city-states was accumulated as a result of these states trading with China. Documentary as well as archaeological evidence from Chinese sites, demonstrate that during the Greco-Roman period, China imported goods such as ambergris, rhinoceros horn, elephant tasks, tortoise shell, and pearls from East Africa. Further, several Chinese sources indicate that prior to the nineteenth century both the imperial court and the nobles consumed products coming from East Africa (Zhao 2015). The East African products that were imported into China during the medieval period consisted of wild birds and animals, elephant tusks, rhinoceros horns, amber, tortoise shells, ebony (*Diospyros ebenum* J. Koenig, *Diospyros melanoxylon* Roxb.), *Physeter macrocephelus* (sperm whale) ambergris, leopard skins, and medicinal plants such as *Aloe barbadensis* Mill. and *Commiphora habessinica* (O. Berg) (Shen 2010). Archaeological evidence also shows that elephant tusks from East Africa were imported into China from the first century CE. From the tomb of the second king of Nanyue (r. 137–122 CE), five pieces of African elephant tusk have been excavated (Guangzhou Shi Wenhuaju 2008). Archaeological excavations of the tenth-century Intan shipwreck has also revealed remains of African elephant tusks (Flecker 2002). During the Song Dynasty (960–1279 CE), elephant tusks were the most important of the commodities in Song maritime trade (Zhao 2015).

Some scholars, notably John Carswell (1977) and Randall Pouwells (2002) argue that before the sixteenth century, the importation of Chinese ceramics into the Swahili coast was primarily done indirectly; these scholars argue that traders involved in this trade went through Southeast Asia, the Persian Gulf, the Red Sea, the Maldives, and northern Madagascar before eventually arriving on the East African coast. There is, however, no conclusive evidence at the moment to support this contention.

## CONCLUSION

Globalization has been defined as the increased interdependence of the world's economies on one another and this is indicated by the circulation of people, goods, information, and money across national boundaries. Since the inception of humanity, different communities were related to one another through territorial spread of ideas, social norms, and trading commodities. This premodern phase of globalization is known as archaic globalization. In his 1974 analysis of global trade, Immanuel Wallerstein presented a theory of a European-centered world-system in which he defined twelve main characters of this system (Wallerstein 1976, 2004). Scholars working on the Indian Ocean have however argued that similar mechanisms already existed in this area several centuries earlier than Europe (Abu-Lughod 1991; Beaujard 2005, 2012). The Maritime trade route, also known as the Maritime Silk Road (Kiriama and Qin 2014) or the Ceramic Road (Mikami 1969; Pirazzoli-T'Serstevens 1985), between East Africa and China is an excellent example of archaic globalization because it was a network of interlinking trade routes across the Indian Ocean which carried trade goods between China, Asia, Persian Gulf, and Africa. Indeed, Tuan Ch'eng-shih, a Chinese explorer who died in 863 CE, wrote about a flourishing trade in ivory, slaves, and ambergris that local East African merchants sold to merchants from Arabia and Persia (Freeman-Grenville 1962), indicating the incorporation of East Africa into the wider network of the Indian Ocean at an earlier in the first millennium CE. As Jacques Gernet (1996) argues, Zheng He's expeditions to Africa, followed well-established trade routes of the eleventh century that continued uninterrupted for several hundred years. In other words, the East African coast for several years had well established trade routes with Asia.

If we accept the notion that globalization is the organization of economic relations between nations that allows for the cross-cultural exchange of ideas, goods, and services (Al-Rodhan and Stoudmann 2006), then the available archaeological and documentary evidence from the coast of East Africa provides strong confirmation that China and Africa had trade contacts long before the arrival of Vasco da Gama on the African shores. Starting from the Han Dynasty (206–220 CE), China practiced globalization when trade took place between the Han Chinese and neighboring people in the North-west through the Silk Route. During the Tang Dynasty (618–901) trade flourished and the Silk Route, which hitherto was overland expanded and included a sea route that saw Chinese trade with other countries on the western Indian Ocean and East Africa in particular. It can thus be argued that globalization is "not a new idea that has been developed only over the last thirty years; rather, it has been shaping the way we think, how we do business, and the way in which we interact with each other for many, many generations" (Al-Rodhan and Stoudmann 2006, 10), and that long before the discovery of America or the start of the Industrial Revolution, China and East Africa were already engaged in global trade. According to Zhao (2015), from their manufacturing sites in China and Southeast Asia, Chinese ceramics came to East African sites, through various regional land and maritime networks. Each network had a precise defined geographical, economic, and social term. This "network existed as a chain-link system, interconnected continuously from one link to the next and so on to the last link, thereby forming a global network. Chinese-style ceramics circulated within this multi-partner global network" (Zhao 2015, 45).

## REFERENCES

Abu-Lughod, J.L. 1991. *Before European Hegemony: The World System AD 1250–1350*. New York: Oxford University Press.

Al-Rodhan, N. R.F and Stoudmann, G. 2006. *Historical Milestones of Globalization*. Geneva: Geneva Centre for Security Policy.

Anshan, Li. 2012. *A History of Overseas Chinese in Africa to 1911*. New York: Diasporic Africa Press.

Beaujard, P. 2005. "The Indian Ocean in Eurasian and African World-Systems Before the Sixteenth Century." *Journal of World History* 16 (4): 411–413.

Beaujard, P. 2012. *Les mondes de l'océan Indien*, 2 tomes. Paris: Armand Colin.

Carswell, J. 1977. "China and Islam in the Maldives Islands." *Transactions of the Oriental Ceramic Society* 41: 121–198.

Chaudhuri, K. N. 1990. *Asia Before Europe: Economy and Civilization of the Indian Ocean From the Rise of Islam to 1750*. Cambridge: Cambridge University Press.

Chittick, N. 1984. *Manda: Excavations at an Islamic Port on the Kenyan Coast*. Nairobi: British Institute in Eastern Africa.

Chittick, N. 1974. *Kilwa: An Islamic Trading City on the East African Coast*. London: British Institute in Eastern Africa.

Duyvendak, J.J. 1947. *China's Discovery of Africa*, Lectures Given at the University of London.

Flecker, M. 2002. *The Archaeological Excavation of the 10th Century Intan Shipwreck*. Oxford: Archaeopress, BAR International Series 1047.

Freeman-Grenville, G. S. P. 1962a. *The East African Coast: Select Documents From the First to the Nineteenth Century*. Oxford: Clareton Press.

Fuwei, Sheng. 1990. *China and Africa-Two Thousand Years of Sino Africa Relations*. Beijing: Zhonghua Press.

Gernet, J.1996. *A History of Chinese Civilization*. Cambridge: Cambridge University Press.

Guangzhou S. W. 2008. *Maritime Silk Road Cultural Heritage in Guangzhou*. Beijing: Wenwu Chubansh.

Hao, F. 1983. *History of East and West Traffic* (1953 reprint). Taipei: China Cultural University Press.

Horton, M. 1996. *Shanga: The Archaeology of a Muslim Trading Community on the Coast of East Africa*. Nairobi: British Institute in Eastern Africa.

Juma, A.M. 2004. *Unguja Ukuu on Zanzibar. An Archaeological Study of Early Urbanism*. Studies in Global Archaeology 3. Uppsala: Uppsala University.

Junyan, Zhang. 1986. *Ancient China's Contact with Central Asia and Africa by Sea*. Beijing: Hai Yang Press.

Kiriama, H.O and Qin, D. 2014. "The Maritime Silk Road: The Indian Ocean and the Africa China Exchange Systems in the Late First/Early Second Millennium CE." *Journal of Indian Ocean Archaeology* 10: 1–11.

Kirkman, J.S. 1963. *Gedi, the Palace*. The Hague: Mouton.

Kusimba, C.M. 1999. *The Rise and Fall of Swahili States*. Walnut Creek: AltaMira.

Liu, Y. Qin, D -S., Kiriama H. 2012. "The Chinese Porcelains Unearthed at Gedi Ruins in Coast. Province, Kenya (Kenniya Binhai Sheng Gedi Gucheng Yizhi Chutu Zhongguo Ciqi." 肯尼亞濱海省格迪古城遺址出土中國瓷器 *Wenwu (Cultural Relics)* 11: 37–78.

Mikami, T.s. 1969. *Road of Ceramics: Materiel Evidence of Eastern and Western Culture contacts.* Tokyo: Iwnami Shoten.

Oka, R., Dussubieux, L., Kusimba, C.M., Gogte, V.D. 2009. "The Impact of Imitation Ceramic Industries and Internal Political Restrictions on Chinese Commercial Ceramic Exports in the Indian Ocean Maritime Exchange, ca 1200–1700." In B. McCarty (ed.), *Scientific Research on Historian Asian Ceramics: Proceedings of the Fourth Symposium at the Freer Gallery of Art,* pp. 175–185. London: Archetype Publications.

Pawlowicz, M. 2017. *Archaeological Survey and Excavations at Mikindani, Southern Tanzania: Finding Their Place in the Swahili World.* Oxford: BAR International series 2859.

Pirazzoli-T'Serstevens, M. 1985. La route de la Céramique." *Le Grand Atlas de l'archéologie,* pp. 284–285. Paris: Encyclopaedia Universalis.

Pouwels, R. 2002. "Eastern Africa and the Indian Ocean to 1880: Reviewing Relations in Historical Perspective." *International Journal of African Historical Studies* 35(2–3): 385–425.

Qin, D.-S. 2015. "Preliminary Analysis on Chinese Ceramics Excavated From Kenya." In Qin, D.S. and J. Yuan (eds.), *Ancient Silk Trade Routes: Selected Works From Symposium on Cross Cultural Exchanges and Their Legacies in Asia,* pp. 61–82. Singapore: World Scientific Publishing Company.

Shen, F.-W. 2010. *Cultural Exchange Between China and Africa.* Ürümqi: Xinjiang Renmin Chubanshe.

Sheriff, A. H. M. 1997. "The Dhow Trade as a Cultural Corridor in the Western Indian Ocean." Paper presented at the Conference on Northwestern Indian Ocean as a Cultural Corridor, Dept. of Anthropology, Stockholm University.

Terada, T. 1988. *Zheng He-The link Between China and Islamic World,* Translation by Zhuang Jinghui, Beijing: Haiyang Chubanshe.

Wallerstein, I. 1976. "A World-System Perspective on the Social Sciences." *The British Journal of Sociology* 27: 343–352.

Wallerstein, I. 2004. *World-Systems Analysis: An Introduction.* Durham: Duke University Press.

Wilson, T. H. and Omar, A. L. 1997. Archaeological Investigations at Pate. *Azania* 32: 31–75.

Xiang, Zhang. 1987. *Four Climaxes of Ancient Sino-African Interaction.* Nan Kai Historiography 2.

Xingliang, Zhang. 1977. *A Historical Compilation of East and West Traffic,* sec.2. Beijing: Zhonghua Press.

Xu Zhou Museum 1980. "On Han Stone Painting in Xu Zhuo." *Wen Wu* 2: 550.

Yongzhang, Xu. 1993. "Investigating Several Ancient Sino-African Relation Issues." *West Asia Africa* 5

Zhao, Bing. 2015. "Chinese-Style Ceramics in East Africa from the 9th to 16th Century: A Case of Changing Value and Symbols in the Multi-partner Global Trade URL: http://journals.openedition.org/afriques/1836; DOI: 10.4000/afriques.1836.

*Chapter 6*

# Siyu Intertwined Exchange Networks from the Early Beginnings to the Fifteenth Century

Ibrahim Busolo Namunaba

This chapter examines the factors that influenced the settlement and growth of the Swahili city state of Siyu (see figure 2.1)[1]. We employed a variety of approaches including site survey, excavation, and analysis of excavated materials to understand and reconstruct the evolution of Siyu city-state. The evidence recovered shows that Siyu first served as seasonal camp for hunters, fishermen, and mangrove cutters subsistence and economic activities. The town was accessible by a navigable creek to its neighbors across Pate island, the immediate hinterland, and other communities beyond. More sand dunes were exposed as the sea receded in the early first millennium CE, creating space and opportunities for more specialized activities, including permanent settlement. Even as it thrived as a city state and became famous for its excellent cottage industries, Siyu was not completely self-sufficient. It's political economy, relied upon strong exchange networks of with neighboring urban and rural regions and across the Indian Ocean. One of the major internal trade networks was in the exchange of local pottery. Our study has revealed that Siyu lacked good local clays and relied trade for all its household needs in pottery. Thus, the role and trade, social and economic networks that linked Siyu to known centers such as Shanga, Pate, Manda, and the mainland were so crucial for Siyu's development into a complex polity. Besides, Siyu was connected to an international exchange network that brought trade commodities from China, Arabia, India, and later Europe.

Extensive archaeological excavations were done at the ancient town of Siyu in order to answer the still unresolved questions of the emergence and sustenance of this Swahili polity that is famous in Swahili oral traditions as Mui wa Mafundi or the city of craftsmen. Excavations sought to understand and place in context the chronological as well as sociopolitical, economic, and ecological factors that influenced the settlement, development of Siyu into a complex city state. This chapter discuss three complementary factors, including (1) factors that influenced Siyu's early settlements; (2) the resource bases and exchange networks; and (3) the settlement sequence.

## SIYU IN HISTORICAL PERSPECTIVE

Swahili oral traditions recall Siyu as Mui wa Mafundi, the city of crafts-people due to its renowned cottage industry in the making and selling of boats, cloth, shoes, beads, and woodcarvings. Today, Siyu is a small settlement in the Lamu Archipelago of 22 hectares and lies midway between Pate and Faza on Pate Island at $02^0$ 06'.072" S, $41^0$ 03'.429" E. Like other island settlements, Siyu is located at the end of a shallow creek that provides a convenient sea access while also protecting it from surprise attack. Due to silting from the nineteenth century, the creek is only navigable only during the spring tide. However, Siyu is accessible by road from Mbui, via Pate in the west and from Faza in the north and by air.

Within the Lamu Archipelago, the average annual rainfall fluctuates between 800 and 1000 mm while dropping to between 500 and 900 mm in the immediate coastal hinterland. The long rains averaging 730 mm occur from April to July and the short rains from August to December with a seasonal average rainfall of 104 mm. The monsoon winds were an important component in maritime economy. Sea travel for trade or fishing almost entirely depended on wind-propelled vessels such as boats and ships (Chami 1998, 36). Local fishing boats have for a long time exploited the offshore and onshore winds as they traveled around the islands. The monsoon winds were therefore the mainstay of the Trans-Indian Ocean trade that thrived between the eighteenth and nineteenth centuries.

There are no large wildlife species on the island. Features observed such as burrows and droppings suggest the presence of wild pig, aardvark, and a variety of small antelopes. The vegetation of Pate Island is highly responsive to natural factors such as marine-derived sandy soils, sea-mud, and coral reefs. However, part of it is influenced by anthropogenic activities. The vegetation around Siyu is characterized by dry coral rag forests that feature open scrubs species such as *Terminalia thorningi* (local name, mwangati), *Acacia seyal* (local name, mkunga) and *Makhamia lutea*. *T. thorningi* is a common hardwood that features a layered canopy and can be seen in most areas towering over thickets. The hardwood is a supplement to mangrove for construction purposes.

Along the brackish creek in Siyu, the vegetation is dominated by three species of mangrove. The most common species that occur on Pate Island is *Rhizophora mucronata*, which is easily recognizable from the buttress-arching roots that support the trunk. Other species are *Sonneratia alba* and *Avicennia marina*. These two are among the first in the ecological succession of the new areas with high saline content. The *Avicennia sp* is a primary colonizer in the front row to the southern shoreline as well as along Siyu Creek. Pockets of grasslands appear in areas northeast of Siyu and to the west toward Pate and Mtangawanda and are important reservoirs of pastureland. The baobab is represented by countable trunks of *Adansonia digitata sp.* (local name, mbuyu) that are interspersed in the thickets.

## ORIGINS AND IDENTITY FORMATION OF SIYU

The question of when and by whom Siyu was inhabited has been studied. Archaeological and historical linguistic studies show that the earliest residents of the coast likely spoke Cushitic and Bantu languages (Allen 1993; Nurse and Spear 1985; Soper 1967). Fishing, herding, and gardening, primarily slash and burn were the main subsistence strategies in the first millennium. The simmering fires from farms on Lamu Island described in the Periplus of the Erythraen Sea may have been the result of a slash and burn activity (Huntingford 1980, 97; see Gearhart 1998, 136). The Periplus further described the inhabitants of the Lamu Archipelago as having their own languages and exchanged animal skins, ivory, tortoiseshell, rhinoceros' horn, and incense with cloth, beads, metal, wire, glass, porcelain, and wine from overseas (Huntingford 1980, 122–23; Freeman-Grenville 1975, 6; see also Ndiema, Kiriama, Ichumbaki, this volume).

Oral accounts claim that Siyu's early inhabitants came primarily from two areas. The first came from Dondo across Siyu Channel and the second from southern Somalia. Dondo migrants were affiliated to modern Mijikenda and/or the Pokomo. Southern Somalia immigrants were the Bajuni and the Katwa. Karisa's (2011) recent study echoes previous studies, which show shared origin narrative that the Mijikenda, Pokomo, Waata, and the Bajuni had at Shungwaya (Allen 1993; Spear 1972; Swaleh 2011, 324). The traditions claim a dispersal from Shungwaya following warfare with the Oromo. The Bajuni settled at coastal sites, including Kiunga, Faza, Lamu, Siyu, Shanga, Tundwa, Ndau, Kiwaynu, Mbwajumwali, and Kizingitini where in time their descendants would establish a thriving maritime economy based on production and exchange of fish, mangrove, and livestock. Thus, Trans-Indian Ocean trade interlocked on an already-thriving local economy.

Siyu monopolized a cottage industry based on carpentry, masonry, weaving, and embroidery. Indeed, upon a visit to Pate Island in 1606, Gasper de Santos Bernadino found Siyu the largest, well organized, and most populous city on the island (Freeman-Grenville 1975, 162). In 1637, Captain Francisca de Seixas Cabreira led a punitive expedition against Siyu, which ended in the bombardment of the city and destruction of the town wall (Kirkman 1974, 18). The town's citizens pledged loyalty and signed a treaty to pay tribute to the Portuguese crown.

Today, Siyu people speak Kisiyu dialect and like all other Swahili dialects, Kisiyu has a significant influence from Arabic, Portuguese, and Gujarat (Nurse and Spear 1985). Some Siyu residents trace their ancestry to immigrants from Yemen and Arabia. These include the Hadrami clan from Hadhramaut (Middleton 2004, 21). The second clan is the Masharifu (also known as Saqqaf) who claim to be descendants of the Prophet Mohamed. This clan plays an important religious and social role in the entire Siyu community. The third clan is that of the Albaury, descendants of the later Omani Arabs who emigrated from Arabia between the mid-eighteenth and the twentieth centuries. Through their Sultanate in Zanzibar, the Omani Arabs enhanced Arabic elements in social life and became the precursor to the later claims of what Middleton (2004, 22) refers to as higher-ranking Swahili families to good Arabic ancestry. The Wafamau form the fourth clan in Siyu.

Oral accounts dispute earlier views that the Wafamau clan did come from Dondo as recorded by Stigand (1913, 18), but from Shanga. Wafamau, or Wafaamai in Kisiyu dialect, refers to the descendants of the survivors of a Chinese shipwreck off Pate Bay (Bwanaheri Ali, personal communication 2012; see also Kusimba, this volume). During one of the legendary Chinese expeditions led by Admiral Zheng He, one of his ships capsized near Pate in the Lamu Archipelago in 1431. After being rescued, these survivors were accommodated at Shanga where they converted to Islam and married the local Muslim girls. The search for the wreckage and traces of its cargo has gained the attention of underwater archaeologists from Kenya and China since the year 2000 (See also Kiriama, and Bita this volume). Other sources indicate that Wafamau are subdivided into three groups, the Bumbuweli, Urdumila, and the Waungwana Ngamia, and are also known as Il Famau, Il Famawi, or Al Famau (Allen 1979). It is also recorded that Wafamau refers to the people whose origin was Indian, Portuguese, Chinese, Persian, and could not be easily fitted into any other. Interestingly, the Wafamau are a large lineage spread all over the Swahili coast and in every Swahili settlement, many people will identify themselves as being Mfamau or of the Wafamau lineage (Allen 1979, 67).

## ECONOMY, PRODUCTION, AND EXCHANGE

The Lamu archipelago has more than 300 square kilometers out of a total area of 500 square kilometers of mangrove forests on the Kenyan coast (GEUS 2006). The Mangrove forest that fringes Siyu creek provides hardwood poles for roofing, charcoal, tanning, and medication. It is a primary source of fuel for burning coral rag (for masonry) and boat construction. The mangrove ecosystem is a spawning ground for fish. The abandoned reef platforms were quarried for coral mortar and stone for construction purposes. The extensive farmlands east and west of the contemporary settlement and on the mainland at Dondo are well-watered. Here, the Siyu residents cultivate coconuts, mangoes, cassava, sesame, and maize. Kitchen gardening is carried out on small plots interspersed within the residential quarters where varieties of vegetables such as peas, beans, eggplant, chili pepper, and tobacco are grown. Livestock include cattle, goats, and chicken. The humped zebu type mainly kept and butchered for food and only sold for cash in rare circumstances. The sea and narrow creeks provide an excellent network of sailing routes between Siyu and other island settlements but also with mainland farming settlements. The town is known for hosting excellent craftsmen who were masters in house construction, boat and ship building, leatherwork, weaving, and carpentry.

## SIYU AND ITS ENVIRONMENTS

Wilding (1973) archaeological surveys at Siyu which included a single test pit led him to conclude that Siyu was not occupied before the sixteenth century CE. Subsequent test studies by Horton (1996, 24) recovered late Sgraffiato pottery of the twelfth century CE and a sample of much older Sassanian-Islamic pottery dated to the sixth century CE. The recovery of a sample of Sassanian-Islamic pottery in a more disturbed context added confusion to a hitherto difficult question of the date of early settlement of Siyu. Although, copious volumes of local pottery associated with the imported wares were recovered, Horton did not discuss them.

This study has employed the theory of exchange systems that states that exchange is a mechanism of human interactions which involves voluntary exchange of trade items from food stuff to exotics into the daily life of a society. Exchange is considered as a form of interrelations such that a system of interrelations operates on a regional level (Torrence 1986). Exchange networks connect peoples (Earle and Ericson 1976). Interacting communities acquire artifacts and/or ideas by exchange media such as trade. Trade occurs through a variety of means of over short and long distances. What is the evidence for trade and exchange at Siyu?

### Approaches to Studying Settlement Patterns

Settlement pattern theory, when applied to archaeology, focuses on the study of how people lived from remains of their living quarters and monuments on the landscape. Gordon Willey (1953) developed this methodology to understand the relationship of living arrangements to geographical features since settlements mirror social structure and cultural process. The comparison of many contemporary settlements should reveal spatial organization across the landscape and thus illustrate how humans interacted with their environment. The environment, habituated locales, economic practices, and technological skills combined to determine the settlement patterns that might emerge from initiatives. Fagan (1991) proposed that in some societies, inherited cultural patterns, and established networks of human behavior influenced settlement patterns. Trade networks also play an important role in the emergence of central places that later develop into city-states. Originally, a settlement pattern based on trade may be determined in part by environment or social considerations, but eventually a vertical hierarchy of sites may grow as technological, demographic, social, and religious forces come into play (Fagan 1991, 419). As a result, a society becomes more complex and exchange networks modified by emerging sociopolitical structures.

From oral traditions, Siyu earliest inhabitants who originated from the mainland may have been attracted to the island for security reason. The islands low nutrient soils could, however, not support the new settlers who continued to maintain agricultural field on the mainland. As population density increased, local resources dwindled and necessitated the development of an exchange network through which resources continued to flow from localities in the hinterland, islands, and overseas. A complex social system emerged which did not need to intensify agriculture for survival; rather it was more convenient to use the network of settlements to intensify external exchange.

## Survey and Mapping

Archaeological survey inside and outside the perimeter wall of the old ruined town and areas along the creek and farms outside the town wall enclosure enabled us to map the extent of town and its resources, including residential, cottage, and farmland. Structural elements of the site including houses, mosques, cisterns, and wells mapped revealed a town that was divided into two zones. Zone 1 was characterized by an altitude from for sea level to 15 m above sea level while zone 2, located mainly at the center of the settlement, was characterized by an altitude 15 m above sea level. The area of interest was the area bound by the shallow creek that circumnavigates the entire northern and western ends of the settlement.

The town wall enclosed an area of 22 hectares which contained the ruins of ancient settlement and as well as modern Siyu. The visible ruins were mainly of mosques, houses, boreholes, and water cisterns. The cemeteries were due north of every mosque. Not everyone who died was buried in designated cemeteries as some tombs occurred outside the mosque area. Most surviving ruins of the ancient settlement are in areas with an altitude of 15 m and above. There is an overlap area between the ancient and the modern settlement, which could indicate that the occupations oscillated within the wall enclosure with time, as people reused coral materials from older houses for new constructions and cultivated crops in the abandoned areas. There is minimal cultivation within the town wall enclosure with about seven agricultural zones identified, five of which are located within the ruins of the ancient settlement while the remaining two are located within the modern settlement. However, major agricultural activities take place outside the town wall enclosure and to the south of the settlement.

## Archaeological Excavations and Finds

A total of four trenches were excavated. Trenches 1, 2, and 4 were all located in Zone 1 toward the southern bastion while trench 3 was in Zone 2. Excavated materials in Trench 1 were dominated by local pottery with 8,128 sherds. Trade ceramics occurred evenly in most levels except for the lower levels, 26 and 27 where none were recovered. Faunal materials and marine shells (quantified separately from other faunal finds) were recorded with totals of 26 and 20 samples, respectively. The faunal materials included bone and teeth fragments from diverse fish species, bovid (cattle, goat/sheep, dik dik), equid, reptilian, rodents, and small carnivores such as domestic cat and dog. Sharpening and grindstones were all quantified under stoneware to a total of eleven pieces, while red ochre was recorded up to ten occurrences. Slag occurred mainly in the middle and lower levels, with the earliest sample appearing in level 25. Beads occurred mainly between level 4 and level 19, while charcoal samples were collected from eight different levels between level 9 and level 25.

Other materials included daub, wall-plaster, charred seeds from date-palm, and spindle whorl made from ivory and pottery. Daub and wall plaster point to the nature of architecture and housing. However, the four samples of daub recorded come from mixed levels making it unreliable for chronological sequencing while only two pieces of wall plaster were recorded at level 20 and could indicate the inception of the use of lime motor for house construction. Seeds of date-palm show a connection of the people of Siyu with the outside world particularly the Arabian Peninsula where date-palms are endemic. Four spindle whorls were excavated each one from levels 7, 11, 15, and 25. The spindle whorls were exclusively recovered from Trench I indicating the concentration of weaving in that locality of town. A variety of raw materials ranging from local, imported pottery, and ivory were used to make spindle whorls (Horton 1996, 337).

In Trench 2, local pottery was the most numerous at 2,111 sherds followed by faunal materials including teeth at 654 fragments. Trade ceramics and pottery was represented by 156 sherds. The rest of the finds were ten samples and below except for samples of bead and copper that totaled twelve and twenty-six, respectively. Trench 3 yielded a variety of finds and like in other trenches, local pottery was numerous at 6,007 sherds with high concentrations at level 23 and 32. Imported pottery totaled to 102 sherds showing a similar pattern of concentration to that of local pottery. Marine shells and other faunal materials were the most numerous in trench three at 155 and 1,663, respectively. Samples of daub (twenty-eight pieces) were significant as they appeared concentrated in the lower levels between levels 24 and 34 at a depth range of 3.10 and 3.30 m below datum point, while wall-plaster occur between levels 17 and 24 and this compares well with the distribution in Trench 1. Trench 4 was excavated to a depth of 3.3 m below datum point. The finds recovered included Square C, a total of 3,610 sherds of local pottery, 61 sherds of imported pottery, 12 pieces of stoneware, 289 faunal materials, and 1 piece of metal ware and iron slag each. There were twenty-four pieces of charcoal and forty-one chunks of daubs. Four fragments of glass were also recovered. It is noted that minimal cultural materials occur after a depth of 3.0 m below datum point. Square K of Trench 4 yielded materials. A total of 3,690 sherds of local pottery, 46 sherds of imported pottery, 4 pieces of stoneware, 267 fragments of faunal remains, daub 25, 15 shells, 1 metal, 10 pieces of iron slag, 22 fragments of charcoal, 10 beads, 4 pieces of wall plaster, 3 glassware, and 2 red ochre.

In summary, total pottery assemblage was 28,786 sherds. Local pottery accounted for 28,197 sherds, while trade ceramics and pottery accounted for 589 sherds.

A total of 23,081 sherds of local pottery were undiagnostic, and these were weighed and returned to their respective trenches. The weight of the undiagnostic pottery was 261 kilograms. Diagnostic sherds totaled 5,115 of rims, bases, and decorated body sherds. In this study, the term "decorative element" is adopted from Hulthen (1974, 426) who identifies some decorative elements as comprising horizontal, zigzag line and a vertical, rectilinear band filled with a rhombic checkered pattern. Decorative structures have taken varying terminologies such as motifs (Collette and Robertshaw 1983, decorative patterns (Nordstrom 1972, 77); structure of design (Hulthen 1974, 25) and decorative format (Sinclair 1987, 164). It is however, agreed that these terms refer to independent impressions or incisions that can be either single or in bands or both in combination.

A total of fourteen decorative elements are recorded on local pottery. Decorative element 1 is common in most Swahili sites and has both TT/TIW and EIA design, although those occurring in EIW designs are in combination with other designs such as vertical or triangular incisions (Chami 1994, 74–5). Continuous stabs shown in element 2 occur in various formats in different sites, either as vertical double stabs, oblique single stabs, horizontal single, or double stabs. Decorative element 4 shows arrow incisions and thumbnail stabs and may occur with a combination of standing triangle with a single vertical incision and thumbnail stabs on body. Decorative element 13, depict cross-hatchings, typical of the EIA described by Soper (1971, 19) as a band of crisscrossing lines with or without horizontal delimiting lines usually incised but occasionally comb-stamped on a flat expanded rim of a shallow bowl. This type of decorative element was reported on a potsherd at Manda, carbon dated c. 600 CE (Chittick 1984, 129) and at Shanga where Horton (1996, 261) classified it as Ceramic Phase B pottery of the Mature Tana Tradition dated between 1000 and 1060+/−110 CE (Horton 1996, 261). Although archaeological evidence from the southwestern port town of Mbui on Pate island show evidence of pottery production there (Chami et al. 2012, 43), apparently only two potsherds with cross-hatches are reported at Mbui.

## TRADE POTTERY AND BEADS

As for the trade pottery, a total of eight decorative motifs were identified as follows: Blue and white floral, chrysanthemum floral, green linear motif, curvilinear, polychrome hand painted, blue-on-white monochrome, greenish brown and finally, light green floral motif. Most the trade wares were glazed. The unglazed ware is mainly Indian brick red wheel-drawn pottery. In summary, the imported pottery is represented by Late sgraffiato ware dated between ninth and tenth century CE from Arabia. From China, the following are recorded; Longquan green-glazed porcelain dated to thirteenth century, blue and white, and white porcelain dated to sixteenth century, powder-blue dated between the late seventeenth and eighteenth century CE. Also represented is blue green under glazed bowls dated between mid-fifteenth and sixteenth century CE. Black-on-yellow pottery is represented by one sherd that came from Khanfur kilns in southern Arabia dated between thirteenth and fourteenth century CE. The few samples analyzed so far provide string evidence that the inhabitants of Siyu were engaged in both regional and Indian Ocean trade and exchange.

Besides the ceramics, two categories of beads were recovered at Siyu. The first category was beads made from shells. Numerous bead grinders were excavated as well as shell beads. The second category was that of imported glass beads. In this work, only wound beads were recorded. One glass bead was a spheroid-wound opaque turquoise 4 mm in diameter. Another bead is wound spheroid, opaque turquoise, and 3 mm in diameter. One was terracotta bicone, reddish brown opaque with a diameter of 8 mm; Glass wound spheroid opaque white with diameter of 8 mm; one wound lenticular, tapered with notches on edge opaque yellow, 6 mm in diameter; glass wound spheroid black in color and 10 mm in diameter. Others include a flat piece of reworked potsherd that may have served as a bead or counter. All the beads were recorded from upper layers except one yellow glass wound bead which was excavated from a depth of 330 cm. According to Horton (1996, 329) and Chittick (1984, 181) colors of earleir beads are predominatly yellow, followed by mid blue or deep blue as recorded at Manda by Chittick. They agree that glass beads were not common in East African coast before 1000 CE. It is established that the eleventh century witnessed increased trade that brought a large number of beads to the East African Coast (Wood 2011). In the fourteenth century, when commercial activity shifted northwards to Mombasa, Malindi, and Pate, more beads were brought into the East African ports (Wood, 2011, 33). Archaeological evidence exist in glass wound beads suggests that these beads were probably made in Egypt or other regions in eastern Mediterrenean. The main type of glass beads found in East Africa are the East coast I-P series (See also Oteyo and Kusimba this volume). Arab and Indian merchants traded commodites in these ports. Horton suggests that due to the low number of beads in most sites, beads were probably exchanged as gifts to cement relations between merchants and the local people rather than as items of trade. Already, it is evident that Siyu had access to both local and international exchange network that enabled her to acquire a wide range of merchandise available to other settlements. Once full analysis of the imported pottery is done, it hoped that more data will reveal an immense network of interaction between Siyu and overseas cities.

## DISCUSSION AND CONCLUSION

From the survey data, Siyu strategic location on the landward side of the Pate Island and on the inner shoreline of a winding Siyu Creek contributed to its attraction for settlement. The navigable creek from the mainland provided access to individual seasonal hunters, fisherman, and mangrove cutters to Siyu, then a coral outcrop on the north-western inner shoreline of Pate Island. The strategic location ensured protection of the settlement from two major threats. First, were the strong oceanic waves that could put boat vessels and fishing activities at risk and, second was the threat of invasion by rival city states. In later periods when Siyu had grown into an important settlement, political insecurity was anticipated from as far as Zanzibar besides threats from close neighbors such as Shanga, Pate, and Faza. The Siyu Creek grew in importance for navigation to the extent that it could anchor relatively large cargo-and-passenger boats during high tide. It could be accessed by foot from the neighboring Shanga, Pate, and Faza settlements.

The second objective was to examine the exchange systems and resource base of Siyu settlement. The rich marine resources in the form of fish and mangrove forest were important items of exchange at the initial stage of occupation. Fish bones formed a major proportion of faunal remains in the excavation. Perennial fishermen used the site as a stopover beach and seasonal camp with minimal settled activities. Erratic fish bone remains in the lower strata indicate that cultural activities in the initial settlement were limited to preservation of fish catch for later transfer to mainland localities. This practice is still in practice by contemporary fishermen who camp on sites such as Parsalia Rocks off Shanga (Bwana Heri Mmaka: personal communication).

The earliest settlements at Siyu were mud and thatch houses constructed to shelter fishermen anchored their boats on the island. Evidence of cultural activities at the site is indicated by the occurrence of daub, charcoal, fish bones, shells, and other faunal materials totaling up to 327 faunal remains. Most of these come from Trench 3 at a depth of 3.40 m below datum point. Archaeological survey revealed that Siyu was endowed with a rich and mature mangrove forest on the northeastern shoreline. Poles harnessed from the mangrove forest were traded between the East African coast, the Arabian Peninsula, and India (Middleton 2004, 81). Besides, serving as primary exports, mangrove poles constituted the bull of construction material for the homes of Siyu's citizenry. Local pottery formed an important trade item for Siyu. Seven pottery types with EIW and TT/TIW affinities were recorded in Stratum I occurring between 3.11 and 3.50 m. One more pottery type not identified with any known local typologies was also recorded. The occurrence of these potteries would mean some form of procurement was done albeit at a small scale going by the number of potsherds at this stratum. The decorative elements found in Siyu pottery also make significant appearances at Shanga site and are identified as Tana Tradition (TT) (Horton 1996, 253). Horizontal line incisions, diagonal incisions, and a pattern of punctuates and thumbnail or otherwise stabs below the rim or on shoulder are common types of decorations on Siyu pottery.

The large amounts of pottery in the subsequent upper strata, presuppose a more elaborate exchange system between the early settlers of Siyu and potters from the mainland. No archaeological evidence of pottery kilns has been located at Siyu and this confirms the hypothesis that Siyu was connected to a wide exchange network that enabled her grow into an important center to procure finished products rather than manufacture her own pottery. Oral information has also shed light to the question of how Siyu acquired finished pots. It is generally agreed that pottery was procured from the mainland. Although archaeological evidence from the southern port town of Mbui on Pate island show evidence of pottery production there (see Chami et al 2012, 43), apparently none of this pottery was exported to Siyu. The early connection of Siyu to the larger international exchange systems beyond East African coast is confirmed by the occurrence of notable imported potteries as presented in the foregoing section. Trade ceramics was regarded as of high status whose utility was restricted to the ruling class. Only a small section of people, the political and economic elite had access to this kind of pottery. The proportion of trade pottery to local pottery 1: 49 implies that only a small population controlled the circulation of high-status pottery. The rest of the population who comprised the subjects and slave workers had at their disposal, locally made clay pottery. The political class imported pottery to Siyu because they had by then developed political ability to maintain the acquisition by tapping into the established trade networks across the Indian Ocean. Due to the growth of political power of Siyu in the fifteenth century, Chinese pottery was sourced directly from China just as they did for other pottery from the Arabian Peninsula. However, since the Wafamau clan is connected to the Chinese descendants, it is tenable to suggest that some of the Chinese pottery was acquired through Shanga as they took advantage of diplomatic relations albeit minimal in a rivalry laden Swahili city states.

The political structures and class division also helped restrict the movement of this kind of pottery within the elite. Even upon breakage such pottery was not disposed ordinarily rather potsherds were used to decorate floors, doorways or tombs of revered personalities who in this case were the ruling class as well as high ranking Islamic scholars or poets. From this study, the residents of Siyu's were connected to other Swahili polities, the hinterland, and the Indian Ocean through social and economic networks of exchange that enabled them to sell their surplus as well import many trade items from the most highly expensive like silk to the most mundane like beads. For its day-to-day survival, local trade with the mainland was every more critical since from the mainland, they not only needed ivory but also utilitarian items such as pottery. Siyu illustrates the importance of trade in shaping culture and taste. Throughout its occupation, Siyu's subsistence economy was dominated by fish resources. The channel provided access to a greater marine resource. Fish was caught either directly or indirectly by local fishermen or indirectly through social exchange networks. Fish bones at Siyu represent not only the fish sourced directly from the nearby sea, rather they would represent fish that would have been caught anywhere else along the coast between Siyu and Mombasa. Cattle, sheep, and goat supplemented fish resources for meat. Stratigraphic sequence also shows that there has been continuous occupation of the site since the ninth through to the nineteenth century. Future studies should endeavor to conduct chromomeric dating on a sample of charcoal to aid in periodization of Siyu. Further survey of more inland sites could discover precise sources of clay that was used in the production of pottery that found utility at Siyu. This would contribute to in depth understanding of the exchange system that placed Siyu in a position to procure more merchandise from the hinterland as well as maintain an international trade link.

## NOTE

1. The Study at Siyu involved many people and institutions. George Gandi, Mohammed Mchulla, Philip Wanyama, and Said Mwakureherwa (Fort Jesus Museum). Dr. Herman Kiriama (Head of Coastal Archaeology Unit, National Museums of Kenya) and Mr. Jimbi Katana (then Principal Curator-Fort Jesus Museum) support me during field work and after. Siyu residents, including Salim Bwana Heri, Masoud Muhammed, Feisal Sheriff, Hussein Athman, and Muhammed Maulana, Saqara Abdalla, and Said Ali gave all the support we required ranging from accommodation, labor, and site surveys. I thank coxswain Anwar Omar, for safely navigating the sea waves. I thank Prof. Wandibba Simiyu and Prof. Ephraim Wahome of the University of Nairobi for their mentor. I am highly grateful to Prof Chapurukha M. Kusimba, Dr. Steven Strohmeier and the President and CEO, John W. McCarter Jr. of the Field Museum and Irene D. Pritzker recommending me for the Irene D. Pritzker Foundation, Inc., Fellowship which supported my graduate studies at the University of Nairobi. I also thank the following institutions for their financial and logistical support; Pwani University Research Board, the National Museums of Kenya and National Council for Science, Research and Technology.

## REFERENCES

Abungu, G. H. O. 1998. "City States of the East African Coast and Their Maritime Contacts." In Graham Connah (ed.), *Transformations in Africa: Essays on Africa's later past*, 204–218. Leicester: Leicester University Press.

Abuodha, P. A. W. 1992. *Geomorphology of the Kenya Coast: Not As a Result of Sea-Level Change Alone*. Unpublished reviews of Literature on Coastal Geomorphology of Kenya.

Allen, J. 1993. *Swahili Origins: Swahili Culture and the Shungwaya Phenomenon*. Athens: Ohio University Press.

Allen, J. V. 1979. "Siyu in the eighteenth and nineteenth centuries." *Transafrica Journal of History* 8(2): 1–35.

Casson, L. 1989. *Periplus Maris Erythraei*. Princeton: University Press

Chami, F., Busolo, I., N., Wanyama, P. and Mchula, M. 2012. The Archaeology Mbui: In Search of Pre-Islamic Settlement on Pate Island. *Studies in the African Past* 10: 21–45.

Chami, F. A. 1994. *The Tanzanian Coast in the First Millenium AD: Archaeology of the Iron Working, Farming Communities*. Uppsala: Societas Archaeological Uppsalinsis.

Chami, F. A. 1998. "A Review of Swahili Archaeology." *African Archaeological Review* 15(3): 199–218.

Chittick, N. 1984. *Manda, Excavations at an Island Port on the Kenyan Coast.* Nairobi. The British Institute in Eastern Africa.

Clark, J. D. 1962. Africa South of the Sahara. In Robert Braidwood and Gordon Willey (eds.), *Courses Toward Urban Life,* pp. 1–33. New York: Wenner-Gren Foundation.

Collett, D. P. and Robertshaw, P. T.1983. "Pottery Traditions of Early Pastoral Communities in Kenya." *Azania* 18, 107–125

Fagan, B. 1991. *In the Beginning: An Introduction to Archaeology* (7th ed.). New York: Harper Collins.

Freeman-Grenville, G. S. P. 1975. *The East African Coast: Select Documents From the First to the Earlier Nineteenth Century* (2nd ed.). Oxford: Oxford University Press.

Freeth, S. J. 1967. "A Chemical Study of Some Bronze Age Pottery and Sherds." *Archaeometry* 10: 104–119.

GEUS. 2006. *Environmental Sensitivity Atlas from Coastal Area of Kenya.* De National Geological Undersea for Denmark and Greenland. GEUS

Horton, M. 1996. *Shanga: The Archaeology of a Muslim Trading Community on the Coast of East Africa.* Memoir No. 14 of the British Institute in Eastern Africa.

Hulthen, B. 1974. *On the Documentation of Pottery.* Lund: Acta Archaeologica Lundensia.

Huntingford, G. W. B. 1980. *The Periplus of the Erythraen Sea.* London: The Hakluyt Society.

Karisa, B. S. 2011. "Chimbuko La Mswahili: Nadharia la Mkoshoro." A paper presented at the Inaugural RISSEA International Scientific Conference held on 18th—20th November 2010 at Travelers Beach Hotel, Mombasa.

Kirkman, J. 1974. *Fort Jesus: A Portuguese Fortress on the East African Coast,*

LaViolette, A. and Fleisher, J. B. 2005. "The Archaeology of Sub-Saharan Urbanism: Cities and Their countryside." In A. B. Stahl (ed.), *African Archaeology,* pp. 327–352. Oxford: Blackwell.

Levitzion, N. 1988. "Islam and State formation in West Africa." In S. N. Eisenstadt, M. Abitbol, and N. Chazan(eds.), *The Early State in African Perspective,* pp. 98–108. Leiden: E.J. Brill.

Middleton, J. 2004. *African Merchants of the Indian Ocean Swahili of the East African Coast.* Long Grove, IL: Waveland Press, Inc.

Mitchell, P. 2005. *African Connections: Archaeological Perspectives on Africa and the Wider World.* Walnut Creek, CA: Altamira Press.

Mutoro, H. W. 1998. Precolonial Trading Systems of the East African Interior. In G. Connah (ed.),*Transformations in Africa: Essays on Africa's later past,* pp. 186–203. Leicester: Leicester University Press.

Nordstrom, H, A. 1972. *Neolithic and A- Group Sites: The Scandinavian Joint Expedition to Sudanese Nubia III.* Stockholm: Scandinavian University Books.

Nurse, D., and Spear, T. 1985. *The Swahili: Reconstructing the History and Language of an African Society 800–1500.* Philadelphia: University of Pennsylvania Press.

Oxford: Oxford University Press.
Pearson, M. N. 1998. *Port Cities and Intruders: The Swahili Coast, India, and Portugal in the Early Modern Era.* Baltimore, MD.: Johns Hopkins University Press.
Phillipson, D. 1995. *African Archaeology.* Cambridge: Cambridge University Press.
Pikirayi, I. 2001. *The Zimbabwe Culture: Origins and Decline of Southern Zambezian states.* Walnut Creek, CA: Altamira Press.
Pwiti, G. 2005. Southern African and the East African coast. In Anne B. Stahl (ed.), *African Archaeology*, pp: 378–391. Oxford: Blackwell.
Sinclair, P. 1987. *Space, Time Social Formation: A Territorial Approach to the Archaeology and Anthropology of Zimbabwe and Mozambique, c 0–1700AD.* Au 9. Uppsala: Societas Archaeologica Upsaleinsis.
Soper, R. 1967. "Kwale: An Early Iron Age Site in South-Eastern Kenya." *Azania: Archaeological Research in Africa,* 2 (1): 1–17, DOI: 10.1080/00672706709511437
Soper, R. 1971. "Early Iron Age Pottery Types from East Africa: Comparative Analysis." *Azania: Archaeological Research in Africa* 6(1): 39–52, DOI: 10.1080/00672707109511546
Stigand, C. H. 1913. *The Land of Zanj: An Account of British East Africa, Its Ancient History and Present Inhabitants.* London: Routledge
Swaleh, H. K. 2011. "The Demise of Religio-Cultural Heritage of the Swahili people of Kenya." A paper presented at the Inaugural RISSEA International Scientific Conference held on 18th—20th November 2010 at Travelers Beach Hotel, Mombasa.
Torrence, R. 1986. *Production and Exchange of Stone Tools.* Cambridge: Cambridge University Press.
Wilding, R. 1973. *A Report on Archaeological Fieldwork on the Northern Kenyan coast, (1971–73.* Copies of Typescript held in Fort Jesus Museum Library, Mombasa.
Willey, G. R. 1953. *Prehistoric Settlement Patterns in the Viru Valley, Peru* (Bureau of American Ethnology 155)
Wood, M. 2011. "A Glass Bead Sequence for Southern Africa from the 8th to the 16th Century AD." *Journal of African Archaeology* 9(1): 67–84.

*Chapter 7*

# Unraveling the Links between the Tanzania's Coast and Ancient China

Elgidius Ichumbaki

## INTRODUCTION

Tanzania's coastal region is part of the Swahili coast that stretches from Mogadishu in Somalia to Sofala in Mozambique, a distance of 3,000 km (see figure 2.1).[1] The Tanzanian segment of nearly one thousand kilometers long represents one-third of the Swahili coast. The coastal littoral and the offshore islands, Zanzibar, Pemba and Mafia (Chami 1998), as well as other islands of Kenya, Mozambique, and Somalia (Kusimba 1999), Comoro Island and northern Madagascar are all parts of the Swahili world (Laviolette and Wynne-Jones 2018). The question that continue to elude archaeologists is how far does the Swahili civilization extend in the interior of Tanzania? Answers to this question have varied over time and space. For instance, although the extension is documented to range from 50 to 300 kilometers between the eleventh and fifteenth centuries CE, it would appear that between the seventh and ninth century (and after the seventeenth century CE), the influence of the coast was limited to 100 kilometers (Chami 2006). Nonetheless, archaeologists have documented evidence for coastal interior interactions as far as five hundred kilometers into the Tanzanian interior (Biginagwa and Ichumbaki 2018; Leakey 1966; Kusimba and Walz 2018; Walz and Dussubieux 2016).

Despite different perspectives, it is evident that for at least 1,500 years, the coastal and hinterlands of Tanzania and other regions of the Swahili coast interacted with other parts of the Indian Ocean world, China inclusive (Kusimba 2017; Kusimba et al. 2013, Walz 2010). This global interaction is revealed in material culture including ceramics and beads as well as shipwreck sites (Bita, this volume). These material records provide evidence indicative of the trade relations that took place not only between the Tanzanian coast and China but also between the coast and the hinterland. This chapter presents the material culture that shows the link between East Asia and Tanzania. The communities settled along the Swahili coast in today's Tanzania have had a history of long and continuous interaction with both the hinterland and the Indian Ocean seaboard. The Swahili people wisely utilized the monsoon winds to develop networks of sailing routes, hence, developed trade (Mitchell 2005).

Bidirectional trade between Tanzania and the Indian Ocean included porcelain, glass, textiles, coins, minerals (copper, lead, and tin; Mapunda 2018) and glass beads as imports and leopard skins, leather, rhinoceros horns, ivory, gold, wild birds, tortoise shells, amber, ebony, and medicinal plants as exports (Kusimba and Kusimba 2018). Material culture, including pottery, glass, beads, coins, and shipwreck found in abundance provide strong and incontrovertible testimony of the millennia links between the southern Swahili coast and China. This chapter reviews published literature, oral testimonies, and archaeological evidence showing the nature and scale of connections between ancient Southern Swahili coastal towns and China.

## HISTORICAL AND ARCHAEOLOGICAL RESEARCH ALONG THE COAST OF TANZANIA

The collection of oral histories from local people is one of the approaches scholars working along the Tanzania's coastal region have used to study the links between China and the coast of Tanzania. At Kilwa Kisiwani, local people maintain a legend about a "dhow-shaped" coral limestone islet called Jiwe la Jahazi meaning a ship (possibly from China) attacking Kilwa that was turned to stone (Pollard 2008; Mahudi 2011; Jeffrey and Parthesius 2013). Jiwe la Jahazi lies on the fringing reef over 1 kilometer south of the entrance to Kilwa Kisiwani Harbour, between two coral- reef causeways. Surveys that followed these local narratives report various black basalt stones on the foreshore, which local people believe were weapons of the "Chinese" invaders. The basalt at Jiwe la Jahazi consists of sub angular to sub rounded small boulders and cobbles concentrated on the seaward edge of the sharp limestone bedrock. These basalt stones, however, are reported as ballast of a ship that had run aground on the reef (Pollard et al. 2016).

Intertidal surveys conducted in the surroundings at Jiwe la Jahazi yielded coarse red ceramics with thickened rims and flat bases, incised and molded bands, some with slips on the inner surface (Pollard et al. 2016). These ceramics, dated to the late eighth to tenth century (Chittick 1984, 84–91; Juma 2004, 113–7; Priestman 2013, 474–6) were also reported in other coastal areas including Manda in Lamu Archipelago, Unguja Ukuu on Zanzibar, Sohar in Oman, and Siraf in the Gulf. Pollard and colleagues' (2016) study interpret the dispersion of both basalt ballast and pottery as an indicator of a shipwreck site. It is noteworthy that oral history played an important role in guiding the discovery of a shipwreck carrying goods imported from the Gulf, hence, links between Kilwa and other parts of the middle and far east as well as Southeast Asia. To complement oral histories, several underwater archaeological surveys at Kilwa Kisiwani and Kaole have been carried out (Pollard 2008). These surveys are building a powerful picture of the social and economic significance of the coast and sea, and the built maritime infrastructure. Through the analysis of previously unknown features such as stone causeways at Kilwa (Pollard 2011) and ports and harbors along the entire coast of Tanzania (Pollard and Ichumbaki 2016) a rich archaeological heritage of interactions between Tanzania and other regions is becoming evident. Furthermore, coastal and intertidal surveys and excavations have revealed sailing routes between settlements and available resources at each port enabling researchers to trace the nature, organization, timing, and scope of maritime trade and travel. As more data becomes available with more intensified research, scholars will be able to answer the questions such as, how far would mariners travel before stopping for supplies, trade, and or transshipment of cargo? The data gleaned from these surveys and excavations will enable archaeologists to figure out factors—from safety, political stability, trading opportunities, marine resources, and climate change—why some ports expanded while others diminished in importance (Pollard and Ichumbaki 2016).

Excavations of coastal archaeological sites allow the researchers to reconstruct Tanzania's maritime history and linkages to the external world. Elinaza Mjema's (2016, 2015) work at Pangani in North Tanzania coast challenges the Zanjian settlements (eighth to thirteenth centuries CE) collapse hypothesis that asserts no connection with formation of the Swahili culture, which arose from the thirteenth to sixteenth centuries CE). He shows continuity in local craft technologies even as local communities became more engaged in Indian Ocean trade and adopted Islam as its primary religion. The results of the analysis of local and trade ceramics, faunal remains and glass beads from Pangani Bay show negligible differences of materials and economical traditions from the late first to second millennia CE. Recovering such a continuous cultural sequence, according to Mjema (2015), indicates that although maritime trade became highly sophisticated during Swahili time, early involvement into oceanic far distance trade contact began in the Zanjian period.

Furthermore, in an effort to reconstruct the ancient trade links of the Tanzanian coast, geophysical and diving surveys have also been undertaken. Geophysical survey using a SwathPlus 468 kHz side scan sonar attached to a motor boat in conjunction with a TSS DMS205 motion reference unit, sound velocity probe, Vector Hemisphere GPS, and Topcon RTK dGPS was conducted around Kilwa Kisiwani Port. Also, a Tritech Starfish 990F side scan sonar at a frequency of 900 kHz and a sonar range of 20 m was also used around Kilwa Kisiwani to get a clearer picture of the environment and anomalies. Scuba diving surveys followed the geophysical survey to ground-truth and investigate in detail the possible shipwreck sites. For safety reasons, the undertaken diving, so far, has been restricted to anomalies at less than 20 m depth (Pollard et al., 2016).

A selection of anomalies was investigated from outside the harbor and within the harbor to gather a wide variety of environments to examine preservation and distinguish natural from cultural features. A circular search pattern with two divers was used for anomalies. Other areas of potential interest were investigated with a swim line search using three to four divers. The dives performed were limited within the harbor environment. Fortunately, both surveys and diving at Kilwa Kisiwani Port revealed a wreck site that is gently dipping about 1–1.5 m over the 1 ha area. At the site researchers recorded an artifact dispersion on the seabed around 100 m from the low water mark that included a medieval stone anchor, local pottery, and imported pottery from Southwest Asia (Pollard et al. 2016: 359).

## DOCUMENTARY AND ARCHAEOLOGICAL EVIDENCE INDICATIVE OF TANZANIA-CHINA CONNECTIONS

Although evidence for the Tanzania-China link abound in numerous publications (e.g., Chittick 1984, 1974; Horton 1984, 1996; Horton and Middleton 2000), little effort has been made to unpack them. These publications generally reveal that, for centuries, trade and cultural interactions existed between the Tanzanian coast and China. Although the question of when such contacts began remains open to debate (Fleisher et al. 2015; Ichumbaki 2017; Kusimba and Walz 2018), multiple corroborating sources including archaeology, historical documents, and linguistic data indicate that the communities that lived along the Tanzanian coast were dynamic (Chami 2001, 2006, 2009, 2017).

Documentary sources by travelers together with chronicles record that for centuries, the inhabitants of along the East African coast developed international trade links (Chami 1999, 237–241, 2001, 7–20; Freeman-Grenville 1975, 1–4). Although several documents do not specifically document the Tanzanian coast a part of the Swahili coast where Chinese visited, they nevertheless report various voyages from China to the East African coast. For instance, during the Ming dynasty, the Chinese launched various missions to the African continent. Two of these voyages made between 1417–1419 CE and 1421–1422 CE have descriptions of the African territories visited, such as Brava, Juba, Muqdishu (Mogadishu), and Muâ-lién/Mo-lin (Malindi) (Inghams 1962, 5; Kirkman 1964, 86–89; Kusimba 1999, 1). The descriptions of these territories are preserved in the official history of the Ming dynasty known as Ming Shih (Inghams 1962, 5) and the Hsing-ch'a sheng-lan; a record of the lands visited by Fei Hsin who sailed as a junior officer on some of the voyages.

The fifth Chinese expedition to Malindi between 1417 and 1419 (Inghams 1962, 5) was a response to a gift of a giraffe of Malindi Sultan (Kirkman 1964, 86–89) via Saif-ud-Din, King of Bengal to the Chinese Emperor. The gift included a "celestial stag" or Oryx, and a "celestial horse" or Zebra. The arrival of an African giraffe in China was made possible by the established seafaring networks between the Kenyan coast and countries bordering the Indian Ocean. The legendary Chinese explorer Zheng He visited Malindi several times during the Ming dynasty, when maritime trade grew unabated (Inghams 1962, 1–5; Kirkman 1964, 88–89). In Zheng He's travel he would have been privy to this commercialization, the most obvious signs of which include a wide range of imported ceramics, beads, glassware, and metal artifacts imported from the Persian Gulf, the Red Sea, India, Southeast Asia, and China. Artifacts of these types have been found in most archaeological excavations along the Tanzanian coast (Chami 2006; see also Kiriama, Kusimba, Namunaba, this volume).

China was known for its porcelain production. Coming from China, the porcelain was traded on the Swahili Coast in exchange for mangrove poles, ambergris, leopard skins, slaves, ivory, gums, rhinoceros' horns, and tortoise shells (Chittick 1979, 273–277; Whitehouse 2001, 411–424). As will be noted in the case of Kunduchi, majority of these ceramics were imported and used either as home utensils and/or decorations on stone-built tombs. Bhing Zhao (2015) reports that Chinese-style ceramics found in East Africa can be arranged into four phases.

The first phase (Phase I: 800–950/80 CE) reported in Tanzania includes green-grazed Yue stoneware and an early Changsha ware dated to between the seventh and ninth century (Juma 2004, 7). Phase II (950/80–1220/50 CE) vessels consist of green and brown-grazed stoneware (monochromes) found at Pemba island (Fleisher 2003) and Sanje ya Kati (Zhao 2012). Phase III (1220/50–1430/50 CE) and IV (1430/50–1500/510 CE) are made of green-glazed porcelain, reported from Sanje ya Kati, Songo Mnara (Zhao 2012) and Kilwa Kisiwani (Chittick 1974).

Chinese coins recovered from Mafia from between the ninth and twelfth centuries contexts are additional evidence for the interactions between the coast of Tanzania and China (Jeffrey and Parthesius 2013). Despite being much corroded, one of the coins was identified as a Kaiyuan tong bao from the Tang Dynasty (618–907 CE). The other was fragmented and could not be easily identified. During its discovery, the Kaiyuan Tong Bao coin was fully intact (24 mm in diameter). Only one side of the Kaiyuan Tong Bao coin was clear enough to identify the marks. There appeared to be no mark on the reverse side, although it could be covered with concretion or corrosion product.

The evidence showing the links between Tanzania and other parts of the Indian Ocean World in particular China is evident at several sites of the Swahili coast. Sites with large monumental structures have received substantial research attention at the expense of smaller more inland sites (Horton 1996, 1984; Chittick 1974; Brown 1970, 1971; Kirkman 1964). Doucmentary evidence (e.g., Freeman-Grenville 1962, 1963, 1975) or inscriptions placed on tombstones and/or mosques (e.g., Sassoon 1966; Garlake 1966; Kirkman 1964), and unfortunate association of monuments with foreign non-African immigrants has distorted the understandings of Indian Ocean globalization (Kusimba 1999; Chami 1998). For instance, Garlake (1966) and Kirkmann (1964) interpreted the majority of the Swahili stone-built towns to have been constructed by Arabs. Likewise, Chittick's excavations at Kilwa and Manda relied heavily on Kilwa Chronicles to inform his research, the same as Brown (1971) at Bagamoyo, whose work was based on written sources, retrieved from across the world. Like Garlake (1966) and Kirkman (1964), Chittick (1974), and Brown (1971) associated the origins of Swahili coastal stone-towns with Arab immigrants. This tendency of focusing on visible monuments (Horton 1996; Chittick 1974; Garlake 1966; Kirkman 1964) and neglecting less obvious sites such as Kunduchi with similar history, overreliance on written texts (e.g., Brown 1971; Freeman-Grenville 1962) and ignoring oral traditions and histories to interpret sites along the coast of East Africa has unfornately excluded local communities from their legacies and histories (Kusimba and Walz 2018; Schmidt and Kehoe 2019). New excavations conducted at Kunduchi on the Tanzanian Coast provide a corrective narrative.

## KUNDUCHI RUINS SITE

Kunduchi site is a tidal inlet and one among several historical settlements found along the coast of East Africa (Horton and Middleton 2000; LaViolette et al. 1989). It is located on a high beach 20 km north of the Dar es Salaam city centre. The site is one among many Swahili towns previously dated to between the tenth and the twentieth century (LaViolette et al. 1989; Masele 2012; Owens 2006, 2004; Sassoon 1966). But the history of the site extends back to the Early Iron Working (EIW) period. Kunduchi's development into a major settlement is owed to its convenient location as a harbor for sailing boats connecting both the interior and other coastal towns. Like many other stone towns along the Swahili coast, Kunduchi exhibits a mosque, stone-built tombs with Arabic epitaphs. Freeman-Grenville and Martin (1973) hypothesized that these dedicatory inscriptions on tombstones along with evidence of trade, including Chinese porcelain and beads, provided evidence of Kunduchi's importance as a major trading port town in Tanzania.

Apart from the ruined mosque, Kunduchi has several tombs both ancient and of recent times. The ancient stone-built tombs are of different styles. Some are pillared, few are stepped, and others are roofed in a quadrangular manner. Although Sassoon (1966) remained silent on the stepped and "star-like" decorated tombs, she explains the pillared ones displaying the fine Chinese porcelain bowls to mean honoring the deceased. To extend this assumption, honoring must have been done in several ways depending on the nature of the deceased person and his/her family. That is, extending the pillar and decorating it with Chinese porcelains was not the only means of honoring the deceased. Instead, some other styles were used, and the Kunduchi Ruins site offers some clues on this. Among others, these styles included decorating the tombs with various types of Chinese porcelain and building the tomb in a unique architectural style. Ichumbaki (2015) is of the view that raising the tomb's pillar, inscribing the tombstone and beautifying the tombs either with steps-like cutting and star-like decorations must have been other means of honoring the deceased. Another tomb had neither steps nor pillars but was decorated with over thirty-five Chinese porcelains of different sizes.

The nineteenth-century accounts by Richard Burton mention Kunduchi but do not discuss its mosque and stone-built tombs as well as the Chinese ceramics placed on tombs (Burton 1872, 331). Probably, the area was too overgrown to be visible (Sassoon 1966). Alternatively, Burton and his team did not find them to be important enough to report. Although the complete history of Kunduchi remained largely unknown, the current research shows that Kunduchi is historically important. As Sassoon (1966, 1) puts it, also as verified by archaeological materials recovered from test pits (Ichumbaki 2015), if not one of the most important, Kunduchi was certainly one of the most attractive sites particularly along the central coast of Tanzania.

Before my work at the Kunduchi ruins, the only archaeological research conducted at the site was in the late 1980s. For two consecutive years (1987–1988), Adria LaViolette and colleagues from the University of Dar es Salaam conducted archaeological field school. Among others, this field school served to train students in techniques of surveys and excavations. The team surveyed and established test trenches at different locations between Dar es Salaam and Bagamoyo including at Kunduchi. At the site of Kunduchi, LaViolette and colleagues (1989) described the tombs, surveyed the site, and excavated two test pits located in the north-western part of the mosque close to the beach. From both surveys and test excavations, different cultural materials including potsherds of probably Tana/TIW tradition and Sasanian Islamic wares, bead grinders, a slag and copper coin of the early Sultan of Kilwa were recovered from the site. Based on these cultural materials, the team concluded that Kunduchi was inhabited at least in the tenth century, and that iron working was one of the village main craft activities (LaViolette et al. 1989). However, this conclusion would have been far more persuasive had the findings been fully analyzed and contextualized. The discussion on the recovered cultural materials is scant. Besides, the materials' context was not documented to coherently establish the site's cultural sequence. Such limitations resulted in a failure to establish the history of the site and make a clear link between recovered cultural materials and the regional links and connections that might have existed. The abovementioned limitations worked against establishing the true chronological foundations of Kunduchi settlement (Ichumbaki 2015).

According to Owens (2004), oral traditions link the foundation of Kunduchi to Debli people whose origin and end remain unknown. The Debli people are said to belong to a local community group that built mosques at many sites along the Tanzanian coast including Kunduchi, Tongoni, and Mbweni (Freeman-Grenville 1962). Nevertheless, documented history of the site states that Kunduchi's mosque dates back to about 1500 CE. Based on a survey of architectural styles of both the mosque and tombs, Sassoon (1966) proposed that building in stones at Kunduchi stopped at the beginning of the sixteenth century or earlier, when the Portuguese sailed to East Africa and monopolized trade in luxury goods such as gold and ivory (Kusimba 1999; Sassoon 1966; Oka et al. 2009). It remained inactive until the late eighteenth centuries; the time to which the majority of its stone-built tombs belong. Despite being limited, this little-known history of Kunduchi is fascinating and features significantly in that of the East African coast. The site's history including its connections with other parts of the Indian Ocean remained incomplete in terms of scope both temporally and thematically. In terms of time frame, the little-known period was that from the fifteenth century onwards, with the construction of a mosque and stone-built tombs with a gap of about 200 years. These monuments are still visible today although in a ruined state.

What makes Kunduchi important are the trade goods mainly imported ceramics and beads. These cultural materials are evidence of trade, and they carry the site's history (LaViolette et al. 1989; Masele 2004, 2012; Owens 2004, 2006; Sassoon 1966). Despite the presence of these material remains on the surface, it remained unclear whether these assets exist in isolation or form part of a greater entity. To address this limitation, test excavation were conducted to recover archaeological data necessary to understand the site's cultural sequence, its spatial-temporal dynamics and place site within a broader global Indian Ocean network.

## Research at Kunduchi Ruins Site

Multiple sources of information were employed in order to reconstruct the origin, nature, and development of Kunduchi. These included written documents, oral sources (notably traditions and histories), and archaeological data. Written documents at the National Archives and libraries of the University of Dar es Salaam, the National Museum of Tanzania, and the Antiquities Division of the Ministry of Natural Resources and Tourism contributed immensely to understanding the site's history and its linkages with the external world. Test excavations were conducted at selected locations, permitting an assessment of the nature, date and extent of structural, artifactual and ecofactual data. All these strategies resulted in obtaining data used for reconstructing the site's history including its interactions with other parts of the Indian Ocean world.

Establishing test pits followed the survey. Originally, the intention was to excavate within the stone-built tombs area and if possible, excavate one of the tombs because of their relatively good preservation. But this was not realizable because the cemetery is still in use.

The first trench was located at the entrance, about 200 m straight from the site's management office. The area has surface scatters of seashells, glass beads, and local pottery. Excavation proceeded by arbitrary levels of 10 cm within the natural layers. The strategy aimed at controlling the distribution of cultural materials vertically because the stratigraphy was relatively unknown. The excavation equipment used to recover materials remains included trowels and brushes. A 4 mm by 4 mm wire mesh was used to sieve the soil so as to collect artifacts that might have escaped the excavators' eyes. The excavation on Test Pit 1 encountered numerous cultural materials including potsherds ($n$ = 988), seashells ($n$ = 801), bones ($n$ =153) and daub ($n$ = 02) amidst the twelve excavated layers. Top layers (topsoil; 0–30) cm comprised dark brown loamy soil. Below this, beginning at 33 cm until 56 cm was dark loamy sandy and produced a good number of seashells and potsherds. Between 60 and 80 cm (60–80 cm), the soil changed from dark to lose brown sandy and produced local potsherds and seashells. While only a few ceramics and seashells came from levels 90–110 cm, level 110–130 cm was composed of white beach sand and produced no artifacts.

The second unit was located at about 80 m northeast of Test Pit 1. The excavation of this unit revealed three layers: dark loamy soil, dark brown loamy soil, and white beach sand. Layers one and two produced both local ceramics and one imported pottery. The imported piece came from a level of 25 cm and belonged to the category of European ware dating to between eighteenth and nineteenth centuries. Apart from this piece, no other imported ceramic of this period was observed in both Test Pit 1 and 2. A good number of seashells came from these two layers. Very few seashells and nondiagnostic local pottery came from the last two levels.

The third Test Pit located close to a baobab tree was the richest of all and produced a large sample of cultural remains. The surface around this trench was relatively flat but with scatters of artifacts. As was the case with the previous trenches, excavation proceeded by arbitrary levels of 10 cm. However, as the excavation continued, materials from the same context were combined and analyzed together. The first layer (0–24) cm made up of dark brown loam sand topsoil produced few plain potsherds and seashells. The second layer (24–56) cm differed from the previous one by soil compactness. It yielded a diverse sample of plain ware; decorated and red-burnished ware, and few pendants. Decorations appear in the form of punctate and large size dots placed on either carination or vessel rim. Diagnostic potsherds exhibit different vessel types including carinated bowls. Additionally, few reddish-brown beads ($n = 3$ and a slag were recovered from this layer).

Layer 3 (56–90 cm) was of mottled loamy sandy with yellowish-brown components. The layer yielded plenty of local potsherds, the majority of which were plain and nondiagnostic. They were in the same context with weathered graffiato. The diagnostic ones indicated that in-turned bowls, necked, and up-turned rim pots were produced at Kunduchi. Other cultural materials recovered from this layer included faunal, a slag, spindle whorls, and bead grinders. The last level with cultural materials extended from 90 to 130 cm. This layer continued to produce nondiagnostic local pottery and copious faunal materials including fish and terrestrial animals' bones and seashells. Some of the local ceramics recovered from this level exhibited beveled and fluted rims. In the same context, daub with wood and stick impressions were found. Furthermore, two bluish beads and green-yellow glazed ceramic were recovered at 97 cm followed by two Sasanian wares at 110 cm deep. Pieces of daub with impressions of woods and sticks and seashells continued to come out down to 130 cm where we recorded a sterile layer.

## DISCUSSION AND CONCLUSION

Results from surveys and excavation conducted at Kunduchi site and its vicinity recorded settlements of early first millennium CE. Recovering daubs bearing pole and stick impressions from the lower levels of Test Pit 1 and 3 supports this assertion. Also, an examination of cross-datable materials, such as bead grinders and daub from surveys and subsequent trenches support this early dating. This early chronological history is neither unusual nor surprising because researchers recorded a similar scenario from other sites of the coast of East Africa (Fleisher 2003; Chami 1994; Horton 1984; Kusimba 2008). The ancient communities of Kunduchi were accomplished ironworkers who subsisted on hunting, herding, fishing, and gardening. Evidence for iron and pottery production in the form of slags large volumes of EIW pottery support this proposition. Thus, early Kunduchi residents were part of the wider Swahili coast cultural and technological landscape that include Mafia Island, Limbo, and Kwale sites of the Rufiji Delta (Chami 1994 1998) and Mbuamaji located about 35 km south of Dar es Salaam (Ombori and Mabulla 2013).

Moreover, like the nearby settlement of Mbuamaji (Ombori and Mabulla 2013) and Kaole (Ntandu 2005; Chami 2002b), ancient communities at Kunduchi were engaged into global trade networks, a proposition supported by the recovery of Sasanian ware, Near-East blue-yellow glazed wares and sgraffiato wares. Similar imports have been reported at Kilwa (Chittick 1974), Tumbe on Pemba Island (LaViolette and Fleisher 2005) and Unguja Ukuu (Juma 2004). Furthermore, the recovery of bead grinders, spindle whorls, pendant, and imported beads and ceramics confirm cultural continuity from Early Iron Working (EIW ≤ sixth century CE), pre-Islamic (sixth to seventh century CE) to Islamic period (eighth to tenth centuries CE) and beyond. The Plain Ware tradition (Mjema 2013, 2015, names it Zanjian B) that followed the Islamic period, dates to between the tenth and thirteenth centuries AD (Chami 2004a-b, 1998, 1994). Although more evidence to strengthen these results is needed, while working along the southern coast of Tanzania, Kwekason (2011) recovered an earlier date of around the eighth century for the emergence of the Zanjian Phase. The Plain Ware tradition recovered at Kunduchi corresponds with the evidence reported from the nearby sites of Kaole in Bagamoyo (Chami 2002a, 1994) and Mbuamaji in Dar es Salaam (Ombori & Mabulla 2013). Following this period is a Swahili tradition dating back to between the twelfth and sixteenth centuries CE. There are several material remains including carinated pottery with punctate decoration treatment, Islamic wares, glass beads, and glass from Kunduchi (Chami 1998, 1994; Walz 2010).

The data reported above indicate that Kunduchi emerged from about the last centuries the Early Iron Age to the second half of the second millennium CE and was connected to other parts of the Indian Ocean until the sixteenth century CE when it remained in isolation for about two centuries until the eighteenth century when it rejuvenated. Results from both surveys and test excavation provide a complete cultural continuity up to this period, thus, confirming the stated argument of decline (LaViolette et al. 1989).

The results also refute the previously popularized claim that the earliest settlement at Kunduchi dates from the fifteenth century (Owens 2004; Sassoon 1966). Nonetheless, the Kunduchi stratigraphy support anthropological and historical studies (Owens 2006, 2004) and analysis of architectural styles and Arabic inscriptions placed on stone-built tombs (Sassoon 1966). These studies maintain that Kunduchi was isolated from other parts of the Indian Ocean between the sixteenth and eighteenth centuries. Lack of trade goods named by Glassman (1995, 38–42) as "prestige goods" such as glass beads and imported ceramics, dating to this period supports this argument of decline of cross-cultural trade during the age of predatory commerce, where Kunduchi like hundreds of other Swahili and inland settlements fell victim to European and Omani Arab predatory commerce (Kusimba 1999; Kusimba et al. 2018).

Based on both oral traditions and epigraphic evidence, Owens (2004) and Sassoon (1966) argue that, Kunduchi was inhabited by the Shomvi during the sixteenth century through the nineteenth century. The questions that need probing into include, what were the reasons for isolation? Was it because Kunduchi sustained and satisfied itself with large herds of cattle and goats, and slaves and commoners? Was it because the qualities that previously attracted other external worlds link-up with Kunduchi ended? These issues and the related hypothesis need a different study to be addressed properly. To conclude, this chapter argues that the developments experienced at Kunduchi during the first millennium continued in the second millennium. Evidence for this includes sgraffiato (trade goods from China) recovered at Kunduchi dating between the tenth and fourteenth centuries (also see Chami 2002b). Trade glass beads dated back to between the fourteenth and sixteenth centuries are additional evidence to prove interaction between Kunduchi and the external world.

## NOTE

1. The author thanks the Division of Antiquities, Ministry of Natural Resources and Tourism for providing permits to conduct the research. Much appreciations go to the African Humanities Program, Gerda Henkel Foundation (grant number AZ 10/BE/17), National Geographic Society (grant number HJ-144C-17) and the University of Dar es Salaam for their financial support. The editor is thanked for all editorial support and invitation to contribute to this volume.

## REFERENCES

Biginagwa, T.G. and Ichumbaki, E.B. 2018. "Settlement History of the Islands on the Pangani River, North-Eastern Tanzania." *Azania: Archaeological Research in Africa* 53(1): 63–82.

Brown, W.T. 1970. "Bagamoyo: An Historical Introduction." *Tanzania Notes and Records* 71: 69–83.

Brown, W.T. 1971. "A Pre-colonial History of Bagamoyo: Aspects of the Growth of An East African Coastal Town." PhD Thesis, University of Boston.

Burton, R.F. 1872. *Zanzibar, City and Coast* (Vol. 2). London: Childs.

Chami, F.A. 1994. *The Tanzanian Coast in the First Millenium AD: Archaeology of the Iron Working, Farming Communities*. Uppsala: Societas Archaeological Uppsalinsis.

Chami, F.A. 1998. "A Review of Swahili Archaeology." *African Archaeological Review* 15(3): 199–218.

Chami, F.A. 2001. "Chicken Bone from the Neolithic Limestone Cave Site, Zanzibar: contact between east Africa and Asia." *Studies in the African Past* 1: 84–97.

Chami, F.A. 2002a. "Kaole and the Swahili World." *Studies in the African Past* 2: 1–14.

Chami, F.A. 2002c. "People and Contacts in the Ancient Western Indian Ocean Seaboard or Azania." *Man and Environment* 27(1): 33–44.

Chami, F.A. 2004a. "The Egypto–Greco–Romans and Panchaea/Azania Sailing in the Erythrean Sea." In P. Lunde and A. Porter (eds.), *Trade and Travel in the Red Sea Region*, pp. 73–101. BAR International Series 1269. Oxford: Archaeopress.

Chami, F.A. 2004b. "The Archaeology of Mafia Archipelago, Tanzania: New Evidence for Neolithic Trade Links." *Studies in the African Past* 4: 73–101.

Chami, F.A. 2006. *The Unity of African Ancient History 3000 BC to AD 500*. Dar es Salaam: E & D Vision Publishers.

Chami, F.A. 2009. "Kilwa and the Swahili Towns: Reflections From An Archaeological Perspective." In L. Kjersti (ed.), *Knowledge, Renewal and Religion: Repositioning and Changing Ideological and Material Circumstances Among the Swahili on the East African coast*, pp. 38–56. Stockholm: GML Print.

Chittick, H.N. 1961. "Kisimani Mafia: Excavation at an Island Settlement on the East African Coast." Dar es Salaam: Annual report of the Department of Antiquities.

Chittick, H.N. 1974. *Kilwa, An Islamic Trading City on the East African Coast: The Finds* Nairobi: British Institute in Eastern Africa.

Chittick, N.H. 1984. *Manda: Excavations at an Island Port on the Kenya coast*. Memoir 9. Nairobi: British Institute in Eastern Africa.

Fleisher, J. 2003. "Viewing Stone Town From the Countryside: An archaeological Approach to Swahili Regional Systems: AD 800–1500." PhD Thesis, University of Virginia.

Fleisher, J., Lare, P., LaViolette, A., Horton, M., Pollard, E., Quintana Morales, E., Vernet, T., Christie, A. and Wynne-Jones, S. 2015. "When Did the Swahili Become Maritime?" *American Anthropologist* 117(1): 100–115.

Freeman-Grenville, G.S.P. 1962. *The Medieval History of Coast of Tanganyika*. London: Oxford University Press.

Freeman-Grenville, G.S.P. 1975. *The East African c\Coast: Selected Documents From the First to the Earliest Nineteenth Century*. Oxford: Clarendon Press.

Garlake, P.S. 1966. *The Early Islamic Architecture of the East African coast. Memoir of British Institute of History and Archaeology in East Africa*. London: Oxford University Press.

Gilbert, E. 2002. "Coastal East Africa and the Western Indian Ocean: Long Distance Trade, Empire, Migration, and Regional Unity, 1750–1970. " *The History Teacher* 36(1): 7–34.

Glassman, J. 1995: *Feasts and Riot: Revelry, Rebellion, and Popular Consciousness on the Swahili Coast, 1856–1888*. Heinemann, Portsmouth, New Hampshire.

Hall, R. 1996. *Empires of the Monsoon*. Harper Collins, London.

Horton, M.C. 1996. *Shanga: The Archaeology of a Muslim Trading Community on theCcoast of East Africa*. Memoir 14. London: British Institute in Eastern Africa.

Horton, M.C. 1997. "Swahili Architecture, Space, and Social Structure." In M. Pearson and C. Richards (eds.), *Architecture and Order: Approaches to Social Space*,pp. 132–152. New York: Routledge.

Horton, M.C. and Middleton, J. 2000. *The Swahili: The Social Landscape of a Mercantile Society*. Oxford: Blackwell.

Ichumbaki, E.B. 2015. "Monumental Ruins, Baobab Trees and Spirituality: Perceptions on Values and Uses of Built Heritage along the East African Coast." PhD Dissertation: University of Dar es Salaam, Tanzania and Roskilde University, Denmark.

Ichumbaki, E.B. 2017. "'When Did the Swahili Become Maritime? A Reply to Jeffrey Fleisher et al., 2015." In L. Harris (ed.), *African Maritime Landscapes: Sea Ports and Sea power*, 1–11, New York: Springer.

Inghams, K. 1962. A *History of East Africa*. London: Longman Ltd.

Jeffery, B. and Parthesius, R. 2013. "Maritime and Underwater Cultural Heritage Initiatives in Tanzania and Mozambique." *Journal of Maritime Archaeology* 8(1): 153–178.

Juma, A. 2004. *Unguja Ukuu on Zanzibar: An Archaeological Study of Early Urbanism*. Uppsalla: Societas Archaeologica Uppsaliensis.

Kirkman, J. 1964. *Men and Monuments on the East African coast*. London: Lutterworth Press.

Kusimba, C. 1999. *The Rise and Fall of Swahili States*. Walnut Creek, CA: Altamira Press.

Kusimba, C.M. and J.R. Walz. 2018. "When Did the Swahili Become Maritime?: A Reply to Fleisher et al. (2015), and to the Resurgence of Maritime Myopia in the Archaeology of the East African Coast." *American Anthropologist* 120 (3): 429–443.

Kusimba, C.M. and Kusimba, S.B. 2018. "Mosaics: Rethinking African Connections in Coastal and Hinterland Kenya." In S. Wynne-Jones and A. LaViolette (eds.), *The Swahili World*, pp. 403–418. London: Routledge.

Kusimba, C.M., Kusimba, S.B. and Dussubieux, L. 2013. "Beyond the Coastalscapes: Preindustrial Social and Political Networks in East Africa." *African Archaeological Review* 30: 399–426.

Kusimba, C.M., Williams, S.R., Monge, J.M., Mohamed, M.M., Oka, R., Oteyo, G., Kusimba, S.B. and Dussubieux, L. 2018. "Mtwapa." In S. Wynne-Jones and A. LaViolette (eds.), *The Swahili World,* pp. 306–318. London: Routledge.

Kwekason, A.P. 2011. *Holocene Archaeology of the Southern Coast of Tanzania*. Dar es Salaam: E & D Publishing.

LaViolette, A. and Fleisher, J. 2009. "The Urban History of a Rural Place: Swahili Archaeology on Pemba Island, Tanzania, AD 700–1500." *International Journal of African Historical Studies* 42(3): 433–455.

LaViolette, A., Fawcett, W.B., Karoma, N.J. and Schmidt, P.R. 1999. "Survey and Excavations Between Dar es Salaam and Bagamoyo: University of Dar es Salaam Archaeological field school." *Nyame Akuma* 52: 74–78.

Leakey, L.B. 1966. "Excavation of Burial Mounds in Ngorongoro Crater." *Tanzania Notes and Records* 16: 123–135.

Mahudi, H. 2011. "Establishing a Maritime and Underwater Cultural Heritage Unit in Tanzania." In J. Staniforth, S. Craig, J. Clyde, B. Orillaneda and L. Lacsina (eds.), *Proceedings of the Asia-Pacific Regional Conference on Underwater Cultural Heritage*, pp. 599–612. Manila: The Museum of Underwater Archaeology.

Mapunda, B.B. 2018. "Metals and Metal-Working Along the Swahili Coast." In S. Wynne-Jones and A. LaViolette (eds.), *The Swahili World*, pp. 517–528. London: Routledge.

Masele, F. 2012. "Private Business Investments in Heritage Sites in Tanzania: Recent Developments and Challenges for Heritage Management." *African Archaeological Review* 29 (1): 51–65.

Mjema, E. 2013. "Preliminary Report on Excavation at Pangani Bay in Tanga Region of Northern Tanzania Coast." *Studies in the African Past* 11: 200–220.

Mjema, E. 2015. *Maritime Community Settlement History in Pangani Bay, Tanga Coastal Region*, Tanzania. PhD Thesis: University of Frankfurt am Main.

Mjema, E. 2016. "The Indigenous Roots of Swahili Culture in Pangani Bay, Tanzania." In K. Sadr, A. Esterhuysen and C. Seivers (eds.), *African Archaeology without Frontiers*, pp. 48–59. Johannesburg: Wits University Press.

Ntandu, C.L. 2005. *Archaeological Investigations of Early Triangular Incised Ware Site at Bwembweni in Kaole, Bagamoyo*. MA Thesis, University of Dar es Salaam.

Oka, R.C., Dussubieux, L., Kusimba, C.M. and Vishwas, G. 2009. "The Impact of 'Imitation' Industries and Imperial Restrictions on Chinese Ceramic Commercial Exports in the Indian Ocean Maritime Exchange, ca. 1200—1700 CE." In *Proceedings of the Fourth Forbes Symposium on Scientific Research in the Field of Asian Art*, pp. 27–29 September. Washington, DC: Smithsonian Institute.

Ombori, T.L. and Mabulla, A.Z.P. 2013. "The Archaeology of Mbuamaji: An Early Iron Working Site in Dar es salaam City, Tanzania." *Studies in the African* 11: 113–139.

Owens, G.R. 2004. On the Edge of a City: An Historical Ethnography of Urban Identity in the Northwest Suburbs of Dar es Salaam, Tanzania." PhD Thesis: University of Wisconsin-Madison.

Owens, G.R. 2006. "The Shomvi: A Precursor to Global Ethnoscapes and Indigenization in Precolonial East Africa." *Ethnohistory* 53(4): 715–752.

Pollard, E. and Ichumbaki, E.B. 2016. "Why Land Here? Ports and Harbors in Southeast Tanzania in the Early Second Millennium AD." *Journal of Island and Coastal Archaeology* 12(4): 459–489.

Pollard, E., Bates, J., Ichumbaki, E. and Bita, C. 2016. "Shipwrecks Evidence from Kilwa, Tanzania." *International Journal of Nautical Archaeology* 45(2): 352–369.

Pollard, E.J.B. 2008. *The Archaeology of Tanzanian Coastal Landscapes in the 6th to 15th Centuries AD (The Middle Iron Age of the Region)*. Cambridge Monographs in Archaeology 76. Cambridge: Bar International Series 1873.

Pollard, E.J.B. 2011. "Safeguarding Swahili Trade in the Fourteenth and Fifteenth Centuries: A Unique Navigational Complex in South-East Tanzania." *World Archaeology* 43(3): 458–477.

Priestman, S.M.N. 2013. A Quantitative Archaeological Analysis of Ceramic Exchange in the Persian Gulf and western Indian Ocean. AD. C. 400—1275. PhD. thesis, University of Southampton.

Sassoon, H. 1966. *Guide to the Ruins at Kundunchi*. Dar es Salaam: Government Printer.

Schmidt, P.R. and Kehoe, A.B. 2019. *Archaeologies of Listening*. Gainesville: University Press of Florida.

Walz, J. 2010. *Route to a Regional Past: An Archaeology of the Lower Pangani (Ruvu) Basin, Tanzania, 500–1900 C.E.*" PhD Thesis, University of Florida.

Walz, J. and Dussubieux, L. 2016. "Research Note: Zhizo Series Glass Beads at Kwa Mgogo, Inland NE Tanzania." *Journal of African Archaeology* 14: 99–101.

Whitehouse, D. 2001. "East Africa and the Maritime Trade of the Indian Ocean A.D. 800–1500." In B.S. Amenoreti (ed.), *Islam in East Africa: New Sources*, pp. 411–424. Herder: Rome.

Wynne-Jones, S. and LaViolette, A. (eds.). 2018. *The Swahili World*. London: Routledge.

*Chapter 8*

# Chinese Porcelain as Proxy for Understanding Early Globalization between China and Eastern Africa

Tiequan Zhu and Chapurukha M. Kusimba

## EARLY CONNECTIONS BETWEEN EAST AFRICA AND ASIA

Archaeological as well as historical investigations reveal the centrality of early global interactions in the development and sustenance of urban societies. Towns and cities that became centers of power were tied to their hinterlands and as their prominence grew, their connection to other regions extended, linking them to many regions abroad. In East Africa, premodern global connections are materially manifested in the ruins of once-flourishing coral towns and associated archaeological artifacts and ecofacts, which originated in many regions of Africa and Asia (Fleisher 2010; Horton 1996; Kusimba 1999, 2; Pollard et al 2012; Sinclair et al. 2012). Foreign artifacts bear witness to the global connections, contributions, and complexity of the past and systematically dismantle the long-held narrative that has served to isolate Africa from Eurasia and, with the exception of North Africa, contributed precious little to global civilization (Abu-Lughod 2008, 188).

Trade played a prominent role in the development of cultures throughout the ancient world (Oka and Kusimba 2008). Trade connected diverse peoples and communities in networks of interactions that qualitatively changed daily life. In East Africa, transoceanic trade served as the main catalyst for building communal and personal wealth, which fostered a steady transformation of villages and hamlets into small towns, cities, and ultimately to city-states with a large and diverse citizenry (Horton 1996; Kusimba et al. 2013; LaViolette 2008, LaViolette and Fleisher 2005; Middleton 2004; Mitchell 2005; Pollard 2007; Wynne-Jones 2005).

Both archaeological and textual data shows that by the second millennium CE, African communities were regular partners in long-distance exchanges that reached as far as the Arabian Peninsula, India, Sri Lanka, and China (Middleton 2004; Mitchell 2005; Pearson 2003; Pouwels 2005; see also Ichumbaki, Kiriama, Namunaba, this volume). A local African urban elite that emerged by the thirteenth century financed, managed, and controlled local, regional, and transoceanic trade and communications along the East African seaboard. Innovations in iron-making technologies aided agricultural intensification and specialization in hunting, fishing, and herding (Chami 1998; Kusimba et al. 1994).

In the late fifteenth century, however, Europe entered into the equation—seeking to benefit from millennia old trade in the Indian Ocean (Acemoglu and Robinson 2012). The rivalry for control of Indian Ocean commerce was economically crippling for Africa and Asia and beneficial for Europe (Fergusson 2012). The consequences of competition for control of transoceanic trade led to warfare in which Dutch, English, Portuguese, and Spanish armies emerged victorious (Kusimba 1999a). The decline and dependence after the sixteenth century paved the way for Europe's colonization of Asia in the seventeenth century and Africa in the nineteenth century (Blaut 1993; Gunder-Frank 1998; Oka et al. 2009; Rodney. 1974). Economic decline and the ceding of sociopolitical power to European nations was a regionwide phenomenon that affected Asian and African political economies. Legitimate and mutualistic regional and transoceanic trade gave way to the now-infamous ivory and slave caravans. Coastal slave raiding expeditions weakened long-standing alliances among peoples, cut off traditions of herding and farming and decimated populations. Today, the ruined walled towns of the East African coast and in the African interior suggest the magnificence of Africa's achievements and contributions to world history (Pikirayi 2001).

While thousands of Chinese Porcelain have been recovered from Eastern and Southern African sites since the Tang Dynasty (ca. 616–907 CE), the provenance of much of the porcelain recovered remains poorly known. As a result, archaeologists cannot sufficiently address concerns beyond chronological and trade connection between Africa and Asia. Relevant questions that need to be addressed today include developing a clear understanding of the nature of relationships that existed within regions, between the regional economic and political power structures, the distribution of the various industrial complexes, the organization of trade and commerce, and the nature and means through which economic and other relations were developed, carried out, and maintained. Some of the key questions that laboratory study of Chinese ceramics recovered in East Africa can help address include how and in what ways did trade reshape Asia and Africa? How did trade and commerce change from Dynasty to Dynasty? How and in what ways did ports of trade thrive as hubs of trading networks that extended across Southeast Asia, South Asia, West Asia, and East Africa? Was trade mostly overland through central Asia or by sea via Southeast Asian port of Malacca, or a combination of both? What major kilns monopolized trade between China and East Africa?

In our attempt to address some of these questions, we studied a small but representative sample of thirty-two Chinese porcelain excavated at the Swahili port city of Mtwapa in Kenya. We used a multimethod strategy involving archaeological classification, micro X-ray fluorescence spectroscopy, and optical microscopy. We were able to determine the provenance of Chinese porcelain exported to East Africa during the Late Ming and Early Qing Dynasty. This chapter presents the results of provenance analyses of this analysis.

## THE MEDIEVAL PORT TOWN OF MTWAPA (CA. 1000–1750 CE)

The earliest evidence for settlement at the site was ca. 1732 BCE when a primarily forager community used the sites. Evidence for a permanent maritime community emerges ca. 1000 CE until 1750 CE when the site is temporary abandoned and reinhabited in the mid-nineteenth century. Located on the Mtwapa Creek some 15 km north of Mombasa, Kenya, the ancient port town of Mtwapa was one of the tenths of port towns that arose on the East African coast following the global trade boom that came to be known as the Silk Road trade. Owing to its strategic location at a natural harbor and navigable creek, Mtwapa served as a main port and conduit for coastal and interior trade as well as a harbor for long-distance maritime trade for a period from ca. 1000 to 1750 CE when it was abandoned (Dussubieux et al. 2008; Dussubieux and Kusimba 2012; Kusimba 1993, 1996, 2008, 2013; Oka 2007; Oka et al. 2009, 2018a, 2018b). In the 1950s, the ruins of the site extended over nine hectares, but human encroachment and resettlement have left four hectares, which still contain standing architecture, including one main congregation mosque, sixty-four houses, some twenty mounds, and thirteen wells. At its height, Mtwapa's estimated population reached 5,000 (Kusimba 1993). As a port, Mtwapa's role in the regional and overseas trade is evident in the nature and distribution of artifacts recovered in excavations.

The ceramic assemblage from Mtwapa town shows the evolution of class distinctions and changes in taste and habit of this society. The ceramic assemblage both native and foreign is characterized by its diversity and complexity. First, 94 percent of all the ceramics were locally produced and bear the imprint of the typical Tana ware with their triangular incised motifs (Abungu 1990; Chami 1994, 1998; Horton 1996; Fleisher and Wynne-Jones 2011).

Jars, bowl, and pots are the dominant ware in the early periods of the settlement, but there is a transition from small eating bowls during the later period to shallow dishes, cooking pots, and jars after the 14th century (Kusimba 1993). This diversity in style and form was indicative of the transformations in tastes, eating habits, and even family sizes that occurred during the fourteenth century as Mtwapa and similar port cities reached their zenith. These emerging primary centers of international commerce attracted and hosted diverse residential populations. They brought with them multiple tastes and habits that influenced ceramic styles, forms, and shapes (Kusimba 1999b; Fleisher and Wynne-Jones 2011; Horton 1996).

A great variety of nonlocal ceramics was excavated. These include South Asian unglazed low-fired hand modeled and wheel-thrown water jars, cooking pots, and serving bowls wares to Islamic glazed wares including Sassanian Islamic, white-glazed ware, green- and-white wares, Lustre wares, Sgraffiato, among others from Southwest and South Asia. Nonlocal ceramics have been crucial for chronologies and mapping of trade networks and connections between East Africa and Southwestern Asia and South Asia (Chittick, 1974 1984; Horton 1996; Kirkman 1954). When carefully studied and analyzed, they have served as a means for understanding class, taste, wealth, and evening identity distinctions between households and within the residential quarters (Oka 2008). As Mtwapa and other similar port towns including Manda where we have an ongoing excavation, trade ceramics, and glassware while universally consumed are nevertheless inconsistently distributed within the town. Some localities have yielded copious amounts during different times, while others had very few; moreover, these associations appear in the earliest levels of the excavations dated to the eleventh century CE and remain consistent throughout the sequence until the upper levels dated to the eighteenth century CE. Thus, the unequal distribution of trade ceramics, including Chinese and Islamic pottery and porcelain at Mtwapa and similar sites reveals great disparities in the distribution of power and wealth within Swahili towns (e.g., Allen 1993; Middleton 2004; Kusimba 1999a, 1999b; Kusimba et al. 2013).

## SAMPLE PREPARATION AND ANALYSIS

We analyzed thirty-two porcelain shards recovered at the Swahili port town of Mtwapa in Kenya. In addition thirteen standard ceramic samples provided by Shanghai Institute of Ceramics of the Chinese Academy of Science (SICCAS) were used for quantitative analysis. Using stratigraphic and classificatory methods of identification places the majority of the samples to the early Qing Dynasty (1532–1751 CE). The samples were cleaned with ethanol solution in an ultrasonic bath and then dried before testing. Optical microscopy (SMZ1500, Nikon, Japan) was first employed to observe the surface and cross-section of the samples. Micro X-ray Fluorescence (EAGLE-III, XXL, USA) was subsequently used to detect the chemical composition of the body, glaze and blue decoration of samples.

The analysis was carried out in the Archaeometry Laboratory of Anthropology Department at Sun-Yat-Sen University. The analytical instrument was operated at 40 kV -230 µA voltage-current of the X-ray tube with the vacuum optical route and the beam spot of 300 µ m. The resolution was 137.5 eV at Mn Kα and dead time was near 30 percent. The software of spectrum retraction and analysis was VISION32 equipped with the instrument. The analytical procedures used for this study have been employed in a previous study by one of us, TZ (Zhu 2009). The results of elements Na, Mg, Al, Si, K, Ca, Ti, Fe, Co, Mn, Cu, Ni, Rb, Sr, Y, Zr. The accuracy of result for most major elements except Na was <6 percent and that of the trace elements was <20 percent.

## RESULTS AND DISCUSSION

Based on external appearance, the porcelains analyzed here include ivory white porcelain, white porcelain, Dongqing Celadon, Celadon of Longquan style, and Celadon of yellowish brown glaze. Li and his colleagues' study of porcelain in north China revealed that potters mainly used the local kaolin clay as material of body, which has the characteristics of higher alumina, Al2O3 > 25 percent (Li et al. 2005). The examples indicate that all but for sample S24 contain lower alumina (Al2O3 > 25%). Lower alumina kaolin has characteristically been associated with kilns in South China so presumably a strong argument can be made that most of samples from Mtwapa-originated from different kiln factories in South China.

### White Porcelain

The Xing, Gong, and Ding kilns in North China are renowned for their world famous white porcelain. These kilns are often credited to be the earliest to produce white porcelain but dominated the market from the Tang (610–907) to the Song Dynasty (960–1279) (Zhu 2009). During the Yuan Dynasty (1279–1368), a major innovation occurred in the ceramic industry with the successful firing of shufu white porcelain at Jingdezhen kilns in Jiangxi province. It marked the beginning of commercial white porcelain production in south of China. During the Ming Dynasty (1368–1644), the production of the highest most technically superior and aesthetically sophisticated white porcelain was mainly produced in Jingdezhen and Dehua kilns, in Jiangxi and Fujian provinces.

Geological analysis of the clay in the vicinity of the Dehua kiln complexes registered high content of potassium. Ancient potters appear to have been aware that when used as flux, high content potassium reduced the melting point of porcelain clay. This was both advantageous for reducing production cost as well as ensuring that the final pieces wound up with a smooth pure white waxy touch, for which Dehua porcelain became renown (Guo 1987). Samples S2 and S8 bear all the characteristics of Dehua porcelain: They are pure white with high potassium, $K_2O$ of 4.04 and 5.25 percent, respectively.

On the other hand, S7 and S9 are tough and dense extremely fine white wares. The calcium of S7 at 1.17 percent and S9 at 2.09 percent is high but within the margin typically associated with white porcelain of Jingdezhen. When used as flux, calcium increases the hardness of porcelain or any other property (Li 1998). Perhaps, this unique property may have served as a catalyst for its popularity among the Jingdezhen potters.

## Qinghua Porcelain

Qinghua, the blue and white porcelain, is a type under-glazed porcelain that rose to become one of best known and arguably the most widely distributed in the world. Although Qinghua porcelain was first made successfully in the Gong Xian kilns of Henan province during the Tang Dynasty (618–907 CE) (Feng 1994; Sun et al 2007), it was during Yuan Dynasty (1271–1368) that the production procedure matured and achieved its global prominence. The kilns of Jingdezhen in Jiangxi Province are widely believed to have pioneered the development of Qinghua porcelain (Feng 2004). During the Ming Dynasty (1368–1644), the Jingdezhen along with the kilns of Zhengzhou in Fujian province monopolized the production and export of Qinghua porcelain. Evidence for interregional innovation, imitation, and competition is indicated in both the internal circulation and export of Qinghua porcelain. Despite these internal dynamics porcelain from the two kiln complexes have clearly distinctive qualities in shape, decoration, texture, body, and glaze.

In contrast to Zhangzhou porcelain, that generally tends to have coarse bodies, all the samples analyzed from Mtwapa have a fine white body. Additionally, these samples have considerably lower levels of iron, $Fe_2O_3$, ranging from 0.90–1.22 percent, which was apparently from that of Zhangzhou kiln, and in the meanwhile, body of Zhangzhou samples also shared the characteristic of lower Na ($Na_2O < 1\%$). These characteristics exclude Zhengzhou kilns as potential sources of Mtwapa porcelain. The analysis also further reveals the dynamism of the industry as potters responded that the forces of demand and supply in time and space. This is seen in the potters use and adoption of different clay sources and recipes in pottery manufacture. This scenario shows the wide range of alumina ranging from 19.72 to 23.45 percent, exhibited in the fabrics from early to late Ming Dynasty. The wide range points to the varying sources of ceramic clays as well as to potters' preferences, expertise, and markets forces. The adoption of native cobalt pigment that has a high content of manganese ranging from 16.84 to 47.96 percent by the Jingdezhen in the Middle Ming Dynasty has been reported (Li 1998).

The Chinese complexity character "大明成化年制," meaning made in period of Ming Chenghua emperor, is printed on the outside bottom of S19. It was common practice for potter to imitate the porcelain of early period to satisfy the requirement of consumers and collectors alike. Thus, the appearances of imitation Ming Chenghua Qinghua porcelain in the Kenyan contexts points to popularity and dominance of Chinese ceramic industry, an observation that warrants further study.

## The Celadon with Longquan style

Longquan kilns factories of Zhejiang were famous for celadon production, which began in the northern Song Dynasty (February 4, 960–March 20, 1127) and achieved its high peak in the Southern Song (1127–1279) and Yuan (1279–1368) Dynasties before declining in the Ming Dynasty (1368–1644). One factor that contributed to the decline of Longquan in Zhejiang was competition from other kilns in South China provinces including Northern Guangdong, Jiangxi, and Fujian, which were favored by geography and came to dominate the market ultimately undercutting Zhejiang's early prominence.

The samples variance ranges in glaze, color—from green, to yellow, to brown, texture, and form. However, all the samples shared the thick fabric ranging from 0.8–1.3 mm. All the Mtwapa celadon samples yielded manganese, Mn, ranging from 2829 to 5634, which conformed to the content consistent with that reported in celadon of Zhejiang Longquan. The study also found that S26 and S28 had lower content of alumina, $Al_2O_2$, of 17.44 and 17.62 percent, respectively, than other samples. Close examination also revealed that that they had numerous smaller bubbles in the glaze. S27 exhibited a clear transparent microstructure with few large size bubbles. The analysis of Longquan celadon reveals that no region dominated the export market to East Africa. Instead based on the differences in chemical composition of body and microstructure in the glaze, we can conclude that celadon with Longquan style exported to East Africa originated in different kilns including those in Northern Guangdong, Jiangxi, and Fujian.

## Dongqing Celadon

Dongqing celadon appeared in the early Qing Dynasty (1644–1912) and was mainly produced in Jingdezhen. S20 is a typical example of Dongqing celadon. It was a shallow green with carved and sculptured flowers on the outside and white glaze on the internal side. The body is fine and white, with small content of iron, $Fe_2O_3$, in the amount of 0. 62 percent and higher calcium, CaO, content of 1.93 percent. This content conforms to the known Dongqing celadon of Jingdezhen made during the Qing Dynasty.

## Other Porcelain

Samples S1, S3, S4, S5, S6, S11, S12, S21, and S22 were different in external appearance but they shared the same characteristic of higher calcium in the glaze, conforming the typical calcium glaze. It is now widely acknowledged that, beginning from the Southern Song Dynasty, major kiln factories in southern China initiated major innovation in ceramic manufacture, which included transformation in the recipe of glaze material. One major innovation in the industry involved the reduction in the use of calcium-alkali glaze or alkali-calcium glaze in finishing the fabric. These innovations progressively resulted in improvement in the quality and purity of the glazes, which simultaneously transformed the quality of porcelain resulting in the Chinese domination of the global market in ceramics.

The industrial complexes and the state often jealously guarded these innovations in science and technology. There were numerous attempts to imitate and wrest control of or get a share of the global demand of porcelain. Imitation porcelain was made was Southeast Asia, West Asia, and eventually even in Europe. Mtwapa was abandoned around 1750 CE before Europeans dominated the Indian Ocean commerce. Therefore, samples with typical calcium glaze found at Mtwapa and other East African sites are very likely from some less well-known Chinese kiln factories or from kilns in Southeast Asia.

## CONCLUSION

The study shows that (1) the identified white porcelain is mainly from Jingdezhen kilns in Jiangxi and Dehua kilns in Fujian provinces; (2) All the Qinghua porcelains originated from Jingdezhen; (4) Celadon originated from diverse kilns, including those in North Guangdong, Fujian, and Jiangxi. (5) Other celadon and white porcelain wares imported to East Africa came from less well-known kilns in China and in Southeastern Asia.

Table 8.1  Macro Description of Mtwapa Samples

| Number | Archaeological number | Sample Description |
|---|---|---|
| s1 | MT95.13058 | White porcelain, white body with shallow yellow, ivory white glaze |
| s2 | MT048-b | White porcelain, white body, and white glaze |
| s3 | MT(2do)181121 | White porcelain, white body with shallow yellow, ivory white glaze |
| s4 | MT141121 | Celadon, white body with shallow yellow, shallow green glaze |
| s5 | MT151121.1 | Celadon, white body with shallow yellow, shallow green glaze |
| s6 | MT151121.2 | Celadon, white body with shallow yellow, shallow green glaze |
| s7 | MT081 | White porcelain, white body and white glaze |
| s9 | MT96.13327) | White porcelain, white body and white glaze |
| s8 | MT96.13549) | White porcelain, white body and white glaze |
| s10 | MT161121 | White porcelain, white body with shallow green, white glaze |
| s11 | MT97.31783 | Celadon, white body with shallow gray, and grayish green glaze |
| s12 | MT96.13270 | Qinghua porcelain, white body and white glaze |
| s13 | MT95.00178 | Qinghua porcelain, white body and white glaze |
| s14 | MT96.13152 | Qinghua porcelain, white body and white glaze |
| s15 | MT96.13226 | Qinghua porcelain, white body and white glaze |
| s16 | MT96.13334 | Qinghua porcelain, white body and white glaze |
| s17 | MT96.13540 | Qinghua porcelain, white body and white glaze |
| s18 | MT96.11622 | Qinghua porcelain, white body and white glaze |
| s19 | MT.048 | Qinghua porcelain, white body and white glaze |
| s19–1 | MT.961331 | Qinghua porcelain, white body and white glaze, with incised character Chenghua nianzhi |
| s20 | MT97.34212 | Dongqing porcelain, white body and green glaze |
| s21 | MT.182 | Celadon, gray body and yellowish-brown glaze |
| s22 | MT.089 | Celadon, gray body and yellowish-brown glaze |
| s23 | Unknown | Celadon, white body with shallow gray, green glaze, thick glaze |
| s24 | MT96.11584 | Celadon, white body with shallow gray, green glaze, thick glaze |
| s25 | MT.130 | Celadon, gray body, green glaze |
| s26 | MT.141121 | Celadon, gray body, green glaze |
| s27 | Unknown | Celadon, white body, green glaze |
| s28 | Unknown | Celadon, white body with shallow gray, green glaze, thick glaze |
| s29 | Unknown | Celadon, white body with shallow gray, green glaze, thick glaze |
| s30 | Unknown | Celadon, white body, green glaze |
| s31 | MT.131121 | Celadon, white body, green glaze |
| s32 | MT.43 | Celadon, white body, green glaze |

Undoubtedly, the provenance of Chinese porcelain analyzed provide important evidential grounds to initiate discussions showing increasingly sophisticate consumption and taste influenced innovation and the global circulation of high-quality well-made and finished trade items. The major innovations in the ceramic industry bespeaks the political, locational, and relational stability that may have fostered trader confidence leading to decisions to invest in technology and science that resulted in the major transformation witnessed in Late Ming and Early Qing Dynasty.

Porcelain as well as other exotic trade goods, including silk, jewelry, and embroidery were expensive (Kusimba et al. 2013). Not everyone at Mtwapa could afford them. Yet the elite of the city were sufficiently wealthy enough to continually sustain the demand of these expensive products throughout the existence of the town. Thus, even as the trade ceramics has served to enable mapping of Africa onto the global network, in particular the determine of chronologies, this study points to the numerous possibilities that the combination of traditional archaeology and laboratory research can yield greater understandings and give voice to the past that once was thought impossibly unknowable.

## REFERENCES

Abungu, G.H.O. 1990. *Communities on the River Tana, Kenya: An Archaeological Study of Relations Between the Delta and the River Basin, 700–1890 AD*. PhD Dissertation. Cambridge, UK: The University of Cambridge.

Acemoglu, D., and Robinson, J.A. 2012. *Why Nations Fail: The Origins of Power, Prosperity, and Poverty*. New York, NY: Crown.

Allen, J. 1993. *Swahili Origins: Swahili Culture and the Shungwaya Phenomenon*. Athens: Ohio University Press.

Blaut, J.M. 1993. *The Colonizer's Model of the World*. New York: Guilford Press

Chami, F. 1994. *The Tanzanian Coast in the 1st Millennium AD: An Archaeology of the Iron-Working Farming Communities*. Studies in African Archaeology. Uppsala: Societas Archaeologica Upsaliensis.

Chami, F. 1998. "A Review of Swahili Archaeology." *African Archaeological Review* 15(3):199–221.

Chittick, H.N. 1974. *Kilwa: An Islamic Trading City of the East African Coast*. Nairobi: British Institute in Eastern Africa.

Chittick, H.N. 1984. *Manda: Excavations at an Island Port on the Kenya Coast*. Nairobi and London: British Institute in Eastern Africa.

Curtin, P.D. 1984. *Cross-Cultural Trade in World History*. Cambridge, UK: Cambridge University Press.

Dussubieux, L., Kusimba, C., Gogte, V., Kusimba, S., Gratuze, B., and Oka, R. 2008. "The Trading of Ancient Glass Beads: New Analytical Data from South Asian and East African Soda-Alumina Glass Beads." *Archaeometry* 50, 797–821.

Dussubieux, L. and Kusimba, C.M. 2012. "Glass Vessels in Sub-Saharan Africa: Compositional Study of Some Samples from Kenya." In Liritzis, I. and Stevenson, C. (eds.), *The Dating and Provenance of Obsidian and Ancient Manufactured Glasses,* pp. 143–156. Albuquerque: University of New Mexico Press.

Duyvendak, J.J.L. 1949. *China's Discovery of Africa.* London: A. Probsthain.

Feng, X.J. 1994 "Origin and Development of Qinghua porcelain." *Journal of History Museum* (2): 29–39 (In Chinese).

Feng, X.M. 2004. *China Ancient Ceramic, Shanghai: Shanghai Chinese Classic.* Publishing House.

Ferguson, N. 2012. *Civilization: The West and the Rest.* New York, NY: Penguin Books Ltd.

Fleisher, J. 2010. "Housing the Market: Swahili Merchants and Regional Marketing on the East African Coast, Seventh to Sixteenth Centuries AD." In Garraty, C.P., and Stark, B.L. (eds.), *Archaeological Approaches to Market Exchange in Ancient Societies,* pp. 141–159. Boulder: University Press of Colorado.

Fleisher, J., and Wynne-Jones, S. 2011. "Ceramics and the Early Swahili: Deconstructing the early Tana Tradition." *African Archaeological Review* 28(4): 245–278.

Gunder-Frank, A. 1998. *Reorient: Global Economy in the Asian Age.* Berkley: University of California Press.

Guo, Y.Y, L G.Z. 1987.*Study on the White Porcelain of Dehua Kiln of Different Period in History, Research of Chinese Ancient Ceramics.* Beijing: Press of Science China.

Horton, M.C. 1996. *Shanga: The Archaeology of a Muslim Trading Community on the Coast of East Africa.* London: The British Institute of East Africa.

Kirkman, J.S. 1954. *The Arab City of Gedi: Excavations at the Great Mosque, Architecture and Finds.* Oxford: Clarendon Press.

Kusimba, C. 1996. "The Social Context of Iron Forging on the Kenya Coast." *Africa: Journal of the International African Institute* 66(3): 386–410.

Kusimba, C.M. 1993. *The Archaeology and Ethnography of Iron Metallurgy of the Kenya Coast.* PhD Dissertation. Bryn Mawr, PA: Bryn Mawr College.

Kusimba, C.M. 1999a. "Material Symbolism Among the Pre-Colonial Swahili of the East African Coast." In Robb, J.E. (ed.), *Material Symbolism: Culture and Economy in Prehistory,* pp. 318–341, Carbondale, IL: Center for Archaeological Investigations, Southern Illinois University.

Kusimba, C.M. 1999b. *The Rise and Fall of Swahili States.* Walnut Creek, CA: AltaMira Press.

Kusimba, C.M., Killick, D., and Creswell, R.G. 1994. "Indigenous and Imported Metals on Swahili Sites of Kenya." *MASCA Papers in Science and Archaeology* II(Supplement). p. 63–77.

Kusimba, C.M., Kusimba, S.B., and Dussubieux, L. 2013. "Beyond the Coastalscapes: Preindustrial Social and Political Networks in East Africa." *African Archaeological Review* 30(8): 399–426.

LaViolette, A. 2008. "Swahili Cosmopolitanism in Africa and the Indian Ocean World, A.D. 600–1500." *Archaeologies: Journal of the World Archaeological Congress* 4(1): 24–49.

LaViolette, A., and Fleischer, J. 2005. "The Swahili." In Stahl, A.B. (ed.), *African Archaeology*, pp. 392–419. Oxford: Blackwell Publishers.

Li, J.Z.1998. *History of Chinese science and Technology. Volume of Ceramic*. Beijing: Science Press of China, pp. 325–359 (In Chinese).

Li, P., Grieg, A., Zhao, J., Collerson, R., Quan, K., Meng, Y., and Ma, Z. 2005. "ICP-MS Trace Element Analysis of Song Dynasty Porcelains from Ding, Jiexiu and Guantai Kilns, Northern China." *Journal of Archaeological Sciences* 32, 251–259.

Middleton, J. 1992. *The World of the Swahili*. New Haven, CT: Yale University Press

Middleton, J. 2004. *African Merchants of the Indian Ocean Swahili of the East African Coast*. Long Grove, IL: Waveland Press, Inc.

Mitchell, P. 2005. *African Connections: Archaeological Perspectives on Africa and the Wider World*. Altamira Press, Walnut Creek.

Oka, R.C. 2008. *Resilience and Adaptation of Trade Networks in East African and South Asian Port Polities, 1500–1800 CE*. PhD Dissertation. Chicago, IL: The University of Illinois, Chicago.

Oka, R.C., and Kusimba, C.M. 2008. "The Archaeology of Trading Systems, Part 1: Towards a New Trade Synthesis." *Journal of Archaeological Research* 16(4): 339–395.

Oka, R.C., Kusimba, C.M., and Gogte, V.D. 2009a. "Where Others Fear to Trade: Modeling Adaptive Resilience in Ethnic Trading Networks to Famine, Maritime Warfare and Imperial Stability in the Growing Indian Ocean Economy, ca. 1500–1700 CE." In: Murphy, A., and Eric, J. (eds). *The Political Economy of Hazards and Disasters*. Monographs in Economic Anthropology. Walnut Creek, CA: Altamira Press.

Oka, R.C., Dussubieux, L., Kusimba, C.M., and Vishwas, G. 2009b. "The Impact of "Imitation" Industries and Imperial Restrictions on Chinese Ceramic Commercial Exports in the Indian Ocean Maritime Exchange, ca. 1200–1700 CE." In *Proceedings of the "Fourth Forbes Symposium on Scientific Research in the Field of Asian Art*. September 27 to 29, 2007, Washington, DC: Smithsonian Institution.

Pearson, M.N. 2003. *The Indian Ocean*. London: Routledge Press.

Pikirayi, I. 2001. *The Zimbabwe Culture: Origins and Decline of Southern Zambezian States*. Walnut Creek, CA: AltaMira Press.

Pollard, E.J.D. 2007. *An Archaeology of Tanzanian Coastal Landscapes in the Middle Iron Age (6th to 15th Centuries AD)*. PhD Thesis. Belfast, Ireland: The University of Ulster.

Pollard, E.J.D., Fleisher, J., and Wynne-Jones, S. 2012. "Beyond the Stone Town: Maritime Architecture at Fourteenth-Fifteenth Century Songo Mnara, Tanzania." *Journal of Maritime Archaeology* 7(1): 43–62.

Pouwels, R.L. 2005. *The African and Middle Eastern World, 600–1500*. New York: Oxford University Press.

Rodney, W. 1974. *How Europe Underdeveloped Africa*. Washington, DC: Howard University Press.

Sinclair, P.J.J., Ekblom, A., and Wood, M. 2012. "Trade and Society on the South-East African Cast in the Later Millennium AD: The Case of Chibuene." *Antiquity* 86(1): 723–37.

Sun, X., Liu, L., Zhao, Z., Guo, M., Bao, M., Zhao, J., Tian, J., Zhang, J., Shen, L., Zhou, Y., Li, Land, and Guo, M. 2007. "Excavation of Huangye Kiln Site in Gong County of Henan Province." *Huaxia Archaeology* 4: 106–129 (In Chinese).

Wynne-Jones, S., and Fleisher, J. 2012. "Coins in Context: Local Economy, Value and Practice on the East African Swahili Coast." *Cambridge Archaeology Journal* 22(1): 19–36.

Wynne-Jones, Stephanie. 2005. Urbanisation at Kilwa, Tanzania. Ph.D. dissertation, Department of Archeology, University of Cambridge.

Zhu, T. 2009. In *Proceedings of the Fourth Forbes Symposium on Scientific Research in the Field of Asian Art.* September 27 to 29, 2007, Washington, DC: Smithsonian Institution.

Zhu, T., Ding, X., Kusimba, C.M., and Feng, Z. 2015. "Using Laser Ablation Inductively Coupled Plasma Mass Spectroscopy (LA-ICP-MS) to Determine the Provenance of the Cobalt Pigment of Qinghua Porcelain from Jingdezhen in Yuan Dynasty of China (1271–1368AD)." *Ceramics International* 41: 9878–9884.

*Chapter 9*

# The Sources of East African Chinese Longquan Celadon and Imitation Celadon

Min Wang, Tiequan Zhu, Khalfan Bini Ahmed, and Chapurukha M. Kusimba

As economists and political scientists debate the impact of China's economic resurgence on the global economy, archaeologists and historians are redirecting their scholarly attention to the earlier global economy, known as the Maritime Silk Road (Millward 2012). The Silk Road trade engaged nearly all regions of the Old World, encompassing Europe, Asia, and Africa. How truly global was the maritime Silk Road phenomenon? What was the impact to states societies and smaller communities? What was its scale and reach? Archaeologically, ceramics does not disintegrate easily and thus archaeologists have relied on this material to understanding the societal social economic, and technological bases and organization, of the Silk Road. Although China exported multiple items to other countries, such as silk, jade, beads, spices, oils, cloth, lacquer ware, tea, and precious metals, it is porcelain and stoneware that today form one of the major exports out of China (Kusimba 2017; Zhu et al 2017; see also Oteyo, Ichumbaki, Kiriama, Kusimba, Namunaba, this volume). Export porcelain first appeared in the Qin and Han Dynasties, mainly through land transport. Chinese porcelain was exported to countries all over the Old World by the Maritime Silk Road in the Tang Dynasty (618–907), and their export porcelain mainly consisted of Changsha-colored, celadon and Yue celadon. With the development of the navigation industry and the further strengthening of foreign trade in the Song (960–1279) and Yuan (1279–1369) Dynasties, Chinese porcelain exports showed an unprecedented prosperity. During this period, the porcelain in Longquan celadon, followed by Jingdezhen bluish-white porcelain, the blue-and-white porcelain of Jingdezhen kiln are also widely used for export in

Yuan Dynasty. In addition, there are Cizhou, Yaozhou, Jian kilns, and the products from the export porcelain kilns in coastal Fujian, Guangdong. In the period of Yongle and Xuande in the Ming Dynasty, Zheng He's seven voyages to the West further promoted the development of foreign trade at sea, and exported porcelain not only exported to Asia and Africa but also began making inroads into the Western European market from the late Ming Dynasty. The export porcelain of the Ming and Qing dynasties was mainly blue-and-white porcelain and glazed porcelain from the Jingdezhen kiln. Among all the porcelains exported from China, Changsha colored, Yaozhou celadon, Cizhou black-and-white colored porcelain, Yue celadon, Longquan celadon, Qingbai ware, and Qinghua ware; Longquan celadon are one of the most representative. The popularity of Longquan celadon in overseas markets increased exponentially in the Song Dynasty (960–1279) and Yuan Dynasty (1271–1368). The popularity of Longquan celadon is indicated in the multiple imitation attempts made by other kiln industrial complexes in different regions of South China, such as Fujian, Jiangxi, and Guangdong (Bureau of light industry in Zhejiang province 1989; Li 1998; Feng 2001).

The ubiquity of Chinese porcelain and other precious stones recovered at archaeological sites in East Africa and Southern Zambezia beginning from the mid-Tang Dynasty (618–907) points to a flourishing intercontinental trade network that crisscrossed different regions, agencies and traders (Oka 2007; Oka et al 2009; Pearson 2003, 85 see Kusimba this volume). The increase in volume and scale of transoceanic trade between the tenth to fourteenth centuries heralded the age of competing partnerships that had a huge impact on the cultural, economic, and technological dynamics (Oka 2018a, 422). To what extend were Chinese exports to Africa consistent? What was the quality of Chinese ceramic products consumed by Africans? Rahul Oka ICP-MS analysis of a large collection of celadons excavated from Mtwapa (800–1750 CE) and Chaul (200 BCE–1750 CE) confirmed that African consumers preferred Chinese porcelain over Islamic and Indian glazed pottery (Oka 2008 2018; Oka et al 2009; Kusimba et al 2018).

Chinese imperial policies during the Yuan Dynasty encouraged Chinese citizens and merchants to invest in long-distance trade with other regions beyond the traditional South China Sea. Yuan Dynasty pro-business policies encouraged private and state-financed corporations and traders to venture further into the Indian Ocean (Pearson 2003, 89). While it remains unlikely that Chinese merchant ships made contact with East Africa during the Tang Dynasty (618–907), the large volume of Chinese porcelain especially celadon and Qinghua reached the shores of Africa and made their way into inland Southeast Africa (Chirikure 2014; Pikirayi 2001; Qin 2015; Zhao and Qin 2018). Longquan celadon, mainly manufactured in Zhejiang and Guangdong during the Ming Dynasty (1368–1644 CE), was one of the most representative porcelains. Its technical and aesthetic superiority made it a highly desirable commodity both in China and abroad. Although all five samples

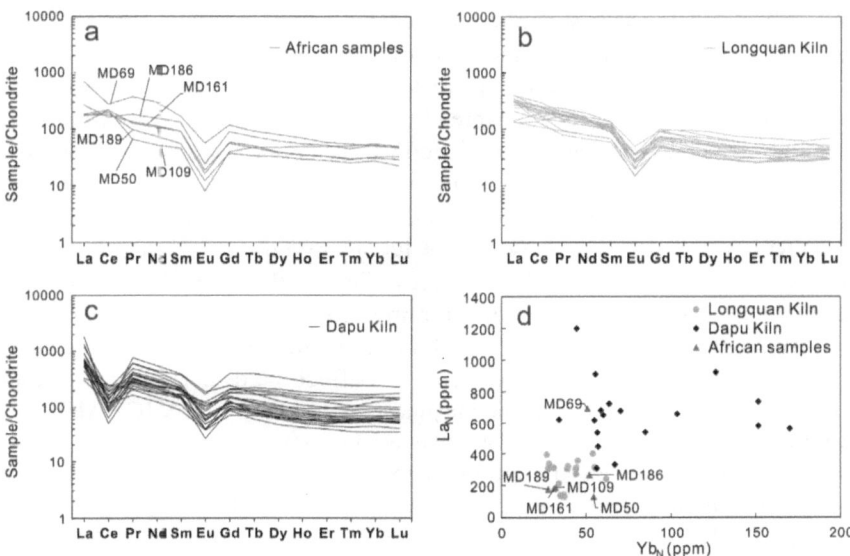

Figure 9.1 Chondrite-Normalized Rare Earth Elements Patterns Spider Diagram Showing Comparison of the African (a), Longquan (b) and Dapu (c) Samples and the $La_N$–$Yb_N$ Scatter-Plot (d) For Various Samples. Chondrite Elemental Values. Photo Credit: Min Wang.

exhibited right leaning REE distribution patterns with an enrichment in light REE (ΣREE) which could also be supported by their (La/Yb)N ratios, sample MD69 displayed the different REE characteristics from others (Figure 9.1).

Do Chinese porcelains recovered in East Africa provide evidence for the early contact between East Africa and China from the Tang (618–906 CE) through Song (906–1279) and Yuan Dynasties (1279–1369 CE)? Was Chinese interaction with their African counterparts predominantly indirect through Persian and Arab merchants? How did Chinese exports from the Tang-Song-Yuan Dynasties reach Africa? To answer these questions, we carried out an analytical study of a group of celadon porcelains excavated from the Kenyan port sites of Mtwapa.

## ANALYTICAL METHODS

In this chapter, we report the results of a LA-ICP-MS analytical study on a group of celadon porcelains excavated at Mtwapa and Manda in Kenya by one of us, CMK. For the analysis of trace elements in ancient ceramics, commonly used methods are neutron activation analysis (INAA), X fluorescence analysis (XRF), and inductively coupled plasma mass spectrometry

(ICP-MS). INAA was first applied to archaeological samples in the 1950s of last century, the chemical composition of a number of famous porcelains in Song Dynasty was measured by this method in 1980s. The popularization this technology, allowed for its widespread use but the accuracy of measurement is variable. There are interference reactions in the analysis process, and the measurement process is complex and expensive. Two analytical methods of XRF are widely used. EDXRF causes the least damage to the sample while WDXRFis the more destructive but it has many advantages including fast analysis speed, high and reliable accuracy. This method is widely used in the determination of chemical composition in ancient ceramics. However, there are also some defects, such as the inability to guarantee that the error caused by the heterogeneity of the sample does not affect the detection result. Laser ablation inductively coupled plasma mass spectrometry (LA-ICP-MS) is a rapid developing microelement analysis technology. The plasma mass spectrometry has high sensitivity and precision, and the detection limit is low. It can simultaneously detect multiple elements and provide isotope ratio information. LA-ICP-MS analysis offers many advantages over other analytical procedures because of the low detection limit, high precision, analysis speed, and micro-in situ sampling. The Kenyan samples were compared with original Zhejiang Longquan celadon and imitation celadon made at the Dapu kiln of Guangdong. We had hoped that this comparative analytical study would provide a good basis for provenance identification necessary to distinguish the types of Chinese celadon that reached Africa as a proxy for defining the nature of competition within China itself. Provenance studies would also enable the identification of articles from royal kilns from those of commercial kilns. The presence of imperial ceramics in East African archaeological contexts would suggest that diplomatic relationships between China and the rest of the world. In China itself, these findings would enable us to map out the extend of domestic competition for external markets.

## Analytical Procedures

Major and trace elemental analyses were conducted on five celadon shards excavated from the site of Manda in Kenya in 2012 were analyzed. These include MD50, MD69, MD109, MD161, MD186. Micro X-ray fluorescence (EAGLE-III, XXL, USA) was used to detect the major element compositions of the samples. The analytical instrument was operated at 40 kV and 610 mA voltage-current of the X-ray tube, with a vacuum optical route and a beam spot of 100 mm. The resolution was 137.5 eV at Mn Ka and dead time was near 30 percent. All the samples were analyzed in three different areas for calculating the average, in order to overcome the potential problems resulting from the inhomogeneity of the samples. The software employed for spectrum retraction and analysis was the program VISION32, associated with the instrument. The analytic procedures used for this study were recorded in a previous study (Zhu et al. 2011). The accuracy of the results for the major elements (except the lighter elements Na and Mg) was in the range of 1 to 6 percent. The accuracy of the result for most of the major elements, except Na, was < 6 percent. The analytical results are illustrated in table 9.1.

Trace element analysis involved sample pretreatment and Trace-element LA-ICP-MS analysis were carried out in the State Key Laboratory of Isotope Geochemistry, Guangzhou Institute of Geochemistry, Chinese Academy of Sciences. Before LA-ICP-MS analysis, a minute piece was cut from the edge of a test sample, using a 1.4 mm-thick diamond wire cutter. The piece samples were then mounted in epoxy to make the standard 2.54 cm-diameter epoxy resin sample target. The targets were polished carefully to expose a cross-section of body.

The LA-ICP-MS system was composed of an Agilent 7500a ICP-MS coupled with a Resonetic RESOLution M-50 ArF-Excimer laser source ($\lambda$ = 193 nm). Laser energy was 80 mJ, and frequency was 10 Hz with ablation spot of 60 μm in diameter. Both double-volume sampling cell and Squid pulse smoothing device were used to improve data quality (Li et al. 2012). The ablated aerosol was carried to the ICP source with He gas. NIST612 was used as an external calibration standard, and NIST 610 was used as monitoring standard, and 29Si as an internal standard. The samples adapted the average concentration obtained by three–four ablations dispersedly distributed in the body/glaze of one sample. The trace elements data were calculated using the software ICPMSDataCal (version 10.2) (Liu et al. 2008; Liu et al. 2010). The detection limit of most trace element was to several ppb, except for some elements including Cr, Ni, Cu and Zn, with detection limit of several ppm. The accuracy of the elements was mostly < 5 percent.

## RESULTS AND DISCUSSION

The analyses revealed that the samples had similar major elements composition, the content of $SiO_2$ were about 70 wt.% (68.7–70.4 wt.%) and alumina content was from 14.7 wt. % to 21.7 wt.% which fell within the range of porcelain produced in southern China (Fang et al. 1990; Zhu et al. 2011). In addition, the study also revealed some differences in the content of certain trace elements. Sample MD69 had much higher concentration of Co (33.0 ppm), Cu (72.1 ppm), Ba (1098.3 ppm) than the other four samples (Co, 1.2–5.8 ppm; Cu, 7.4–21.7 ppm; Ba, 338.5–605.5 ppm). Especially, the content of Nb and Ta were lower than those of the other four samples. But they had similar Nb/Ta radio, just the same as in samples in Guangdong Dapu kiln

**Table 9.1  Analytic Results of Manda Samples by EDXRF (wt.%)**

| | $Na_2O$ | $MgO$ | $Al_2O_3$ | $SiO_2$ | $P_2O_5$ | $K_2O$ | $CaO$ | $TiO_2$ | $Fe_2O_3$ | $MnO$ |
|---|---|---|---|---|---|---|---|---|---|---|
| MD50  | 0.75 | 0.54 | 14.72 | 78.02 | 0.09 | 3.68 | 0.15 | 0.14 | 1.72 | 0.03 |
| MD69  | 0.70 | 0.54 | 20.96 | 70.41 | 0.07 | 4.65 | 0.06 | 0.22 | 2.17 | 0.05 |
| MD109 | 0.75 | 0.48 | 20.49 | 70.34 | 0.08 | 5.74 | 0.09 | 0.08 | 1.73 | 0.06 |
| MD161 | 0.74 | 0.41 | 20.47 | 69.96 | 0.09 | 5.86 | 0.44 | 0.12 | 1.72 | 0.09 |
| MD186 | 0.50 | 0.54 | 21.66 | 68.69 | 0.07 | 6.45 | 0.14 | 0.10 | 1.58 | 0.10 |

and Zhejiang Longquan kiln (Wang et al. 2018). Geochemically, Nb and Ta, high field strength elements (HFSE), have the similar electrovalence, ionic radius, and electronegativity. Therefore, they are very similar in geochemical properties and have very similar geochemical behavior in various geological processes (Ding et al. 2013). Given that Nb and Ta are immobile during weathering and pedogenesis of the parent rock, they can truly reflect the characteristic of the parent rock. Overall, higher Nb and Ta in the Longquan samples than that of the Dapu ones, suggesting that the porcelain clay and related adamellite in Longquan also have higher Nb and Ta. This is consistent with the higher fractionated extent for the Longquan adamellite, comparing to the Dapu biotite granites (Wang et al. 1997a, b).

Rare earth elements (REE) in celadon body are mainly controlled by the minerals of their porcelain clay, but scarcely interfered by human activities. Therefore, the REE can be especially used as tracers to discuss the source of the raw material (Laveuf and Cornu 2009). Although all five samples exhibited right leaning REE distribution patterns with an enrichment in light REE (ΣREE) which could also be supported by their $(La/Yb)_N$ ratios, sample MD69 displayed the different REE characteristics from others. The total rare earth elements content (ΣREE) of MD69 is 608 ppm which was significantly higher than those in other four samples (ΣREE ranging from 244 ppm to 334 ppm) probably resulting from the climate difference, weathering degree of parent rock and their ΣREE background value. In addition, MD69 had a distinct negative Ce anomaly ($\delta Ce = 0.54$), which could come from the weathering of biotite granites, staying in a redox environment, and/or the removal of Ce-rich heavy minerals (McGill 2000) during the elutriation process. By contrast there were positive Ce anomalies or almost no Ce anomalies in the other four ($\delta Ce = 0.84-1.52$). The REE characteristics of MD69 are similar to samples in Guangdong Dapu kiln while other four samples are similar to the Zhejiang Longquan kiln.

## CONCLUSION

The distinction of the trace elements, especially REE, indicates that the provenance of the five celadon were not all produced in the same kiln or from the same sources of clay. And, based on its composition, sample MD69 was probably produced in Guangdong. The study points to multiple sources of Longquan celadon consumed at Manda, with Zhejiang and Guangdong Dapu kilns serving as strong candidates.

Archaeologists and economic historians recognized and to a large extent attributed material traces to interregional interactions and globalization (Curtin 1984; Oka 2018; Kusimba 2017). Ongoing archaeological investigations at ancient city-states along the East African Coast show that preindustrial urbanism in East Africa arose, was sustained and evidentially declined following its relationship and connections to wider regional and interregional interaction spheres. These included the African hinterland and the wider Indian Ocean trading networks (e.g., Kusimba 1999; Kusimba et al 2013; Kusimba and Walz 2018; LaViolette 2008; LaViolette and Fleisher 2005; Wynne-Jones and LaViolette 2018).

Ancient trade between East Africa and Asia was a complex affair that involved many communities and took several routes. On the one hand, Africa's commodities in high demand in Ancient Asia included ivory, ambergris, gold, rhinoceros' horns, sandalwood (Freeman-Grenville 1962, 21; Horton 1996, 418). On the other hand, Africans were interested in ceramics and silk from China, beads and cloth from India. Consumption of African and Asia products was bidirectional and appears to have begun during the Tang period (618–907) and continued to the contemporary times. Archaeological evidence from early Swahili settlements including Manda, which dates to the fifth century, and Shanga in the eighth century, show that trade between Africa and China is traced to the beginnings of these settlements. From the Tang (616–907) through the Yuan Dynasties (1271–1368), it would appear that the volume of trade between East Africa and China was slightly lower compared to that from Southwest Asia and South Asia (Junker 1990; Miksic 2013). Distance factors into the equation. However, trade between the two regions was for the most part conducted indirectly (Zhao and Qin 2018). There were two principle routes of trade: first, the overland caravan through central Asia and southwest Asia via the Persian Gulf and India Ocean, and second, the direct maritime route through the South China Sea and Indian Ocean via Sri Lanka along the West Indian Seaboard to East Africa via Aden (Pearson 2003, Seland 2014). Mark Horton (1996, 418) has suggested that:

> During the eighth and ninth centuries, contact with China was through the Gulf ports, specifically, Siraf. One of the reasons why the Gulf merchants were interested in high-value commodities from East Africa may have been because of their potential in China, where they could be used to obtain manufactured goods such as silk and ceramics.

The arrival of significant quantities of whitewares made in Fujian, mainly Ding, qingbai, and molded whitewares, the use of Chinese and Indian coins, the close similarity of Chinese greenwares recovered at ports, such as Homs, Syria; Chaul, India; Shanga, Manda, and Mtwapa, Kenya; and Kilwa in Tanzania (Horton 1996, 418; Whitehouse 1976, 146), points to the major advances that China had made in technology and which, though indirect linked the two regions global commercial networks.

Scholars have argued that the so-called "Ming Gap" (ca. fourteenth–sixteenth centuries), was a period of intensive state regulation: foreign goods into and out of Chinese ports were limited and heavily taxed. In Southeast Asia, archaeologists have documented sharp decline in the proportion of Chinese ceramics found in shipwrecks and terrestrial sites from that period (Junker 1990). In contrast to East Africa, such documentation is still in infancy. To what extent did overregulation of seaward trade affect commerce between China and the rest of the world? What role did smuggling, black marketeering, and corruption play in redirecting trade between China and the rest of the world? Moving forward, one of the goals of future research should be to explore possible avenues through which trade may have continued, especially overland trade between China and West Asia. Through systematic analysis ceramics and other finds, the sourcing of these artifacts and determination of their life histories should be possible. Only then can we begin to confidently address more salient questions regarding the organization of trade, the role of state and private corporations' in enabling these exchanges.

To be sure, the presence of imperial ceramics would suggest that diplomatic relationships between China and the rest of the world continued despite the official policy to the contrary. Second, methodologically employing advanced and science methodologies such as laser ablation-inductively coupled plasma-mass spectrometry (LA-ICP-MS), X-ray fluorescence (XRF), and scanning electron microscopy-energy dispersive spectroscopy (SEM-EDS) employed in this study will contribute new ways of understanding China's relationships with world regions and the interconnectedness of Africans and Asians in history. Trade is an important human institution: it promotes friendship, knowledge-transfer, fosters interdependence, and tolerance, but it is also of the source of global inequality and conflict. This study provides a unique context in which to study trade and the economic, political, and social relationships that made it succeed for nearly two millennia. Lessons derived from archaeology will inform contemporary practices, ensuring their success of failure.

## REFERENCES

Bureau of Light Industry in Zhejiang Province. 1989. *Study on the Longquan Ware*: Beijing: Press of cultural Relics.

Chirikure, Shadreck. 2014. "Land and Sea Links: 1500 Years of Connectivity Between Southern Africa and the Indian Ocean Rim Regions, AD 700 to 1700." *African Archaeological Review* 31, 705–724.

Curtin, P.D. 1984. *Cross-cultural Trade in World History*. Cambridge, UK: Cambridge University Press.

Ding, X., Y. H. Hu, H. Zhang, C. Y. Li, M. X. Ling, and W. D. Sun. 2013. "Major Nb/Ta Fractionation Recorded in Garnet Amphibolite Facies Metagabbro." *Journal of Geology* 121(3):255–274.

Fang, Y. S., J. M. Fang, and C. R. Liu. 1990. *Mineral material of Chinese Ceramic*. Nanjing: Press of Nanjing University.

Feng, X. M. 2001. *Chinese Ceramics*. Shanghai: Shanghai Chinese Classic Publishing House.

Freeman-Grenville, G.S.P. 1962. *The Medieval History of Coast of Tanganyika*. London: Oxford University Press.

Horton, M. 1996. *Shanga: The Archaeology of a Muslim Trading Community on the Coast of East Africa*. Memoirs of the British Institute in Eastern Africa; no. 14. London: The British Institute in Eastern Africa.

Kusimba, C. M. 199. *The Rise and Fall of Swahili states*. Walnut Creek: AltaMira Press.

Kusimba, C. M., S. R. Williams, J. Monge, M. Mchula, R. Oka, G. Oteyo, S. Kusimba, and L. Dussubieux. 2018. "Mtwapa, Betwixt in Between Land and Sea: Foundings of an African City State." In Stephanie Wynne-Jones and Adria LaViolette (eds.), *The Swahili World*, pp 226–230. London: Routledge.

Kusimba, C.M., S. B. Kusimba, and Dussubieux, L.2013. "Beyond the Coastalscapes: Preindustrial Social and Political Networks in East Africa." *African Archaeological Review* 30(4):399–426.

Kusimba, Chapurukha M. 2017. "The Swahili and Globalization in the Indian Ocean." In Tamar Hodos (ed.), *The Routledge Handbook of Archaeology and Globalization*, pp. 104–122. London: Routledge Handbooks.

Kusimba, Chapurukha M., and J. Walz. 2018. "When Did the Swahili Become Maritime?: A Reply to Fleisher et al. (2015), and to the Resurgence of Maritime Myopia in the Archaeology of the Swahili Coast." *American Anthropologist* 120(3):429–443.

Laveuf, C., and S. Cornu. 2009. "A Review on the Potentiality of Rare Earth Elements to Trace Pedogenetic Processes." *Geoderma* 154 (1–2):1–12.

LaViolette, A. 2008. "Swahili Cosmopolitanism in Africa and the Indian Ocean World, AD 600–1500." *Archaeologies*, 4(1):24–49.

LaViolette, Adria, and Jeffrey Fleisher. 2005. "The Swahili." In Anne B. Stahl (ed.), *African Archaeology*, pp. 392–419. Oxford: Blackwell Publishers.

Li, H., M.X. Ling, C.Y. Li, H., Zhang, X. Ding, X.Y. Yang, W.M. Fan, Y.L. Li, and W.D. Sun. 2012. "A-Type Granite Belts of Two Chemical Subgroups in Central Eastern China: Indication of Ridge Subduction." *Lithos* 150:26–36.

Li, J. Z. 1998. *A History of Science and Technology in China: Ceramics*. Beijing: Science Press.

Liu, Y. S., S. Gao, Z. C. Hu, C. G. Gao, K. Q. Zong, and D. B. Wang, 2010. "Continental and Oceanic Crust Recycling-Induced Melt–Peridotite Interactions in the Trans-North China Orogen: U–Pb Dating, Hf Isotopes and Trace Elements in Zircons from Mantle Xenoliths." *Journal of Petrology* 51(1–2):537–571.

Liu, Y. S., Z. C. Hu, S. Gao, D. Günther, J. Xu, C. G. Gao, and H. H. Chen. 2008. "In Situ Analysis of Major and Trace Elements of Anhydrous Minerals by LA-ICP-MS Without Applying an Internal Standard." *Chemical Geology* 257 (1–2):34–43.

McGill, I. 2000. "Rare Earth Elements." In H. Siegel and M. Eggersdorfer (eds.), *Ullmann's Encyclopedia of Industrial Chemistry*, pp. 41–57. Weinheim: Wiley-VCH Verlag GmbH and Co.

Millward, J.A. 2012. *The Silk Road: A Very Short Introduction*. Oxford: Oxford University Press.

Oka, R. 2008. *Resilience and Adaptation of Trade Networks in East African and South Asian Port Polities, 1500–1800 CE*. Ph.D. Thesis. University of Illinois at Chicago.

Oka, R. 2018. "Trade, Traders, and Trading Systems: Macromodeling of Trade, Commerce and Civilization in the Indian Ocean." In K. Kristiansen, T. Lindkvist, and J. Myrdal (eds.), *Trade and Civilization*, pp. 279–319. Cambridge: Cambridge University Press.

Oka, R., L. Dussubieux, C.M. Kusimba, and V.D. Gogte. 2009. "The Impact of Imitation Ceramic Industries and Internal Political Restrictions on Chinese Commercial Ceramic Exports in the Indian Ocean Maritime Exchange, ca. 1200–1700." In *Scientific Research on Historic Asian Ceramics: Proceedings of the Fourth Forbes Symposium at the Freer Gallery of Art*, pp. 175–185. London: Archetype Publications Ltd.

Pikirayi, I. 2001. *The Zimbabwe Culture: Origins and Decline of Southern Zambezian States*. Walnut Creek: AltaMira Press.

Qin, D.-S. 2015. "Preliminary Analysis on Chinese Ceramics Excavated From Kenya." In D.S. Qin and J. Yuan (eds.), *Ancient Silk Trade Routes: Selected Works From Symposium on Cross Cultural Exchanges and Their Legacies in Asia*, pp. 61–82. Singapore: World Scientific Publishing Company.

Sun, S. S., and W. F. McDonough. 1989. "Chemical and Isotopic Systematics of Oceanic Basalts: Implications for Mantle Composition and Processes." *Geological Society, London, Special Publications* 42(1):313–345.

Wang, M., T. Zhu, X. Ding, Z. Hui, F. Wu, C. Liu, and W. Sun. 2018. "Composition Comparison of Zhejiang Longquan Celadon and its Imitation in Dapu kiln of Guangdong in the Ming Dynasty of China (1368–1644CE) by LA-ICP-MS." *Ceramics International* 44(2):1785–1796.

Wang, Y. X., Z. H. Zhao, Z. W. Bao, and X. H. Li. 1997. "Geochemistry of Granitoids from Zhejiang Province and Crustal Evolution—I. Phanerozoic Granitoids." *Geochimica* 26(5):1–15.

Wang, Y. X., Z. H. Zhao, Z. W. Bao, and X. H. Li. 1997b. "Geochemistry of Granitoids from Zhejiang Province and Crustal evolution—II. Proterozoic Granitoids, *Geochimica* 26 (6):57–68.

Wynne-Jones, S., and A. LaViolette. 2018. *The Swahili World*. London: Routledge.

Zhao, B., and D. Qin. 2018. "Links with China." In S. Wynne-Jones and A. LaViolette (eds.), *The Swahili World*, pp. 430–444. London: Routledge.

Zhao, B. 2012. "Global Trade and Swahili Cosmopolitan Material Culture: Chinese-Style Ceramic Shards from Sanje ya Kati and Songo Mnara (Kilwa, Tanzania)." *Journal of World History* 23(1):41–85.

Zhu, T. Q., H. Huang, H. M. Wang, L. M. Hu, and X. B. Yi. 2011. "Comparison of Celadon from the Yaozhou and Xicun kilns in the Northern Song Dynasty of China by X-ray fluorescence and microscopy." *Journal of Archaeological Science* 38(11):3134–3140.

*Chapter 10*

# The Consumption of Glass Beads in Ancient Swahili East Africa

Gilbert Oteyo and Chapurukha M. Kusimba

Earlier work by Chittick (1984) at Manda recovered over 1,000 beads, most of them made of glass. The glass beads were concentrated (83.2% of them) in the Period II layer ( mid-eleventh to late thirteenth CE) with 13.0 percent of the beads in earlier contexts and 3.8 percent in later ones. Most of the beads were drawn (74.1%) and the others were mostly wound (23.4%) and more rarely, molded (2.3%). Typologically, the collection of glass beads of Manda was fairly similar to that of other sites along the East African coast such as Kilwa, Mafia, Songo Mnara, Songo Mnara, and Sanje ya Kati (Morrison 1984). African glass beads research was in its infancy when the data from Manda were published. Davison (1972) work was the only one providing compositional data obtained with sophisticated analytical techniques (X-ray fluorescence spectrometry and instrumental neutron activation analysis). However, her approach provided incomplete dataset with some crucial elements for glass classification (Mg, K or Ca) missing. More than twenty years passed before another impulse was able to create significant progress on this topic. Indeed, only recently have we begun to see chemical analysis used in a more systematic and meaningful way since the advent of laser ablation—inductively coupled plasma—mass spectrometry (LA-ICP-MS) that has the advantage to be almost nondestructive, fairly fast, and capable of generating compositions, including a wide range of major, minor, and trace elements (Saitowitz 1996; Saitowitz et al. 1996; Robertshaw et al. 2003). The combination of elemental composition obtained with LA-ICP-MS has greatly improved glass bead research in sub-Saharan Africa from creating a chronology of glass beads circulation in the southern part of Africa (Robertshaw et al. 2010) to discovering an original ancient glass production in Western Africa (Babalola et al. 2018). In this context and the framework of a very active Swahili archaeological research, the study of new glass beads excavated at Manda fits perfectly into the current effort to understand glass bead circulation in connection with the socio-cultural changes that occurred on the eastern coast of Africa starting at the end of the first millennium CE and during the second millennium CE.

## THE ARCHAEOLOGICAL SITE OF MANDA

The ancient town of Manda was one of more than a dozen settlements that emerged in the Lamu archipelago during the period ca. 700 and 1500 CE (Horton 1996; Kusimba et al. 2018; see figure 2.1). Manda, located on the island that bears the same name, rose to prominence between the seventh and mid-fifteenth centuries when it precipitously declined. Despite repeated attempts to revive its shattered economy, it remained a minor player in relation to its more powerful neighbors, Takwa, Lamu, and Pate. Today, the island is home to a small hamlet of Internally Displaced Persons who settled the island in the early 1970s and two exclusive resorts, Manda Bay and Manda Toto (Mzee Ali 2012). The remains of a once powerful stone town are scattered over an area about eight hectares in size. Neville Chittick estimates the town at its greatest extent to have ranged between fifteen and twenty-five hectares (Chittick 1984; Horton 1996). Neville Chittick who carried out extensive multiyear excavations at the site in the 1970s and 1980s believed that Manda provided an excellent case study for the Asiatic migration and foundation of modern Swahili civilization. His memoir published posthumously remains the major work on the site (Chittick 1984). Although carefully illustrated, Neville Chittick's conclusions were immediately found to be incorrect (Horton 1986).

Manda consists of three distinct areas: (1) a northern urban zone of stone-built walls, homes, tombs, and a mosque; (2) a southern stone-built urban zone bordered by a town wall; and (3) an open space devoid of stone architecture immediately to the east. Excavated material indicates that Manda's settlement began in the seventh century CE and steadily rose to prominence due to its residents' participation in commerce, as a result of Manda's development as a local hub for local African products that were highly desirable in Persia, Arabia, and India (Kusimba et al. 2018). Although Manda does not exhibit uniqueness in comparison to other sites in the Lamu Archipelago cluster, its excellent location, including shelter from direct sea, its proximity to the mainland—separated by a shallow wadable channel—permitted and indeed enabled regular intercourse between Manda's residents and their neighbors, while simultaneously protecting it from surprise or unsolicited intrusion and even attacks. Manda's still standing architecture betrays a comparatively earlier experimentation and adoption of stone architecture that is now characteristic of elite house forms of the Swahili world (Ghaidan 1976). Manda first exhibits stone architecture after the mid-tenth century CE, has been linked to the shift in its primary external contact to the Red Sea at this time (Horton and Middleton 2000). Although there is no evidence of Islamic worship at Manda in this early period, the site of Shanga on Pate Island 10 km to the north exhibits a sequence of timber mosques found below the remains of a series of stone-built mosques (Horton 1996). The precise chronology of the only standing mosque at Manda has not been determined, but the style places it to the eleventh century. Future excavations of the mosque may not be feasible because the issue of conversion and adoption of Islam by East African coastal and interior residents—Swahili, Somali, and Oromo, among others has already been determine by excellent work within the cluster and on the mainland. Thus, our assumption here is that Manda's adoption of Islam mirrors that of Shanga (Horton 1986).

Our renewed work at Manda has the central aim to reevaluate Manda's biological and cultural heritage and place Manda within a regional and interregional context as a node from which we can discern the process of integration of Eastern Africa into the Afrasian commercial network and the general impacts and influences that derived from this interaction (Pearson 1998, 2003). Geophysical explorations combined with full-coverage survey and mapping by total station have been completed. Seven out of nine trenches earmarked for excavation have been completed. Two middens context trenches (Trenches 1 and 7) directed at understanding site chronology, one each in the northern and southern urban zones of the site have been excavated. In addition, seven religious/burial context trenches (Trenches 2–5 and 8–10), one of which may be a domestic context with a burial (Trench 3), directed at assessing the biological profile of Manda's residents were also excavated; two in the northern zone, four in the southern zone, and one outside the town wall in Manda's eastern sector.

## THE BEADS IN ARCHAEOLOGY

Throughout the Late Stone Age and, more intensively, in the Iron Age, objects of personal body adornment in the form of beads constitute one of the most common materials in the African archaeological record. Virtually all archaeological sites excavated have yielded beads on one form or another, from stone, molluscan, and avian shell, and glass. It would appear that the bead making, and consumption was one of the major craft activities since their demand across regional, ethnic, age, sex, and gender boundaries was high. To walk about without beads would have rendered the offending individual's identity hard to fathom. Beads were significant markers of identity, age, class, marital status, and were in many ways used both as currency and personhood (Dussubieux et al. 2008). Trade in beads across different regions was high. Investment in this cottage industry was very likely highly desirable creating opportunities for specialization and competition among the makers. Indeed, glass beads made in South Asia reached the shores of Eastern Africa; they found an already long-established tradition of bead making and use and with ease, interlocked on this thriving market. Across Africa, archaeological settlement over 1,000 years old have yielded a combination of local and imported beads.

The East African coastal settlements were no exception to this widespread phenomenon. Here archaeologists have recovered large volumes of beads (see Wood 2018). All glass beads recovered from the coast are assumed to have been imported from different regions outside Eastern Africa. But the diversity of local beads recovered at these sites shows the existence of many active bead production centers which were located both at coastal settlement and inland.

## THE EVIDENCE FOR BEAD PRODUCTION AND CONSUMPTION AT MANDA

The beads recovered from Manda were dominated by two types, locally manufactured and imported beads. Locally manufacture beads made up more than 98 percent of the entire bead collection. Large quantities of locally produced beads made using local sandstone and marine shells were recovered. Evidence for bead production comes from the large quantities of bead grinders that have been recovered during both seasons 2012 and 2017 of our excavations. Besides bead grinders and actual beads as evidence of production, this industry is further confirmed by the multiple finds of unfinished bead products, remains of chipped pieces of shell and calcite stones and pebbles, and whole cores of such material that was mines and transported to the site as raw material. Local beads ranged in color from white, brown, purple among others.

Large volumes of small drawn glass beads were recovered from float samples. Every flat bag of 2017 excavations would have almost the same ration of 1:9 of the glass beads versus shell/stone beads of similar sizes. Although imported beads were on an array of colors.

Under what conditions were these beads made, who made them and who consumed them? Were they made for the local and regional market? Explore these questions further.

## BEAD MAKING AND CONSUMPTION AT MANDA

### The Raw Material

Local beads were primarily made from marine shells, mainly bivalves and stone. There was also evidence for *Achatina achatina*, fresh water land snail shell beads recovered at Manda and other coastal sites. Stone beads were primarily made from calcite material and other stones that ranged in color from white, brown, light brown, purple, and so forth. The evidence for bead manufacture is contained in the beads themselves, chipped and unfinished beads, and the grooved and polished coral slabs that could have been either hand-held or placed in a surface for polishing the beads, hence the name bead grinders. Animal bones and fish bones were also worked into beads.

### The Working Process

Shell and calcite beads were mostly flat and smooth trimmed circular generally averaging 2 mm in diameter and less than 1 mm in thickness. They were almost similar in size to the imported glass beads. The shell and stone beads were made with holes bored at the center very likely with hot pointed object or drill. It there not surprising that the amount of loss due to drilling, chipping, or grinding was relatively high. This also partly supports the hypothesis that bead production was carried out at a household level, from start to finish, with every member of the family participating in production, including drilling.

### The Volume and Scale

Spatial and temporal data from 2017 excavations show that bead working at Manda was an intensive household craft. Reference here is made to finds recovered in the floatation samples. We are convinced that the volume of beads made at Manda huge. Since on average few carried out flotation on about two out of fifteen buckets and recovered approximately two beads per bucket, we estimate that the number of beads recovered would run in thousands of beads if 100 percent and recovery process is carried out.

### The Trend over Time

All excavation levels at Manda produced beads pointing to this industry as a continuous craft. There were hardly any fluctuations in either stone/shell bead production or glass bead importation throughout Manda's existence. But ongoing laboratory analysis of the collections from the 2012–2017 and

2017 seasons partially reported in this chapter highlights the intensity of production. Future work will explore the relationship through time between local and nonlocal beads. How and in what ways did fluctuations in any one material affect production of another?

In sum, the local bead industry at Manda continued throughout the history of the settlement. As such, beads have been recovered in every level of the 2017 excavations that were very highly controlled, and everything recovered in situ. Beads were recovered in every area in different units, whether in the courtyard or inside the house. The large number of beads shows how beads as personal body adornment was highly desirable among a part of the communities' identity. The presence of beads and bead-making tools in all areas of the sites coupled by the absence of clear bead making areas suggests that this was a cottage industry. People worked in their homes. Some activities could be working inside the homes and others outside in the courtyards, as suggested in Units 11 and 12 in the 2017 excavations.

## GLASS BEADS CONSUMPTION

From the more recent excavations at Manda 227, glass beads were catalogued. The proportion of drawn (73%) and wound (26%) beads are extremely close to what was excavated by Chittick. The 1 percent remaining includes beads manufactured with another technique and beads with unidentified manufacturing technique. A little more than one-third or eighty-four beads were analyzed for elemental composition. The list of the analyzed samples is provided in Table 10.1.

## ANALYTICAL RESEARCH

The elemental compositions of the beads from Manda were determined at the Field Museum of Natural History in Chicago, USA, with a Varian Inductively Coupled Plasma-Mass Spectrometer (ICP-MS) connected to a New Wave UP213 laser for direct introduction of solid samples. This analytical method

Table 10.1  Kenyan Sites with v-Na-Al Glass Beads

| Site | Period |
|---|---|
| Gede | 13-17th |
| Jumba Ruins | 14-15th |
| Manda | 13-16th |
| Mnarani | 14-beg. 15th |
| Mbaraki | 14th |

combining the low limits of detection of ICP-MS with the microsampling capability of laser ablation and is now widely used for the study of ancient glass (e.g., De Juan Ares and Schibille 2017; Wood et al. 2017).

The diameter of the laser beam is 100 µm. A preablation time of 20 s is set in order to eliminate possible surface contamination or light corrosion before carrying out the measurement of the glass compositions. For each glass sample, the average of four measurements corrected from the blank is considered for the calculation of concentrations. To improve reproducibility of measurements, the use of an internal standard is required to correct possible instrumental drifts or changes in the ablation efficiency. The isotope Si29 was used for internal standardization. Concentrations for major elements, including silica, are calculated assuming that the sum of their concentrations in weight percent in glass is equal to 100 percent (Gratuze 1999).

Full quantitative analyses are possible by using external standards. To prevent matrix effects, the composition of standards has to be as close as possible to that of the samples. Two different series of standards are used to measure major, minor, and trace elements. The first series of external standards are standard reference materials (SRM) manufactured by NIST: SRM 610 and SRM 612. Both of these standards are soda-lime-silica glass doped with trace elements in the range of 500 ppm (SRM 610) and 50 ppm (SRM 612). Certified values are available for a very limited number of elements. Concentrations from Pearce et al. (1997) were used for the other elements. The second series of standards were manufactured by Corning. Glass B and D are glasses that match compositions of ancient glass (Brill 1999, vol. 2, 544). More in details are available in Dussubieux et al. (2009).

## ANALYTICAL RESULTS

A total of eighty-four beads were analyzed resulting into eighty-seven compositions as the different colors of polychrome beads were measured separately (table 10.2). Four different glass types were identified: (1) fifty-five glass samples have a mineral soda composition with relatively high alumina concentrations; (2) twelve glass samples were obtained from soda plant ash and a low alumina sand; (3) eleven glass samples were also manufactured from soda plant ash but exhibit higher alumina concentrations and (4) five glass samples have high lead concentrations.

### The m-Na-Al glass beads

More than half of the beads from Manda (55) belong to the mineral—soda—high alumina (m-Na-Al) glass group. The m-Na-Al glass was manufactured

Table 10.2 Other Sites on the Eastern Coast of Africa and around with M-Na-Al 2 and M-Na-Al 6 Glass Beads

| | m-Na-Al 2 | m-Na-Al 6 | Chronology (c. AD) |
|---|---|---|---|
| Mtwapa | x | | 10th–18th |
| Bungule | x | | 17th–19th |
| Muasya | x | | 16th–19th |
| Ungwana | x | x | 9th–16th |
| Takwa | x | | 16th–17th |
| Gede | x | x | 13th–17th |
| Fort Jesus | x | | 16th and onward |
| Songo Mnara | x | | Late 14th–early 16th |
| Juani Primary School, Mafia Is | | x | Post 1000 |
| Antsiraka Boira | | x | 12th–13th |

in India and its composition can be explained by the selection of rather immature sands, with compositions very close to that of the granite from which it derives, containing relatively high proportion of feldspar. These sands also contain high concentrations of a range of trace elements, including titanium, zirconium, the rare earth elements, uranium, and so forth. High concentrations of sodium in a glass is generally due to the addition of soda, found either in mineral form or produced from halophytic plants (growing in salt-rich soils) that are reduced to ashes. Ethnographic data as well as scientific experiments (Kock and Sode 1995; Brill 2003; Gill 2017) indicate that in several parts of India, glass makers were using a sand naturally mixed to sodic efflorescence called reh containing large amounts of sodium salts (carbonate, bicarbonate, and sulfate) and varying proportion of calcium and magnesium salts. It occurs in areas where river-draining mountains contain dissolved salts that percolate through the subsoil until saturation. Rains dissolve these salts, which travel upward through the soil during the dry season by capillary action and form white efflorescence on the surface (Wadia 1975, 489, 501, 502). They are present in arid or semiarid regions.

In Dussubieux et al., (2010), five m-Na-Al glass groups are described. One of them (m-Na-Al 5) is not relevant to this study as it was quite likely manufactured in modern Turkey (see Schibille 2011). More recently another type of m-Na-Al glass was identified on the East Coast of Africa: m-Na-Al 6. Previously, a strong correspondence between the m-Na-Al 2 composition of some glass samples from Chaul in India and from Mtwapa was identified showing that some glass beads found on the eastern coast of Africa were quite likely imported from the Western coast of India, possibly through the port of Chaul (Dussubieux et al. 2008). Further analysis of glass beads coming from different sites located on the eastern coast of Africa identified a new type of m-Na-Al glass. This glass type was named m-Na-Al 6. This glass seems to arrive earlier in this region as it corresponds to contexts dating from the ninth to thirteenth century CE, whereas the m-Na-Al 2 glass type is associated with beads dating from the late fourteenth century and onward. Including the concentrations of MgO, CaO, Sr, Zr, Cs, Ba, and U (Dussubieux et al. 2010) of samples belonging to the m-Na-Al 1, 2, 3, 4, 5 glass groups and the m-Na-Al glass from Manda, principal component analysis (PCA) was carried out using the Gauss 8.0 routine. The majority of the m-Na-Al samples from Manda (52) fits with the m-Na-Al 6 glass group. Only thirteen samples fall in the same area than the m-Na-Al 2 samples (Dussubieux et al. 2008), m-Na-Al 3 (Dussubieux and Kanungo 2013), m-Na-Al 4 (Dussubieux 2009), and m-Na-Al 6 (unpublished) and Manda.

Two samples taken from the same bead have a composition similar to that of the m-Na-Al 1 glass. This bead (BMA033) is a polychrome bead with a black background, and white stripes obtained using the drawing technique (M-Na-Al 1) glass beads are fairly rare on the eastern coast of Africa. One bead with such a composition was found at Ungwana (ninth to nineteenth century CE). The m-Na-Al 1 glass and glass beads were quite likely manufactured in Sri Lanka at the site of Giribawa (third century BCE to second century CE), located in the northwestern part of Sri Lanka (Gratuze et al. 2000; Dussubieux 2001; Bopearachchi 1999, 2002). In South India, the presence of the same type of glass is also attested, suggesting that it might have been manufactured in South India. At this point, no primary glass manufacturing center has been fully excavated in South India, but preliminary evidence for glass bead making is available (see Abraham 2016).

Glass samples in the m-Na-Al 2 groups are all drawn except for three beads that are wound. One drawn bead is polychrome with a greenish translucent background and white and yellow stripes. In this group, five beads are opaque red. They contain copper (0.2–0.3%) and sometimes relatively high concentration of iron (1.5–4.1% compared to 0.8 to 1.8% in the other colored glass samples of this group). Three yellow samples contain significant concentrations of tin (0.3–2.0%) and lead (2.2 to 12.0%). Small concentrations of these two elements were detected in the two green beads (0.2% of $SnO_2$ in both beads; 0.5 and 0.8% of PbO). Copper was also measured in these two beads with concentrations of 0.6 and 0.7 percent. A turquoise bead contains 0.8 percent of CuO. Two dark beads have no specifically high element to explain their color (e.g., iron, cobalt, manganese).

One-third of the beads in the m-Na-Al 6 glass group are wound, and the other beads are drawn. More than half of the beads are turquoise blue (36%) or opaque yellow (30%). The turquoise blue color is due to the presence of copper (0.4–0.8%). Yellow beads contain variable but correlated concentration of tin (0.3–4.4% of $SnO_2$) and lead (1.4–44% of PbO). Green glass beads also contained significant proportion of tin (0.3–1.0%) and lead (2.3–6.4%)

and also copper (0.5–0.7%). Seven beads have a dark color. They do not contain significant quantities of cobalt or manganese but some of them have higher iron concentrations than the other beads (BMA901 has 3.5% of $Fe_2O_3$). Two beads are opaque red: they contain 0.2–0.4% of copper (and not significantly high iron concentrations). Two glass beads amber, one differs from all the other beads by its high iron concentration (6.5%), the other one has 1.8 percent of iron.

The larger proportion of m-Na-Al 6 glass type at Manda compared to the m-Na-Al 2 one seems to indicate more active exchange with South Asia through the Indian Ocean trade network at early dates when the m-Na-Al 6 glass was predominant (ninth to thirteenth century AD). Later (fourteenth century AD and onward), the ties with the South Asia still existed, but the exchange was less intense.

## The v-Na-Al

Eleven beads are made from vegetable-soda alumina or v-Na-Al glass. This type of glass contains potash and magnesia concentrations higher than 1.5 percent suggesting the use of plant ash as a soda source. Alumina concentrations are higher than 4 percent, but the silica source is different from that of the m-Na-Al glasses as much lower trace elements are associated with these high alumina concentrations.

The provenance of that kind of glass is very uncertain. Soda plant ash glass with high alumina are fairly common in regions including Afghanistan (Brill 1999), Uzbekistan (Abdurazakov 2009; Rehren et al. 2010), and Pakistan (Dussubieux and Gratuze 2003a) for a wide period ranging from the second century BC to the fourteenth century AD. If the glass from Pakistan that is much earlier than the glass from Manda, which also has very different trace element patterns with fairly high trace elements such as uranium, can be excluded, comparison with the other regions is more difficult due to the fact that compositions that are available do not include trace elements.

This type of glass was described by Robertshaw et al. (2010) for glass beads found in Southern Africa and two subgroups were identified. These two subtypes correspond to the Mapungubwe oblate (MO) and the Zimbabwe (Z) bead series. The MO v-Na-Al glass has lower zirconium concentrations compared to the Z v-Na-Al glass type. The Manda v-Na-Al glass seems to belong to the MO v-Na-Al sub-type.

Forty-five percent of the v-Na-Al glass is shaped using the wound technique and 55 percent of them are drawn. One bead is dark blue and contain ~500 ppm of cobalt along with roughly the same concentration of arsenic that could suggest that the cobalt was extracted from erythrite or cobaltite. Six beads are green, only one of them being translucent, all the other being opaque. Opaque green beads contain tin (0.6–1.6% of $SnO_2$), lead (0.4–7.0% of PbO), and copper (0.9–1.4% of CuO). The translucent green bead contains 1.06 percent of copper. Two red beads are part of the v-Na-Al group, and they were colored using different elements: one bead contains 1.2 percent of copper and no other element in significant quantities. The other red beads contain not only fairly similar concentrations of copper (1.4) but also high concentrations of iron (4.3%) and lead (3.2%).

Robertshaw et al. (2006) identified v-Na-Al glass beads (Zimbabwe series) at the sites of Mahilaka (thirteenth to fifteenth century AD) and Sandrakatsy (thirteenth to sixteenth century CE) on the Island of Madagascar.

Unpublished data from glass beads from Kenya indicate that v-Na-Al glass beads are systematically present at sites occupied during the fourteenth to fifteenth century CE period. These v-Na-Al Kenyan beads belong to the MO v-Na-Al glass groups. Beads made from v-Na-Al glass in Eastern Africa are mostly drawn (~72%) and then wound (~26%). In Robertshaw et al. (2010), the v-Na-Al glass associated with the Mapungubwe Oblate bead series is dated from 1240 to 1300 CE. It seems that in Kenya, that type of glass is abundant during the fourteenth to fifteenth century period.

## The v-Na-Ca

Twelve glass beads have a soda-rich composition with potash and magnesia concentrations relatively low (<1.5%) and also low alumina concentrations (< 4%). This type of glass (also called v-Na-Ca glass) is well known and results from the mix of rather pure sand with soda-rich plant ashes. The earliest glass, found in Mesopotamia, was manufactured using soda plant ash as a flux. Starting around the 8th century BCE, soda from mineral deposits (e.g., natron) replaced soda plant ash. Particularly during the fourth to eighth centuries CE, mineral soda glass was produced in Egypt and the Syro-Palestinian region, then distributed widely throughout the Mediterranean basin. Toward the end of the first millennium CE, the use of natron declined (Shortland et al. 2006) and a return to plant ash occurred. However, the soda plant ash glass tradition may have continued in Mesopotamia, and Sasanian glassmakers produced such a glass from the third to the seventh century CE (Mirti et al. 2008; 2009). If the Arab invasion of the seventh century CE caused the fall of the Sasanian Empire, the expansion of the Muslim world may have served as a vector of diffusion for the soda plant ash glass that became the dominant glass type again after the eighth century CE through the Middle-East and the Mediterranean region (Gratuze and Barrandon 1990; Henderson et al. 2004).

In sub-Saharan Africa, several subgroups were identified for that type of glass suggesting distinct producing centers sharing a same recipe but using raw materials with slightly different trace element signatures. This could indicate glass procurement from different glass-making workshops operating in different areas and/or at different periods. In Southern Africa and more especially at the site of Chibuene, Mozambique, three main v-Na-Ca (previously called v-Na) glass types were identified. First, V-Na-Ca 1: it is the most abundant v-Na-Ca glass type and was found similar in composition to Middle-Eastern glass such as the one found at the site of Nishapur. At Chibuene, it was associated with the eighth to tenth century CE period. Second, V-Na-Ca 2: this glass type has significantly high amount of chromium correlated with the presence of nickel. It was found in samples in the forms of glass sherds or wastes. At Chibuene, it was associated with the eighth to tenth century CE period. Third, V-Na-Ca 3: this glass usually in the form of bluish or greenish drawn glass bead contains higher trace elements such as Rb, Ce, Cs, Ba, La and U. It was associated with Chibuene with the earliest context possibly ranging from the seventh to the ninth century CE.

PCA was conducted on the Manda v-Na-Ca glass samples taking into account the concentration of MgO, $P_2O_5$, CaO, Cr, Rb, and La that were found useful to separate soda plant ashes found at the site of Chibuene (Wood et al. 2012). The comparison of the compositions of the Chibuene v-Na-Ca glasses and of the Manda v-Na-Ca glass appears in Fig X. Most of the Manda samples fit within the v-Na 1 glass group, whereas two samples match the v-Na 3 glass. Two samples are found away from the Chibuene v-Na glasses.

Among the v-Na-Ca glass samples from Manda, six are drawn: the two v-Na 3 glass beads are drawn, and the others have a v-Na1 composition. If most of the drawn beads, regardless of their composition, were cut while the glass was cold, one the v-Na1 glass beads is segmented meaning that the glass tube was pinched while hot to then facilitate the separation of the beads by snapping the tube when solid. One the v-Na1 glass beads seem to have been shaped from powdered glass, the individual particles being still visible. A pendant is also part of the v-Na1 glass type: it is drop-shaped with the perforation located in the narrower part of it. Two wound beads are part of the v-Na-Ca beads, with one belonging to the v-Na 1 glass type and the other one to the unidentified one.

In the v-Na1 subgroup: two glass beads are corroded, and their colors are difficult to determine. Another corroded glass bead belongs to the outlier group. It contains significant concentration of tin (1.6% of $SnO_2$) and lead (10.7% of PbO). The other glass bead in the outlier group contains also significant concentrations of tin and lead, although in higher concentrations (3.8% for $SnO_2$ and 32.2% for PbO). Other beads (in the v-Na1 group) contain manganese (1.1–1.4%) and appear to be dark blue Two beads containing lead and tin also have significant concentrations of copper. The two v-Na3 beads have higher iron concentrations and low but significant amount of manganese (0.3%), copper (0.4–0.5%) in agreement with what was found in the Chibuene v-Na3 glass beads.

The v-Na-Ca glass seems to appear at the earliest periods, as early as the seventh century CE and before the tenth century CE based on the dating of the Chibuene glass.

In East Africa, beads with a v-Na-Ca composition are fairly rare. They were identified at the site of Tumbe on Pemba Island in Tanzania (eleven beads) and at Shanga in the Lamu Archipelago in Kenya (one beads) (Wood 2011). Ten v-Na-Ca 1 glass beads were found at Kwa Mgogo, Tanzania, 700–1250 CE (Walz and Dussubieux 2016).

## LEAD GLASS

Chinese glass beads dating to the period under discussion—that is roughly the middle of the second millennium CE—have not been widely studied, so compositional data for comparison are rather scarce. But fortunately, data from two sets of beads made of potash lead silicate glass with dates and compositions similar to those found on the East Coast are available. The first consists of beads from Singapore that date to the fourteenth century (Dussubieux 2010). They form part of 8,000 wound beads that were recovered at Fort Canning Hill (Borell 2010). They appeared in several different colors and translucencies including transparent red, dark blue, and turquoise blue as well as opaque yellow and white. The second set of wound beads is from the Philippines and was excavated by Karl Hutterer at Tanjay. They came from a burial that was dated to the late fifteenth to early sixteenth century based on associated porcelain ceramics (Laura Junker, personal communication). These beads are transparent red, opaque black, white, and green.

When the trace elements lithium and rubidium are plotted, trends begin to appear. The fourteenth century beads from Singapore have higher concentrations of lithium and lower and less variable levels of rubidium compared to the beads from the Philippines that date to the late fifteenth to early sixteenth century. Similar glass beads were found at Songo Mnara.

## DISCUSSION

This study is showing that glass beads arrived in Manda possibly as early as the seventh to eighth century from the Middle East. The earliest beads represent a very small proportion of the total number of beads (10%), but they testified of an early connection with the Indian Ocean network that was facilitating at that time exchange with the Middle East. Subsequently, beads from South Asia arrive to Manda. They could have arrived as early as the ninth century CE. Their abundance (51% of the analyzed beads) is indicating that the exchange was fairly intense. If the exchange with South Asia did not stop, a shift appears around the thirteenth to fourteenth century with the identification of m-Na-Al 2 glass beads. If the exact origin of the m-Na-Al 2 glass beads within South Asia is unknown, it seems that the m-Na-Al 2 glass beads were manufactured in the western part of Africa where they were found at the site of Chaul. Around the same period (fourteenth to fifteenth century CE), a more diverse procurement pattern emerges suggesting that the interaction through the Indian Ocean involved a more varied range of traders or traders that would procure goods from more diverse origins.

## CONCLUSION

Glass beads in particular were imported as already manufactured goods, but those beads of other materials were probably manufactured on the site as evidenced by the recovery of bead grinders. A range of these beads and identification notes put alongside the drafts. The collection of glass beads recovered here is wonderful and range from wound, drawn to cut glass beads of many colours and shapes. This motivates further archaeological glass beads in Africa, and particularly local beads have been the least studied materials. We therefore emphasize the further study of this collection plus those earlier excavated from this site and indeed all other sites of East African coast and interior.

## REFERENCES

Abdurazakov, A.A., 2009. Central Asian Glassmaking During the Ancient and Medieval Periods. In Fuxi, G., Brill, R., Shouyun, T. (eds.), *Ancient Glass Research Along the Silk Road*, pp. 201–219. Singapore: World Scientific.

Abraham, S.A., 2016. Glass Beads and Glass Production in Early South India: Contextualizing Indo-Pacific Bead Manufacture. *Archaeological Research in Asia* 6: 4–15.

Babalola, A.B., Dussubieux, L., Keech McIntosh, S., Rehren, Th., 2018. Chemical Analysis of Glass Beads from Igbo Olokun, Ile-Ife (SW Nigeria): New Light on Raw Materials, Production, and Interregional Interactions. *Journal of Archaeological Science* 90:92–105.

Bopearachchi, O., 1999. Sites Portuaires et Emporia de l'ancien Sri Lanka, Nouvelles Données Archéologiques, *Arts Asiatiques* 54: 5–23.

Bopearachchi, O., 2002. Les Relations Commerciales et Culturelles Entre Sri Lanka et Inde de sud: Nouvelles Données Archéologiques et Épigraphiques. *Cahier du Cercle d'études et de Recherches Sri Lankaises* 4: 1–16.

Borell, B., 2010. Glass from China and from India: Finds of Vessel Glass from Fourteenth Century Singapore. *Archipel* 80: 139–196.

Brill, R.H., 2003. The Glassmakers of Firozabad and the Glassmakers of Kapadwanj: Two Pilot Video Projects, Annales du 15e Congrès de l'Association Internationale pour l'Histoire du Verre, pp. 267–268. New York: Corning.

Brill, R.H., 1999. *Chemical Analyses of Early Glasses*. New York: The Corning Museum of Glass, 2 vol.

Chittick, N., 1984. *Manda, Excavations at an Island Port on the Kenyan Coast*. Nairobi: The British Institute in Eastern Africa.

Davison, C.C., 1972. Glass Beads in African Archaeology: Results of Neutron Activation Analysis, Supplemented by Results of X-ray Fluorescence Analysis. PhD Dissertation, University of California, Berkeley.

de Juan Ares, J., Schibille, N., 2017. Glass Import and Production in Hispania During the Early Medieval Period: The Glass from Ciudad de Vascos (Toledo). *PLoS ONE* doi.org/10.1371/journal.pone.0182129

Dussubieux, L., 2001. *L'Apport de l'ablation laser couplée à l'ICP-MS à l'étude du verre archéologique de l'Océan Indien*. PhD Thesis, Université d'Orléans, France.

Dussubieux, L., 2009. Compositional Analysis of Ancient Glass Fragments from North Sumatra, Indonesia. In Perret, Daniel, Surachman, Heddy (eds.), *Histoire de Barus III: Regards sur une place Marchande de l'océan Indien (XIIe-milieu du XVIIe s.)*, pp. 385–417. Paris: Association Archipel/EFEO.

Dussubieux, L., 2010. Glass Material from Singapore. *Archipel* 80: 197–209.

Dussubieux, L., Gratuze, B., 2003. Nature et origine des objets en verre retrouvés à Begram (Afghanistan) et à Bara (Pakistan). In Bopearachchi, O., Landes, C., Sachs, Lattes, C. (eds.), *De l'Indus à l'Oxus: Archéologie de l'Asie Centrale*, pp. 315–323. Musée de Lattes : Association Imago.

Dussubieux, L., Gratuze, B., Blet-Lemarquand, M., 2010. Mineral Soda Alumina Glass: Occurrence and Meaning. *Journal of Archaeological Science* 37: 1645–1655.

Dussubieux, L., Kanungo, A., 2013. Trace Element Analysis of Glass from Kopia. In Kanungo, A. (ed.), *Glass in Ancient India: Excavations at Kopia*. KCHR, Triruvananthapuram, 360–366.

Dussubieux, L., Kusimba, C.M., Gogte, V., Kusimba, S.B., Gratuze, B., Oka, R., 2008. The Trading of Ancient Glass Beads: New Analytical Data From South Asian and East African Soda-Alumina Glass Beads. *Archaeometry* 50(5): 797–821.

Dussubieux, L., Robertshaw, P., Glascock, M.D., 2009. LA-ICP-MS Analysis of African Glass Beads: Laboratory Inter-Comparison with an Emphasis on the Impact of Corrosion on Data Interpretation. *International Journal of Mass Spectrometry* 284: 152–161.

Gill, M.S., 2017. A Single Ingredient for Primary Glass Production: Reassessing Traditional Glass Manufacture in Northern Indi. *Journal of Glass Studies* 59: 249–260.

Gratuze, B., Barrandon, J.-N., 1990. Islamic Glass Weights and Stamps: Analysis Using Nuclear Technique. *Archaeometry*, 32(2): 155–62.

Gratuze, B., 1999. Obsidian characterization by laser ablation ICP-MS and its application to prehistoric trade in the Mediterranean and the Near East: Sources and

Distribution of obsidian within the Aegean and Anatolia, Journal of Archaeological Science, 26: 869–81.

Gratuze, B., Dussubieux, L., Bopearachchi, O., 2000. Etude de Perles de Verre Trouvées au Sri Lanka, IIIe s. av.—IIe s. ap. JC., Annales du 14e Congrès de l'AIHV, Italia\Venezia-Milano 1998, pp. 46–50.

Henderson, J., McLoughlin, S.D., McPhail, D.S., 2004. Radical changes in Islamic Glass Technology: Evidence for Conservatism and Experimentation with New Glass Recipes from Early and Middle Islamic Raqqa, Syria. *Archaeometry* 46(3): 439–468.

Horton, M., 1988. Early Muslim Trading Settlements on the East African Coast: New Evidence from Shanga. *The Antiquaries Journal* 68: 290–325.

Horton, M., 1996. *Shanga: The Archaeology of a Muslim Trading Community on the Coast of East Africa*. Memoirs of the British Institute in Eastern Africa; no. 14. London: The British Institute in Eastern Africa.

Kock, J., Sode, T., 1995. *Glass, Glassbeads and Glassmakers in Northern India*. Vanlose: THOT Print.

Mirti, P., Pace, M., Malandrino, M. and Negro Ponzi, M.M., 2009. Sasanian Glass from Veh Ardašī. *Journal of Archaeological Science* 36(4): 1061–9.

Mirti, P., Pace, M., Negro Ponzi, M.M. and Aceto, M., 2008. ICP-MS Analysis of Glass Fragments of Parthian and Sasanian Epoch from Seleucia and Veh Ardasir (Central Iraq). *Archaeometry* 50(3): 429–50.

Morisson, H., 1984. The Beads. In Chittick, N., *Manda, Excavations at an Island Port on the Kenyan Coast,* Nairobi. The British Institute in Eastern Africa, Memoir Number 9.

Pearce, N.J.G., Perkins, W.T., Westgate, J.A., Gorton, M.T., Jackson, S.E., Neal, C.R., Chenery, S.P., 1997. A Compilation of New and Published Major and Trace Element Data for NIST SRM 610 and SRM 612 Glass Reference Materials, *Geostandards Newsletter*, 21: 114–115.

Rehren, T., Osório, A., Anarbaev, A., 2010. Some notes on Early Islamic Glass in Eastern Uzbekistan. In Zorn, Bettina, Hilgner, Alexandra (eds.), *Glass Along the Silk Road From 200 BC to AD 1000*, pp. 93–103. Mainz: Verlag des Römisch-Germanischen Zentralmuseums.

Robertshaw, P., Glascock, M.D., Wood, M., Popelka, R.S., 2003. Chemical Analysis of Ancient African Glass Beads: A Very Preliminary Report. *Journal of African Archaeology* 1: 139–146.

Robertshaw, P., Rasoarifetra, B., Wood, M., Melchiorre, E., Popelka-Filcoff, R.S., Glascock, M.D., 2006. Chemical Analysis of Glass Beads from Madagascar. *Journal of African Archaeology* 4: 91–109.

Robertshaw, P., Wood, M., Melchiorre, E., Popelka-Filcoff, R.S., Glascock, M.D., 2010. Southern African Glass Beads: Chemistry, Glass Sources and Patterns of Trade, *Journal of Archaeological Science* 37(8):1898–1912.

Saitowitz, S.J., 1996. *Glass Beads as Indicators of Contact and Trade in Southern Africa ca AD 900 – AD 1250*. PhD Dissertation, University of Cape Town, South Africa.

Saitowitz, S.J., Reid, D.L., Van der Merwe, N.J., 1996. Glass Bead Trade from Islamic Egypt to South Africa c. AD 900–1250. *South African Journal of Science* 92: 101–104.

Schibille, N., 2011. Late Byzantine Mineral Soda High Alumina Glasses from Asia Minor: A New Primary Glass Production Group. *PLoS ONE* 6(4): e18970. doi:10.1371/journal.pone.0018970

Shortland, A., Schachner, L., Freestone, I. and Tite, M., 2006. Natron as a Flux in the Early Vitreous Materials Industry: Sources, Beginnings and Reasons for Decline. *Journal of Archaeological Science* 33: 521–30.

Wadia, D.N., 1975. *Geology of India,* 4th edition. New Delhi: Tata Mac Graw Hill Publishing Co.

Walz, J., Dussubieux, L., 2016. Zhizo Series Glass Beads at Kwa Mgogo, Inland NE Tanzania. *Journal of African Archaeology* 14(1): 99–101.

Wood, M., 2011. A Glass Bead Sequence for Southern Africa from the 8th to the 16th Century AD. *Journal of African Archaeology* 9(1): 67–84.

Wood, M., Dussubieux, L., Robertshaw, P., 2012. Glass Finds from Chibuene, a 6th to 17th century AD Port in Southern Mozambique. *South African Archaeological Bulletin* 67(195): 59–74.

Wood, M., Panighello, S., Orsega, E.F., Robertshaw, P., van Elteren, J.T., Crowther, A., Horton, M., Boivin, N., 2017. Zanzibar and Indian Ocean Trade in the First Millennium CE: The Glass Bead Evidence. *Archaeological and Anthropological Sciences* 9(5): 879–901.

*Part II*

# CONTEMPORARY FLOWS

*Chapter 11*

# Six Hundred Years of Harmony

## *Comparing Zheng He's West Ocean Navigation with China's African Policy*

Xinfeng Li

It has been more than 600 years since the beginning of Zheng He's seven West Ocean navigations. How and in what ways did this great historical event which took place during China's Ming Dynasty transform China and the rest of the world? Do these events that occurred so long ago have any bearing on contemporary China's African policy? What relationships still exist between ancient and contemporary relationships between China and Africa? This chapter discusses how China's Ming Dynasty foreign policy buoys with today's policy. We will also discuss within today's relations as remarkable elements of cultural and economic continuity. I draw insight from the historic voyages of Admiral Zheng He to the "West Oceans" into Africa and today's China's African Policy.

First, let me note from the outset that Admiral Zheng He's four visits to Africa via the West Ocean navigations and China's contemporary strategy for Africa are fundamentally different from Africa's colonial and postcolonial relationship with the West (Rodney 1973). The rise of the Great Ming Empire into a powerful economic, political, and military state during the fourteenth and fifteenth century was not achieved by invading or plundering other countries. Admiral Zheng He's seven West Ocean navigations were neither conquest, colonization, nor imperial expansionist expeditions. The Ming Dynasty emperor Zhu Di's "active contact with foreign countries" was to "moralize and placate foreign people" and to establish friendly relations with Asian and African states, kingdoms, and empires. China had no intention to establish colony or economic bases abroad, as Chinese people at the time, unlike Europeans or Muslims, were uninterested in expanding China's territory to other areas but were, instead, anxious to forge business connections with other peoples (Podell and Anzovin 2007, 296–297). So the Zheng He mission was to establish equal and friendly relationship with the local people wherever they visited.

Five decades after the termination of Zheng He's seven West Ocean navigations, Portuguese colonialists landed in the African continent, constructed strongholds, business stations, and engaged themselves in other dirty deals. European colonialists including the Dutch, English, and Spanish, hot on the heels of Portuguese, established colonies in Africa, occupied land of Africa, plundered natural resources of the African continent, and enslaved the local people (Rodney 1973). European activities sharply contrast with those of the Chinese who made no attempt to occupy a single inch of the Africans land, did not plunder any of the African wealth and did not enslave or sell a single African (Kusimba 1999, 2). The historical record is clear who is right and who is wrong. Speaking at the tenth anniversary of Republic of South Africa and the China-Africa Partnership Forum, President Mbeki stated:

> History tells us that hundreds of years ago, neither Africans nor Asians had taken the other side as barbarians. Oceans apart, both sides deemed that their happiness depended on the happy life of the other. This basic idea reflected from this aspiration is shining with the glory of human nature. Guided by this aspiration, the 15th century Chinese fleet visited African ports and brought Africa mutual benefit and cooperation, not slave-trade or colonialism-resultant destruction or despair brought by Arabians and Europeans. (Li 2005, 292)

Even today, the former European masters, unable to let go their "African complex," regard Africa as their own "hunting ground" and "backyard," arrogantly order African people about from above and arrogantly say this and that about African affairs. On the contrary, China has consistently pursued a policy of equality and honesty with Africa, engaging Africans like good brothers, friends, and partners. Based on this principle, the China-Africa relationship, featured by "friendship, peace, cooperation, and development," has been universally recognized and praised by African countries and peoples.

Second, Zheng He's voyages to Africa differed from those of Europeans. His mission to the West Oceans was often followed by the reciprocal establishment of diplomatic missions in China. The establishment of diplomatic relationship between China and the Kingdom of Malindi during the Ming Dynasty reflects great official concern and importance attached by China and African countries to the development of China-Africa friendly cooperation. The historical fact that the Zheng He fleet made four visits to Africa during his seven West Ocean navigations is not open to debate. It is a fact. However, some scholars have continued a false claim that Zheng He had never visited

Africa but executed his distant command of the fleet navigations by staying in the Southeast Asia area (Chen 2003).[1]

Admiral Zheng He's voyages to Africa are recorded in different sections of the History of the Ming, vol. 326:

> Mogadiscio 20 days and nights travel by water from Minor Kollam. In the 14th year of Yongle reign, the kings of Brava and Malin dispatched envoys to present tributes to the Chinese emperor. Zheng He was ordered to accompany the envoys back and to reward the kings with money. When the kings paid tributes again, Zheng He was again ordered to accompany the envoys and to reward the kings and queens with wealth and money . . . Brava adjoins Mogadiscio . . . Zheng He was twice dispatched to the kingdom. In the 5th year of Xuande reign, Zheng He was dispatched to the kingdom again . . . Djubo also adjoins Mogadiscio. This kingdom presented tributes to China in the middle period of Yongle reign. Its people, not diverse, are honest. Zheng He had been to the place.

Besides, in the History of the Ming (Ming shi), there are also records of Zheng He's visit to the African kingdoms Bila and Suna, "There are also two kingdoms, known as Bila and Suna. Zheng He had been dispatched there with imperial gifts. It is so extremely far from China that envoys of the two kingdoms had never come to China" (History of Ming: vol. 326, Biography no. 214, Foreigner no. 7). Professor Zheng Yijun, a well-known expert in Zheng He studies, points out, "The Zheng He fleet paid four visits to Africa in its seven West Ocean navigations. Zheng He was present each time, three times during Yongle reign, one time during Xuande reign, as clearly recorded in related historical works." History of Mogadiscio records that Zheng He visited African countries in the thirteenth year of Yongle reign: "In the 14th year of Yongle reign, envoys were dispatched by the imperial court to accompany envoys from Brava and Malin to present tributes" (History of Ming: vol. 326). There are also records about Mogadiscio envoys' second visit to China to pay tributes to China. As a return, "Zheng He was ordered to accompany the envoys back with rewards in the form of gifts and money." This was the second visit Zheng He paid to Africa. After that, envoys from Mogadiscio "presented tributes again" and "Zheng He was again ordered to accompany the envoys" to ensure their safe return to their countries. This was the third visit Zheng He paid to Africa. The above visits were made during Yongle reign. Later, "In the 5th year of Xuande reign, Zheng He again brought the Chinese emperor's orders to the kingdoms." The four visits Zheng He made to Africa are a full reflection of the importance the Ming imperial court attached to the development of China-Africa relations (Professor Zheng Yijun Personal Communication with Li Xinfeng, September 25. 2009).

The Fei Xin (b. 1388) edited book, *The Overall Survey of the Star Raft* (Xingcha shenglan), provided the first description of people of the three African kingdoms, Mogadiscio, Brava, and Djubo, accurately and discussed on the geological locations, architectural styles, residential features, seasonal climate changes, economic activities, natural resources, trade and commerce, social customs, and military situations. In the mission of Zheng He, Ma Huan, and Fei Xin were probably senior interpreters of the mission leaders. The later description made by Portuguese about the architectural styles of the tribal states in the East African coastal areas are similar to those made by Fei Xin decades earlier. This historical fact convinces us that Zheng He and Fei Xin did arrive in the states in the East African coastal areas. This hard evidence has convinced scholars abroad that Zheng He did visit Africa, though controversies exist as to whether the Chinese had arrived in Africa in the historical periods of the Song and Yuan dynasties when oceangoing navigation had fairly developed. The British scholar Basil Davidson, in his book, *Old Africa Rediscovered*, points out, "The well-known navy commander Zheng He landed the East African coast," "It seems that the Chinese had not gone beyond the eastern waters of the Indian Ocean, though their ships and equipment might well bring them to places much farther" (Davidson 1973, 271–272). Despite some degree of bias, Basil Davidson confirms that Zheng He's visit to Africa reflect the fact that he left an unforgettable historical memory in people's mind as a historical evidence to the fact that the Chinese reached this "New Continent" much earlier than the Europeans (Professor Zheng Yijun Personal Communication with Li Xinfeng, September 25, 2009).

Zheng He's visits to Africa also find evidence from the following records. In the nineteenth year of Yongle reign (1421), Brava and Mogadiscio "dispatched envoys to present famous horses and local specialties as tributes and the Ministry of Rites treated the envoys to a feast at the imperial order." "When the envoys were to return home, they were granted money and gifts. Zheng He was again ordered to grant the African Kings silk fabrics and other gifts" (Veritable Records of Emperor Chengzu of the Ming Dynasty, vol. 119). Zheng He was ordered to grant the kings such gifts in person and the term "dispatched again" indicates his second visit. This record is a clear statement that Zheng He paid two visits to Africa.

When Zheng He visited Africa, the African kings and envoys visited China in Zheng He's fleet ships. The missions of Zheng He's later visits to Africa were to accompany the envoys home, a clear indication that such envoys were high-ranking officials. Ancient Chinese books record that the king of the ancient kingdom Mala died while on a state visit to China of a disease he may have contracted during the voyage and was buried with full honors in Minxian County of Fujian. According to the Records of Ming Dynasty Emperors' Social Laws (Ming Huang shi fa lu), "The ancient kingdom Mala

(Malin) is located in the Southeastern Sea. In the 18th year of Yongle reign (1420), the King Ganlayiyidunben had visited with his queen and ministers and presented gifts to the Chinese Emperor. Upon his sudden death, he was posthumously granted the title Kangjing and was buried in Minxian County and following the imperial order, the anniversary of his death was commemorated every year." The event is also recorded in Records of Advices in an Alien Land (Shu yu zhou zi lu), edited by the Ming scholar Yan Congjian: "During the Yongle reign, the (Malin) King Walaidunben came to China with his ministers, died in China [while on a state visit], was granted the title Kangjing, buried in Minxian County at an imperial order and was offered official sacrifices every year" (quoted from Ai and Mu 1966: 77). Professor Zheng Yijun believes that the "Ancient Mala" kingdom is not the "Malin" in East Africa, but a kingdom in Southeast Asia, in the present-day Philippines or in Mindanao Island or Cabarruyan Island near Bolinao on Luzon Island.

Historical events often seem to repeat. In the twenty-first year of Yongle reign (1423), over 1,200 envoys from sixteen countries came to visit China at the same time. In 2006, state leaders and high-ranking officials from forty-eight countries gathered in Beijing as participants in the Forum on China-Africa Cooperation and the Third Ministerial Conference. These two grand occasions, seldom seen in the history of China, are wonders in the history of communication between China and other countries of the world and are brilliant chapters in the history of the Chinese nation. The Communist Party of China and state leaders of China speak highly of Zheng He's visits to Africa. In 1964, Premier Zhou Enlai, during his visit to East Africa, pointed out in his speech that Zheng He was a great navigator as he visited East African countries such as Somalia and Kenya and made great contributions to the friendship between China and Africa. President Hu Jintao and Premier Wen Jiabao also highly praised the Zheng He fleet's visits to Africa for their contribution to the development of the relations between China and Africa. In 2005, all kinds of activities were held in China to mark the 600th anniversary of Zheng He's West Ocean navigations and all the African countries Zheng He had visited also made their responses to the celebration activities.

It has been 600 years since the first of Zheng He's seven West Ocean navigations, but today, "high-level reciprocal visits" still feature the relationship between China and Africa, though interruptions and setbacks exist in their communication. Along with the advance of times and the development of communication means, such reciprocal communication is far beyond that in Zheng He's time in frequency and scale. Nevertheless, the basic philosophy remains the same and that is equality, sincerity, seeking common ground while keeping differences, mutual complementation and benefit, and cooperative development.

## TRADE AND ECONOMIC EXCHANGE BETWEEN CHINA AND AFRICA

Zheng He was the pioneer of official trade between China and Africa. His fleet paid four unprecedented visits to distant African countries, operated free commercial trade with East African coastal countries and people, realized a degree of large-scale goods exchange by which the Chinese people and the African people broadened their vision and enriched their material and spiritual life. This complementary bilateral trade connection is the major momentum of such overseas trade, which was guided by the basic principle of equality, willingness, and equivalent exchange. Local products such as myrrh and mastic were common products in African countries of that time but to the distant China, they were rare treasures and even African giraffes were regarded as a rare treasure in the eyes of the Chinese people in the Ming Dynasty, an auspicious animal known as "sacred animal." This complementary and coequal trade of the Zheng He mission enabled China and Africa to supply their needs for mutual benefit as a major factor in the smooth development of trade between China and Africa. Six hundred years later, the bilateral complementariness still features the trade between China and Africa as a major factor in expanding China-Africa trade networks. China's mechanical and electrical products, textile products, and light industry products are favored by the African public for their high quality and reasonable prices, whereas the abundant African mineral and power resources are urgently needed by China for her national economic construction, in addition, the rich tourist resources of Africa are getting more attractive to the Chinese people. The deepening and expanding economic and trade cooperation is an inevitable result of the development of the relationship between China and Africa, which was impossible in Zheng He's time. All this vigorous and prospective development is based on the principle of equality and willingness.

Zheng He's courageous missions to the distant Africa is comparable to Chinese diplomats' efforts in Africa. Both point to spiritual continuum and testimony to hard work, commitment, and selfless service work, commitment, and selfless service to one's motherland and a glorious tradition of patriotism. The great achievements made during Ming Dynasty China was due to the emperor's desire to establish friendly relations with foreign countries and the dedication and loyalty of diplomats such as Zheng He. His efforts prevailed over poor communication, limited knowledge of world geography, and the vast distances between China and Africa. Zheng He and Wang Jinghong tried every means to communicate with East African coastal countries and to establish friendly relations, despite dangers, hardships, and self-sacrifice. Indeed, some sailors lost their lives to diseases, accidents, and shipwrecks. For example, survivors from the shipwreck would become permanent residents in foreign lands. One such shipwreck that occurred on the Kenyan coast opposite Island has been recorded in the area's oral traditions, and descendants of the union between the Chinese sailors and local Swahili people were recently identified by geneticists.

In Africa of today, the spirit of Zheng He is evident in Chinese diplomats to Africa: diligence, dedication, and commitment to their work and mission to make outstanding contributions toward the development of amicable China-Africa relations. For example, for a long time, the Chinese embassy to Angola was located in one of the poorest areas, local slum districts being the nearest neighbors. Chinese diplomats to South Africa are often harassed by criminals; Chinese diplomats still work in war-torn conditions. In July 2006, Premier Wen Jiabao addressed Chinese diplomats on his visit to seven African countries in the following terms: "I am thankful to you. You are really living a hard life here. 30 or 40 years back, China was not very well-off. Comparatively speaking, the life is much harder here. So I am thankful to you for your determination to work here and to win glory for our motherland" (Li 2006, 17).

## COMPARING AND CONTRASTING ANCIENT AND CONTEMPORARY CHINA-AFRICA POLICIES

There exist great similarities and continuity in the Chinese diplomatic protocol of the Ming Dynasty and contemporary People's Republic of China relationship with other nation states. In East Africa, the first major postcolonial project was the construction of Tanzania-Zambia Railway. This project symbolizes China's age-old practice of "hou wang bo lai," or "Giving-more-for-less" that was initiated by the Ming Dynasty emperors. The "Giving-more-for-less" philosophy is a manifestation of the important role and function of unconditional aid and a mutually willing principle in the bilateral friendly diplomatic communication between China and Africa. In this respect, we must be clear about the concepts "Giving-more-for-less," "Tribute Trade," and "Overseas Trade." First of all, "Giving-more-for-less" and "Tribute Trade" are different in nature, the former is a diplomatic manner which is within the category of politics and the latter foreign trade within the category of economy. In the first lunar month of the fifth year of the Hongwu reign (1372), Zhu Yuanzhang addressed his central secretariats thus: "West Ocean is secluded, known as distant countries. Their envoys come here over oceans and seas, spending months and years, whether their tributes are abundant or sparse, we may give them much and get back little in return" (Veritable Records of Emperor Taizu of the Ming Dynasty, vol. 71). He also stipulated that "all tribute personnel and all officials with noble titles are granted gifts" (Administrative Laws of the Ming, vol. 111, Ministry of Rites no. 69). This was the conciliation policy toward overseas countries who presented tributes to China. Zheng He studies expert Zheng Yijun is convinced that the policy "Giving-more-for-less" meant that tribute by foreign nations was reciprocated with abundant gifts, regardless of quality or quantity or times of tributes, to encourage foreign countries to come and engage with China. This policy was carried out at an economic expense, but its political benefits were immeasurably rewarding. We must be clear that "Giving more" meant the gifts the imperial court granted to tribute-presenting envoys from abroad. Envoys from overseas countries, when visiting China, presented gifts to the imperial court, which were understood as "tributes," and in return, the Ming imperial court granted them generous "rewards" that were considered huge by Chinese standards. "Tributes" to the imperial court and the Ming imperial court granted them generous "rewards." These were not exchanges of "tribute" and "reward" in a commercial transaction. That "Giving-more-for-less" action was not a commercial transaction but a diplomatic protocol. At the same time, China's "Giving more" "Rewards," though generous, were not "unlimited" at an unaffordable economic expense on its part but standardized and specified.

Emperor Yongle himself decreed the Giving-more regulation, "The imperial court commands the surrounding countries with kindness and all tribute presenting envoys should be granted rewards according to their official ranks, even with generosity" (Veritable Records of Emperor Chengzu of the Ming Dynasty, vol. 119). For instance, in the sixth year of the Yongle reign (1408), King Abdul Majid Hassan of the kingdom of Borneo visited China with a "golden wire list of tributes: Borneo camphor, crown, waistband, Borneol, crane top (鹤顶) Eretmochelys imbricata, rhinocerous horn, turtle scales, gold and silverware and other local treasures" (Veritable Records of Emperor Taizong of the Ming Dynasty, vol. 82). The Chinese side reciprocated with, "ceremonial weapon, folding chair, water tub and water basin, all made of silver; umbrella and fan, all made of white silk; two sets of gold saddle and horse, golden fabric, gauze and ten silk and satin dresses. The princess and the king's brothers and sisters as well as his attendants, regardless of gender, were all rewarded with corresponding gifts" (Veritable Records of Emperor Taizong of the Ming Dynasty, vol. 83). Besides, as Abdul Majid Hassan was taken ill and died during the visit, his son Awng was granted a hundred ounces of gold and three thousand ounces of silver as a special comfort on the eve of his return. All the precious utensils at the Guest Reception Office were granted to Awng as a gift.[2] As Abdul Majid Hassan was the first foreign king to visit China in the Ming Dynasty and in the history of China, the Yongle emperor attached great importance to him. The "Giving-more-for-less" grants as such, they were nothing to the prosperous and strong Ming Empire. Such grants were regulated. Ten days after the arrival of Abdul Majid Hassan, the Ministry of Rites told the emperor that the King of Borneo's visit to the emperor was not regulated yet. Zhu Di instructed, "As the king of Borneo is a vassal king, he is approved to see the emperor as a prince" (Veritable Records of Emperor Chengzu of the Ming Dynasty, vol. 59). So the Ming court received the Borneo king "as a prince." Since then, later overseas visiting kings and envoys were accorded this same principle. In terms of gift quantity and grade, the gifts granted by the Ming court to Abdul Majid Hassan and his son Awng were about the same or even less than those granted to its own ministers.

The gifts granted to ordinary envoys were much less than those granted to kings (Zheng 2005, 13). In the nineteenth year of Yongle reign (1421), the imperial court specified its regulations on gifts granted to foreign tribute envoys: "Each of third or fourth grade envoys is granted 150 ingots, one piece of brocade and 3 rolls of silk. A fifth-grade envoy is granted 120 ingots and 3 rolls of silk. A sixth or a seventh envoy is granted 90 ingots and 2 rolls of silk. An eighth or ninth envoy is granted 80 ingots and 1 roll of silk. A low rank envoy is granted 60 ingots and 1 bundle of silk" (Veritable Records of Emperor Chengzu of the Ming Dynasty, vol. 119). In the very year when this regulation was promulgated, Brava and Mogadiscio "dispatched envoys to present rare horses and local specialties and the envoys were treated to a banquet," "On the eve of the envoys' return, they were granted ingots and fabrics. The Admiral Zheng He was again dispatched to grant rewards to the kings, such as brocade, silk, gauze, satin and thin silk" (Veritable Records of Emperor Chengzu of the Ming Dynasty, vol. 119).

Tribute Trade means equal and fair bilateral trade of foreign envoys' goods, performed at fixed time and place in accordance with the imperial court's regulations after the giving-more-for-less ceremony. It was in fact an international trade performed in China. As international trade was monopolized by the state, tribute trade was the sole form of international trade in China and the sole form of international trade in the period of Zhu Yuanzhang's reign, no other forms of commercial trade performed abroad. In the period of Zheng He's West Ocean navigation, the state's foreign trade included two divisions, one was a continuation of tribute trade which was much limited in scale and the other was the Zheng He fleet's large-scale trade abroad and folk trade activities.

Second, tribute trade and overseas trade were similar but with minor differences. They were similar as both followed the trade principle of equivalent exchange in a foreign trade setting. They were different in transacting places, the former in China, at the Chinese emperor's guest reception office and the latter was performed in foreign countries, countries overseas, that is, countries Zheng He visited. They were also different in transacting time, the former completed in a fixed duration, usually three to five days and the latter not limited by this regulation. Administrative Laws of the Ming records provide details of this regulation in the following language: "If traffic permits, all people should begin their trades within three to five days after tribute presentation and gift exchange ceremony, with the exception of the unlimited Koreans and Loochooans" (quoted from Zheng 2005, 12). There are detailed records in Ma Huan's (fl. 1413–1451) Wonders Overseas (Yingya shenglan) about the time of overseas trade performed by the Zheng He's mission. In each transaction performed in Kolkata, merchants met fellow merchants, wealthy people, and accountants to inspect goods and negotiate prices, "A transaction was not made in one day, but in one month, if quick, or in three months, if slow" (Ma 2005, 60).

Third, the marketing operation modes were different, the former performed regular management of market and policies toward foreign guests relatively loose and comfortable. The latter followed local customs in equal and even transactions with foreign merchants. Emperor Yongle expected that "all envoys from vassal states were treated with sincerity and the trade in their local specialties at the market were performed at their free will. In case of violation to laws due to ignorance of laws, all foreigners were forgiven as a concern for guests from afar" (Veritable Records of Emperor Chengzu of the Ming Dynasty, vol. 12, Part I). But, all foreign guests participating in "Tribute Trade" at the guest reception office must first of all "pay tributes," "Before paying tributes, transactions at market were not permitted" (Zheng 2007, vol. 2, 85). If Emperor Yongle's edict was much general, the regulations in the Administrative Laws of the Ming were more specific. People of all trades enter the guest reception office with their goods as equals to trade. Dyed goods or fabrics must be traded on the spot in cash. Cases of purchase on credit or deliberate delay, cheating, and/or blackmailing of foreign guests led to delayed departure of foreign guests. In cases of private trade, traders would be detained in the office as a punishment. In case of deliberate violation of regulations on the part of foreign guests or sneaking into households for trade, their private goods were confiscated by the office and rewards reduced. Frontier guards were not to escort criminal foreigners to the capital. In cases involving purchase of forbidden goods by army men or civilians living in the immediate areas of the office on behalf of foreigners, the culprits were punished with one-month detention after which they would be exiled to remote places as penalty (Zheng 2005, 12).

Fourth, the giving-more-for-less trade, tribute trade, and overseas trade shared a common ground: equality, honesty, and trade at the traders' own will. For instance, in a giving-more-for-less trade, foreign envoys had full right to decide on the variety and quantity of their tributes and the Ming court was not specific about their local specialties as tributes. The variety and quantity of the Ming Imperial reward was decided by the Emperor. Usually, this was several times or dozens of times better than the tributes paid. The imperial court regularized the tribute trade to ensure justice and honesty in trade and to avoid cheating. The Zheng He mission's overseas trade operated on the principle of justice, honesty, and free trade at traders' own will. Bilateral trade had a long history in China at the time of Admiral Zheng He's mission to Africa.

Turning our attention to contemporary times, principle of giving-more-for-less is epitomized by China's construction of the Tanzania-Zambia Railway. First, both the economic giving-more and the economic aid were politically considered and realized as diplomatic rituals. That is to say, both of them politicized economic events to win political trust and high political value at a degree of economic expenses or losses. The Yongle Emperor Zhu Di "Admires the prime of the Tang and the Song dynasties with all countries obedient to China," for world peace, for respects from all countries, for "shared peace" with China and for in the words of the Ming scholar He Qiaoyuan, "surpassing the prime of the Han and the Tang as well as the three grand dynasties including Xia, Shang and Zhou in three generations" (He 1993, vol. 104).

This was done by moralizing foreign countries and Giving-more-for-less was the best choice. Compared with feudal emperors, leaders of New China do not pursue the splendor of "being worshiped by all foreign peoples when the heavenly palace opens" (Wang 1991, 183) but made the strategic decision to construct the Tanzania-Zambia Railway on the basis of internationalism. At the request of the leaders of the two countries, Chairman Mao pointed out when meeting Zambian president Kaunda, "The countries that win national independence earlier are obliged to assist the countries that win national independence later" (Zhang 1999, 107). China regards aid to the construction of the Tanzania-Zambia Railway as a model of Chinese aid to foreign countries. It is inseparable from the fact that China in that period took aid to foreign countries as her support to the colonial and semicolonial countries and peoples in their struggle for national independence and her aid to newly independent countries in their economic construction.

In January 1964, Premier Zhou Enlai, when visiting Mali, comprehensively expounded the eight principles of China's economic and technical aid provided to foreign countries. China's Eight Principles for Economic Aid and Technical Aid to Other Countries are outlined as follows:

1. The Chinese government always bases itself on the principle of equality and mutual benefit in providing aid to other countries. It never regards such aid as a kind of unilateral alms but as something mutual.
2. In providing aid to other countries, the Chinese government strictly respects the sovereignty of recipient countries, and never attaches any conditions or asks for any privileges.

3. China provides economic aid in the form of interest-free or low-interest loans and extends the time limit for the repayment when necessary so as to lighten the burden on recipient countries as far as possible.
4. In providing aid to other countries, the purpose of the Chinese government is not to make recipient countries dependent on China but to help them embark step by step on the road of self-reliance and independent economic development.
5. The Chinese government does its best to help recipient countries complete projects which require less investment but yield quicker results so that the latter may increase their income and accumulate capital.
6. The Chinese government provides the best-quality equipment and materials manufactured by China at international market prices. If the equipment and materials provided by the Chinese government are not up to the agreed specifications and quality, the Chinese government undertakes to replace them or refund the payment.
7. In giving any particular technical assistance, the Chinese government will see to it that the personnel of the recipient country fully master the technology.
8. The experts dispatched by China to help in construction in recipient countries will have the same standard of living as the experts of the recipient country. The Chinese experts are not allowed to make any special demands or enjoy any special amenities.

China considers this unconditional give-more assistance as its responsibility, not a charity, and does not expect economic gain in return. Making economic events emotional is an expression of sincerity and a means to make friends and to win over their hearts. The Ming court's give-more to tribute payers was to politically influence foreigners and to convince them to willingly and peacefully obey to the great power of the Ming Empire, not for selfish gains or for conquest or plunder of other nations. New China takes her economic aid to developing countries as her duty because she takes them as her true friends. Mutual assistance between friends is based on equality and not for anything in return, but for development of their national economy and for the enhancement of people's livelihood. Just as Chairman Mao Zedong said to the Tanzanian president Nyerere, "We are pleased to see you. We are of one family. We have no ill-intentions towards you and neither do you towards us. We are not exploiting each other; we are helping each other. Neither my country nor yours are imperialist countries. Imperialism is ill-intended. We must be cautious" (Zhang 1999, 56).

In the light of China's national strength and the China-Africa communication condition at that time, this timely give-more aid was valuable and commendable. In other words, the moralization of economic problems is an expression of the Chinese nation's traditional virtues—hospitality, broad mind toward foreigners, eagerness to meet the needs of others and willingness to help people in need. The Ming court's give-more-fore less principle was a preferential treatment for guests, whereas New China's aid to the construction of Tanzania-Zambia Railway was an expression of her eagerness to meet the needs of others. "A friend in need is a friend indeed." China, with her national strength at that time, spent so much financial, material, and human resources on such a large-scale construction of the Tanzania-Zambia Railway, motivated by political and economic factors as well as by the traditional virtues of the Chinese nation.

In a word, the give-more-fore less policy of the Ming Dynasty and the contemporary China's aid in the construction of the Tanzania-Zambia Railway are a reflection of China's growing economic strength, comprehensive national strength, and international influence. It bears witness to the fact that development, power, prosperity, and the civilization process are not only benefit the Chinese nation but also the world. Some Western scholars have pointed out that "China's economic growth will not only greatly benefit the developing countries but will also unfold its significance in the future. The values, the development mode and the foreign policies which China advocates will yield even greater resonance and influence among the world public." (Peoples' Daily, October 5, 2009). Just as President Hu Jintao pointed out at the sixtieth anniversary of the People's Republic of China, "The Chinese people are confident and competent in building their country and are also confident and competent in making their due contributions to the world" (Hu 2009, 2).

The Tanzania-Zambia Railway was a milestone in the contemporary relations between China and Africa, an ode to the China-Africa friendship and a materialization of the "Bandung Spirit" and China's "Eight Principles" in foreign aid. Its influence was far beyond a railway. It signaled and symbolized the huge potential in future China-Africa relationships.

The essential Differences between contemporary China's African Policy and Zheng He's West Ocean navigation is that contemporary China' African policy is much more strategic, much more interactive and much more international, compared with the time of Zheng He's West Ocean navigation. Contemporary China's African policy has overcome the historical limitations of Zheng He's West Ocean navigation. It is a sustainable, stable, and comprehensive development agenda. Zheng He's China was a feudal society which relied on imperial power and supremacy. Therefore, despite a series of political, economic, military, and cultural achievements of Zheng He's West Ocean voyages, the dark side of feudalism abruptly put an end to this great human endeavor to engage the world. Why was Zheng He's West Ocean navigation not continued? Both Zhu Di, the emperor who initiated the West

Ocean navigation and Zheng He, the commander, were confined by their limitation of times. The historical limitation made Zheng He's West Ocean navigation unsustainable and the China-Africa relations interrupted as a result.

In contrast, contemporary China's African policy is sustainable because it is based on solid political foundation, on affection, and regular cooperation. Equality in China-Africa relations is the foundation of contemporary China's African policy, reinforced by the historical experience shared by China and Africa, by their common task of development, and by their shared fate and goal. In addition, after decades of development, China-Africa relations have created a new cooperation mechanism, the Forum on China-Africa Cooperation, which ensures periodical meetings to review progress towards strengthening sustainable development of bilateral relations. Contemporary China's African policy implements and ensures stable development on the basis of mutual economic benefit, win-win cooperation and bilateral cultural exchanges and mutual learning. International communication is inseparable from benefit and the relation between China and African countries is no exception, but their relation is one of mutual benefit and win-win cooperation, and in cultural exchange, a mutual learning and respect for each other's cultural tradition and life style. Emperor Yongle Zhu Di, when relating Zheng He's West Ocean navigation, said, "Envoys are often dispatched to disseminate education to vassal states, to inform them of fine manners and to change their tribal customs." (Zhu 1983, 856). Wherever Zheng He went, he issued Chinese calendar to foreign countries for them to follow as examples, such as the Ming Dynasty politics, society, social customs, and other social practices. In other words, Zheng He, in his West Ocean navigation, unilaterally spread Chinese culture, not a bilateral cultural exchange.

Contemporary China's African policy is ensured of comprehensive development as it is oriented to the entire African continent for multichannel, wide-range, all-dimensional, and multilayered diplomatic activities, whereas the Zheng He fleet, restricted by limitation of geological knowledge and communication conditions, only visited some countries along the East African coast, staying away from the inland of Africa and the bilateral trades in these two historical periods cannot be equal in terms of goods quantity and variety. The relation between contemporary China and Africa is one of all-weather friends and is oriented to all African countries. The range of bilateral exchange covers all fields of all-round diplomacy between friends, partners, and brothers. Premier Wen Jiabao points out that the China-Africa commercial and trade cooperation is deepening:

> In 2008, the China–Africa trade value exceeded $100 billion and fifty-three African countries are in commercial and trade connection with China; China is executing construction projects in six commercial and trade cooperation areas and nearly 1600 Chinese enterprises are registered in African countries, with

a direct investment stock of $7.8 billion. Project contracting, and labor supply cooperation are expanding in scale and financial cooperation is well under way. Cultural and educational exchanges are in full swing. Exchange and cooperation in culture, education, healthcare, human resources training are developing with great vigor, the number of Africans trained by China will reach 15,000 and exchanges between youth, women and sister-cities and sister-provinces are gaining in frequency. All these are deepening our mutual understanding and traditional friendship. (Wen 2009)

Premier Wen Jiabao's speech clearly stipulated China's holistic, inclusive, and comprehensive African policy aimed all integrating all of Africa without isolating or favoring particular regions or countries. Second, this new-type strategic partnership between China and Africa is based on equality between all countries, regardless of territory size or differences in wealth, or abundance or shortage in natural resources of African countries. The view that China develops the relationship between China and African countries for the purpose of seizing African resources and the label "Neocolonialism" is groundless.

Since the founding of New China, Chinese leaders have employed, on the principle of proletarian internationalism to support the African people's justified struggles for national liberation and independence. Since independence, China has assisted development of African national economies in order to improve people's livelihoods. In other words, Chinese leaders attach strategic importance to China-Africa relations, leaders of the older generation opening the gate to China-African relations since that foundation was laid by Chairman Mao Zedong, successive leadership has continued to attach importance to China-Africa relations, emphasizing that aids to Africa should focus on major projects that involve national economy and people's livelihood and should also focus on strengthening African countries' capacity for their independent development, stressing that Chinese enterprises should build their fine images, protect the environment, and treat local people with respect.

The strategy of Chinese diplomacy has also found expression in dispatching her naval forces to convoy oceanic navigation for the first time. As the Somali pirates are rampant and Chinese merchant ships are gravely threatened when they pass the Gulf of Aden and other Somali waters, a Chinese naval fleet has been dispatched to the Gulf of Aden and other Somali waters at the invitation from the Somali transitional government to safeguard Chinese merchant ships and Chinese seamen. Foreign media has characterized this decision as a "Repetition of Zheng He's Navigation." Zheng He opened up the first nonwar application of Chinese n to anti-piracy operation in Southeast Asia and was praised by people of the world. Zheng He met with pirates and removed evils during his West Ocean navigation. This time, the Chinese navy's expedition to Aden and Somali waters is to ensure safe navigation of Chinese ships is a non-war expedition of the Chinese navy to safeguard China's interest in oceans. This is a very important measure taken by the Chinese navy.

The interactive relation means that the China-Africa relation is not a unilateral aid or support but is a bilateral cooperation with a win-win result. As Premier Wen Jiabao writes:

> As early as the 1950s and 1960s of the last century, China and Africa have been fighting side by side in the historical resistance against imperialism, colonialism and hegemony and had been advancing together in their arduous common efforts to revitalize their national economies. The Tanzania-Zambia Railway, the Africa-aiding medical teams and the young volunteers are vivid examples of China's selfless aid to Africa. The facts that China was "carried" into the United Nations, that the Beijing Olympic Torch concluded smoothly in Africa and that the African people enthusiastically donated money to the earthquake-stricken Wenchuan area of Sichuan Province are mirroring African people's true friendship towards the Chinese people. (Wen 2009)

Contemporary China's African policy based on a firm foundation has made unprecedented development as evidenced by the successful hosting of Forum on China-Africa Cooperation Beijing Summit Conference and the full implementation of the eight policy measures. At the November 2006 Forum on China-Africa Cooperation Beijing Summit Conference, President Hu Jintao proclaimed that, to promote the development of the new-type strategic partnership between China and Africa, to promote China-Africa cooperation in even broader scales, the Chinese government would take policy measures in eight fields. Three years later, the Chinese government had implemented all the eight policy measures as promised. At the fourth ministerial conference of Forum on China-Africa Cooperation held in Egypt in November 2009, Premier Wen Jiabao proclaimed another eight policy measures for deepening all-round pragmatic cooperation between China and Africa encompassing the complete implementation of the eight policy measures, old and new, has upgraded China-Africa relation to new levels of unprecedented development.

Contemporary China's African policy manifests the basic principle of her diplomatic policy and the clear characteristics of our times—open, inclusive, and international. This policy is an integral part of China's diplomatic policy in Africa and is a model for South-South cooperation. This is this cooperation manifest the basic concept of China's diplomatic policy. As President Hu Jintao points out, "It is the correct principle of sincere friendship, equality, mutual support for common development in developing our mutual relation that has withstood historical challenges and changes of international environment" (Hu 2006). Premier Wen Jiabao emphasizes that China-Africa friendly relation is "based on shared and mutual support, respect, equality, and cooperation for common development" (Wen 2009).

Zheng He's mission followed the principle "Cherishing the world with China as the center and making the world obedient with no bias" (Veritable Records of Emperor Chengzu of the Ming Dynasty, vol. 23) but what the feudal emperors pursued were "respect from all countries" and obedience from all four seas," in the hope of "moralizing people on Earth under Heaven within the reach of ships and vehicles" (Zheng and Zheng 1952, 863). The "unbiased attitude" means that the countries Zheng He had visited were equal with the powerful Ming empire commanding from above, being paid "tributes" and "obedience." The former colonialist suzerains of Africa in the colonial days enslaved the African countries, and today, they are still regarding and treating Africa as if they were "Master" of African countries. In contrast, it is China's sincere respect for Africa and her equal treatment of Africa that has won her respect from Africans.

The fact that China develops her relationship with African countries on equal terms and that she treats African peoples on the principle of equality do not mean that China rejects other countries and peoples in developing normal diplomatic relations with Africa. On the contrary, China welcomes other countries to support and assist the development of Africa. The China-Africa relation is an open and transparent strategic partnership relation, not an alliance, nor a joint opposition to any third party, nor a hindrance to African countries in their friendly cooperation with other countries. Indeed, strengthening bilateral mutually beneficial cooperation will help draw more international attention to Africa and will be of help in realizing the millennium development goal of Africa. China-Africa relation is highly inclusive, strategic, and international, each dimension adding to another.

The internationalism in China-Africa relation finds expression in mutual consultation and coordination between China and Africa in international affairs, in mutual accommodation of each other's concerns and in their joint effort in coping with all global threat and challenge to security and in promoting balanced and harmonious development of the world. At the same time, the mutual trust and coordination between China and Africa in international affairs will jointly help safeguard the legitimate interest of developing countries. China is the largest developing country in the world and Africa is the continent where developing countries concentrate. The population of China and Africa accounts for over one-third of the world population. This fact alone testifies the importance of China-Africa relation in the world today.

## NOTES

1. Chen Hsin-hsiung held that Zheng He had never been to Africa, the evidence being no Guan ware, or "official" ware had been discovered in Africa. In recent years,

a kind of Guan ware, the Longquan celadon, has been found along the Kenyan coast in East Africa. Therefore, Chen's argument has insufficient grounds today.

2. Guest Reception Offices (Huitong guan) were in charge of receiving minority ethnic officials and foreign envoys in the period Yuan, Ming, and Qing dynasties. They were established in the thirteenth year of the Yuan Dynasty (1276). The offices were in charge of interpretation, escorting, inspecting tributes, and tribute trade in the imperial palace.

## REFERENCES

Administrative Laws of the Ming (Ming hui dian). 2009 [1587]. Beijing: Beijing Library.
Ai, Z. and T. Mu (eds.). 1966. *History of China: Africa Relations*. Shanghai: East China Normal University Press.
Chen, H-H. 2003. "Where on Earth Did Zheng He's Fleet Arrive." In C. Hsin-hsiung and C. Yuh-Nue (eds.), *Proceedings of the International Conference on Zheng He's Voyages to the West Oceans*. Taipei: DowTien.
Davidson, B. 1973. *Old Africa Rediscovered*. Trans. by Tu Erkang and Ge Ji. Beijing: SDX Joint Publishing House.
He, Q. 1993 [1640]. *History Reserved in Famous Mountains (Ming Shan Cang)*. Nanjing: Jiangsu Guangling Ancient Books Printing House.
History of the Ming (Ming shi), by a group of historians led by Zhang Tingyu. 2011 [1645–1739]. Book 28, vol. 326. Biographies 214, Foreign countries 7, *History of Mogadiscio History of Brava History of Djubo*. Beijing: Zhonghua Book Company.
Hu, Jintao. 2006. "Speech at the Opening Ceremony of China-Africa Cooperation Forum Beijing Summit Conference," *People's Daily*, November 5.
Hu, Jintao. 2009. "Speech at the 60 Anniversary of the People's Republic of China," *People's Daily*, October 2.
Kusimba, C.M. 1999. *The Rise and Fall of Swahili States*. Walnut Creek: AltaMira.
Li, X. 2005. *Following Zheng He Footsteps in Africa*. Kunming: Aurora Press.
Li, X. 2006. "Moving People by Emotion, Convincing People by Reasoning and Being Considerate of Other People – Notes on Premier Wen Jiabao's Visits to Seven African Countries," *The Earth*, no. 14.
Ma H. 2005 [1451]. *Wonders Overseas*. Collated and Annotated by Wan Ming. Beijing: Ocean Press.
People's Daily Commentator. 2009. "The Proud Power of China," *People's Daily*, October 5, p. 1.
Podell, J. and S. Anzovin. 2007. *They Changed the World*. Trans. Chen Huiying. Beijing: Zhonghua Book Company.
Professor Zheng Yijun's letter to Li Xinfeng, September 25, 2009.
Rodney, W. 1973. *How Europe Underdeveloped Africa*. London: Bogle-L'Ouverture Publications.
Veritable Records of Emperor Taizong of the Ming Dynasty (Ming Taizong shilu) also known as Veritable Records of Emperor Chengzu of the Ming Dynasty (Ming

Chengzu shilu), by royal historians in the Ming Dynasty (1368–1644). 2016, photocopied and published, Beijing: Zhonghua Book Company.

Wang, W. 1991 [758]. "Matching the Poem 'Dawn Audience in the Palace of Great Brightness' by Secretary Jia Zhi" (He Jia Sheren zaochao Da Minggong zhi zuo). In Liu Kezhuang, (ed.), *Poems of the Masters* (Qian jia shi), p. 158. Annotated by Li Muhua. Lanzhou: Gansu People's Press.

Wen, Jiabao. 2009. "Promoting All-Round New-Type Strategic China-Africa Partnership – Speech at the 4th Ministerial Conference of China-Africa Cooperation Forum," *People's Daily*, December 9.

Zhang, T. (ed.). 1999. *Road to Friendship: Notes on the Construction of Tanzania-Zambia Railway*. Beijing: China International Economy and Trade Press.

Zheng, H. and Y. Zheng(eds.). 1983. *Collected Documents on Zheng He's West Ocean Navigation*, vol. 2. Jinan: Qilu Publishing House.

Zheng, R. 2007 [1562]. *Nautical Chart Illustrations (Chou Hai Tu Bian)*. Beijing: Zhonghua Book Company.

Zheng, Y. 2005 *On Zheng He's West Ocean Navigations*. Beijing: Ocean Press.

Zhu, D. 1983. "Nanjing Imperial Hongren Puji Goddess Temple Monument." In Zheng Hesheng and Zheng Yijun (eds.), *Collected Documents on Zheng He's West Ocean Navigation*, vol. 2. Jinan: Qilu Publishing House.

*Chapter 12*

# Impacts of Chinese Influence in Contemporary East Africa

Angela Kabiru

The number of Chinese nationals living and working in Kenya has been growing steadily in the last ten years. The number is now estimated at over 40,000 and is expected to rise quickly in the next several years. Although cultural and linguistic barriers still remain major obstacles, the Chinese influence can be felt in nearly all sectors of the economy. According to available data, Chinese companies now own 31 percent of infrastructure projects in Kenya, a figure that rises to over 50 percent when considering construction and education programs. In 2008, the Export-Import Bank of China lent Kenya US$84.07 million to finance two bypasses in Nairobi, Kenya's capital and largest city. The contract was awarded to China Road and Bridge Corporation, CRBC. In May 2014, Kenya secured a loan to construct the Standard Gauge Railway, SGR line, along with sixteen more loans estimated in billions of dollars. This trend of over-borrowing from one nation is deeply troubling to critics and economists (Sanghi and Johnson 2016).

China's strategy of global engagement is based upon a political philosophy of non- interference in internal affairs of other nations (Xi 2015). This strategy is attractive to debtor nations like Kenya who have found in China a partner willing to offer critical financing in the sectors that Euro-American investors and donors had overlooked such as the Standard Gauge Railway, SGR. Kenya's external debt estimated at US$2.85 billion in 2011 had grown to US $4.7 billion in 2015 primarily due to Chinese lending. During this period, loans from China increased by 657.33 percent to US$2.73 billion, overtaking Japan, Germany, and France as the major loan sources.

Besides infrastructural projects, China's influence is growing in other sectors of Kenya's political economy, including tourism, education, and retail. The numbers of Chinese tourists has increased following aggressive marketing by Kenyan and Chinese tourist board campaigns through business fairs and in the Chinese media. The establishment of Confucius centers at Kenyan universities is also a growing trend. Supermarket chains across Kenya's towns now stock Chinese delicacies. Along with these trends has also emerged tensions. For example, the rising incidents of illegal poaching and trafficking of animal products from endangered species, including rhino, elephants, lions, and recently the donkey has been associated with Chinese nationals. This chapter discusses the nature of Kenya's collaboration with China, impacts of this relationship, and Kenyans' perception of the Chinese. What short and long-term effects will this have for Kenya? What factors have contributed to the rapid rise of Chinese influence in Africa?

## CHINESE INVESTMENTS IN KENYA

On June 1, 2017, Kenya's President Uhuru Kenyatta commissioned the Standard Gauge Railway (SGR) linking Mombasa and Nairobi. The 472 km railway estimated to have cost the Kenyan tax payer $3.6 billion is the largest infrastructural project in Kenya since independence. The SGR was constructed by the state-owned China Road and Bridge Corporation (CRBC) and financed by China's Eximbank, which provided nearly 90 percent of the total cost. Of $3.6 billion in financing, $2 billion is a fifteen-year loan at Libor plus 360 basis points. The remaining $1.6 billion is on concessional terms of 2 percent interest, repayable over twenty years, according to the China-Africa Research Initiative at Johns Hopkins University (Pilling and Feng 2017). CRBC will operate the rail for the first five years to recoup some of this cost.

While the SGR project ranks among the most important in East Africa, it is just one of the few large-scale infrastructural projects financed by the People's Republic of China in Africa. For example, the first fully electrified cross-border railway line in Africa is a 750-km project linking Djibouti and Ethiopia. In contrast to the SGR, the fully electric Ethiopia-Djibouti railway cost $3.4 billion. The Kenyan railway will initially run on diesel, to be upgraded to fully electric in four years when power supply "becomes dependable." And that will cost an additional 15 percent of the money already spent (Mutambo 2017)

Proponents of these investments argue that the rail will transform the regional economy by improving the speed and capacity of rail transportation by lowering the cost of ferrying passengers and freight from the port of Mombasa to Nairobi and eventually, beyond to Uganda, Rwanda, South Sudan, and the eastern parts of Democratic Republic of Congo (Muriri 2017).[3] In May 2017, President Kenyatta secured an additional $3.59 billion from China to extend the Standard Gauge Railway from Naivasha to Kisumu on the shores of Lake Victoria (Ilado 2017).

China has gone from having little presence in Kenya in the past ten years to becoming one of its most important trading and investment partners. Kenya's imports from China tripled to nearly $5 billion in 2016, against $780 million from the United States. Between 2013 and 2017, Chinese investments and commitments to Kenya reached $ 6.5 billion (Muraya 2016) making China Kenya's largest bilateral lender, with debts amounting to $ 3.5 billion, or 19.4 per cent of the total external debt in the second quarter of the 2016/17 fiscal year. Kenya's external debt in Chinese currency nearly doubled between September and December 2016, pushed up by a Sh20.7 billion ($200 million) semi-concessional loan. Statistics from the Central Bank of Kenya show that this external debt stood at 6.6 percent at the end of the second fiscal quarter of 2016/2017, increasing from 3.9 percent at the end of September. In contrast, the percentage of debt denominated in the other hard currencies—the Euro, British pound, and Japanese yen—decreased. Total external debt stood at $17.7 billion at the end of 2016 (Mwaniki 2017).

In 2016, Kenya secured a $600 million loan from China toward paying a $6 billion budget deficit for the year, reducing the deficit from 8.7 percent of gross domestic product to 7.9 percent. World Bank statistics show that China is now Kenya's largest creditor, accounting for 72 percent of the country's total external debt, eight times more than the next lending partners gave to Kenya. Chinese loans to Kenya grew an annual rate of 54 percent between 2010 and 2014 while loans from other lenders like Japan and France fell (Dahir 2018, 8).

The latest statistics from the Treasury, courtesy of Quartz Africa. https://qz.com/1324618/china-is-kenyas-largest-creditor-with-72-of-total-bilateral-debt/. Since 2003, China has funded seventy development projects in Kenya, most which have been completed. An estimated fifty Chinese companies have been contracted to work on various projects in energy, roads, water, housing, and transport in Kenya, with a combined value of $2 billion (Xinhua 2017). Since 1964, Kenya has received KES 488.82 billion in financial support from China (www.treasury.go.ke). Examples of Chinese funded projects include Moi Sports Complex Kasarani, Moi Teaching and Referral Hospital, Eldoret, Thika Road Development (Lot 3), Nairobi Eastern and Northern Bypass Project, and Mama Lucy Kibaki Hospital. Ongoing projects include Kenyatta University Teaching and Referral Hospital, Nairobi Southern Bypass Project, and drilling of eighty geothermal wells at Olkaria. The Thika Superhighway, University of Nairobi Towers and Nairobi North and East Ring Road are being funded at the tune of $360 million, $26 million, and $108 million, respectively.

China Electric Power Equipment and Technology (CET) has begun construction of the $1.26 billion Ethiopia-Kenya power project, a 500 KV transmission line with a capacity of 2,000 MW stretching 445 km into Ethiopia

(NEPAD[11] 2017). China Power Global is one of the companies investing US$2 billion in the construction of a coal plant in Lamu (Wesangula 2017; Kamau 2018). In May 2017, the Guangdong New South Group Limited signed an agreement with the Kenya government to build a US$1.9 billion industrial park in Eldoret, a special economic zone that is part of the Africa Economic Zones. The company is also investing in Zimbabwe (PSCU 2017). Avic International plans to build the Global Trade Center in Nairobi, a 30,000 square-meter mixed use complex, Chinese News Agency, Xinhua) reported.

A total of 1,046 projects, including railways with a total length of 2,233 km and highways with a total length of 3,530 km have been funded by China in Africa. These projects have made tangible improvements in transportation infrastructure in Africa. Sino-African cooperation has contributed over 20 percent to Africa's economic growth (Xinhua[1] 2015). In 2010, China surpassed the United States as Africa's largest trading partner, amassing trades totaling to nearly $200 billion. Across African nations, Chinese contractors and laborers are engaged in railway, road, housing, and office construction (Brown 2012).

China's contribution to Africa's development are funneled through the African Development Bank (AfDB) and the African Development Fund (ADF) which it joined in 1985. Since its initial contribution of US$14.59 million to the AfDB in 1985, China's contributions to African programs exceed US$486 million, US$122 million of which was for the ADF XI (2008–2010). China contributed UA 83,921,666 (US$125,815,361.67) to ADF-XII, which corresponds to a 5 percent increase from its ADF-XI contribution. Its burden share represents 2.052 percent of ADF-XII (AfDB 2017). Assistance is also provided through the People's Bank of China, the China Development Bank, the Export-Import Bank of China and China-Africa Development Fund. China is keen to further expand investments in African countries in support of economic growth and development. Trade between China and Africa totaled US $26.4 billion in 2012 and rose to US $85.3 billion in 2017. This rise has been attributed to China's change in trade policies in 2015. Chinese imports from Africa have reached US $38.4 billion, while exports to Africa stand close to $47 billion (AfricaNews17 2017).

In spite of rhetoric around equality and win-win mutualism (see the previous chapter), China-Kenya trade is heavily skewed in favor of China, partly because of the type of goods being exchanged by the two countries. For example, Kenya commodity exports are mainly agricultural products, while Chinese exports to Kenya are manufactured goods. In 2015, Kenya imported US$5.9 billion worth of Chinese goods, of which US$4 billion was railway steel and other construction equipment. Kenya exported only US $99 million worth of goods to China. Beijing must "begin . . . to appreciate that, if their win-win strategy is going to work, it must mean that, just as Africa opens up to China, China must also open up to Africa" (Pilling and Klasa 2017). Without a fair and equitable balance in trade, a long-term equal friendship so critical to China-Africa is doomed.

Attempts to improve the trade imbalance have begun in the form of financial subsidies to Chinese companies to facilitate importation of Kenyan coffee, tea, and flowers. Trade fairs in China promote awareness of Kenyan products to the Chinese market. Kenyan exporters and companies get preferential treatment in the form of free exhibition spaces at trade fairs in China (Odhiambo 2011). At the same time, the number of Kenyans commuting between Kenya and China for business opportunities is increasing. Companies such as the China Information and Culture Communication Limited (CICCK) based in Nairobi, regularly flies Kenyans to Guangzhou for business tours that seek to link them with producers of goods. The company assists business people with the logistics of travel and goods transportation (Mutegi 2011). A round trip ticket per person costs US$1,400 including an 8 day stay in a three-star hotel with breakfast. On the other hand, as more Chinese nationals invest in Kenya, and their companies compete for Kenya's lucrative market, businesses that cater to Chinese interests are emerging. For example, the Chinese real estate firm Avic International is constructing a US$960 million complex in Nairobi to house its Africa headquarters. The complex includes a 43-floor office block and four apartment blocks (Wasuna 2015). In June 2017, Kenya hosted the third edition of China Week which attracted 450 exhibitors representing industries in building, construction, lighting, consumer electronics, auto parts, furniture, textiles, stationary and jewelry (Xinhua 2017). A delegation representing 40 Chinese companies from Shenzhen came to Nairobi to meet local investors to discuss investment opportunities in the energy, trade, finance, and agriculture sectors. The Chinese delegation, comprised of entrepreneurs from various sectors was led by Lu Pengqi, the vice chairman of China Council for the Promotion of International Trade, and Chen Biao, the deputy mayor of Shenzhen municipal government (Xinhua 2017).

## THE CHINESE ARE COMING, LEARN MANDARIN QUICKLY

Compared to Europe, the cultural and linguistic divide between China and Africa is wide, yet Chinese interactions with the east African coast is nearly 1,200 years old (see chapters 10, 11, and 12, this volume). These millennial old contacts were sporadic and of a noncolonial nature and so Mandarin, a language spoken by more than a billion people, never spread outside East Asia in the way English or French did. What factors have enabled the Chinese influence to spread so fast in Africa, without a common language and culture? How do people communicate?

Despite the growing number of Chinese nationals living and working in Kenya, now estimated at 40,000, cultural and linguistic barriers continue to pose major obstacles and to produce tensions (Kelly 2016). Chinese language classes are being taught at Kenyan colleges and universities with instructors' salaries subsidized by the Chinese government. In 2005, the first Confucius Institute in Africa was established at the University of Nairobi. Since then three other Confucius Institutes started in Kenyan public universities, giving Kenya and South Africa the highest number of such institutes on the African continent (ACRP 2013). Confucius Institutes are not-for-profit schools funded by the Chinese government to promote Chinese mandarin language and culture. They are attached to universities as independent departments awarding certificates, diplomas and degrees in Chinese language studies (Xinhua[5] 2015).

Kenyans are keen to learn Chinese language and culture because of the growing influence of the world's most populous country. One Kenyan student interviewed stated, "China is taking over the whole of Africa in investments and infrastructure development. It is better to learn the Chinese language and their culture because they are taking over everything." Another student adds, "Nowadays the Chinese are many in Kenya, if you know how to communicate with them, then it will be easier to interact. If we understand them better, we can do much more." Enrollment in Chinese language and culture courses is high. In line with its global strategy, China aims to have at least 1,000 Confucius Institutes globally by 2020. Africa currently has more than forty institutes (Penn 2014).

In addition to college students, Chinese language is being taught to younger children. For example, the Chang Rong Light Centre in Mathare, a low-income neighborhood in Nairobi where most of its residents an un- and underemployed, teaches children and young adults Chinese language and culture (Kelly 2016). Other initiatives include developing a research center for population studies in Kenya which teaches population data management (Mutambo 2017).

The center for population studies is part of a series of collaborations between Kenyan and Chinese research institutes in higher education and research. Grants for training and infrastructure cover all levels of education, from primary, technical courses, professional training and higher education. For example, Mcedo Beijing School in Mathare received donations from the Chinese Embassy to renovate classes and increase the enrollment capacity of the pupils; furthermore, the Communication Construction Company (CCCC) together with the Kenyan government sponsored sixty high school graduates to study at Chinese universities to develop skills in railways construction.

Huawei, in conjunction with the Kenyan government, selects outstanding ICT college students for professional training at its headquarters, where they learn cutting edge technical knowledge and hands-on understanding of the industry (Makori 2017).

China Road and Bridge Cooperation (CRBC), the builders of the Standard Gauge Railway (SGR) in 2017 offered full scholarships to thirty-five Kenyan students for bachelor's degree railway engineering courses at Beijing Jiaotong University in China for a period of four years. The program aims to sponsor up to 100 Kenyan high school graduates to the course (Mutethya 2017). In August 2017, 150 Kenyan students left for China to pursue various degree programs at all levels (Mueni 2017).

The Chinese Government's Kenyan scholarship program began 1982 and its quota doubled in 2011. About 200 academic scholarships are offered each year, in addition to more than 500 training opportunities to study in China in various disciplines for PhD, Masters and undergraduate degrees at reputable universities (Nyambura 2016). The Chinese Ambassador to Kenya Liu Xianfa said that Beijing has so far provided about 1,000 government scholarships to Kenyan students in a bid to upgrade their skills and enhance their ability to survive in a fiercely competitive job market.

The number of hotels and restaurants owned and run by the Chinese have also increased. There are supermarkets that mainly cater for Chinese clientele. Supermarket chains such as Nakumatt have introduced Chinese foodstuffs on their shelves, and local farmers are growing Chinese vegetables such as bok choy (Morangi and Liqiang 2015). The number of Chinese visitors to Kenya is rapidly increasing. The Kenya Tourist Board (KTB) has stepped up efforts to market Kenya in China. Available statistics show that the number of Chinese tourists has been steadily increasing for the last eight years, and is projected to reach 100,000 in 2017, up from 69,000 in 2016. (www.ktb.co.ke).

China is now the second largest tourist destination for Kenya in Asia after India (Table 12.1). Kenya is looking to Asia to boost falling tourism numbers

Table 12.1  The Number of Chinese Tourists Visiting Kenya Has Been Rising Steadily Since 2009

| Year | Tourists |
| --- | --- |
| 2016 | 47857 |
| 2015 | 29774 |
| 2014 | 33199 |
| 2013 | 37062 |
| 2012 | 41303 |
| 2011 | 37432 |
| 2010 | 28479 |
| 2009 | 20292 |

caused by terrorism attacks, and subsequent travel advisories by the European Union and the United States which caused sharp decreases in tourists from Europe and the Americas. Increased marketing boosted by Chinese television (CCTV) airing Kenya's attractions has paid off (Watila 2014; Siwei 2017).

## SOFT POWER AND DIPLOMATIC POWER

China's interests in Africa are not confined to infrastructure and construction. There are fifty-two diplomatic missions in Africa, compared to forty-nine for the United States. China is a member of the UN Security Council and has deployed more than 2,000 peacekeeping troops in Congo, Liberia, Mali, Sudan, and South Sudan (Pilling 2017). China has also provided US$16.2 million in grants for humanitarian support for repatriation of Somali refugees from Dadaab. China gave The United Nations World Food Program (WFP) US$5 million to buy 9,000 tons of cereals for 420,000 refugees in Dadaab and Kakuma camps for about four months. The Chinese government has also provided US$120 million for the construction of a new Confucius Institute at the University of Nairobi and provided a grant in the amount of US$30.5 million for the rehabilitation of Moi Sports Centre Kasarani (Xinhua 2017).

## WHAT DOES CHINA HAVE TO GAIN?

A study by the John L Thornton Institute found that China contributes about one-sixth of all lending to Africa (Pilling 2017). Africa's abundant natural resources in the form of oil from Angola, Nigeria, and Sudan; copper from Zambia and the Democratic Republic of Congo; and uranium from Namibia are of major import to the sustenance of the resource hungry Chinese economy. Congo has the world's largest reserves of cobalt, which is used in the production of electric car batteries. State-owned Chinese companies have invested multibillion-dollar stakes in Congolese mines. Across the continent Chinese companies and businessmen have gained a reputation for raw material extraction—from timber, oil, gold, or illegal ivory (van de looy 2006, 41). All these minerals and raw materials are necessary to feed China's industries. Many of the finished products are then exported to other countries, including Africa, whose market is rapidly growing in tandem with its increased demands for infrastructure and population. Chinese manufacturers and construction companies seek markets for their products in Africa—especially for products that would not normally be exported to the West—in part because of a perception that Africans (and their governments) can be induced to accept substandard products that are specifically manufactured for their markets (van de Looy 2006, Alden 2005). Finally, Chinese loans for infrastructure projects are often contingent on a Chinese company being contracted to complete those projects thus ensuring employment for Chinese surplus labor (Alden 2005). It is a case of the Chinese looking after their own money and kind.

Howard French in his book *China's Second Continent: How a Million Migrants are building a new Empire in Africa*, hypothesizes that Africa is an opportunity to experiment in a low-risk environment, a workshop of ideas that have a much bigger scale and strategic significance (Kleven 2015). There are signs that Africa is becoming a trial ground of policies for China's envisaged future global role. For example, early in 2015, Beijing sent its first ever contingent of troops to South Sudan as part of a U.N. mission and assumed the role of mediator between the two warring sides. It has also been interested in a military base in Djibouti. These military interventions might be the beginning of China's re-evaluation of its traditional strategy of non-interference (Alden 2005). Thus, Africa is a promising vehicle for Chinese geopolitical influence. Having fifty-four friendly nations on the second largest continent with more than a billion potential customers is important for China (Kleven 2015).

## WHY HAS AFRICA TURNED TO CHINA?

The West has long viewed Africa as a place without history where little innovation occurred, as a region inhabited by people without history (Wolf 1990). In contemporary times, Africa is viewed as an epicenter of political instability and terrorism and a source of migrants. The European Union and the U.S. governments have sought to restrict the movement of Africans in their countries (Pilling 2017). Where Europeans and Americans have seen Africa as a lost cause (Pilling 2017), China has seen opportunity and strategically developed policies of embracing Africa. China's official policy of noninterference in internal affairs of other nations have made it an attractive partner to African leaders fed up with lectures from former colonial powers about human rights or democracy (Alden 2005).

The critics of China-Africa assistance programs have pointed out that Chinese loans are unfavorable to African countries, yet African governments still consider the terms "favorable" as their financial needs exceeds the limits of African Development Bank or World Bank loans. Africans are cognizant of the fact that while their engagement with China has risks, it brings tangible benefits. More importantly, it brings a choice welcome for African governments that have, for decades, been locked in often unproductive relationships with European and American donor nations who have brought billions of dollars in aid often tied to significant and detrimental social changes such as structural adjustment requirements (Alden 2005).

The relationship between China and Djibouti is an excellent example of China-Africa friendship. A decade ago, it would have seemed improbable for tiny Djibouti to feature high on Beijing's security agenda. Since becoming president in 1999, Omar Guelleh had mostly relied on aid from the United States and France, but after being criticized in the U.S. Congress for his human rights record, kleptocratic rule, and intentions to run for a fourth presidential term, Guelleh turned to China which offered financial assistance; in turn, Djibouti allowed China to build the first military base on continental Africa. Djibouti's former ally, the United States now fears possible restrictions on their access to the region, which will have repercussions on their activities to combat terrorism in the Middle East and Northeast Africa (Kleven 2015).

The China-Africa relationship is strategic as well as opportunistic. Uwe Wissenbach from the China Africa Research Initiative (CARI), has pointed out that rather than Beijing carving up the world, there is now a scramble for Chinese state funds by African governments (Pilling 2017). African governments need money to develop infrastructure, and this is the easiest way to do it. The real danger lies in the amounts of money already owed to China and in the ramifications of nonpayment of these debts for Africa's future. Underlying these large-scale multimillion-dollar projects is the opportunity for illicit gain for both the perennially corrupt political elite and for Chinese contractors who may funnel money outside (Campbell 2008, Alden 2005).

## KENYAN PERSPECTIVES ABOUT THE CHINESE?

For a long time, Kenyans have perceived Chinese products to be of inferior quality. Before the influx of Chinese nationals on mega-infrastructure projects, most of these products consisted of small household items and children's toys. When imports of larger machines and equipment began coming in, many Kenyans were skeptical and kept referring to the country of origin whenever new things were bought. Thus, it is no surprise that perception spread to cover projects where the Chinese were concerned. Part of this attitude toward the Chinese was partly due to the belief that China is a poor country, and therefore did not have the expertise to build complex equipment. The very first major taste of Chinese capability was the construction of Kasarani Sports complex in 1987. But it did little to change people's opinions. Later large-scale projects, including the construction of the Nairobi-Mombasa Highway, began to change perceptions.

However, several publicized incidents have reversed the trend and placed the quality of Chinese workmanship into question. In the 2017 long rains

Figure 12.1 How Did a $ 12 Million Chinese Built Bridge in Kenya Collapse Days after Been Officially Inaugurated? Photo Credit: Angela Kabiru.

season, sections of the Standard Gauge Railway (SGR) protection slope were washed away by flood waters. Although engineers tried to dispel fears of poor workmanship this incident ignited fierce debate (Muasya 2016). How could a project that was already costing much more than it should have not withstand floods caused by normal long rains? A second example is that in 2017, a bridge constructed across the River Nzoia in western Kenya at a cost of US$11.5 million collapsed a few days after it was commissioned by President Uhuru Kenyatta. No reason was given for the collapse (Kuo 2017; Linder 2017; see figure 12.1).

These highly publicized engineering disasters have reignited the question in many people's mind; why does the projects cost so much if the workmanship is of inferior quality? One of the conditions of Chinese funding is that a Chinese company is contracted to complete a particular project. That has a bearing on the quality of the end project. The increasingly skeptical Kenyan public points to the Thika Highway in Nairobi that was completed with much fanfare in 2012 but is already showing signs of intensive wear. Thus, the large majority of Kenyans are unconvinced that Chinese technology is superior to Kenyan work.

Chinese nationals have on several occasions been accused of being racist and treating Africans badly. For example, in 2015, a Chinese restaurant in Nairobi was ordered shut down after it was accused of denying entry to Africans after 5 pm. Chongquing Chinese Restaurant only allowed entry to Africans accompanied by Chinese, European, or Indian patrons, claiming they were taking measures to avoid an attack by Al Shabaab terrorists

(Shankar 2015). The Chinese Embassy in Nairobi reprimanded the owner of the restaurant pointing out that the establishment did not have any right to have selective admission of certain persons and denial of admissions to others (Kangethe 2015). It emerged that the owner did not have a valid liquor license and had not complied with the public health requirements. The manager was also charged with not having a work permit to work inside the country. This seems to be a widespread problem as many Chinese may not have valid work permits (New Vision 2015).

The Chinese have taken advantage of the corrupt executive and civil service in Kenya to cut corners. It is alleged that they routinely take and give bribes and kickbacks and thus gain unfair advantage in negotiating for contracts of large-scale projects. At the same time, they bribe low-level officers to get illegal residence and work permits to set up business after their official visas expire. It is now common knowledge in Kenya that the cost of the Standard Gauge Railway (SGR) railway was inflated to accommodate kickbacks (Michira 2017). Accusations of discriminatory practices in hiring Kenyans and allocation of jobs and salaries at SGR and stealing local jobs from Kenyans have been made. For example, While Kenyan train drivers earn a basic salary of Sh30,000, Chinese cleaners earn two to three times more. By comparison, Kenyan cleaners only earn between Sh15,000 and Sh18,000 (Mwangi 2015). Kenyans see the employment of Chinese workers as sweepers as an act of betrayal by the government that has failed to negotiate labor policies that protect local jobs. The hiring of more Chinese than Kenyans and offer of better terms of employment fits in with the accusation of Chinese racism. Kenyans hired by the SGR passenger train operator are said to be working without contracts, leaving them without legal protection and exposing the service to industrial action. The ticketing operators and coach attendants who were employed in October 2016 were initially offered six-month probation terms that had since expired in April 2017, but by the end of July 2017 had still not been offered permanent employment contracts (Otieno 2017). At the SGR staff restaurant, the Chinese do not share tables with Kenyan crew, and neither do they share staff vans on their way to and from work (Wafula 2018)

Other Chinese in the country now engage in all sorts of work to earn them a living. They are engaged in street side hawking, they run shops stocked with Chinese delicacies and some work as tour guides. In downtown Nairobi, Chinese sell household items. Most of the Chinese living in Kenya initially came on large infrastructure projects such as SGR, or the planned Lamu Coal power plant. According to Amu Power, the owners of the coal plant, 40 percent of about 3,500 workers needed for construction will be foreign, mostly Chinese. In their defense, Chinese companies point out that most of these foreign workers will eventually be replaced by local staff, mainly for reasons of saving costs, since a work permit costs up to $4,500 annually (Otieno 2017).

## GROWING UNEASE AS CHINESE INFLUENCE RISES

A 2016 Afrobarometer survey of thirty-six African countries found that 63 percent of Africans found China's influence "somewhat" or "very" positive. The United States was thought to provide the best development model for Africa, followed by China (Strauss 2013, PRC 2013). Africans' view of China may still be positive, but there is increasing evidence of a widening fissure. Africans welcome the infrastructure but insist their governments should not be taken for a ride by overpaying, accepting shoddy work or allowing Chinese companies to use all their own labor and materials (Pilling 2017). Contrary to a belief that Africans are complacent when it comes to corruption, Africans resent it when corrupt governments inflate the price of projects to make space for kickbacks. Chinese companies often come under scrutiny that they are international land grabbers. Many Africans are suspicious of what they see as a neocolonial land grab, in which companies acting as proxies for the Chinese state extract minerals in return for infrastructure and finance that will saddle governments with large debts (Pilling 2017). China's interest in Africa is also thought to be an effort to recreate colonial trading patterns by flooding the continent with manufactured goods while extracting raw materials and gobbling up construction contracts (Strauss 2013; Manero 2017). The behavior of Chinese actors in Africa, in common with those from the west, has often fallen short of international standards. There have been legitimate complaints about Chinese companies employing few locals, mistreating those it has and paying scant regard to the environment.

Among local communities, there is growing skepticism about the motivation for Chinese investment in educational programs in low-income areas of Nairobi. Critics believe that the initiative to teach Chinese in Nairobi's slum areas is a front for business. They point out that as these lessons to children in the slums have received wide publicity, the Chinese are quietly setting up businesses in these slums. The local residents are increasingly suspicious of their motives (Kelly 2016).

Arting Luo from the Sino-Africa Centre of Excellence, thinks that this is an unjust representation of Chinese intentions. Lucy Liu from China House, a not-for-profit organization that seeks to promote engagement between Chinese companies and Kenyan communities, acknowledges that there is a lot of misperception about Chinese business interests. This is mainly caused by linguistic barriers which are proving to be a major obstacle. The lack of communication between the Chinese and Kenyans has spawned several myths about Chinese behavior. Most of the Chinese construction workers brought in to work on infrastructural projects keep much to themselves and most hardly speak a word of English. Thus, was born the myth that companies recruited prisoners to work on government projects, due to the many hours they put in at work, and the fact that they do not speak English. Apparently, there have been similar claims in Benin and Zambia, something the Chinese authorities deny (Brautigam 2010). There are also reports of dogs disappearing form neighborhoods close to Chinese living quarters. Whether this is true or not, it is known that dog meat is a delicacy in China. If this initially started off as a fabrication, the allegation that the Chinese in Kenya have been feeding on dog meat was substantiated when dog legs were found hanging from beams in the kitchen of the restaurant that restricted Africans' entry after 5 pm. It seems this was one of the motives for keeping Africans out, the other is its use as a brothel. The Nairobi senior public health officer said that his officers did not inspect the dogs allegedly served at the Chinese Restaurant, and that dog meat consumption is banned in Kenya. In this regard, Kenyan authorities do not inspect dog meat nor approve slaughtering of dogs (Ndunda 2015; The Star 2015).

With well over 40,000 Chinese people now living and working in Kenya, cultural and linguistic barriers will remain major obstacles if no steps are taken to remedy the situation. Currently, not many Chinese speak English, let alone Kiswahili. Communicating requires an interpreter or by resorting to sign language. Unless the Chinese make more effort at interacting with Africans, these myths will continue to grow. Better communication and interactions will help bridge the gap between the two cultures, as every community sees the other from their own perspective.

Chinese companies like to be seen to be transferring skills. Huawei, which earns 15 percent of its global revenue in Africa, trains 12,000 students in telecoms a year at centers in Angola, Congo, Egypt, Kenya, Morocco, Nigeria, and South Africa. According to Johns Hopkins researchers, 80 percent of workers on Chinese projects are African, even if many are in low-skilled jobs such as trench-digging (Pilling 2017). The availability of so much Chinese money is not accidental, but a well-orchestrated strategy to revamp the Chinese economy. Analysts also view it a geopolitical strategy, with China getting more actively involved in world affairs.

## OTHER NEGATIVE ASPECTS: POACHING

China's economic boom is believed to be driving elephant poaching in Africa and Asia. Statistics show that the number of ivory items on sale in Southern China has more than doubled since 2004, with most being traded on the black market. There is also a dramatic rise in rhino poaching in many parts of Africa, and thefts of rhino horns from European museums and auction houses (Neale and Burton 2011). Chinese workers building tarmac roads in northern

Kenya are believed to be behind the sharp rise in elephant poaching in the area, leading to the deaths of dozens of animals. According to the Kenya Wildlife Service (KWS), there may be a link between the workers' arrival and the increase in poaching. In the first eight months of 2008, fifty-seven elephant carcasses were found across Kenya with their tusks pulled out, a 15 percent increase to the 2007 total and the third annual increase in a row. More than half of these elephants have been killed in areas where Chinese construction crews were working (Pflanz 2008).

There are no elephants in China, but the demand for ivory products is very high. In 2014, a court in Kenya fined a Chinese man, Tang Yong Jian 20m shillings (£140,000; $230,000) or seven years in prison for possessing an ivory tusk weighing 3.4 kg (7.5 pounds), under tough new antipoaching laws. He was arrested at the Jomo Kenyatta International Airport (BBC 2014). In neighboring Tanzania, a court sentenced two Chinese men to thirty years in prison each after they were found guilty of illegally possessing 706 elephant tusks, the equivalent of 226 elephants. The two men are said to have entered the country in 2010 under the pretense of being garlic and marine product importers; they were arrested in 2013 with the tusks hidden in garlic bags (MacDonald 2016).

China is the world's largest market for ivory with up to five tons of ivory permitted to be sold every year. However, the demand for ivory in China exceeds this amount at around 100 tons annually, and it has proven impossible to separate the limited amount of legal ivory from the black-market supply available on the market (Kelly 2016). Ivory researchers have since called for China to tighten its enforcement of ivory trading regulations, to reduce the number of elephants being killed illegally. If this is not done, demand for ivory products will remain high with considerable amounts still in circulation. Activists have spent many years lobbying Chinese officials to ban all ivory sales. The Chinese government finally announced that after 2017, it will no longer be legal to sell or trade ivory. Highly anticipated, this announcement will hopefully help to save what's left of Africa's elephant population. According to experts however, it is not practical to believe that "when the buying stops, the killing can too." With huge demand and so much stock still in circulation, the trade will most likely go underground and flourish on the black market as illegal ivory. Widespread corruption and ineffective regulation framework may allow highly organized international crime syndicates to continue with the trade. Neighboring countries such as Vietnam may also be used to smuggle ivory into China (Kelly 2016). While China's ban alone may not be enough to stop the killing, there have been efforts to persuade the Chinese working in Kenya not to get involved in poaching. How this pans out is yet to be realized (Kelly 2016).

## The Donkey

Elephants are not the only animals in danger. Across the continent, the price of donkey skins has rapidly increased in the last five years, fueled by demand in China. Donkeys are used to carry and transport goods, mainly by pastoralist communities, but also by water vendors to ferry water in places without water piping. This great demand for donkey skin is fueled by ejiao, a 2,500-year-old traditional Chinese remedy prepared with gelatin from the animals' skins. Ejiao is used for the treatment of anemia, dementia, infertility, respiratory problems, insomnia, and excessive menstrual bleeding, as a boost for libido, sweets, liqueurs, and as an ingredient in beauty products. About 250 g of the gel can sell for up to $350 or higher (Gardner 2017; de Greef 2017). Up to 4 million skins are used for ejiao each year, and the high cost of the gelatin reflects a demand that is higher than supply. Donkey meat is also a delicacy.

Increased demand for imported donkeys is because of a massive decrease in China's donkey population brought about by industrialization. The country is in the grip of a massive donkey shortage and local animals are being stolen from farmers. Demand for ejiao has doubled since 2010, reaching nearly 15 million pounds a year in 2015. In the past, it was only affordable by royalty, because one donkey yields 2.2 pounds of the substance. One block made in 2007 was valued at $47 a gram, making it more expensive than gold (Gardner 2017). With this high demand, it is not surprising that informal supply chains are wreaking havoc on rural economies that depend on donkeys for transport. Across Africa, syndicates have begun raiding farms in order to steal donkeys and to smuggle the skins to Chinese middlemen, many of whom also deal in other illegal wildlife products. Agents travel around the farms, looking for willing sellers while ignoring export bans and other regulations such as when and how the animals can be slaughtered. Reports indicate that before the boom, donkeys cost as little as $8 per head. Now they attract a price of more than $150 each, generating tens of millions of dollars each year (de Greef 2017).

Chinese importers began asking about donkeys in South Africa in 2014, a total of seven companies each looking for 10,000 skins. It was certainly a big opportunity for rural development, and for farmers to earn income. But because it was a new thing, and there were no frameworks to support a legal trade, traders and middlemen resorted to illegal practices, including the sale and slaughter of stolen donkeys. The sudden increase in hide prices made it prohibitively expensive for rural farmers who rely on donkeys to buy new ones. Reports indicate that in Niger, for instance, average donkey prices rose from $34 to $145 in less than five years. In 2016, 80,000 donkey skins were shipped out in just nine months. In September 2016, Niger banned all donkey exports. In 2017, Uganda joined the list of countries that have banned the export of their donkeys to China, just like Senegal, Mali, Botswana, Tanzania, and Burkina Faso in the recent past. The big fear was that the high demand would make the supply unsustainable (de Greef 2017).

In Kenya, the average price of an adult donkey has gone up by about 225 percent in the six months since February 2017, from US$40 to the current price of US$130. However, instead of banning exports, Kenya has allowed the Chinese to set up donkey slaughterhouses in areas with high donkey populations, such as Nakuru and Baringo (Kenyan News 2017, Chacha 2017). Kenya's first donkey slaughter house is doing brisk business since it opened in 2016. The Goldox abattoir, owned by Lu Donglin, located at Mogotio in Baringo County, reportedly receives between 400 and 600 donkeys daily, and slaughters 300 on average (Chacha 2017). Suppliers source donkeys from Tanzania, Turkana, Trans Mara, and Maralal and sell each at $77. However, Kenyan law does not allow local consumption of the donkey meat, and is therefore only for export (Kenyan News 2017). The downside to this trade is that although it may create jobs, generate revenue for farmers, and encourage commercial donkey breeding, it is believed to attract other wildlife traffickers out to export other animal products disguised as donkey products (de Greef 2017). A UK-based charity, The Donkey Sanctuary, has pointed out that demand for donkey hide is fast outstripping supply; 1.8 million donkey hides are traded every year, while global demand is estimated at between 4 and 10 million skins (Chacha 2017).

China now has between 3 and 5 million donkeys, from 11 million thirty years ago. But China is consuming them faster than they can be replaced. Even with intensive breeding programs, donkeys do not breed fast, and usually have one foal every two years. This is the reason there are only 44 million donkeys worldwide. According to Donkey Sanctuary, ejiao trade is unsustainable in its current form, and donkeys are simply facing extinction (de Greef 2017[1]). Back in Africa, the natural shortage of donkeys has left rural communities vulnerable to theft, poaching, and surging prices. If the trade can be regulated and monitored, and commercial breeders are able to meet demand, this may be the most viable export product to the Chinese market (Gardner 2017).

## THE INTERTWINED RELATIONS OF KENYA AND CHINA

In 2015, Chinese President Xi Jinping announced that his country had put side a massive budget of US$15 billion for what he termed the world's most ambitious infrastructure project, the Belt and Road Initiative (BRI), which includes the Silk Road Economic Belt and the 21st Century Maritime Silk

Road (MSR). In a ceremony attended by twenty-nine Heads of State and Government in June 2017, President Xi said besides the Sh15 trillion, China had also set aside US$1 billion for a South-South Cooperation fund and another US$1 billion for cooperation projects in countries on the new Silk Road (PSCU 2016).

The Silk Road Economic Belt is a land route starting in western China going through Central Asia and on to the Middle East, while the twenty-first century MSR is a maritime route that goes around Southeast Asia, the Persian Gulf, and the Horn of Africa. The entire initiative includes more than two-thirds of the world population, more than one-third of global economic output, and could involve Chinese investments totaling up to $4 trillion (Parameswaran 2017). Kenya is part of the twenty-first century MSR. The twenty-first century MSR begins in Fujian province, will pass through Guangdong, Guangxi, and Hainan before heading south to the Malacca Strait. From Kuala Lumpur, it heads to Kolkata and Colombo, then crosses the Indian Ocean to Nairobi. From Nairobi, it heads north around the Horn of Africa, through the Red Sea into the Mediterranean, stopping in Athens before meeting the land-based Silk Road in Venice (Parameswaran 2017).

The Belt and Road initiative is also seen as a political strategy aimed at controlling several naval bases in Asia and the East African coast. The Chinese government has already signed a ten-year agreement with Djibouti to set up a naval base to serve as a logistics hub for the People's Liberation Army-Navy (PLA-N) ships engaged in anti-piracy operations off the coast of Yemen. It is interesting to note that the base will be located in the Obock region where an American outpost was earlier evicted, and that it would cost $100 million a year to run (Pilling 2017). The base offers China strategic access to the Red Sea and Indian Ocean (Manero 2017).

The Chinese, however, insist that the initiative is also designed to meet other economic rather than geopolitical objectives. China's leaders hope it will help ease oversupply of labor at home while spurring growth in its underdeveloped border regions. Boosting economic growth is critical to the survival of the Chinese Communist Party (CCP). Internationally, the initiative is also a means for Beijing to advance diplomatic and strategic objectives to consolidate China's position in Eurasia. The greatest fear is that this will ultimately undermine Washington's control of these affairs (Parameswaran 2017).

Chinese scholars claim that the initiative is part of China's "opening up" strategy. Since China is facing challenges of overproduction and overcapacity, especially in the steel and construction industries, this initiative aims to create more demand overseas, and thus help in addressing China's domestic economic problems. So this could be a way for China to reform economically; the initiative is expected to promote development initiatives in the less-developed regions of China to narrow income gaps in the population.

The initiative could also be an excellent overseas investment opportunity for the Chinese private sector (Parameswaran 2017).

The Belt and Road initiative features five major areas of cooperation—policy communication, road connectivity, unimpeded trade, money circulation, and cultural understanding. It will directly impact 4.4 billion people, around 63 percent of the world's population, and deal with an economic aggregate of $21 trillion which is 29 percent of the global volume. It also aims to improve the Chinese geostrategic position in the world. This ambitious initiative will receive funding from seven capital pools, among them, the Silk Road Fund, the AIIB, BRICS Bank, and the SCO Development Bank which are likely to play major roles (Parameswaran 2017).

The China-Africa Development Fund (CAD) is a Chinese private equity fund wholly funded by the Chinese government policy bank, China Development Bank. The CAD Fund is one of the eight measures for Sino-African relations announced at the Beijing summit of the Forum on China-Africa Cooperation (FOCAC) by President Hu Jintao in November 2006. It was subsequently established in June 2007 with an initial funding of US$1 billion by the China Development Bank, projected to grow to US$5 billion in the future.

The aim of the fund is to stimulate investment in Africa by Chinese companies in power generation, transportation infrastructure, natural resources, manufacturing, and other sectors. The fund's primary purpose is therefore to identify potential investment opportunities and to connect African projects to Chinese investors. It further aims to bridge the finance gap for realization of these projects and to offer specific managerial and financial advice. By the end of 2010, the fund had invested in thirty projects in Africa worth around US$800 million. In 2009 alone, the fund invested US$140 million of China's total US$1.3 billion invested in Africa that year, focusing primarily on industrial development (Parameswaran 2017). With so much money at their disposal, African governments will continue to look to China to develop their infrastructure.

## THE FUTURE OF CHINA-AFRICA RELATIONSHIPS

The number of Chinese nationals returning to China from Africa has reportedly increased mainly due to a fall in commodity prices in individual countries' economies. According to World Bank statistics, sub-Saharan Africa grew at 1.5 percent in 2016, its slowest in two decades, while some countries went into recession. The Chinese population in Africa, most of them small-scale entrepreneurs, was about 1 million in 2013. For example, 150,000 Chinese are estimated to have left oil-rich Angola in the past four years alone. All over Africa, the number of contract workers serving Chinese state-owned enterprises fell by 32,000 last year to 233,000, according to the China International Contractors Association. The decline in the number of migrants reflects a slowing down in trade and investment between China and Africa which reached more than US$200 billion in 2015 but now stands at US$150 billion.

In East Africa, however, there has been an increase in Chinese nationals due to the huge projects being undertaken under the China Belt and Road infrastructure initiative in manufacturing and green field investments (Hancock 2017). Judging from the number of projects being funded and constructed by the Chinese in Kenya alone, this number is likely to increase. "I think the Chinese know what they want. It is the Africans who don't know what they want . . . China wants to control. China wants to be a world power," says PLO Lumumba, director of the Kenya School of Law. He adds that African governments are taking on so much Chinese debt that they will be in economic and political dependence to Beijing. "It's the same old story: now you have the Chinese conquering Africa, but what is Africa getting out of it?" (Pilling 2017).

Confucius institutes play a key role in the Chinese government's foreign policy as it seeks a bigger footprint in Africa. It has already had relative success in wielding soft power on the continent through no-strings funding for development programs and infrastructure, unlike that of western countries. While the Chinese are using soft power to increase their influence in Africa, there's nothing subtle about their marketing of the Chinese language and culture (Penn 2014). Jeffrey Sachs, director of the Earth Institute at Columbia University, calls China's newfound enthusiasm "the most important single development for Africa in this generation." Beijing, he says, can help transform the continent. "They know how to build big projects," he says, referring to the dams, ports, airports, railways, telecommunications networks, and roads that Chinese groups are building in even the most obscure corners of the continent. "They know how to get them done." (Pilling 2017).

## CONCLUSION

China has an active and growing presence in almost all African countries, but there is currently no dominant framework or narrative for conceptualizing engagements between China and Africa in the twenty-first century (Strauss 2013). As Campbell (2008) points out, two things have endeared the Chinese leadership to Third World leaders: challenging the Bretton Woods institutions and raising the question of reparations. There are now broadening and deepening relations in diverse sectors as mining, migration, public diplomacy, investment, agriculture, infrastructural projects, and manufacturing. When compared to Western Europe and the United States five factors distinguish the relationship between Africa with China. First, China was never a participant in the transatlantic slave trade. Second, there is no tradition of Chinese colonialism, genocide, and occupation in Africa. Third, China embraced the African liberation process with diplomatic, political, material, and military support. Fourth, both China and the AU formed the part of the South-South bloc in the WTO. Fifth, China had nothing to do with the structural adjustment policies that impoverished Africa over the past thirty years. These factors, he points out, must be borne in mind when analyzing the medium- and long-term implications of the Chinese engagement with Africa (see also Xinfeng, this volume).

Sino-African trade and bilateral relations have great implications for Africa. The continent is currently China's third biggest trading partner, after the United States and France. China has provided African states with more choice and less dependence on the West. Increasing oil production and export to China is boosting the revenue of African states (van de Looy 2006). The international community's view of Chinese investment in Africa is not wholly positive. Today, Chinese construction firms regularly outbid their western corporations in large infrastructural projects in Africa. Western critics believe that this success is due to corruption and the fact that China attaches no conditions to their loans and grants, a process which undermines local efforts at increasing transparency and good governance. Bretton institutions, the IMF, and the World Bank no longer control the terms of aid to the Global South (Strauss 2013; van de Looy 2006).

Within Africa itself, cynicism towards Chinese intentions is emerging. There is a growing unease concerning China's military assistance. For example, China provided Mozambique's army with uniforms, training and some light equipment in the late 1970s, it sold fighter jets to the government of Zimbabwe, sent helicopters to Angola and Mali, light arms to Namibia and Sierra Leone and, during the Ethiopian–Eritrean war, it reportedly sold multibillion dollar worth of arms to both sides of the conflict, and provided various arms to the Democratic Republic of the Congo during the war with Rwanda. China has been the largest arms supplier and supporter of the Sudanese government in their war with the South Sudan. China's record of providing diplomatic and economic support and arms shipments to boost African countries notorious for human-rights violations is unsettling (Alden 2005).

In terms of the economic balance, China is a clear winner. Production costs in manufacturing are lower in China (Alden 2005). Chinese companies import migrant labor into Africa, which does not alleviate unemployment and underemployment in host African nations. The closure of African factories due to bankruptcies arising from competition from cheap textiles and household utensils from China has increased unemployment and poverty in affected regions, especially Mozambique and Botswana (Alden 2005; van de Looy 2006).

China's top priority is to meet the current demands of fuel for her industries. Its balance of trade in African oil has increased exponentially. Ironically, Africa's total trade with China amounts to only 2 percent of its international trade (van de Looy 2006). Is China only driven by its own interests? Alden (2005) argues that China's diplomacy toward Africa is aimed at fostering mutual economic interests and maintaining sovereign protection against the influence of the West. We will have to find proper ways to engage the continent, including using approaches that go beyond satisfying African elites interests. Without these, China risks becoming a superpower that befriends dictatorial regimes that violate the civil and human rights of their own peoples. Strauss (2013) cautions that China's principles of noninterference and nonconditionality have the potential to keep weak and extractive regimes in power.

China's participation in UN-sanctioned operations that promote stability by sending peacekeepers to Liberia and the DRC, donations to UN agencies that target Africa, such as the UN Trust Fund for African Development and the UN Environment Program, have been substantial. It has also given financial support to fight drought in the Horn of Africa and Darfur (Alden 2005). The Chinese must accept that policy choices and outcomes are open to criticism. In addition, "Beijing also seems to have misjudged the power of human-rights ideals and agendas to influence events in Africa as elsewhere. Africa is as complex as any other region and assumptions that have guided Chinese action there, based to a great extent on its relative material superiority over the continent, are an insufficient guide to conducting a successful foreign policy" (Alden 2005, 160).

Alden (2005) concludes that Africans should have a short-term, medium-term, and long-term view of the relations with China. In the short term, they should hasten the break with the Western imperial forces over Africa. In the medium term, they should strengthen African co-operation leading to a united government of Africa, and in the long term, Africans must guard their independence so that the new relations between Africa and China do not repeat centuries of underdevelopment and exploitation.

> Africa must be vigilant; China is seeking to diversify its holdings away from the dollar. Investment in Africa in the long run will prove to be more profitable than holding dollars. This ensures that the role of China in Africa will intensify in the short term. African peace activists will have to work with the international peace movement to ensure that the old competition of capitalism does not lead to another global war. (Alden 2005, 160)

The year 2013 marked the fiftieth anniversary of the establishment of diplomatic ties between the People's Republic of China and the Republic of Kenya (MFAPRC 2014). In 2013 China supported Kenya in its efforts to seek a proper settlement of the issue involving the trials against Kenyan leaders at the International Criminal Court (ICC), called on all parties to give positive responses to relevant appeals of Kenya and other African countries, and voted in favor of the UN Security Council draft resolution on suspending trials against Kenyan leaders at the ICC. In 2017, Kenya announced plans to model its manufacturing sector after China's Special Economic Zones (Xinhua 2017). The relationship between the two countries continues to deepen. But to what end and to what uncertain future?

## REFERENCES

ACRP. 2013. "Why Kenyan Students are Hooked on Chinese." Africa China Reporting Project, October 22 2013. http://africachinareporting.co.za/2013/10/kenya-mandarin-chinese/ Accessed June 7, 2017.

Africa News. 2017. "Business Booms for Kenya's Donkey Slaughterhouse Despite Local Ban on meat." http://www.africanews.com/2017/03/07/business-booms-for-kenya-s-donkey-slaughterhouse-despite-local-ban-on-meat//. Accessed July 25, 2017.

Africa News. 2017. "Chinese Investment in Africa Rises in First Quarter of 2017." Africa News, May 11 2017. http://www.africanews.com/2017/05/11/chinese-investment-in-africa-rises-in-first-quarter-of-2017/. Accessed June 5, 2017.

African Development Bank Group.2017. "China: Partnership Overview." https://www.afdb.org/en/topics-and-sectors/topics/partnerships/non-regional-member-countries/china/. Accessed July 4, 2017.

Alden, C. 2005. China in Africa. Survival, Vol. 47 no. 3 Autumn 2005 pp. 147–164. DOI: 10.1080/00396330500248086.

Asian Survey, Vol. 38, No. September 9, 1998, pp. 867–879.

BBC. 2014. "Chinese Ivory Smuggler Gets Record Kenyan Fine." BBC News 28 January 2014. http://www.bbc.com/news/world-africa-25925176. Accessed July 25, 2017.

Brautigam, D. 2010. "Is China Sending Prisoners to Work Overseas?" China Africa Research Institute, August 13, 2010. http://www.chinaafricarealstory.com/2010/08/is-china-sending-prisoners-to-work.html. Accessed October 15, 2017. http://allafrica.com/stories/201211130124.html 71 Accessed October 15, 2017

"China's Plan To Ban Ivory Sales Will Not Save Africa's Elephants." The China Africa Project, January 2 .2017. http://www.chinaafricaproject.com/china-africa-ivory-ban-2017-kenya-tanzania-wildlife/58 Accessed July 25, 2017.

Campbell, H .2008. "China in Africa: Challenging US Global Hegemony." *Third World Quarterly* 29(1): 89–105, DOI: 10.1080/01436590701726517.

Chacha, G. 2017. "Chinese Appetite for Donkey Meat Cause for Worry." East African Standard Online version, May 21, 2017. https://www.standardmedia.co.ke/lifestyle/article/2001240557/flawless-skin-sex-drive-push-up-china-s-craving-for-poor-donkey. Accessed July 26, 2017.

Chaturvedy, R. R. 2017. "The 21st Century Maritime Silk Road." Observer Research Foundation, February 10, 2017, http://www.orfonline.org/research/the-21st-century-maritime-silk-road/76 Accessed August 10, 2017.

Dahir, A. 2018. "China Now Owns More than 70% of Kenya's External Debt." Quartz Africa, July 10, 2018 https://qz.com/1324618/china-is-kenyas-largest-creditor-with-72-of-total-bilateral-debt/. Accessed July 20, 2018.

de Greef, K[1]. 2017. "Rush for Donkey Skins in China Draws Wildlife Traffickers." National geographic September 22, 2017. http://news.nationalgeographic.com/2017/09/wildlife-watch-donkey-skins-china-wildlife-trafficking/. Accessed July 25, 2017.

De Greef, K. 2017. "Chinese Smugglers Are Buying Up Hundreds of Thousands of Illegally Slaughtered African Donkeys." World Press May 21, 2017. https://srilankatwo.wordpress.com/2017/05/21/chinese-smugglers-are-buying-up-hundreds-of-thousands-of-illegally-slaughtered-african-donkeys/. Accessed July 26, 2017.

Gardner, H. 2017. "China Has a Donkey Shortage—and Why that Matters." USA TODAY July 17, 2017. | https://www.usatoday.com/story/news/world/2017/07/17/china-donkey-shortage/456034001/. Accessed July 25, 2017.

Hancock, T. 2017. "Chinese Return from Africa as Migrant Population Peaks." The Financial Times, August 28, 2017. https://www.ft.com/content/7106ab42–80d1–11e7-a4ce-15b2513cb3ff.

Ilado, P. 2017. "Uhuru Secures $3.59 Billion More from China to Extend SGR to Kisumu."http://www.the-star.co.ke/news/2017/05/15/uhuru-secures-359-billion-more-from-china-to-extend-sgr-to-kisumu_c1561750 The Star, May 15, 2017. Accessed May 17, 2017.

Kamau, J. 2018. "Power, Politics and Economy of the Coal-fired Plant in Lamu." Daily Nation April 10, 2018. https://www.nation.co.ke/news/Power--politics-economy-of-coal-fired-plant-in-Lamu-/1056–4379590–112cm0xz/index.html. Accessed May 20, 2018.

Kangethe, K. 2015. "Chinese Embassy Slams Restaurant over Racism." Capital News, March 26, 2015 https://www.capitalfm.co.ke/news/2015/03/chinese-embassy-slams-restaurant-over-racism/. Accessed August 12, 2017.

Kelly, N. 2016. "Teaching Mandarin: Chinese influence in Kenya's Slums" November 16, 2016 http://www.bbc.com/news/business-37679954. Accessed May 23, 2017.

Kenya Tourism Board. 2017. "International Arrivals." www.ktb.co.ke. Accessed June 05, 2017.

Kenyan News. 2017. "Donkey Prices In Kenya Skyrocket By 225% in Six Months on Strong Demand from China." Kenyan Wall Street August 30, 2017. http://kenyanwallstreet.com/donkey-prices-kenya-skyrocket-325-six-months-strong-demand-china. Accessed July 25, 2017.

Kleven, A. 2015. "Is China's Maritime Silk Road a Military Strategy?" The Diplomat, December 08, 2015 https://thediplomat.com/2015/12/is-chinas-maritime-silk-road-a-military-strategy/. Accessed August 05, 2017.

Kuo, L. 2016. "The Worst Thing About Kenya's New Power Plant Isn't that Chinese Workers are Being Brought in to Build it." Quartz Africa July 28, 2016 https://

qz.com/743461/the-worst-thing-about-kenyas-new-power-plant-isnt-that-chinese-workers-are-being-brought-in-to-build-it/. Accessed August 12, 2017.

Kuo, L. 2017. "A Chinese-built Bridge Collapsed in Kenya Two Weeks After it was Inspected by the President." Quartz Africa, https://qz.com/1015554/a-chinese-built-bridge-collapsed-in-kenya-two-weeks-after-it-was-inspected-by-the-president/. Accessed July 25, 2017.

Linder, A. 2017. "Bridge in Kenya Being Built by Chinese Company Collapses 11 Days after President's Visit." Shanghaiist News Jun 29, 2017. http://shanghaiist.com/2017/06/29/kenya-bridge-collapse.php Accessed July 25, 2017.

Lloyd Thrall, L. 2015. "China's Expanding African Relations: Implications for U.S. National RAND Corporation." http://www.jstor.org/stable/10.7249/j.ctt15zc655.8.

MacDonald, F. 2016. "Two Chinese Poachers Have Been Jailed for 30 Years After Slaughtering 226 Elephants." Science Alert March 22, 2016. https://www.sciencealert.com/two-chinese-poachers-have-been-jailed-for-30-years-for-the-slaughter-of-226-elephants. Accessed July 25, 2017.

Makori, P. 2017. "Chinese Businesses Showcase CSR Projects in Kenya." Business Today, June 22, 2017. https://businesstoday.co.ke/chinese-businesses-showcase-csr-projects-in-kenya/ . Accessed May 27, 2017.

Manero, E. 2017. "China's Investment in Africa: The New Colonialism?" Harvard Political Review, February 3, 2017. http://harvardpolitics.com/world/chinas-investment-in-africa-the-new-colonialism/. Accessed December 23 2017.

MFAPRC. 2014. "China and Kenya" Ministry of Foreign Affairs of the People's Republic of China http://www.fmprc.gov.cn/mfa_eng/wjb_663304/zzjg_663340/fzs_663828/gjlb_663832/3014_664044/

Michira, M. 2017. "SGR Train Moves 70,000 but Delays Inter-county." East African Standard, July 2 2017 https://www.standardmedia.co.ke/business/article/2001245657/sgr-train-moves-70-000-but-delays-inter-county49. Accessed August 12, 2017.

Miriri, D. 2017. "Kenya Inaugurates Chinese-built Railway Linking Port to Capital" Reuters, May 31, 2017. https://af.reuters.com/article/topNews/idAFKBN18R2OS-OZATP. Accessed June 5, 2017.

Morangi, L. and Hou Liqiang. 2015. "Growing Demand for Vegetables Follows Influx of Chinese." China Daily, October 16, 2015 http://africa.chinadaily.com.cn/weekly/2015-10/16/content_22202458.htm. Accessed June 15, 2017.

Muasya, P. 2016. "Floods Wash Away Part of Standard Gauge Railway SGR Project." East African Standard, November 21, 2016 https://www.standardmedia.co.ke/article/2000224139/floods-wash-away-part-of-standard-gauge-railway-sgr-project . Accessed July 20, 2017.

Mueni, J. 2017. "150 Kenyans Head to China on Academic Scholarships." Capital News, August 15, 2017. https://www.capitalfm.co.ke/news/2017/08/150-kenyans-head-to-china-on-academic-scholarships/ Accessed September 14, 2017.

Muraya, J. 2016. "Chinese Investments in Kenya Hit Sh663bn." Capital Business August 10, 2016 http://www.capitalfm.co.ke/business/2016/08/chinese-investments-kenya-hit-sh663bn-fm-wang-says/. Accessed May 17, 2017.

Mutambo, A. 2017. "Nairobi to Host Africa's Chinese-Built Population Centre." Daily Nation April 19, 2017. http://www.nation.co.ke/news/Nairobi-to-host-Chine

se-built-population-centre-/1056–3894658–129ybei/index.html. Accessed May 22, 2017.

Mutambo, A. 2017. "SGR to be Upgraded to Electric Railroad in Four Years." Daily Nation March 22 2017 http://www.nation.co.ke/news/SGR-to-be-upgraded-to-electric-railroad/1056–3860944–99bjol/index.html . Accessed May 17, 2017.

Mutegi, M. 2011. "Kenya-China Trade Opens Doors for Tour Consultants." Business Daily May 27, 2011 http://www.businessdailyafrica.com/news/Kenya-China-trade-opens-doors-for-tour-consultants/539546–1170016-rotc7wz/index.html20 . Accessed May 25, 2017.

Mutethya, E. 2017. "Chinese Firm Offers Scholarships to Kenyan Students to Study in China." Chinadaily.com.cn,February 2, 2017. http://www.chinadaily.com.cn/world/2017–02/23/content_28317220.htm. Accessed May 22, 2017.

Mwangi, J. 2017. "Chinese Sweepers Earn Three Times More than Kenyan Train Operators." City News. https://www.sde.co.ke/thenairobian/article/2001249551/chinese-sweepers-earn-three-times-more-than-kenyan-train-operators. Accessed August 12, 2017.

Mwaniki, C. 2017. "Kenya's Yuan Debt Doubles on Sh20.7bn Chinese Loan." http://www.businessdailyafrica.com/markets/news/Kenya-yuan-debt-doubles-on-Sh20–7bn-Chinese-loan/3815534–3926686–71778h/index.html.

Ndunda, J. 2015. "Dog Meat Not Food in Kenya, Says City Hall." The Star, March 26, 2015. https://www.the-star.co.ke/news/2015/03/26/dog-meat-not-food-in-kenya-says-city-hall_c1107948. Accessed October 15, 2017.

Neale, G and James Burton. 2011. "Elephant and Rhino Poaching 'is Driven by China's Economic Boom." The Guardian August 14, 2011. https://www.theguardian.com/world/2011/aug/14/china-boom-fuels-africa-poaching. Accessed July 25, 2017.

NEPAD. 2017. "Chinese Firm Launches Construction of Ethiopia-Kenya Power Project." http://nepadippf.org/chinese-firm-launches-construction-of-ethiopia-kenya-power-project/. Accessed May23, 2017.

New Vision. 2015. "Racist Chinese Restaurant Owner Charged in Kenya." March 27, 2015 https://www.newvision.co.ug/new_vision/news/1323156/racist-chinese-restaurant-owner-charged-kenya. Accessed August 12, 2017.

Nyambura, R. 2016 ."Kenya: 120 Kenyans Get Full Scholarships to Study in China." Capital News. http://allafrica.com/stories/201608260541.html. Accessed August 22, 2017.

Odhiambo, A. 201.1 "Kenya-China Bilateral Trade Hits Record Sh144 billion." Business Daily February 24 2011 http://www.businessdailyafrica.com/Kenya-China-bilateral-trade-hits-record-Sh144-billion/539552–1113600-u0bkbjz/index.html. Accessed May 19, 2017.

Otieno, B. 2017. "Kenyan SGR Workers Yet to Get Contracts." Business Daily July 28, 2017 http://www.businessdailyafrica.com/news/Kenyan-SGR-workers-get-contracts-/539546–4035350-mcag92/index.html. Accessed August 12, 2017.

Parameswaran, P. 2017. "The Real Trouble with China's Belt and Road." The Diplomat, May 11, 2017. https://thediplomat.com/2017/05/the-real-trouble-with-chinas-belt-and-road/. Accessed August 10, 2017.

Payne, R. J. and Cassandra R. Veney. 2008. "China's Post-Cold War African Policy RAND Corporation." http://www.jstor.org/stable/10.7249/j.ctt15zc655.8.

Penn, M. 2014. "The Chinese are Coming, Quick Learn Mandarin." Mail & Guardian Africa May 8, 2014 http://m.mgafrica.com/article/2014-05-08-the-chinese-are-coming-quick-learn-mandarin. Accessed May 22, 2017.

Pflanz, M. 2008. "Rise in Kenya Elephant Poaching Linked to Arrival of Chinese Workers." The Telegraph October 3, 2008. http://www.telegraph.co.uk/news/worldnews/africaandindianocean/kenya/3129550/Rise-in-Kenya-elephant-poaching-linked-to-arrival-of-Chinese-workers.html. Accessed July 25, 2017.

Pilling, D. 2017. Chinese Investment in Africa: Beijing's Testing Ground | Financial Times June 13, 2017. https://www.ft.com/content/0f534aa4-4549-11e7-8519-9f94ee97d996 . Accessed June 26 2017.

Pilling, D. and A. Klasa. 2017. "Kenya President Urges Rebalance of China-Africa Trade." The Financial Times, May 14, 2017. https://www.ft.com/content/947ea960-38b2-11e7-821a-6027b8a20f23.

Pilling, D. and E. Feng. 2017. Kenya's $4bn Railway Gains traction from Chinese policy ambitions. The Financial Times April 4, 2017. https://www.ft.com/content/d0fd50ee-1549-11e7-80f4-13e067d5072c?mhq5j=e1. Accessed May 17, 2017.

PSCU. 2017. "Kenya Set to Gain From China's Sh15 Trillion Budget for Silk Road." Capital News, May 14, 2017. http://www.capitalfm.co.ke/news/2017/05/kenya-set-gain-chinas-sh15-trillion-budget-silk-road/. Accessed August 10, 2017.

Sanghi, A. and D. C. Johnson. 2016. Deal or No Deal: Strictly Business for China in Kenya ? Policy Research working paper; no. WPS 7614. Washington, DC: World Bank Group. http://documents.worldbank.org/curated/en/801581468195561492/Deal-or-no-deal-strictly-business-for-China-in-Kenya.

Shankar, S. 2015. "Chinese Restaurant In Kenya Shut Down After Refusing Service To Africans." International Business Times March 3, 2015. http://www.ibtimes.com/chinese-restaurant-kenya-shut-down-after-refusing-service-africans-1858536. Accessed August 12, 2017.

Siwei, P and Xinhua. 2017. "Chinese Tourists to Kenya to Double in 2017." http://news.xinhuanet.com/english/2017-06/11/c_136356851.htm. Accessed June 20, 2017.

Strauss, J. C. 2013. "Conclusions: China and Africa Rebooted; Globalization s, Simplificaticns and Cross-Cutting Dynamics in 'South-South' Relations." *African Studies Review* 56(1): 155–170.

The Star. 2015. "Racist' Chinese Restaurant That Banned Africans After 5pm Served Dogs, Has a Brothel." The Star March 24, 2015. https://www.the-star.co.ke/news/2015/03/24/racist-chinese-restaurant-that-banned-africans-after-5pm-served-dogs_c1107351. Accessed October 15, 2017.

Van de Looy, J. 2006. Africa and China: A Strategic Partnership? ASC Working Paper 67/2006 African Studies Center, Leiden, The Netherlands.

Wafula, P. 2018 "Exclusive: Behind the SGR Walls." The East African Standard July 8, 2018. https://www.standardmedia.co.ke/article/2001287119/exclusive-behind-the-sgr-walls. Accessed July 24, 2018.

Wasuna, B. 2015. "Kempinski Blocks Building of Rival China Firm's Hotel." Business Daily Africa September 28, 2015 http://www.businessdailyafrica.com/corpo

rate/Kempinski-blocks-building-of-rival-China-firm-s-hotel/539550–2887798-w 2v8an/index.html . Accessed June 7, 2017.

Watila, A. 2014. "Kenya Turns to China to Boost Tourist Numbers." East African Standard, April 14, 2014 https://www.standardmedia.co.ke/business/article/2000109373/kenya-turns-to-china-to-boost-tourist-numbers. Accessed June 05, 2017.

Weller, C. 2017. Africa's Carbon-Copy Cities Show How Much it Wants to Be the New China. Business. http://www.businessinsider.com/african-cities-now-look-like-chinese-cities-2015–8?IR=T. Accessed June 20, 2017.

Wesangula, D. 2017. "Kenya Signs China Deal for Coal Plant Beside UNESCO Site." Climate Home News May 23, 2017. http://www.climatechangenews.com/2017/05/23/kenya-signs-china-deal-coal-plant-beside-unesco-site/. Accessed May 23, 2017.

Xinhua. 2015. "China Opens Fourth Confucius Institute in Kenya." China Daily March 31, 2015. http://www.chinadaily.com.cn/world/2015–03/31/content_19961978.htm Accessed May 22, 2017.

Xinhua. 2017. "China Donates $5m Food to WFP to Support Refugees in Kenya." China Daily, June 8, 2017. http://www.chinadaily.com.cn/world/2017–06/08/content_29670720.htm. Accessed June 20, 2017.

Xinhua. 2017. "Chinese Delegation in Kenya to Look for Investment Opportunities." ChinaDaily.com June 17, 2017 http://www.chinadaily.com.cn/business/2017–06/17/content_29782052.htm Accessed June 20, 2017.

Xinhua. 2017. "Kenya to Host China Trade Expo." China Daily June 06 2017 http://www.chinadaily.com.cn/world/2017–06/06/content_29643045.htm . Accessed June 10, 2017.

Xinhua. 2017. "New Chinese Development Projects Greatly Improve Lives in Kenya." http://www.coastweek.com/3806-Chinese-development-projects-greatly-improvinging-lives-in-Kenya.htm. Accessed May 23, 2017.

Xinhua. 2017. Kenya to Model Manufacturing Sector after China Success: New China, November 24, 2017. http://www.xinhuanet.com/english/2017–11/24/c_136777418.htm. Accessed December 5 2017.

## Chapter 13

# Becoming Mitumba

## *Transnational Secondhand Clothing Trade between China and Kenya*

### Boyang Ma

In the new millennium, China has become an important player in the global market of used clothing. In this chapter, I discuss a transnational supply chain of secondhand clothing between China and Kenya. I foreground the ways in which economic value is constantly generated, transferred, and extracted through this process and argue that used clothing is not a simple commodity that is being bought and sold in the transnational supply chain. Instead, it is a certain kind of raw material that is continuously collected, processed, transported, and redefined in the different sectors of this system. These sectors are not independent and isolated but are mutually interconnected. The emerging online-based economy has generated a new economic form that assists clothing collectors to increase margins and expands their business influences in Chinese society. In the processing sector of the transnational supply chain, the factory owners have adapted a unique strategy to create clothing bales and determine the portion of good clothing and rags within the bales, which helped them to earn a substantive market share in Kenya. Chinese wholesalers of used clothing in Kenya also utilize an efficient market strategy to localize Chinese used clothing bales and consolidate business relationships with Kenyan buyers. The description of this hidden global supply chain reveals the social life of Chinese used clothing and how value is created and added into a used clothing item combined with the changes of its commodity status. Furthermore, this case also offers a new perspective on economic relations between China and Africa. African countries are not passively controlled by globalization; instead, they are actively reshaping globalization as well.

## "FAKE" CHARITIES AND REAL BUSINESSES

As the world's largest exporter, importer, and consumer of textile products, China is responsible for a staggering quantity of textile waste. According to the China Association of Circular Economy, Zhong Guo Xun Huan Jing Ji Xie Hui, over 26 million tons of used textiles are generated by Chinese families and industrial sectors each year (Gu Mingming and Tang Shijun 2012, 27). In addition, the nation's accumulated textile waste amounts to nearly 100 million tons. However, compared with their counterparts in developed countries, China's textile recycling industry is less efficient. Only less than 1 percent of used textiles is recycled, which is much less than European countries and the United States, where the textile reutilization rate is around 12 to 16 percent.

Paradoxically, a large number of Chinese textile companies are thirsty for acquiring textile materials, while massive recyclable textile products are discarded in landfills. Therefore, the Chinese government treats textile recycling as one of the most important sectors for textile industry development. According to the Chinese Thirteenth Five-Year Plan for Textile Industry (National Development and Reform Commission China 2016). China has established a textile recycling and reutilization system and standardized the processes of recycling used textiles such as collecting, sorting, and classified utilization.

Even though the Chinese government has an ambitious plan for promoting the textile recycling industry, the current market for it is in a turmoil. The standard and rules for this industry remain vague. Recycling companies might in fact be contributing to market disruption.

The Chinese used clothing export industry began to boom in 2011. By 2016, the nation became the world's fifth biggest exporter in the global used clothing market. The strong demand for used clothing in the foreign market attracted many investors. In the domestic market, the textile industry and other industrial sectors have a strong demand for recycled textiles because various kinds of fibers can be reutilized through a recycling process. Many companies and entrepreneurs have identified this potential business opportunity. Millions of yuan (¥, Chinese monetary unit) are spent in collecting and sorting used clothing and other textile products from Chinese families.

Traditionally, used clothing was widely circulated across the nation, while most Chinese families were materially impoverished. Old clothing might be shared by different family members for a long time. Since the economic reform in 1978 and the development of the textile industry, the supply of clothing has been increasing, and the excessive consumption of textile products has become a social issue. Many families have accumulated a great amount of used clothing, but there has not been an adequate system implemented to deal with the recycling demand. As a consequence, in the last two decades, the government and some social organizations have encouraged Chinese citizens to donate their used clothing to poverty-stricken areas to help the poor populations there.

However, many scandals have been exposed in recent days. For instance, according to a TV clip from Qingdao TV Station, a textile recycling charity Yiyibushe (衣衣不舍) put numerous recycling bins out for used clothing in different residential communities and claimed that the collected old clothing would be donated to people and areas in need. However, it just acted under the guise of a charity and actually used the old clothes for commercial repurposing. Reporters from the Qingdao TV Station found out that they were exporting the donated clothing to Africa.

Such negative news aroused a strong wave of social suspicion against recycling organizations and charities like Yiyibushe. People were agitated by these kinds of "fake" recycling charities and questioned the real destination of their donations. While it is reasonable for people to be angry, recycling used textiles and clothing is facing numerous difficulties in China. First, the cost of recycling is extremely high. Recycling organizations must spend a huge amount of money collecting, sorting, cleaning, and storing clothing donations. Most organizations do not have enough funds to run without the profits from selling used clothing. In addition, the demand of used clothing is constantly decreasing as fewer and fewer poor people really want, or need, clothing that used to be worn by others. Meanwhile, the total amount of used and donated clothing is increasing. The contradiction between weak demand and strong supply contributes to accumulate a massive amount of used clothing in Chinese society. Even though the recycling industry is being promoted by the government, its capability to reutilize used textiles is still limited. As a result, exporting the used clothing to other countries has become the only solution for used clothing accumulation.

This situation has created a new supply chain of used clothing for the global used clothing market. As a new comer to this market, in the last five years China has become the world's fifth largest exporter of used clothing. However, this supply chain is not simply constructed through the economic relationship between the global demand and supply, it is also closely related to the social and political environment. Even though textile recycling organizations are facing the same issues in both China and the West, Chinese recycling organizations are struggling to survive, and their solutions have a strong "Chinese character," which will be illustrated below.

One day in June 2017, I was walking on a street in a suburb of Shanghai. I was on my way to interview a leader of the recycling company, Flying Ants 飞蚂蚁. Which is one of the most famous and influential textile recycling companies that has been established in recent years. Various forms of media had reported on the startup story and founder of this company, Ma Yun 马云. He was invited to present his startup story on a popular Chinese TV talk show, Yixi 一席. I was going to interview Lin Xi 林夕, cofounder of this company, and we had never met before.

When I got out of the cab, I found out I had been taken to an extremely remote place on the outskirts of Shanghai city. Old residential buildings and new housing were located side by side. There were at least five employment agencies on that street. Most license plates on the cars were registered in Jiangxi province, some 800 km to the southwest. I was the midst of a large Jiangxi enclave of job-seeking migrants.

After two-hours of waiting, Lin Xi finally showed up with his SUV. He was a young, energetic, and talkative man. He was also an immigrant from Jiangxi province. He apologized many times for his late presence and invited me to a local restaurant. After a joyful and sumptuous feast, I could not resist asking why he decided startup in the textile recycling industry. He smiled, lit his cigarette, and asked me back, "why do you want to learn about the used clothing business?" I explained to him that I was a graduate student and had stayed in Africa for half a year. I had seen a lot of used clothing sold in Africa, and I wanted to know the source of it. It was important for my research project. His eyes were clear and listened to my answer carefully. Upon hearing my response, he smiled and replied:

I do not know what the value is for your research project, for me, it is just a business. I was born in a poor village in Jiangxi, my parents were both farmers. They spent most of their money to finance my education, I could not let them down. I graduated from Shanghai University of Technology, but I was never a good student. I spent most of my time starting up a business when I was on campus. I had several small businesses in college, all of them were quite good, but just too small. Before graduation, I met Ma Yun. He had some experience in the used clothing business, even though most of them had failed in the end. He knew that I had some connections with a few logistic companies when I was running my small businesses in university. I also wanted to start up an entrepreneur career after graduation, so we joined forces and began to do this business.

The Chinese government policy strongly encourages young Chinese people to become entrepreneurs due to the decline of the traditional manufacturing industry. Many local governments have invested on this issue by offering low-interest loans and free "talent apartments" to newly graduated students who interested in starting their own businesses. As expected, Internet-based start-ups including software engineering, the sharing economy, artificial intelligence, and other emerging economies have attracted the largest pool of talented graduates. Lin Xi and Ma Yun are a part of this group.

The business model of Flying Ants is different from traditional recycling organizations. In a traditional sense, recycling companies or organizations set up numerous recycling bins for storing used clothing in different neighborhoods. Recycling organizations will collect donated clothing at a fixed time. However, its influences are limited because it does not have any other incentives to encourage donation. And recycling bins may not cover all families in this community.

Flying Ants are aware of the shortcomings of traditional recycling and have taken advantage of the Internet to source and extend their influence. As a result, most of their recycling activities are based on the Internet. They have created their own WeChat public account for donors to order pick up services, at no cost. Flying Ants pays all costs. Before collecting used clothing, they inform clients that the donated clothing are commodities rather than a simple donation to be distributed among the poor in China. Donors are informed that some of their collections will be recycled to factories for reutilization, while others will be resold to international traders for export to other countries.

Lin Xi finds recycling of the used clothing problematic and advocates other measures to break the dependency syndrome that might be created by the culture of handing down used garments to the poor:

Used clothing and textiles are a severe problem in our society. People want to solve this problem, but they have all failed. Why? Because most people believe that recycling used textiles should be a charity, donated clothing should be sent to impoverished areas freely. To some extent, they are right, but who should pay the cost? In addition, as far as I know, used clothing collected from Shanghai alone can satisfy nearly all the demand of clothing in poor districts of our country. This is a tiny amount of used clothing generated in China every year. Do poor people really like or need donated clothing from outside? I really doubt it. People need capital, they need means of production to enable them to improve their live permanently rather than rely simple donations. Donations of used clothing do not help to solve the problem of poverty!

The mitumba business is no picnic. Dealers barely break even and for the most part struggle to keep the business afloat. Lin Xi explains the Flying Ants experience at length below:

Some people think we are cheating people and making a lot of profits from selling donated clothing. Let me clear this up first. It is not a donation! People are generating used clothing all the time. When a clothing item is no longer desired by its owner, the first thing that comes to the owner's mind is to get rid of it. Of course, they want their abandoned clothing to be useful to society instead of simply being discarded in landfills. Therefore, we pay the delivery company to collect their discarded clothing from their hands and help them to recycle the used clothing. We do sell clothing to others, however, the money we earn from selling it is all used for compensating the delivery cost. Until last year, we even cannot fully pay the delivery company through the sales of the used clothing. Without selling used clothing to others, the whole business is unable to run, and nothing can be recycled. Therefore, what I understand about this business is that the selling of used clothing is the cost of recycling it. About 40 percent of used clothing we get is recycled and reutilized by the society. However, without the 60 percent of clothing we sell, this 40 percent recycling rate is extremely hard to reach within a traditional recycling model.

Lin Xi defined Flying Ants as an Internet company rather than a recycling company because the majority of the profits they earned were not through directly sale of secondhand clothing but from other sources connected with the internet.

Indeed, selling used clothing covers transportation and warehouse costs. Our company's earnings come from the advertisement in our WeChat public account. We also run an online store that is connected with the account. Every time people donate their used clothing to us, they get a discount coupon from our store, so that people can visit it and buy commodities cheaply.

In WeChat, all public accounts can post advertisements on their own pages and share articles. The price of an advertisement for a public WeChat account is decided by how many people are following this account and how many "likes" an account can receive in an article. It is basically a flux economy in which the economic performance relies on the flow of people. According to Lin Xi, the Flying Ants account has one million followers. The market price for an advertisement with such popularity is around fifty thousand Chinese yuan (around $8,000), and WeChat allows them to post four to five advertisements a month. As a consequence of this advertising income, Flying Ants has grown relatively rapidly. There were only four members on this team at the beginning of 2015. In 2017, it had become quite an influential WeChat based company with a team of more than twenty people.

Ma Yun and Lin Xi have an ambitious plan for their recycling business. With a growing customer base and the amount of used clothing they receive increasing exponentially, Flying Ants are trying to enlarge its business and diversify its portfolio to more professional fields. They have contacted more professional recycling companies to process used clothing into sound insulation materials, which are extensively used in making sound proof layers of vehicles. If they succeed in this endeavor, Flying Ants has the potential to become a more viable and legitimate company to the public.

Donating used clothing has become a spontaneous behavior in postindustrial societies. On the one hand, the excessive consumption of clothing and other textile products has created severe environmental and social issues. On the other hand, though donation itself might not be so effective on limiting the overconsumption of textile products, it provides an excuse to simultaneously consume more and have a peace of mind. Therefore, the donation behavior becomes a part of the "salvage accumulation" process. Anna Tsing (2015, page) defines salvage accumulation as "the process through which lead firms amass capital without controlling the conditions under which commodities are produced . . . all kinds of goods and services produced by pericapitalist activities, human and nonhuman, are salvaged for capitalist accumulation." In this case, a recycling company does not need to "produce" used clothing by themselves, it has been constantly produced and generated by consumers in the industrial world. The only task for those companies is to simply collect them from the society and the people willing to spontaneously donate them.

Donated clothing as understood by the public is clothing that should be distributed freely to other people. However, there is no such thing as a free lunch. Like other objects in our capitalist society, donated clothing and the system that generate and collects it is organized and utilized by capitalist production. Lin Xi and his team have successfully commodified secondhand donated clothing. However, the central part of this commodification is not as simple as transforming a donated clothing item into a commodity. Instead, it redefines the property of the donated item. Under their operations on the Internet and WeChat, collecting and selling used clothing becomes a mandatory cost for recycling textile products. A part of these donations collected from the society must be sold to the global market in exchange for the recycling of other donated clothing. Through this process, the commodification of used clothing is justified. In addition, in their business model, instead of being a commodity for sale, donated clothing and all the efforts used for collecting them are turned into a strategy for attracting customers to "follow" their WeChat account and shop in their online store. Therefore, it is not only donated clothing that is commercialized, rather, the entire process and activities of recycling are commoditized. In this process, Flying Ants and other emerging Chinese recycling companies are effective in utilizing the power of the Internet and successfully transforming a charity behavior into an efficient business model. In this process, donated clothing is not only redefined into a commodity but also a tool to attract public attention and create conducive conditions for growing an Internet economy.

Marx proposed that labor in production is the major source of commodity value German sociologist Simmel (1978) believed that the major economic value within a commodity is originated from the exchange. More recently, Appadurai (1986) defined a commodity as a situational thing that only in some certain circumstances, a thing can be transformed into a commodity stage, and through this process, the economic value of a commodity can be generated. However, in the Internet era, the economic value generated from a commodity is not simply limited by the production or exchange. The

Internet itself becomes a major source of value generation. In this new business model, what is being sold or bought is insignificant. It focuses on how to create a flow of people which can be utilized by the Internet companies to extract value.

In the case of the used clothing transactions, in the supply sector of this global market, even though donated used clothing goes into the commodity situation in which it is sold and bought by different players, what is really traded is not used clothing itself but the social and cultural identity within it. Companies like Flying Ants do not directly make profits from the use value of a donated clothing item to some extent, instead, they benefit from its identity as an abandoned thing. Because the abandoned clothing is too abundant and too valuable to be discarded (this needs to be clarified. Is not the value being sought that of donation and helping the poor?), the society hopes it could be reutilized. Chinese companies like Flying Ants exploit this social opinion and develop a sophisticated online economy based on the donations and transactions of used clothing in Chinese society. This online economic model reveals that in the internet era, the definition of a commodity has become ambiguous. On the surface, donated used clothing become a commodity that is traded; however, it is the public environmentalism and the hope for a recycling economy being consumed in this business model.

The social life of a commodity is much more complicated in today's world and this life has been deepened and widened in today's online economy. In the case of used clothing, its use value is expanded. A used clothing item is not only a piece of cloth that can be exchanged by diverse groups of people, it also becomes a vital resource that can be recycled and utilized by different industries. The internet helps companies to collect used clothing more efficiently. From the vertical perspective, the meaning of used clothing is being pulled by the internet economy and being manipulated and processed into a concept that can be exploited by online virtual economy. Therefore, the used clothing commodity situation in China uses an extremely complex and intricate system.

New meanings and values are constantly added into the donated used clothing in different sectors of the global secondhand clothing network. The case of Flying Ants reveals how donated used clothing is collected and redefined in the supply sector of this network. However, it is just the beginning of its transformation from a donation to a commodity. Before the used clothing can be traded in the global market, there is still a significant step to process it into a standard commodity that can be traded all over the world, which is packing. Even though donated clothing is commercialized through the transactions between recycling companies and global used clothing traders, it is still not an intact commodity because it is just a "raw material" for a commodity that has not been processed and managed. In next section, I provide a detailed account about how used clothing is processed in factories and how this procedure totally transforms used clothing into a real worldwide commodity.

## PRODUCING MITUMBA: STRATEGIES FOR PRICE-SETTING AND PROCESSING USED CLOTHING BALES

A grain of rice is not a commodity until it is packed with other rice in a bag. A drop of wine is not a commodity until it is bottled by its producer. For the same reason, in the transnational trade of used clothing, instead of trading a single piece of used clothing, global dealers mainly trade bales of used clothing. In Kenya, used clothing is called Mitumba, a Swahili word referring to the plastic bales used to pack foreign used clothing from overseas. In international trade, everything should be standardized in order to create a universal and unified criterion for the sake of traders from different parts of the world. For instance, International Standard Organization (ISO) containers are produced by the same sizes and standards, so they can be efficiently loaded, uploaded, stacked, and transported over long distances. In the global trade of used clothing, the size and the weight of a used clothing bale are also standardized. Two weight categories, 45 kg and 75 kg, are standard, but the former is the most universal one. This international standard is the most fundamental unit in the global used clothing market. To some extent, a piece of used clothing is not directly traded by global buyers and sellers, instead, it becomes an element of another kind of commodity, used clothing bales.

The transnational used clothing market between China and Kenya can be divided into four major sectors: global trade, wholesale, retail, and street business. Global traders bring foreign secondhand clothing bales to the Kenyan market. Wholesalers transport those bales to their warehouses, negotiate the price with retailers and finally sell bales to next sector. Retailers also have their relatively small warehouses that are close to the major secondhand market. Sale of specific types of clothes to other vendors and street hawkers takes place here. A single piece of used clothing is not an independent commodity until the bales move to the street market and are opened by the retailers and the clothes bought by the street hawkers for sale in their shops. In fact, except the final transaction, used clothing bales are the major commodity being exchanged.

Furthermore, setting the price of used clothing is a complex affair involving different criteria at each stage. Before cloth is sent to the sorting factory for packing, the price is only related to its weight. A ton of used clothing might only cost a few hundred dollars. After the used clothing gets sorted and packed in the factory and transported to other markets, the price of the used clothing bales increases. In the wholesale stage, the price of one bale depends on various factors: the quality of the clothing, the types of clothing, and the original country in which the bales are produced and packed. The bale price varies from a hundred dollars to a few hundred dollars. My observations revealed that bales with secondhand men's shirts are the most expensive. The reason for its high price is complicated. First, men's shirts are light. A bale might contain 200 to 300 shirts, which means more clothing can be sold to the market in each bale. Second, the unit price of a man's shirt is relatively high in this retail market. Therefore, selling men's shirts is one of the most profitable businesses in the local street markets, which contributes to a high demand of secondhand man's shirts bales.

Sorting and processing used clothing into bales demands processors to have superb skills and a strategic vision. Indeed, the price in the wholesale and retail sectors can be controlled and manipulated through processing and sorting in factories. In the Kenya local market, Chinese traders concentrate on the wholesale sectors. Most of them also have their own processing factories in China. In most situations, they are processors, transnational traders, and wholesalers in the Kenyan local market. Therefore, the performance of their business in Africa really depends on how they sort, and process used clothing in their Chinese factories.

Guangzhou, the capital of Guangdong province in southeast China, is the major center of Chinese light manufacturing. A large number of textile and garment factories are located around this city. It also hosts Asia's biggest international trading center of textile products. Meanwhile, it is also the major consuming center for textile products. Guangdong province yields the highest GDP in all of the Chinese provincial political units. As a traditional center of manufacturing and global commerce, it has a strong consuming culture. One Chinese trader, Zhang Ying, informed me that most Chinese used clothing brought to Africa were collected from the Pearl River Delta where Guangzhou is located and the Yangtze River Delta which is close to Shanghai. Because both districts are economically developed, the quality of used clothing collected from these places is much better than those from other regions. Thus, numerous sorting and packing factories for used clothing were established in Guangzhou and Shanghai due to the increasing demand from the foreign used clothing market. Most owners of these factories also have their wholesale branches in Africa or there are some close business partners that help them sell their goods in African countries.

Wang Xunying, a used clothing trader in her thirties, has an MBA graduate from Sun Yat-Sen University. Before she entered this business, she was an agent for a trading company. In 2010, many members of her extended family lost their jobs because of the global financial crisis. Wang Xunying entered the used clothing business when she noticed that there was a strong global demand for this product. When she was a trade agent working in a commercial company, numerous clients contacted her and inquired whether her company could help them connect with some Chinese suppliers of used clothing who were willing to import this commodity from China. Following a year of intensive market study and preparation, she established her first processing factory in Guangzhou in 2011.

As one of the pioneers, Wang Xunying's business was highly successful. During the first month, she successfully exported ten containers weighing around 200 tons of clothing. Most of her clients were Africans, and she was surprised by the high demand for used clothing in Africa. Subsequently, in 2013, she visited several East African countries to investigate local markets for secondhand clothing. In 2014, she established her first wholesale branch in Kenya. She asked her uncle to take over the processing factory and she moved to Kenya and ran a local business herself. Two years later, in 2016, she established another wholesale branch in Uganda and let her brother run the business. At the end of 2016, her family business had reached large scale, she owned three processing factories in China, as well as two overseas wholesale centers for used clothing in Uganda and Kenya. She could transport 300 to 400 tons of used clothing to Africa each month.

Her family members take different, but clear duties in this family business. Generally, it is her uncles who are responsible for managing and operating processing factories in Guangzhou. She and her brother concentrate on foreign markets. Their united and efficient market strategy is the key to guaranteeing a successful business for this family company. One of the biggest advantages they have is the total control of their supply chain, which means they can easily manipulate the quality and price of their used clothing bales by themselves.

As mentioned above, the price of a bale is largely decided by the quality of clothes and the types of clothing within the bale. The better the clothing, the higher the price. Furthermore, the price of used clothing bales is also influenced by how much salable clothing can be selected by street hawkers in the retail sector. If the bale has more salable clothing, its price is higher than others.

During her market investigation in East Africa, Wang Xunying found that bales from Western countries were dominant in the local markets. Because most Western used clothing sold in Africa comes from charities, the quality and condition of the clothing are extremely well kept. For instance, a bale of used men's shirts from Britain with an estimated 300 shirts cost $300 in the local market. Local hawkers can select around one hundred and fifty shirts from the bale and sell them in their own stores. The Chinese used clothing she can collect is not as good as Western ones in terms of quality and condition. And she cannot promise that the salable used clothing in her bales can be as plentiful as British bales. Wang Xunying realized she could directly compete with Western bales at the same price and thus adjusts her bales to be cheaper than Western ones in order to remain competitive.

At that time, massive Chinese used clothing was also flowing into the market. She found that clothes brought by other Chinese traders were in worse condition than hers; the price of each bale was only around $100, or even less. Compared to her Chinese competitors, her clothing had much better quality because most of them were collected from the Pearl River Delta. She believed she should be able to sell her clothing at a better price if she adjusted the quality of her bales cleverly.

Sorting or processing used clothing is not an easy work. Used clothing must be collected by street vendors, recycling companies, and charities. The quality of Chinese used clothing is extremely diverse. Furthermore, normally, a bale only contains one certain kind of used clothing. For instance, a bale can only have long sleeve coats or short jackets. Otherwise, it will be difficult to determine an appropriate price. Therefore, the task of processing factories is not simply packing those clothes into bales, but categorizing them with strict standards. However, united standards and criteria of sorting used clothing has not yet been established in China. Each factory uses its own standards of categorizing its commodities into jeans, jackets, shirts, skirts, and so on. Under these broad categories are numerous types defined by different factors such as gender, material, seasons, styles of fashion, among others.

When used clothing is transported to the factory, sometimes it has been packed into bales or other containers. However, no matter what the original packing standard is for the bales, factory workers will open the bales and pull all the clothing out. The clothing will be sorted and recategorized based on each factory's own set of standards. Factory workers will identify the classification of this clothing and sort it into various categories. For instance, the best quality jeans will be put in the same stack, lower quality jeans will be arranged into another stack. Normally, a skilled and experienced worker can sort hundreds of clothing items in one hour.

Generally, clothes in good condition and high quality are relatively rare in a batch of donated clothing. Again, used clothes are not factory products, they are collected from the society and their quality cannot be guaranteed. For example, owners of processing factories do not know how many good clothing items can be found in a bale with a thousand kilograms. This business is like gambling, processing factories buy a massive amount of clothing, and their potential profits are based on their fortune. Indeed, not all of the used clothing can be sold in the African market, only the clothing in decent quality can be chosen and bought by local hawkers. Therefore, the quantity of good clothing is significant for factory owners, they are the most valuable resources in this business.

Because secondhand clothes in good condition are rare and valuable, they cannot be put in the same bale, otherwise, the cost for the factory owners will be extremely high. Except clothing in good condition, there are still a large amount of clothes whose quality and condition are less favorable. Factory owners will utilize all of the clothing to create a commodity that can meet the demand of the African market with an appropriate price.

Thus, the strategy is to strike a healthy balance between low and high quality used clothing. This is important because the higher the percentage of good quality clothing, the higher the price of a used clothing bale. In order to maximize their economic profits, factory owners have to mix good quality clothing with rags at a proper ratio so that the price of the bales can be competitive in the local African markets. It demands that factory owners have a comprehensive knowledge about the African markets, and a deep understanding about their competitors.

After a full investigation of the Kenyan market, Wang Xunying decided to take over the middle market of used clothing in Kenya. She chose to produce a kind of used clothing bales whose quality is relatively lower than Western ones, but higher than other Chinese bales. Thus, the price of her bales would be cheaper than Western ones but had a better quality than other competitors. This market strategy gave her an advantage to seize a considerable market share through lower prices. At the same time, she could also keep substantial profits because the quality and the price of her bales were relatively higher than her Chinese competitors. She also developed a sophisticated classification system for her products. Her bales would be divided into three different levels. The first-class bales were as same quality as Western bales, but the quantity of them were limited. These kinds of bales would only be sold to her most loyal and long-term clients. The middle-class bales were the major products she created. The lowest-class bales were extremely cheap, but they were also quite popular for local retailers who have limited funds and capital.

Her market strategy contributes to a successful business in Africa. In 2016, she could export twenty containers of used clothing to Africa in each month, which was around 400 tons. During the peak season, the clothing she exported to Kenya could reach 600 hundred tons, or around thirty containers, monthly.

This successful business relied highly on her full control on her own supply chain. Because she owned processing factories and managed them wisely, it gave her an advantage on manipulating the quality and the price of her products. However, the output of her factories sometimes could not feed her demand in peak seasons. To meet the supply shortage, she would have to buy used clothing from other factories and pack them with her own bales.

With her training in business, Wang Xunying understood the strength of branding. All her used clothing bales had a unified logo, "Beauty." She printed this logo on all bales. Wang Xunying insisted that all of her bales should be packed in same way with the same materials and logos on them. She believed this was useful to improve the brand identity of her products. Wang Xunying was also eager to maintain a good relationship with her customers. Long-term clients sometimes would receive small gifts from her company such as electronics and imported food. She also gave them considerable discounts if clients are loyal to her company.

In the processing sector, a single piece of used clothing is not a commodity, but it is an important element of another commodity, used clothing bales. Even though used clothes are packed, processed, and transported in bales, they do not become a commodity until the bales are opened by retailers and sold to street hawkers. During the processing procedure, new values are added to used clothing through packing. The mixture of good clothing and rags redefine the value within them. Abandoned, or donated quality clothes contain little economic value until they are sorted and packed by factory labors. At this point, its use value is "rediscovered" by factory workers through the identification and sorting process. The exchange value is also added to them when they were packed in bales. For rags, the value is also added to them when they are packed together with quality donated clothing. As discarded clothing, rags have little use value and few people want to buy them. Therefore, their economic value is zero before they are mixed with good quality used clothing. After the mixture, because the price of bales is decided by both quality clothes and rags, a portion of economic value of the bales is distributed to the rags. As a consequence, the packing sector of the used clothing network generates a new kind of commodity, and through creating this commodity, used clothing bales, with both quality used clothing and rags become valuable. In other words, both of them are recommodified through this process even though they are not the direct commodity that is traded by global dealers to some extent.

## WHOLESALE AND DISTRIBUTION OF USED CLOTHING BALES

After being packed, Chinese used clothing bales will be uploaded into heavy trucks and transported to ports for export. They are finally loaded into containers which will be carried by a container vessel and transported to Mombasa, the major port of Kenya. It costs a container ship twenty days to sail across the South China Sea, the Malacca Strait, and the India Ocean. After the ship arrives in the port of Mombasa, the used clothing bales will be unloaded and stored in dock warehouses. It will cost a wholesaler three days of dealing with paperwork, as demanded by local customs. Then, a wholesaler will hire a transportation company to upload used clothing bales from the dock warehouses and transport them to their own warehouses in Nairobi.

The major roads that connect Nairobi and Jomo Kenyatta Airport is called Mombasa Road. Major industrial zones and commercial warehouses are built along this road. Thousands of trucks, Matatus (minivans for public transportation in Nairobi) bring cargo and people to this district every day. Economically, that is the most vibrant area of the Nairobi metropolis. For most Chinese wholesalers who sell used clothing bales, the Mombasa Road is the major base for their commercial activities. Normally, a wholesaler has at least one warehouse in this district. For some big wholesalers, it is normal to own even three or four warehouses along the Mombasa Road.

Mr. Lyu is the biggest Chinese wholesaler of used clothing bales in Kenya. He and his company own three large warehouses in Nairobi as well as a business branch in Kisumu, another large city in western Kenya. His company also owns and manages dozens of processing factories in China. Their factories not only offer bales to their own business in Africa but also sell used clothing bales to other customers in the world. Mr. Lyu is also the first Chinese wholesaler who ventured into the Kenyan used clothing market.[1]

Mr. Lyu was around forty years old when he came to Kenya in early 2011 to investigate the used clothing market. Through his investigation, he found the Kenyan market held good potential for their business. First, the local market had a strong demand of all kinds of clothing. Even though Kenya was located along the equator, most of its territory is based in the plateau. The temperature fluctuated during the day: relatively low in the morning and night but quite high at noon. Due to its unique climate, clothes for different seasons were all needed in the local market. Second, the exchange rate between the Kenyan shilling and the US dollar were relatively stable compared with other African countries. This would help his company to avoid currency risk. Third, with its population size, Kenya itself provided a large market for used clothing. With a population of around 46 million, the nation only had a small textile and garment industry whose products were majorly exported to Western markets. As a result, cheap, used clothes were extremely welcome in the local clothing market.

Mr. Lyu spent three months establishing a wholesale branch of used clothing for his company in Kenya. It was not easy work. There were many things that needed to be taken care of, such as renting warehouses, finding transportation companies for both maritime and land transportation, hiring local employees, building up commercial relationships with local customers, and dealing with legal issues with the Kenyan government. After three-months of preparation, the first three containers were transported to Kenya at the end of 2011. Unfortunately, the business was not successful at the beginning. Only one-third of his bales could be sold at a decent price. Due to the lack of knowledge about the local demand of used clothing, the used clothing bales within the first three containers were not accepted by local clients. He had to sell the rest of his products at an extremely low price. But he was not disappointed about this failure. Through this first business attempt, he began to understand the local market. He contacted his colleagues who were responsible for managing and processing factories in China and asked them to adjust the quality of their bales based on local demand. The adjustment of bales was a long process. He spent three months selling different clothing bales to the local market. He assessed what was happening and finally figured out the most appropriate types of bales that would be accepted by the local retailers. Since then, his business started to improve. More and more local retailers placed orders for used clothing bales from his warehouses. At the end of 2016, he could sell around 600 tons of used clothing bales each month.

Warehouses are the central part of the wholesale business of used clothing. The warehouse is not only a place to store used clothing bales, but also the major place to negotiate the price, build up personal and business relationships, and connect two remote markets together. Mr. Lyu's warehouse is around 600 sq m. The major space is used for storing used clothing bales. A warehouse will be divided into different sectors according to the types of clothing in the bales. The warehouse also includes two small offices, a small bathroom and a tea room for people working in this place. The quality and the price of bales are a major concern for clients to evaluate wholesalers. New customers can open a clothing bale to check whether the used clothing within it is good enough.

Customers who buy clothing bales from Mr. Lyu vary in their financial capability. Some big customers can buy hundreds of bales in a single purchase. However, some small-scale customers can only afford one to two bales when they visit this warehouse. The price for different customers is different as well. For loyal customers that do a lot of business, the price for each used clothing bale is negotiable. In order to keep and maintain a good commercial relationship, Mr. Lyu always gives them a cheaper price. If big customers do not have enough money, Mr. Lyu can lend them credit and allow them to pay it later. For small-scale dealers, the price is nonnegotiable, and they must pay on site. Once bales are sold, customers cannot return it to the warehouse. Even though Mr. Lyu has a quality standard for his bales, and there is quality control in company's processing factories, the quality for a single clothing bale is still hard to estimate. That means customers buy these bales at their own risk, and small-scale traders have to undertake a higher risk than big traders because they can only buy a limited number of bales in one purchase. During my fieldwork in Nairobi, I have seen many unsatisfied small customers came back to the warehouse with the bales they purchased from Mr. Lyu's stock. They complained that the condition of the clothing is not up to par. Many items are damaged or torn. Even so, Mr. Lyu did not allow them to return.

A small desk is always arranged at the entrance of the warehouse. A Chinese or a Kenyan employee sits behind the table and records how many bales are transported in the warehouse and how many bales are sold to customers every day. At night, Mr. Lyu checks the recording books and examines whether the number of bales recorded on the books is as same as numbers of bales stocked in the warehouse. If they are not equal with each other, Mr. Lyu will ask the employee who made the records to explain the situation, and cut their monthly salary, or extend their hours. Even with such careful managing strategies, some of his bales always disappeared without any trace. Mr. Lyu said it must be his African employees who stole those bales from his warehouse.

"Those Africans are not reliable. I pay them quite well, but they still steal bales from me. Some of them are bribed by my clients. When clothing bales are transported in my warehouse, they record it in a smaller number. Therefore, the number of bales that should be recorded never exist in my inventory. And when clients come to buy clothing bales, they can sell those 'nonexistent' bales to them. They are quite cunning, but never use their cleverness in the right way," claimed Mr. Lyu.

Even though Mr. Lyu never fully trusted his African employees, he did need their assistance to deal with some local issues. He hired a manager to help him manage another warehouse in Nairobi. He also hired local Kenyans as accountants, porters, securities, and sales agents who know better about the local used clothing market than him. Nonetheless, the core business is still supervised by his Chinese employees. All the sale income will be collected by Chinese employees rather than Kenyans. And there are two different account books in his warehouse, one is only used for recording daily income and cost, another account book has all the transaction records since he started his business. Mr. Lyu's Kenyan accountant only helps him record daily transactions; the accountant does not have the authority to read or use the real account book for his company.

Indeed, compared to the retail sector, the wholesale sector of the used clothing business is less profitable. However, the local business society is reluctant to share this business with Chinese businessmen. When Mr. Lyu started his business in Kenya, he also implemented a retail store in a large city market for used clothing. A month later, someone sent him a message through his Kenyan manager in his retail store. The message was simple, that for Chinese merchants, doing wholesale business is fine, but local Kenyan dealers did not welcome his presence in the retail sector. The message did not say what would happen if he continues his retail business, however, it was an obvious threat. Based on the consideration of his personal safety and the safety for his business, Mr. Lyu finally surrendered and closed his retail business.

In the transnational used clothing network between China and Kenya, the sourcing, processing, and wholesale sector were all directly controlled by Chinese entrepreneurs. However, each sector is created due to African demand on used clothing. Used clothing bales must be constantly adjusted according to the local demand in Kenya Therefore, it is not China that dumps used clothing to Africa, instead, it is the demand from Africa that creates and reshapes this transnational business. To have a better business performance in the local market, Chinese entrepreneurs also need to constantly study local knowledge, culture, and social rules. Through this process, Chinese entrepreneurs in Africa have begun to give up their racial prejudices against Kenyans and have started to understand the local society and culture.

"People who are out of this business might think we are dumping rags and tatters to the local market, and Kenyans are just buy everything that we bring from overseas. That is totally wrong. To some extent, I have to admit that local Africans have a great taste in clothing. If you walk on the streets of Nairobi, local residents, especially young people, are dressing much better than most ordinary Chinese. They are fastidious about the quality of used clothing. There are thousands of bales exchanged in local market every day. Therefore, it is not an easy business, you need to understand Africans, and offer them appropriate products, otherwise, they can easily switch to other wholesalers and abandon you . . . Some Chinese here think we are superior to the local Africans, they always say that Kenyans are lazy, stupid, and unreliable. Well, I must admit that is totally wrong as well. They are just living in their own way. As foreigners, we do not have the right to judge local people. What we need to do is try to understand them, and make money from them, hah!" Mr. Lyu told me.

In warehouses, used clothing bales are localized. In this sector, Kenyan retailers directly encounter used Chinese clothing. Clothing bales from China are evaluated by local retailers in terms of their quality and condition. Even though the price of bales is decided by Chinese wholesalers, it is a result of the continuous negotiation between wholesalers and Kenyan retailers. It is based on the wholesalers' knowledge of the local used clothing market. After the transaction between wholesalers and retailers, clothing bales leave the transnational used clothing network between China and Kenya and enters the local market system.

The transnational used clothing network between China and Kenya is a result of the used clothing demand in Africa. Various social organizations, charities, and companies actively participate in this business. Even though it is traded by different players, its value is reflected through clothing bales instead of a single piece of used clothing. The real commodity flowing in this network are the clothing bales. Through sourcing, processing, and wholesale, different values are constantly generated in different sectors, and the new value is added into the clothing bales. In the sourcing sector, a new model to acquire the used clothing supply for the global market is closely related with the internet business. The Internet advertisement and Internet business successfully transform the collection of used clothing into a profitable business. In the processing sector, the portion of good clothing and rags are important. Through adjusting the portion of good clothing, the price and quality of clothing bales can be manipulated by processors. During this process, clothing bales are produced, clothing within it begins to transform from donations into elements of a commodity. Economic value is added to both good clothing and rags. In the wholesale sector, Chinese used clothing bales enters into the local market system. They are evaluated by local dealers based on their standards. They finally become a popular local commodity and leave the transnational network of used clothing between China and Kenya.

The transnational network of used clothing between China and Kenya reflects the business pattern of global used clothing trade. Used clothing is not only a simple commodity traded through this network. Instead, it is a certain kind of "raw material" that is constantly collected, processed, and redefined by various players in different business sectors. The final products of this global used clothing system are packed clothing bales. However, when used clothing bales move into the local market system in Kenya, the meaning of clothing bales changes.

In the local used clothing market, clothing bales will be opened by retailers, and clothing within bales will be selected by local hawkers. In this sector, the selection of used clothing is based on a complicated local knowledge system. Local consumers have a totally different understanding about used clothing compared with the consumers in the industrial world. Doing used clothing business and consuming used clothing from overseas are important activities for the social life of local citizens. In next chapter, I am going to introduce: (1) the local knowledge system regarding used clothing in Kenya; (2) how this system generates a strong demand of used clothing in this country; (3) how this demand reshapes the global used clothing market. It will offer us a better understanding about the hidden used clothing world under globalization.

## NOTE

1. Before he started this business in 2011, he had offered used clothing bales to other African clients for years. Mr. Lyu is a business partner of this company. This company is actually owned by another Chinese businessman called Mr. Han. Mr. Lyu is the director of the East African market, managing all the business in East Africa.

# REFERENCE

Arjun Appadurai. (1986). *The Social Life of Things: Commodities in Cultural Perspective.* Cambridge: Cambridge University Press.

Marx, K., 1818–1883. 1991. In Fernbach D., Fowkes B. and Mandel E. (eds.), *Capital: A Critique of Political Economy.* New York: Penguin Books in association with New Left Review.

Mingming, G. and T. Shijun. 2012. "The current Situation of Reutilization of Used Textile Products in Our Country." *Renewable Resources and Circular Economy* 5(1), 27–29.

顾明明, and 唐世君. 2012. 我国废旧纺织品综合利用现状及发展方向. 再生资源与循环经济 5(1), 27–29.

Simmel, G. 1978. *The Philosophy of Money*, trans. Tom Bottomore and David Frisby. London: Routledge and Kegan Paul.

Tsing, A. L. 2015. *The Mushroom at the End of the World: On the Possibility of Life in Capitalist Ruins.* Princeton: Princeton University Press.

*Chapter 14*

# The Potentials, Opportunities, and Challenges of Underwater Cultural Heritage for Understanding Early Global Networks

Caesar Bita

East African coastal communities have had a long and continuous history of interactions with the Indian Ocean (see figure 2.1). For centuries, they sailed using different types of water craft between and along lands that surrounded it.[1] Voyages also occurred between this coast and the Atlantic to as far as Europe and the Americas. Similarly, this occurred between the Swahili coast and Pacific Ocean to lands as far as China (Freeman-Grenville 1975; Kirkman 1964). Sailing across these lands has been (and is still) based on regular and predictable monsoon winds. Maritime interactions, as well as oceanic changes, have left behind on the seabed and foreshores, material evidence of this past. These material traces are in the form of tangible heritage such as shipwrecks and artifacts. Further, some of the maritime cultural practices are still active, for instance, religious practices, traditional boat building styles continue to play a role in the lives of the coastal people. That the East African Coast has had long-standing global networks, and together with its potential for underwater cultural heritage, makes it an important area of study. The potential of underwater archaeology of this coast, however, comes to light from researches, accidental discoveries by fishermen, written records, and oral traditions. This chapter will explore the maritime cultural heritage of the East African coast and its potential for understanding ancient global networks. It will also outline the opportunities and challenges in the region for managing this heritage.

The East African Coast has a 3,000-km long coastline, popularly known as the "Swahili coast." This coast, also referred to as the Western Indian Ocean contains vast maritime resources which have been exploited in various ways by the local communities for centuries. Seafarers from Greece, China, Persia, and India have sojourned to this coast leaving traces of their voyages and interaction with East Africans in the form of monumentality, shipwrecks, and socio-linguistic traces, religious practices, boat building styles, among others (Hourani 1963; Matthew 1963; Kusimba 1999; Kirkman 1964; Wilson and Omar 1997). Further, some of the maritime cultures and activities are still practiced, for instance, traditional boat building styles that have been practiced for centuries continue to play a role in the lives of coastal people (Bita 2008; 2009a; 2009b; 2010; Prins 1962).

Multiple historical sources make reference to ancient seafaring on the Swahili coast. The Periplus of the Erythraen Sea mentions the East African coast as early as 2000 BCE (Casson 1989; Huntingford 1980). It refers to routes, ports, and goods involved in trade across the Indian Ocean seaboard (Freeman-Grenville 1975). Chinese sources mention the presence of cattle economy on the Somali coast by late 800s CE, as well as their involvement in trade with foreigners from the Far East (Kirkman 1964). Arab geographers of mid 900 CE allude to thriving maritime communities along the East African coast (Datoo 1970; Kirkman 1964; Freeman-Grenville 1975). Ongoing underwater archaeological investigations on the Kenyan coast are recovering data that corroborates these historical literary sources (Breen and Lane 2003; Forsythe et al. 2003; Bita 2008; 2011; 2014c; 2015b; Pollard and Bita 2017). Preliminary results show that the highest concentration of shipwrecks is around Mombasa, Malindi, and Lamu (Bita and Wanyama 2007; Bita 2010; 2014c; 2015b). The finds bear evidence to East Africa's role in long-distance international maritime trade networks and the potential for underwater archaeology in furthering knowledge about the deep buried history of East Africa and the Indian Ocean.

## ANCIENT INTERNATIONAL MARITIME CONTACTS WITH EAST AFRICAN COAST

Bidirectional interaction between East Africans and other communities around the Indian Ocean over the last 2,000 years has facilitated the cultural and technological transfers among participants and created one of the longest and most stable international economic system (Mitchell 2005; Kusimba 2017). The coast is an integral part of Africa and its inhabitants maintained economic and social networks with inland neighbors creating a network that made possible the bidirectional movement of products, some of which found their way to the international markets (Kusimba et al 2013; Kusimba and Kusimba 2018; Kusimba and Walz in Press; Ndiema, this volume). Similarly, global trade between the East African coast and the rest of the world was facilitated through after the discovery by mariners that the monsoon winds and oceanic currents could reliably permit rapid seasonal navigation across the Indian Ocean to western and southern Asia (D'Souza 2008). Although the precise chronology of premodern trade between Africa and Asia is unknown, what is certain is that when these interactions became more regular, the Swahili coast became the link, a gateway, from which trade products left and entered Africa (Chami 2009). African residents of the coast were thus poised to benefit from this trade and were the most impacted by these networks of interaction.

East African exports were primarily animal products (skins and horns) metal, timber, and incense (Chami 1994; 2006; 2009; Kusimba 1994; Sheriff 2000; 2002). Spices including cinnamon, cloth, glass beads came from Asia (Kusimba and Kusimba 2018). The high demand for labor, which included soldiers-initiated demand for African enslavement and East Africans may have been recruited as well as kidnapped to serve as soldiers, domestic workers, and agricultural laborers to the Middle East (Kusimba 2013). Reports exist of Zanj slaves reaching China as early as seventh century CE (Kusimba 2004; Mathew 1963; Sheriff 2002; Duyvendak 1939; 1949).

Chinese also visited and wrote about this coast (Freeman-Grenville 1975). Earliest Chinese references to Africa appear as early as the T'ang Dynasty (618–906 CE). The revised Tang history of Ou-yang Hsiu and Sung-Ch'I, T'ung Tien, an encyclopedia compiled by Tu yu in 812 CE, T'ai- P'ing Huan Yü Chi accounts by Yüeh Shih between 976 and 983 CE, T'ung Chih, an historical compendium by Cheng Ch'iao in about 1150 CE, Ma Tuan lin's, encyclopedia wen-hsien T'ung- K'ao which was published in 1319 CE. All these accounts identified Mua-lien as the town of Malindi on the Kenyan Coast. Later during the Ming Dynasty, between 1417–1419 CE and 1421–1422 CE, various Chinese missions visited Muqdishu (Mogadishu), Brava, Juba, and Malindi (Freeman-Grenville 1975). The most famous of these missions was one led by Admiral Zheng He who visited the East African coast where he received a giraffe as a present by the king of Malindi for his Chinese counterpart the Yong Li emperor (Kusimba 1999, 19). During these voyages, one of his ships is believed to have wrecked in Lamu Archipelago near Pazzalia rocks off the Island of Pate near modern-day Shanga (Boxer 1960; Freeman-Grenville 1975; Kusimba and Zhu, this volume). The understudied underwater heritage of the East Africa coast is a fertile site for the study of the millennial interaction between the East Africa, South Asia, Southwest Asia, and East Asia.

## POTENTIAL FOR UNDERWATER ARCHAEOLOGY IN EASTERN AFRICA

Systematic scientific underwater archaeological survey of the waters of the Swahili coast has only began recently, so we are only becoming aware of the rich heritage that remains largely unknown (Patience 2006; Bita 2008; 2010; 2013b; 2015a). Patience (2006) has documented over 100 shipwrecks, the majority of which are contemporary and of European origin. Portuguese shipwrecks lost off the Kenya coast, including *Nossa Senhora da Graca* (suspected to have sunk in the 14th century), the *Nossa Senhora do Guadalupe, Joao Soares Henriques, El Rei, Salvacao, Nossa Senhora dos Remedios,* and *San Filipe* have been discovered during these surveys. The British have several shipwrecks lost in Tanzania, Kenya, and Uganda, while the Germans have many shipwrecks in Tanzania (Patience 2006). Discoveries of underwater cultural heritage tend to be largely accidentally by fishermen and divers who encounter sites from the sea (Bita 2013b). Similarly, in East Africa underwater sites have come to light largely through nonarchaeological ventures. For example, the shipwrecks of *Santo Antonio de Tanna* in Mombasa and the Ngomeni vessel in Malindi, were both discovered by fishermen (Bita 2013b). Recent maritime surveys have successfully uncovered and documented many submerged sites (Bita and Wanyama 2007; Bita 2008; Bita 2011; 2013b; 2015a; Tripati and Bita 2015).

## MARITIME ARCHAEOLOGICAL POTENTIAL IN KENYA

Kenya's maritime and underwater cultural heritage landscape consists of shipwrecks, traditions, sites, and monuments that are spread along the coastline. The National Museums of Kenya have mounted underwater archaeological studies in an effort to identify, document, and understand Kenya's underwater cultural heritage (UCH). The majority of ancient shipwreck sites have been recovered around the ancient cities of Mombasa, Malindi, and Lamu have been documented. Associated finds including pottery, beads, ivory, glass, porcelains, and daggers serve as proxies for understanding the nature and intensity interaction between East Africa and the Middle East, Indian subcontinent and China (Piercy 1977; 1978; Sassoon 1980; Patience 2006; McConkey and McErlean 2007; Bita 2008; 2009a; 2009b; 2011; 2014b; 2014c).

## MARITIME ARCHAEOLOGICAL POTENTIAL IN LAMU

The Lamu Archipelago is composed of several islands with ancient settlements that have provided important landmarks for understanding the history of the Swahili Coast and its relationships to the Indian Ocean world (Kusimba 1999; Chittick 1984). Studies undertaken collaboratively between National Museums of Kenya and National Museum of China recovered sites with anchors, wooden features, and Chinese porcelain. Along Pate Bay, near Shanga, a pot with dragon emblems typical of Chinese motifs of the Ming Dynasty period was recovered (Bita and Wanyama 2007; Bita 2013b; 2015a). This is the bay one of the junks belonging to legendary Admiral Zheng He sunk during voyages to East Africa. The discovery of this pot suggests the likelihood of this junk in the sea as fishermen continue to collect Chinese pottery and report of unusual finds. A strong oral tradition in Pate has it that the survivors of this Zheng He shipwreck stayed at Shanga where they intermarried with the local population (Namunaba, this volume). Today, there is a generation of locals who claim ancestry from this shipwreck tragedy and whom locals refer to as "Chinese" due to their unique physical appearance (Bita and Wanyama 2007).

## MARITIME ARCHAEOLOGICAL POTENTIAL IN MALINDI

Malindi is one of Kenya's and Swahili coast ancient towns that had contact with the outside world since the early centuries of the last millennium CE (Martin 1973; 1975). Vasco Da Gama was repulsed from Mombasa but was warmly welcomed by the Malindi Arab King (Martin and Martin 1978). Throughout the sixteenth century, the Portuguese controlled the Indian Ocean trade with Malindi as their headquarters. Maritime archaeological surveys in Malindi have documented several sites, some yet to be confirmed as shipwrecks. One unconfirmed interesting find is a site off Leopard Bay with fourteenth to fifteenth century Chinese and Indian porcelains (Patience 2006; Bita 2013b). Another is an object in Mambrui which rises about 100 feet from the sea floor and which has been called the "Mambrui lump." This feature has been sighted by sailors who comment on unusual structures in the seabed of Ungwana Bay (Bita 2005; 2008; 2012). Recent studies undertaken collaboratively between the National Museums of Kenya and National Museums of China under the Sino–Kenya underwater archaeology project, recovered, surveyed, and excavated the sixteenth century Ngomeni shipwreck 30 km north of Malindi Town. Large quantities of Islamic and Far Eastern wares were recovered inside the shipwreck in addition to ivory, cinnabars, bone, lead strips, and mercury (Bita 2014b; 2014c).

Studies of the typology of a few of the copper ingots revealed that they were made in varying size. All are Plano-convex, or half-moon shaped, and their weights varied from 5 kg to 10 kg and have diameters ranging between 12 and 15 cm. Some had a visible trident seal similar to the Fugger family crest, a prominent merchant and banking family from Augsburg, Germany (Bita 2014a; 2014c). These attributes are similar to those of copper recovered in the Oranjemund Shipwreck (Sinamai 2010). Together with others such as the Welser family, the Fuggers are known to have supplied merchandise that formed part of the commercial artery of the Portuguese crown (Chalmin 1987).

Recently, surveys and excavations have been undertaken at the ancient town and port of Kilepwa along Mida Creek off the ancient city of Gede in Malindi (Pollard and Bita 2017). The studies were done of the boat illustrations and graffiti as mentioned by Kirkman (1952; 1964). It was found that these boat graffiti depict probably the mtepe type of boat that plied the Indian Ocean in the last centuries BCE, referred to by the Portuguese and believed to have been in use in the Swahili Coast until the early centuries of the Christian era.

## MARITIME ARCHAEOLOGICAL POTENTIAL IN MOMBASA

The potential of Mombasa underwater archaeology is incomplete without mentioning Santo Antonio de Tanna, a Portuguese frigate brought to Mombasa in 1696 by the Portuguese when Fort Jesus was under siege by the Oman Arabs. During attempts to free the Fort, it was sunk by the Arabs in 1698 in front of the Fort (Boxer 1960; Sassoon 1980; Lynch 1999). This shipwreck was excavated between 1976 and 1982 resulting in the recovery of Indian, Chinese, and Burmese artifacts (Piercy 1977: 331–347; 1978: 301–319; Bita 2013a). While more artifacts remain preserved in situ, some are in conservation and exhibition at the Fort Jesus Museum. Following this project, the wreck is today gazetted as a national monument and is protected by the country's legislation. Other studies have documented the sites of Globe Star, Kota Menang, Sussex, and Ahmadi shipwrecks all near Fort Jesus and in shallow depth (Patience 2006; Bita 2016).

Other surveys have documented several submerged sites, some of which are likely to be shipwrecks (Forsythe et al. 2003; Rory et al. 2007; McConkey and McErlean 2007; Bita 2009a). Recent maritime surveys at the channel entrance to the ancient port of Mombasa recovered one Indo-Arabian and two composite stone anchors, caves, and ivory concentrations (Bita and Wanyama 2011; Bita 2013b 2015a; 2015b; 2016; Tripati and Bita 2015). The shape and size of the three stone anchors resembles those used by mariners in India, Sri Lanka, Oman, and the Mediterranean region (Tripati et al. 1998; 2003; Souter 1998; Vosmer 1999). Thus, the recovery of these anchors in East Africa points to a rich, diverse, and interlinked maritime cultural heritage. Similarly, ongoing underwater archaeological surveys at the ancient port of Kilwa in

Tanzania by Edward Pollard and his colleagues have recovered a wide array of material cultural including a stone anchor and diverse artifacts of imported pottery and glass jars (Pollard, et al. 2016).

## MARITIME STRUCTURES AND PRACTICES

In addition to the submerged underwater cultural heritage sites, there are multiple marine structures that bear witness to the region's engagement with foreign colonizing powers that have sought to control Indian Ocean commerce since the sixteenth century. These installations were constructed at various times by the Portuguese, Omani Arabs, British, Germans, and Italians as they vied to control and monopolize Indian Ocean commerce (Oka et al. 2009; Kusimba and Oka 2008). Defined as colonial heritage, these structures include jetties, fortified fortresses, chalets, and military bunkers (Kirkman 1974). Other natural structures such as caves were also converted into habitable sites that were widely used (Abungu 2018; Kiriama 2018). These include Vasco da Gama pillar in Malindi, Lamu, and Siyu Forts in Lamu, Fort Jesus in Mombasa, and so forth. The rich maritime heritage of East Africa is still visible in the complex sailing and boat building traditions. In the Lamu Archipelago towns such as Siyu, Pate, Faza, and Matondoni, traditional boat building still continues alongside new technologies. Among the Swahili and other coastal communities, the relationships with the sea is ingrained in everyday life, offering fertile opportunities for ethnoarchaeological research that would inform greater Indian Ocean practices that have been lost elsewhere (Bita 2013b cf. Vosmer 2013).

## OPPORTUNITIES IN UNDERWATER CULTURAL HERITAGE IN KENYA

The sea has played and continues to play an incredibly significant role in the daily lives of the global community. Today's global tourist industry is so intertwined with the sea that nations in the global south have increasingly invested in the tourism sector through marketing the beautiful and enchanted attractions of sun, sand, and fun. In recent years, however, Underwater Cultural Heritage (UCH) has begun to attract the attentions of the global tourism industry leading nations bordering the sea to invest in developing their UCH heritage sites for visits. Underwater archaeological surveys in Kenya, Tanzania, and Mozambique reveal rich heritage that if carefully developed could be sustainably managed through tourism. As ongoing research and training in underwater archaeology continues to recover sites of great significance so does the need for a maritime museum and underwater cultural heritage training institute that will curate, exhibit, and preserve this rich heritage.

## DEVELOPMENT OF MARITIME MUSEUM AND UCH TRAILS

As discussed above, underwater archaeological studies in Kenya have documented many shipwreck sites around Mombasa, Malindi, and Lamu. With warm clear tropical waters that offer underwater visibility to over 5 m and a fully developed diving industry, these shipwrecks have a huge potential to be developed into underwater cultural heritage tourist sites. For example, in Mombasa, the shipwrecks of Santa Antonio De Tanna, Globe Star, Kota Menang, Sussex, and Ahmadi located near the UNESCO World Heritage Site and Museum of Fort Jesus are less than 700 m offshore and at depths between 5 m and 12 m (Bita 2015a; 2015b). The high visibility of the waters makes these sites extremely suitable developing an underwater cultural heritage trail.

In Malindi, the sixteenth-century Ngomeni Shipwreck is not only the oldest shipwreck but also the best preserved in East Africa. Located about 500 m from the shore in a well-protected area of Ras Ngomeni, the shipwreck lies in shallow waters of 5 to 7 m deep. The wreck still retains most of its major components including timber frames, ribs, the base and cargo of ivory, ceramics, copper, and other articles still trapped inside the ship. The site is ideal for an underwater museum and a companion photographic mosaic ideal for a traveling exhibit. In Lamu, potential sites for underwater cultural heritage trails include one site with a massive anchor embedded in coral and several with hordes of submerged material culture opposite Manda and Shela. Despite the huge potential for underwater archaeology, the prohibitive cost of developing and sustaining a vibrant program in this emerging field has contributed to the slow embrace and adoption in sub-Saharan Africa. In Kenya, following very successful surveys by the National Museums, plans are now afoot to invest in a maritime museum and underwater training institute that will serve the region. The institute will integrate approaches in conservation and management of underwater cultural heritage through inter-country and interdepartmental capacity building. Once developed, it will offer short and long-term courses that are suitable and relevant for the regional heritage institutes including museums, universities, local communities, and other stakeholders. These are to range from three-day training workshops to a whole year diploma and in partnership with universities. Trainees will include archaeologists, heritage experts, historians, or conservationists working in government institutions such as museums, and allied organizations and including tourism docents. The institute will also train local communities on how to identify and promote conservation of UCH. Courses will be tailor-made for different stakeholders from government personnel to technical staff and the general public dealing with cultural heritage.

The potential for an underwater archaeology/underwater cultural heritage training institute exists in Kenya. Several suitable underwater heritage sites have been identified along the entire coastline. Further, National Museums of Kenya has many undeveloped and potential areas that can be utilized to build such a facility. In addition, all major universities in the country including Nairobi University, Kenyatta University, Moi University, Egerton University, and Mount Kenya University have campuses in all Kenya's major coastal towns. Related to this, universities in the neighboring countries of Tanzania, Uganda, Rwanda, Burundi, Sudan, Mozambique, Congo, and Ethiopia stand to benefit since a majority of these university offer anthropology, history, archaeology, and cultural heritage-related courses. Several of the international cultural heritage nongovernmental organizations based in Kenya including Centre for Heritage Development in Africa (CHDA) and UNESCO can partner with the UCH training institute. Additionally, the National Museums of Kenya's Kenya Heritage Training Institute (KeHTI) based in Mombasa that offers basic cultural heritage courses. Other support facilities include Kenya National Library Services, a government body that has resource centers in all major coastal towns. National Museums of Kenya also operates libraries that, in addition to books, can offer trainees and researchers good and conducive environment to undertake research.

## Management of UCH in Kenya

Kenya and Ghana have initiated an underwater archaeological expedition and legally recognizing the value of underwater cultural heritage[2]. This was during the discovery and excavation of Santo Antonio de Tanna shipwreck in the 1980s. However, after this expedition, no efforts were made to develop underwater archaeology in the country until 2006 when, in a bilateral cooperation with China, two Kenyans were trained (Bita 2014a). With the immense potential of underwater archaeology in Kenya, a new research and heritage management perspective is required. Underwater archaeology training and research will lead the way in the management and preservation of this rich heritage. Legal framework based on international instruments such as UNESCO 2001 Convention on the preservation of underwater cultural heritage and United Nations Convention on the Law of the Sea (UNCOLOS) should guide policy and legislative framework in UCH preservation for posterity in Kenya. In Kenya, National Museums and Heritage Act (NMHA) forms the legal basis for formal protection, conservation, presentation, research, and management of cultural heritage resources. This legal instrument establishes and gives the National Museums of Kenya powers to put in place sound policies for managing cultural heritage in the country. The Act recognizes and provides that any shipwreck more than fifty years old is a declared National monument and therefore protected. In addition, it empowers NMK to undertake UCH Impact Assessments for projects likely to impact on UCH (Republic of Kenya 2006; 2010).

National Museums of Kenya is the custodian of the national heritage in the country. The institution has over the years undertaken underwater archaeological surveys and documented the UCH in Kenya's coastal waters. The museum is also putting in place underwater archaeological programs, has trained two personnel in the field of underwater archaeology, and an underwater artifacts conservation laboratory. Further, the museum has developed a database of the maritime and UCH and coordinates underwater archaeological research in collaboration with local and international institutions. The museum enjoys good rapport with stakeholders and endeavors to stimulate public awareness in the field of maritime cultural heritage both to the general public and in schools.

Recognizing the limited capacity in underwater cultural heritage management in the country, there is need for a collaborative approach of harnessing intellectual and financial resources to address this problem. The Museums embraces collaborative engagement and promotes bilateral and multilateral partnerships with countries that have similar coastal and maritime cultural heritage. These include joint research agreements and partnerships in capacity building/staff trainings. An example is the Sino-Kenya Underwater Archaeological Project that provided training of the first two Kenyan underwater archaeologists, collaboratively carried out the maritime archaeological survey of Kenya coast and partial excavation the Ngomeni Shipwreck (Bita 2011; 2014a; 2014b; 2014c). The National Museums of Kenya close working relationships with her UCH stakeholders such as local communities, universities, Kenya Wildlife Services, Kenya Ports Authority, Kenya Marine and Fisheries Research Institute, Ministry of Fisheries, Tourism, Education has contributed to early successes.

## CHALLENGES IN THE MANAGEMENT OF UCH IN EASTERN AFRICA

Managing underwater cultural heritage resources represents a balance among competing forces and is subject to changing political and financial climates.

Without proper management, the exploitation of marine environments would result into a conflict and endanger resources of which underwater cultural heritage is part thereof. World over, UCH is under serious threat from treasure hunters, development, climate change, and poor management. This is compounded by rapid industrialization and increasing population density as experienced by many countries in Eastern Africa. With each and every development, the environment is impacted either positively or negatively and more often cultural heritage is never spared the impact. This scenario is no different from Kenya where UCH is in real danger from treasure hunters, development, and climate change.

Although Kenya was the first sub-Saharan country to initiate an underwater archaeological expedition, has trained personnel in the field of underwater archaeology, the country is yet to ratify the UNESCO 2001 convention on protection of the underwater cultural heritage. This makes the country miss out on technical, professional as well as financial support from major international sponsors of UCH. Similarly, many legal frameworks in the country, as is the case in many other countries in the region, are yet to be tailored to include underwater archaeology and underwater cultural heritage. Only in one case like Kenya's constitution that recognizes and declares any shipwreck more than fifty years of age as a protected National monument. Underwater archaeology and UCH management is in its infancy in East Africa and as such many museums in the region and cultural heritage agencies are yet to develop UCH management strategies. In Kenya, managing of UCH is challenged by inadequate personnel due to lack of underwater archaeology programs in local universities despite there being archaeology, anthropology and history departments. Lack of a training facility in the region and since underwater archaeology is not an established academic discipline in local universities makes training of underwater archaeologists expensive as the country incurs huge costs taking personnel to Europe, America, China, or Australia. Lack of maritime cultural heritage policies and funds for management programs are also major challenges.

For a long time, National Museums of Kenya has been taking over land, declaring and gazetting land-based historical sites and monuments. However, due to lack of adequate funding and requisite personnel, not much attention goes to the underwater archaeological sites. Amidst this, NMK has been holding onto rich and tourist potential heritage resources. Despite the challenges, Kenya now recognizes UCH and is encouraging relationships and promoting bilateral and multilateral relationships with countries with more highly developed coastal and maritime archaeology management capability. This is anticipated will lead to a demand for underwater archaeology academic programs in the local universities.

## CONCLUSION

Kenya and the Eastern Africa region as a whole have an immense potential of underwater heritage. As such, there is need to embrace new perspectives in UCH management such as research and documentation, public awareness, and enactment of relevant legislations as guided by UNESCO and UNCLOS. The growing public interest in UCH in the region provides great opportunities for building collaborative initiatives for maintenance and preservation of these resources once they are found. This will ultimately lead to greater community support. Development of underwater cultural heritage trails will create direct and indirect employment necessary for sustainable management of these underwater cultural heritage. Training of underwater archaeology personnel is the first-step. Development of underwater archaeology and underwater cultural heritage training institute will build capacities in UCH Management, create demand for underwater archaeology academic that teach effective preservation and management of this invaluable heritage resource for posterity.

## NOTES

1. The author thanks The School of Anthropology and Sociology at Sun Yat Sen University China, Department of Anthropology American University, USA, and National Museums of Kenya.
2. The Ghanaian initiative is led by Christopher DeCorse around El Mina funded by National Geographic Society, editors

## REFERENCES

Bita, C. 2005. *Malindi: A Review of the History of a Coastal Town at the Mouth of River Sabaki, Kenya.* Research Report. Malindi: National Museums of Kenya.

Bita, C. 2008. *The Western Indian Ocean Maritime Heritage: An Overview of the Maritime Archaeological Heritage in Malindi.* Nairobi: British Institute in Eastern Africa.

Bita, C. 2009a. *Intertidal and Foreshore Survey of Pate Island.* Survey Report. Mombasa: Fort Jesus Museum.

Bita, C. 2009b. *Intertidal and Foreshore Archaeology of Mombasa Island: An Inventory of Maritime Sites.* Survey Report. Mombasa: Fort Jesus Museum.

Bita, C. 2010. *Protection of Maritime and Underwater cultural heritage in Kenya.* Paper presented at the International Conference on Maritime Cultural Heritage, Alexandria: Egypt.

Bita, C. 2011. *Underwater archaeological survey in Malindi and Lamu.* Preliminary report, SINO-Kenya Underwater Archaeology project, Research Report. Mombasa: National Museums of Kenya.

Bita, C. 2012. *The Origin of Malindi Town. A Case Study of Mambrui*. M.A. Thesis. Dar es Salaam: University of Dar es Salaam.

Bita, C. 2013a. "Martaban Jars Found in Kenya. *Southeast Asian Ceramics Museum Newsletter.* 7 (1):3.

Bita, C. 2013b. "Ancient Afro-Asia Links: Evidence from a Maritime Perspective." *Journal of Indian Ocean Archaeology* 9, 1–12.

Bita, C. 2014b. *Ngomeni Shipwreck, Report and Future Plans. Underwater Archaeology Project Report*. Mombasa: National Museums of Kenya.

Bita, C. 2014c. *Underwater archaeological survey and excavation of Ngomeni Shipwreck, in Malindi Kenya. SINO-Kenya Underwater* Archaeology Project Research Report. Mombasa: National Museums of Kenya.

Bita, C. 2015a. "The Potential of Underwater Archaeology in Kenya. A Short Communication." In Sila Tripati (ed.), *Shipwrecks Around the World. Revelations of the Past*, pp. 485–510. New Delhi: Delta Book World.

Bita, C. 2015b. "Historical Period Stone Anchors from Mombasa, Kenya: Evidence of Overseas Maritime Trade Contacts with Asia and Middle East." *International Journal of Environment and Geoinformatics* 2(3): 13–24.

Bita, C. 2016 *Heritage Impact Assessment for the Construction of a Retaining Seawall at Fort Jesus World Heritage Site, Mombasa, Kenya*. Nairobi: National Museums of Kenya.

Bita, C. 2018. "Ngomeni Shipwreck: Its discovery and What It Tells Us About the 16th Century Transoceanic Trade." *Kenya Past and Present.* Issue 45. Kenya Museum Society. Nairobi.

Bita, C. and Wanyama, P. 2007. *Preliminary Intertidal and Underwater Archaeological Survey of Lamu archipelago*. Research Report, Mombasa: Fort Jesus Museum.

Bita, C. and Wanyama, P. 2011. *Underwater Archaeological Impact Assessment for the LION 2 (Telkom / Orange) Undersea Fibre Optic Cable*. Mombasa, Kenya.

Boxer, C.R. 1960. *Fort Jesus and Portuguese in Mombasa*. London: British Museum.

Breen, C. and Lane, P. 2003. "Archaeological Approaches to East Africa's Changing Seascapes." *World Archaeology* 35 (3): 469–89.

Casson, Lionel. 1989. *Periplus Maris Erythreai. Text with Introduction, Translation and Commentary*. Princeton: Princeton University Press.

Chalmin, P. 1987. *Trade and Merchants: Panorama of International Commodity Trading*. London: Harwood Academic Publisher.

Chami, F.A. 1994. *The Tanzanian Coast in the First Millennium A.D: An Archaeology of the Iron Working, Farming Communities*. Uppsala: Societas Archaeological Uppsaliensis.

Chami, F.A. 2006. *The Unity of African Ancient History: 3000 BC to 500 AD*. Dar es Salaam: E and D Vision Publishers.

Chami, F.A. 2009. "The *longue Duree* of Zanzibar and the Western Indian Seaboard." In F.A. Chami (ed.), *Zanzibar and the Swahili Coast from c.30 000 Years Ago*, pp 194–222. Dar es Salaam: E & D Vision Publishers.

Chittick, N. 1984. *Manda: Excavations at an Island Port on the Kenya Coast. Memoir No. 9*, Nairobi: British Institute in Eastern Africa.

D'Souza, B.R. 2008. *Harnessing the Trade Winds. Story of the Centuries Old Trade with East Africa Using the Monsoon Winds*. Nairobi: Zand Graphics.

Datoo, B. 1970. "Rhapta. The Location and Importance of East Africa's First Port." *Azania* 5: 65–77.
Duyvendak, J.J.L. 1939. "The True Dates of the Chinese Maritime Expeditions in the Early Fifteenth Century." *T'oung Pao*, Second Series 34(5): 341–413.
Duyvendak, J.J.L. 1949. *China's Discovery of Africa. Lectures Given at the University of London on January 22 and 23, 1947*. London: A. Probsthain.
Forsythe, W., Quinn, R., and Breen, C. 2003. Subtidal Archaeological Investigations in Mombasa's Old Port. In P. Mitchell, A. Haour, and J. Hobart (eds.), *Researching Africa's Past: New Contributions from British Archaeologists*, pp. 133–138. Oxford: Oxbow Books.
Freeman-Grenville, G.S.P. 1975. *The East African Coast: Selected Documents from the First to Earliest Nineteenth Century*. Oxford: Clarendon Press.
Hourani, F.G. 1963. *Arab Seafaring in the Indian Ocean in Ancient and Early Medieval Times*. Beirut: Khayats.
Huntingford, G.W.B. 1980. *The Periplus of Erythraen Sea*. London: Hakluyt Society.
Kirkman, J. 1952. "The Excavations at Kilepwa: An introduction to the Medieval Archaeology of the Kenya Coast." *The Antiquaries Journal* 32: 168–184.
Kirkman, J. 1964. *Men and Monuments on the East African Coast*. London: Lutterworth.
Kirkman, J. 1974. *Fort Jesus: A Portuguese Fortress on the East African Coast*. Oxford: Oxford University Press.
Kusimba, C.M. 1999. *The Rise and Fall of Swahili States*. Walnut Creek: Altamira Press.
Kusimba, C.M. 2004. "The Archaeology of Slavery in East Africa."*African Archaeological Review* 21: 59–88.
Kusimba, C.M. 2017. "The Swahili and Globalization in the Indian Ocean." In Tamar Hodos (ed.), *The Routledge Handbook of Archaeology and Globalization*, pp. 104–122. London: Routledge Handbooks.
Kusimba, C.M. and Kusimba, S.B. 2018. "Mosaics: Rethinking African Connections in Coastal and Hinterland Kenya." In S. Wynne-Jones and A. LaViolette (eds.), *The Swahili World*, pp. 403–418. London: Routledge.
Lynch, M. 1999. "A 17th Century Portuguese East Indian: The *Santo Antonio de Tanna*." *INA Newsletter* 18(2): 1–3.
Martin, E.B. 1973. *A History of Malindi*. Nairobi: East African Literature Bureau.
Martin, E.B. 1975. *The History of Malindi: A Geographical Analysis of an East African Coastal Town from the Portuguese Period to the Present*. Nairobi: East African Literature Bureau.
Martin, E.B. and Martin, C.P. 1978. *Cargoes of the East: The Ports, Trade and Culture of Arabian Seas and Western Indian Ocean*. Nairobi: Elm Tree Books.
Matthew, G. 1963. "The East African Coast Until the Coming of Portuguese." In R. Oliver (ed.), *The History of East Africa*, pp. 94–127. Oxford: Clarendon Press.
Mitchell, Peter. 2005. *African Connections: Archaeological Perspectives on Africa and the Wider World*. Walnut Creek: Altamira.
McConkey, R. and McErlean, T. 2007. "Mombasa Island: A Maritime Perspective." *International Journal of Historical Archaeology* 11(2): 99–121.

Patience, K. 2006. *Shipwrecks and Salvage on the East African Coast*. Dar Akhbar Al Khaleej, Bahrain.

Piercy, R. 1977. "Mombasa Wreck Excavation, Preliminary Report." *International Journal of Nautical Archaeology* 6(4): 331–347.

Piercy, R. 1978. "Mombasa Wreck Excavation, Preliminary Report." *International Journal of Nautical Archaeology* 7(4): 301–319.

Pollard, E. and Bita, C. 2017. "Ship Engravings at Kilepwa Mida Creek, Kenya." *Azania: Archaeological Research in Africa* 52 (2):173–191.

Pollard, E., Bates, R., Bita, C., and Ichumbaki, E. 2016. "Shipwreck Evidence from Kilwa Tanzania." *The International Journal of Nautical Archaeology* 45(2): 352–369.

Prins, A.H.J. 1962. *The Swahili Speaking of Zanzibar and the East Africa Coast*. London: Africa International African Institute.

Republic of Kenya. 2006. *National Museums and Heritage Act*. Nairobi: National Council for Law Reporting.

Republic of Kenya. 2010. *The Constitution of Kenya*. Nairobi: Government Printer.

Rory Q, Forsythe, W., Breen, C., Lane, P. and Lali, A. 2007. "Process –Based Models for Port Evolution and Wreck Site Formation at Mombasa, Kenya." *Journal of Archaeological Science* 34: 1449–1460.

Sassoon, H. 1980. *Mombasa Wreck Excavation*. Interim Report, National Museums of Kenya, Nairobi.

Sheriff, A. 2000. "Coastal Interactions." *Journal of African History* 43: 317–318.

Sheriff, A. 2002. *Slaves, Spices and Ivory in Zanzibar*. Oxford: James Carrey.

Sinamai, A. 2010. *Maritime Archaeology and Transoceanic Trade. A Case Study of the Oranjemund Shipwreck Cargo, Namibia*. New York: Springer Science Business Media.

Souter, C. 1998. "Stone Anchors Near Black Fort, Galle, Sri Lanka." *International Journal of Nautical Archaeology* 27(4): 331–342.

Tripati, S., Sunjaya, G. and Sundaresh. 1998. "Historical Period Stone Anchors from Vijaydurg on the West Coast of India." *Bulletin of the Australasian Institute for Maritime Archaeology* 22: 1–8.

Tripati, S., Sunjaya, G. and Sundaresh. 2003. Anchors from Goa Waters, Central West Coast of India: Remains of Goa's Overseas Trade Contacts with Arabian Countries and Portugal." *Bulletin of the Australasian Institute for Maritime Archaeology* 27: 97–106.

Tripati, S. and Bita, C. 2015. "Historical Period Stone Anchors from Mombasa, Kenya: Evidence of Maritime Contacts with Indian Ocean Countries." *Bulletin of the Australasian Institute for Maritime Archaeology* 39: 84–91.

Vosmer, T. 1999. "Indo-Arabian Stone Anchors in the Western Indian Ocean and Arabian Sea." *Arabian Archaeology and Epigraphy* 10: 248–263.

Whitehouse, David. 2001. "East Africa and the Maritime Trade of the Indian Ocean 800–1500 AD." In B.S. Amenoreti (ed.), *Islam in East Africa, New Sources*, pp. 411–424Rome: Herder.

Wilson, T.H. and Omar, A. L. 1997. "Archaeological Investigations at Pate." *Azania* 32: 31–76.

## Chapter 15

# Opportunities and Challenges of Preserving Cultural Relics in a Globalized World

Zhan Changfa

As ancestral creations, cultural relics bear witness to the fruits of their wisdoms and labors. We there have a responsibility to harness essential ways and means to safeguard these cultural relics because they play an important role in defining who we were as a human community. At the same time, we need bear in mind that in our time, promoting culture in all its forms is not only culturally, intellectually but also economically beneficial. Also, cultural relics tend to be rare, distinctive, and nonrenewable, they have the potential of marketability making it possible to sustainably invest in their management. The global demand for antiquities provides strong evidence for why investment in the protection of cultural heritage include both tangible and intangible heritage is paramount. The gradual rise of heritage tourism also reflects the changing taste in the societies' consumption patterns and appreciation of the past achievements, which is vanishing at such great speed.

Cultural heritage sites bear witness to the artistic, scientific, and technological accomplishments that has accompanied our civilization. They convey the evolution of many aspects of our experiences including how people in particular regions of the world exploited local resources, build enduring bonds with their neighbors and others beyond their region, how they build, maintained, and sustained their ethnic and national identities. In short, cultural heritage plays a huge role in the development of nation, country, and even human civilization. Said another way, our heritage serves as a custodian of our being as humankind and cannot be monopolized by individuals or some groups for their own benefits. Culture belongs to all us! Despite the centrality of cultural heritage in our lives, not everyone appreciates or is aware of the importance of protecting cultural heritage sites. Sites of great significance across the globe continue to be irreversible destroyed. There is a growing awareness on the urgency to protect heritage sites of great significance and meaning. To do this, a series of laws and policies for the protection of heritage sites and antiquities must be promulgated.

In some countries, especially in formerly colonized nations, the losses to local forms of knowledge during periods of colonial rule provides great challenges to heritage managers tasked with formulation of laws and policies. At the same time, there are innumerable obstacles that heritage managers must confront in protecting these heritage sites and landscapes, and objects. Under this background, nations also consider the benefits of cultural heritage protection against the national development agenda. It is under this backdrop that legislations policies are implemented. This chapter discusses the history of cultural heritages management in China in light of the perspective raised here.

## SYSTEM OF SEPARATION OF CULTURAL RELIC PROTECTION AND MARKET ECONOMY.

The protection and management system of cultural relics in China is determined by a national agenda. That agenda generally will be complied by specific administrative department responsible for the protection and management of ethnic cultural heritages. The cultural relic protection and management policy is not determined in any way by market economy.

First, the economic value of a cultural relic is not contained in the definition when laws and policies of cultural heritages and their values are promulgated. The antiquities and monuments law covers three areas of classical history, art, and science. Cultural sensitization campaigns by heritage managers have resulted in a growing awareness and acceptance of the importance of protecting cultural relics since these relics express national traditional cultures and ways of making a living in the past. Intangible cultural heritage sites have also entered into the conversation and laws are being promulgated to protect these sites. Some cultural heritages, without extremely high historic and artistic values, play a crucial role in representing and maintaining local traditional cultures. Some scholars have argued that besides their historic, artistic, and scientific values, cultural heritage sites have cultural and social values. These values have been integrated into the 2015 China Cultural Relics Protection Standards. The rise of internal heritage tourism in China has inspired local governments to initiate economic development programs designed to exploit heritage tourism. There are innumerable examples of such investments across China, where the practice of protecting cultural relics sites has become intimately linked to wealth generation. Despite this reality, the heritage laws of the land, the antiquities laws, do not favor this approach but focus almost exclusively on the significance of a site over its potential the economic value.

The antiquities and monuments law promoted the country's protection and management of cultural heritages without consideration of the social public welfare value and the market economy.

Second, the current cultural relics protection law stipulates that the basic principle of antiquities in China is "protection as essence, rescuing first, rationally using and strengthening management." Thus, the law prioritizes the protection of antiquities and stipulates that the circulation of antiquities should be driven by availability. In 2015, the Legislative Affairs Office of the State Council released the terms of Revised Draft of Cultural Relics Protection Law for public comments. Many senior cultural heritage experts objected to the chapter on "reasonable utilization" that had been added in the revised draft, on grounds that the protection and utilization of sixteen character policy was far from a parallel relationship. They proposed that as a basis of legislation of antiquities protection and management, the law ought to protect antiquities whose use is likely to drive their commercial value at the expense of their historical and cultural values.

There are few provisions on the use of cultural heritages in current fundamental cultural relic legislation, especially the commercial use related to economic value, and they are chiefly restrictive or prohibitive rules. For instance, the antiquities law stipulates that, "state-owned immovable cultural relics must not be transferred or mortgaged and museums, storage facilities, and those state-owned cultural relic protection units classified as tourist sites cannot be managed as assets of enterprises." Privately owned immovable cultural relics must not be transferred or mortgaged to foreigners and when they are transferred, mortgaged, or changed for another purpose, they shall be reported to relevant administrative departments according to their degrade (the twenty-fifth rule). State-owned cultural relic collection units are prohibited from giving, renting, or selling collections to other units or an individual (the forty-fourth rule). Even to ethnic cultural relic collections, the law restricts their range and place of exchange as well. The protection and inheritance of many intangible cultural heritages and intellectual property rights are closely related. However, the protection methods stipulated in the law of Intangible Cultural Heritage is entirely administrative. There is no mention of the problem of intellectual property related to commercial usage.

The new restrictive antiquities laws are aimed to protect China's rich cultural heritages and responsive to old and largely ineffective laws that failed to protect the nations' heritage from suffering a great losses as a result of wartime damage, looting, and sale to foreigners and illegal export outside. Therefore, strengthening the protection and management of antiquities and institutions preventing conservation of national cultural relics and curbing illegal export is a major priority of China's antiquities laws. The success of these new initiatives will depend on state's powerful intervention in the antiquities import and export market by implementing these restrictive provisions. The limitation of cultural relic market circulation, particularly the transnational cultural relic exchange via administrative intervention, is an essential means of preventing the loss and illegal export of antiquities. In this process, people will attach due importance to the historic, social, and cultural values for the nation and state rather than the economic value.

The idea of 'large in size and collective in nature' in the early stage of the socialist system intensified the neglect of privately owned property interests in the process. For another thing, in the period of socialist construction, though under the guidance of "double emphasis and benefits"[1] thought and policy, some important historic sites with outstanding values were not supported by capital and thus suffered neglect. Some of the sites that were deemed of less importance were "sacrificed" in favor of economic development of new China. These resulted in the destructions of a great many sites that had not been protected by the old antiquities laws. Many were looted and their finds sold on the antiquities black market. In some instances, the restrictive laws played a role in stimulating the development of the illicit trade in antiquities.

Thus, because the 1982 antiquities laws failed to address the economic value by separating antiquities protection from market economy, the laws that were meant to protect cultural antiquities and monuments ended up playing a role in their destruction. Today, forty years after the reform of the Chinese economy began, the new antiquities and monuments law passed in 2011 still does not adequately address the economic ramifications of the antiquities. This silence has had the unfortunate consequences of emboldening some local governments to destroy archaeological sites including monuments to create space for modern development investments. Thus, protection of cultural heritage is a long-term undertaking that required requires continuous investment of human, material, financial capital. Emphasizing profit as the modus operandi in decision-making will irreparably harm China's heritage.

One positive development is that despite these problems, effort to safeguard and protect China's rich cultural heritage has continued to expand. The conservation of marine ecosystems, building of museums at major archaeological sites. This has exponentially increased the cost of construction, maintenance, protection, and restoration of these heritage sites. Regions that lack adequate funding from the local governments have borne a huge burden. The antiquities and monuments law also now requires the owners to protect and repair sites, including building that are designated as monuments by the law. The restrictions imposed on private owners of designated monumental building have forced some owners to lose interest in their properties leading to disrepair. The tension between ownership and the government agencies has been continued unabated and need to addressed, including finding ways to fund privately owned monumental structures. Resoling this issue will reassure the public about the value assigned to antiquities and monuments to the national and global community and reaffirm the importance of protecting them.

One way in which antiquities can be enhanced is for museums and other institutions to exhibit them widely instead of confining them to cabinets where they are only accessible to a select few owners, their friends, and scholars. When members of the public know that the cultural objects they finds and donate to the museum and other public institutions will be seen by many, they become more motivated to become better custodians of their heritage. This will required concerted efforts to educate them on the economic and social significance of the culture. The economic value of cultural heritage is inexorably connected to our progress as a nation. Thus, it makes little sense to separate the protection and management of cultural relics from the market economy system. Doing so only creates avenues for illegal trade, illegal export, the destruction of cultural sites caused by developing economy, the irrational use of cultural relics. This kind of "one-size-fits-all solution" is actually detached from reality.

## INCENTIVES AND GUARANTEES OF THE ECONOMIC GAIN

In reality, the preservation of cultural heritage needs the security of economic development. A compromise must be found to ensure a win-win situation between antiquities and monuments protection and economic development. This can be achieved through provision of fund guaranteeing the protection of cultural heritage. Cultural tourism is in great demand, providing an excellent resource for sustainably managing these heritage sites. The rising middle class is increasingly patronizing the local museums and cultural sites and landscapes. This provides the much-needed revenue, creates jobs, and improved allied sectors including arts and crafts and horticulture.

The average expenditure on the protection of monuments in the top five and bottom five provinces is illustrated in table 15.1, below (Blue Book 2017, 299–300).

Although remains unclear whether the expenditure on management of monuments and antiquities is directly proportional to regional economic development grade, nevertheless these data indicate that economic development significantly influences expenditure on monuments. We need to balance public interest and private interest in the protection of cultural relics and to promote public enthusiasm and confidence. Owners of private protected sites and monumental structures should be allowed to rationally use their possessions including for economic gain. Not only can we convert those noneconomic values like culture and art of cultural heritage into economic

Table 15.1 Investment in Antiquities and Monuments by Province in 2016/17 Final Year

| Province | Millions Yuan |
| --- | --- |
| Beijing | 26861 |
| Shanghai | 12414.2 |
| Chongqing | 7093.5 |
| Hainan | 6997.6 |
| Tianjin | 6867.7 |
| Guizhou | 2186.3 |
| Qinghai | 1973.1 |
| Yunnan | 1992.9 |
| Heilongjiang | 1888.8 |
| Tibet | 357.5 |

value to lessen the subjects' burden of possessing or using cultural relics, but we can also stimulate and accelerate their cultural relic protection enthusiasm via stressing the tight connection between subjects and cultural relics. This has been done so successfully in Japan and Taiwan and we can borrow from these models where rural villagers realized economic renaissance and cultural development through investment in cultural tourism.

## CULTURAL HERITAGE AND ECONOMIC CONSTRUCTION

The intertwined relationship between cultural heritage protection and economic development is beneficial to both. It is estimated that museums, sites, and monuments contribute up to 73.25 billion to the national economy up, 2.3 times more than the annual investment in their upkeep. The museum system's direct contribution to the national economic (only be measured by the increasing value of museum industry, since museums open for free overall, and thus their direct economic contribution is weakening) is up to 9.33 billion yuan, which covers 19.5 percent of the museum system's contribution. Two kinds of indirect contributions, the increasing value of building industry driven by the expense of museums' maintenance and the increment augment of museum tourism, are respectively 0.24 billion yuan and 39.99 billion yuan, with respective occupancy of 0.5 percent and 83.5 percent (Blue Book 2017: 49–50). The data above provide powerful evidence that there exists no fundamental opposition and contradiction between cultural heritage and economic development. On the contrary, the cultural heritage can meet the cultural needs of social public while creating opportunities for economic development. In a word, the cultural heritage is beneficial to economic reconstruction.

## SUMMARY AND CONCLUSION

In sum, cultural heritage and economic development are more closely related and mutually reinforcing. The economy must play an important role in protecting cultural heritage. A comprehensive, coordinated, and sustainable concept requiring us to pay more attention to improving mechanisms of interaction need to be become part of the mentality of leadership and the publics. At the same time, we must adopt a scientific and sustainable approach to rationally utilize cultural relics and be attentive to their significance and value in all aspects of contemporary society. This requires that on the basis of grasping the new pattern, we must change the mode of development and rationally make use of cultural relics to unleash their economic potential. I suggest how this could be done below.

First, change the mode of development, take the road of sustainable development, and face the role of culture in sustainable development. As a low-carbon environmental protection and sustainable use of cultural resources, cultural heritage plays an increasingly important role in economic development. Changing power, innovating models, and improving the level are our future efforts. Second, pay attention to the economic value of antiquities and monuments. It is incumbent that we think critically through the perfection of institutional norms and market behaviors related to cultural relics in cultural heritage protection. Third, encourage and guide the use of antiquities and monuments through scientific planning and effective regulation and supervision to prevent their destruction in short-sightedness rush for social and economic benefits that might arise from contemporary economic investments. Fourth, promote economic development with cultural industries to nurture heritage protection. To develop a culture of self-confidence we must rely on cultural heritage and profoundly explore its cultural elements to create high-quality creative products and focus on integrating both their economic and cultural value.

## NOTE

1. The double emphasis and benefits thoughts were proposed during socialist basic destruction period. "Double emphasis" means key excavation and key protection. "Double benefits" means that we should "both benefit basic construction and cultural relic protection" when coordinating with protecting cultural relics in basic construction.

## REFERENCES

CASA. 2017. *The Blue Kook of Cultural Heritage: The Development Report of the Development of Chinese Cultural Heritage* (2016–2017). Beijing: Social Science Literature Press.

*Chapter 16*

# China and East Africa Ancient Ties and Contemporary Flows

## *A Critical Appraisal*

Augustin F. C. Holl

The book *China and East Africa: Ancient Ties and Contemporary Flows* marks the culmination of a new round of archaeological and historical research on the relations between China and Africa, from the origins to the present. American, Chinese, Kenyan, and Tanzanian scholars debated and presented the results of their new and current research at the Lamu Conference that took place in July 27–29, 2017. The amplification of historical scholarship is now bringing back to life very complex and intricate networks of connections that crisscrossed the Indian Ocean and surrounding lands, and linked Africa to East Asia. It all started with the first expansion of humans—*Homo erectus*—around 2–1.8 million ago. Some of these early humans took hold in a handful of places in China and Indonesia. The second expansion, this time of *Homo sapiens*, reached China between 85,000 and 80,000 BP. The expansion of speakers of Austronesian languages, whose ancestral homeland is suggested to be located along southeast coastal China, reached Madagascar in the east flank of Africa in the early centuries of the present era. The diffusion of domesticated plants, like bananas, from New Guinea to South Asia and Africa where phytoliths are dated to the mid-fourth millennium in Uganda and mid-first millennium BCE in southern Cameroon, provide additional evidence on early interactions between Africa and Asia (Denham *et al.* 2003, Holl 2018, Perrier *et al.* 2011). Africa and Asia have always been in constant contact, through land and seas. This book is focused on the Africa side of the China-Africa relations. It explores the different facets of these connections from their earliest manifestations to the present.

## THE RESEARCH FRAMEWORK

### Chinese Presence in Africa

Ongoing research is unearthing more and more evidence of contact between China and Africa (Li 2015). It is not yet known precisely when Chinese goods reached Africa for the first time in the past. Archaeological research, always in progress with sometime challenging results, provides a number of clues. An Austrian expedition excavating in Thebes, at Deir el Madina found the remains of silk in the hair of a thirty- to fifty-years-old female mummy discovered in the burial ground of the kings' workmen. The burial is dated to the Hyksos period, belonging to the Twenty-First dynasty, that is, 1075–945 BCE (Anshan 2005, Lubec *et al* 1993, *Renmin Ribao*—April; 2 1993). The silk industry certainly originated from China where archaeologists "have found textiles in a mysterious tomb dating back nearly 2,500 years in eastern Jiangxi Province, the oldest to be discovered in China's history" (*People's daily* Online, August 26 2007). The silk industry, trade, and consequently the Silk Road are thus much older than thought and probably reached Egypt through Persia. The silk found in the Thebes burial could have been introduced by the Hyksos. Trade and cultural exchanges between China and Egypt were well established during the Han Dynasty (206 BCE–220 CE) (Sun Tang 1979 in Anshan 2005).

Evidence of Chinese material culture has been recorded along the eastern flank of the African continent, from Egypt to Zimbabwe and South Africa, along the coast as well as in the hinterland. Chinese porcelain represented by "Longquan wares, Jingdezhen Qingbai wares, Fujian celadon and Qingbai wares, and blue and white, copper red wares from Jingdezhen were all found in the coast of Kenya . . . Changsha wares were found in Shanga, celadon shards produced in Guangdong found in Shanga and a Fanchang ware made in the 10$^{th}$ century was discovered in Manda" (Anshan 2015, 49).

Numerous coins from different historical periods were also found in different parts of East Africa: "Coins of the Song Dynasty were found by the British in Zanzibar, the Song coins made in the 11th and 12th centuries were found in Mogadishu in 1898. In 1916, Chinese coins were discovered at Mafia island in Tanzania, including one of Song Emperor Shenzong (1068–1085). Qinyuan *Tongbao* of Song Emperor Ningzong (1168–1224) and Shaoding *Tongbao* of Song Emperor Lizong (1205–1264) were discovered in Gede of Kenya. In Kilwa, six coins were found, i. e., one Chunhua *Tongbao*, four Xining *Tongbao* and one Zhenghe *Tongbao*. The most significant discovery is in Kazengwa of Zanzibar in 1945, when 176 coins were found. Among them 108 are of the North-Song Dynasty, 56 of the South-Song Dynasty, four of the Tang Dynasty, and eight not identical. In 1991, the coins of the Song were discovered in Aihdab in the Sudan by a Japanese archeologist, this was the first time for this type of discovery in the region" (Li 2015, 49).

According to Anshan (2005, 60), Du Huan, a Chinese from the Tang Dynasty (618–907 CE) and war captive at Baghdad where he spent several years, visited Africa in the eighth century, sometime around 762 CE. The book he wrote when he returned to Guangzhou, *Jingxingji* (经行记,"Record of My Travels," was lost and is now known only through quotes in other books. It is therefore not known which part of Africa he may have visited, even if Egypt and Northeast Africa appear to have been the most reachable.

In the first half of the fifteenth century, the Ming Dynasty decided to project Chinese naval power all over the Indian Ocean. The Yongle Emperor (1403–1424) appointed Zheng He as the chief admiral of a large fleet—the "Treasure Fleet." The later organized a number of expeditions, seven in total, from 1405 to 1433, generally termed "Zheng Ho travels" (Deng 2005; Dreyer 2006; Ferrand 1919, 1922; Filesi 1970; Levathes 1997; Viviano 2005). The "Treasure Fleet" sailed to the East Africa coast in the fourth voyage (1413–1415), fifth (1416–1419), and sixth (1421–1422), docking at Mogadishu, today in Somalia, Malindi, and Mombasa in today's Kenya. They exchanged Chinese goods for African ones, including live animals like zebras and giraffes. (Prinsloo *et al* 2005, Beaujard 2007). In addition, some of the descendants of Chinese sailors from Admiral Zheng He fleet living in the small island of Pate were interviewed by Kristof (1999) for the *New York Times*.

In summary, there are scattered but significant evidence for the presence of Chinese goods and people in African past. These interactions started in the early first millennium BCE, became more frequent with time through the Han (206 BCE–220 CE), Tang (618–907 CE), Yuan (1271–1368), and Ming (1368–1644) dynasties, peaked in the fifteenth century and were cut short by an imperial ban on foreign trade and naval expeditions.

## African Presence in China

Beyond the presence of surprising animals like the zebra and the giraffe (Chou Ju-Kua 1911; Ferrand 1919; 1922; Filesi 1970; Wheatley 1961; Talib and Samir 1988), a number of Africans, through different indirect channels ended up living in China as early as the first quarter of the eighth century. According to the Chronicle of the T'ang Dynasty, the king of Srinijaya from Palembang in Sumatra offered a Zandj (black) girl, among other things, as tribute to the Emperor in 724 (Talib and Samir 1988, 732; Ferrand 1922). This practice was repeated several times during the next centuries, in 813, 818, and 976 CE. In 813 and 818 CE, the rulers from Kalinga, an Indonesian kingdom, offered several Zandj boys and girls in three successive missions to the T'ang emperor Hsien Tsung. In 976 CE , under the Sung Dynasty, the Imperial court received "a black K'un Lun slave with deep set eyes and black body" (Chou Ju-Kua 1911) from an Arab trader (Talib and Samir 1988, 732)

Although, indirectly and through Arab and Indonesian middlemen, the slave trade reached China, principally through the entry port and distribution hub of Guangzhou. The enslaved Africans were "employed on shipboard to caulk leaky seams below the water-line from the outside as they were expert swimmers who do not close their eyes under water" (Chou Ju-Kua 1911, 31–2; Talib and Samir 1988, 732; Wheatley 1961, 55). Others were gate guards and household servants for the wealthy families in metropolitan areas. According to Chou Ju-Kua (1911, 32), "many families buy black people to make gatekeepers of; they are called *kui-nu*, or 'devil-slaves' or *hei siau ssi* (black slaves or servants)." There is clearly much more research to be done in this direction, if oral histories and archives of ancient Cantonese elite families and landowners can be collected systematically.

The great Moroccan world traveler and explorer Abu Abdullah Muhammad ibn Abdullah Al Lawat Al Tanji Ibn Battuta—Ibn Battuta for short—visited China in the middle of the fourteenth century. He was born on February 24, 1304, at Tangiers and died at Marrakech in 1377. He traveled all over the Ancient world, covered some 120,000 km in twenty-nine years. Ibn Battuta arrived at Guangzhou in China in 1345 (Ibn Battuta 1982). He was particularly interested in local crafts, boat construction, porcelain making, and visited a number of places and towns. He traveled north to Hangzhou, he presented as the largest of the cities he had ever seen. He could not reach Beijing and returned to Guangzhou in 1346 to sail to Sumatra.

It is also claimed that Admiral Zheng He "Treasure Fleet" took some foreign dignitaries back to China to visit and pay homage to the Ming emperors. It is not clear if some Africans from the Swahili city-states of Mogadishu, Malindi, or Mombassa, were involved in this visits. In summary, from as early as the eighth century, Africans were present in Chinese imperial courts and in some wealthy families from southern China.

Available data provide significant evidence on interactions between China and Africa. Discovering additional evidence in new sites is always interesting. It expands knowledge and helps tracing the contours of the overlapping spheres of interaction. It is however more important to investigate and decipher the intimate characteristics of the documented interactions, rigorously assess the precise "factuality" of the documented connections, as well as their economic, social, and political meanings, and their historical implications. These are some of the goals of the contributions assembled in this volume.

## TIES AND FLOWS: THE NARRATIVE THREAD

The concepts of ties and flows are both polysemic. Ties refers to a broad array of connections and flows refers to movement through space and time.

The book narrative is staged in two parts featuring "Ancient Ties" in the part I and "contemporary flows" in part II. The former is made of eleven chapters and the latter of five. The coeditors introduction sets the tone. They clarify the main goal of the conference and the book. It is not only intended to display and describe new discoveries—they are obviously important—but to theorize the China-East Africa relationships in their own terms and analyze early patterns of globalization that developed in the Indian Ocean sphere of interaction. The contributions assembled in part I can be arranged into four thematic categories: (1) initial stages; (2) formation and consolidation of exchange networks; (3) local impact and development; and finally, (4) transferred commodities.

## Initial Stages

As far as Africa-China relationships are concerned, the most ancient ties are clearly those generated by the expansion of early humans. L. De Weyer examines the emergence of early stone tools technologies through a comparative analysis of a sample of African and Chinese Early Stone Age assemblages. The sites under consideration range from 2.2 to 1.4 million years ago. Variability is the dominant characteristic of the reviewed assemblages. Functional imperatives and technological convergences are probably the most parsimonious explanations for the few cases of stone tools similarity.

## Formation and Consolidation of Exchange Networks

The formation and consolidation of local, regional, and long-distance exchange networks are addressed directly in three contributions. E. K. Ndiema's chapter 2 explores the background of the development of the Indian Ocean exchange system linking East Africa to East Asia. The sociocultural conditions for the development of regional and inter-regional trade network are articulated on food acquisition strategies, the emergence of hinterland economic networks, and their connections to their coastal partners. The writer reviews diverse strands of archaeological evidence to flesh out what can be called pre-Swahili regional and extra-regional trade and exchange networks linking East Africa to East Asia. C.M. Kusimba and H. Kiriama, respectively in chapters 3 and 5, look at the time depth and nature of the connections between East Asia and East Africa. The former analyzes different facets of this connection with a special focus on Chinese material culture, essentially pottery, recorded in East African sites. The latter examines the formation of the Indian Ocean Sphere of interaction in the first half of the second millennium CE, considered as initial stages of incipient globalization.

## Local Impact and Development

Four contributions deal with different aspects of local impact and development. J. Monge et al., analyze a sample of burials to craft a cultural and biological profile of ancient coastal Swahili peoples in chapter 4. I. B. Namunaba (chapter 6), and E. Ichumbaki (chapter 7) contributions are area and place specific. They look at the development along a site occupation sequence for the former and the areal deployment of eastern Asian material culture for the latter. The use of East African modern states names—Kenya, Tanzania, and so forth—is however partly misleading and anachronistic. A simple geographic terminology such as Northern, Central, and Southern Swahili Coast would have been preferable. The name Tanzania, for example, a contraption of Tanganyika and Zanzibar, is an astute but modern creation with shallow historical depth.

## Transferred Commodities

Different classes of commodities collected in archaeological contexts transferred from East Asia to East Africa are described and discussed in four successive chapters. C. Kusimba explores the multiple economic and social implications of the presence of Chinese porcelain and examines its provenience in the archaeological record of the ancient city of Mtwapa in chapter 8. The different provenances of Chinese porcelain from the ancient city of Mtwapa are assessed in chapter 9 by T. Zhu and C. Kusimba. M. Wang *et al.* trace the sources of Longquan and imitation Celadon in chapter 10 and finally, G. Oteyo and C. Kusimba analyze patterns of distribution and use of glass beads in chapter 11.

The second part of the book entitled "contemporary flows" deals with present-day relations between China and East Africa. Today, the People's Republic of China is the dominant economic partner of many African countries, particularly in East and South Africa. The flows examined in six contributions are unfortunately one-sided. Xinfeng Li's chapter 11 compares the imperial policy at work during the time of Admiral Zheng He voyages (Ming Dynasty: 1368–1644) and present China Africa diplomacy. Beside the formulaic statements, there are profound differences between the economic and diplomatic systems of these distinct historical periods. A. Kabiru analyzes the determining and expanding influence of China and Chinese in Africa in general and East African countries in particular in chapter 12. From heavy investments in infrastructure and real estate, to students' scholarships, financial services and loans, China's economic might is at full display in East African countries. Chapter 13 focuses on a relatively new commodity, second-hand clothing, that has entered the market, its shares of the China-East Africa trade being on the rise. B. Ma examines the cycles of that commodity, from the collection of unused clothing donated by concerned citizens to charities, bought and processed by merchants, and shipped and sold in Kenya in this case. Marketing strategies and relations with the locals vary, with constant adjustment as an imperative.

The last two chapters deal with cultural heritage issues. C. Bita discusses the high potential of underwater archaeology to identify the range of transportation technology that sustained the formation of early inter-oceanic global networks in chapter 14. Finally, in Chapter 15, Zhan Changfa proceeds to a cost-benefit analysis of the preservation of cultural heritage in an open world. Unfortunately, the heavy reliance on economic costs overshadows the very idea of cultural heritage that in the end appears more like burdens than inspiring opportunities.

## GREAT OPPORTUNITY AND IMPORTANT IMPLICATIONS

This volume offers a great opportunity to correct profound distortions of world economic history. The Indian Ocean sphere of interaction can be traced back a few thousand years. How did the cultural and economic connections and exchanges systems operate from the beginning to the present is a key question to address (Dalton 1968; Polanyi et al. 1957; Renfrew 1975; Rotstein 1970; Sabloff and Lamberg-Karlovsky 1975). The East African side of the equation is addressed directly in this book, with trade and exchange as central focus. These terms are synonymous and can be defined as "the mutual appropriative movements of goods between hands" (Polanyi 1957, 266). Relying on exchange systems spatial manifestations, C. Renfrew (1975, 41) has identified ten trade modes ranging from Direct Access to Port of Trade. Whatever the case however, trade requires personnel, commodities, organization, transportation, and value. There are different organizational forms of economic life and as shown in this book, different patterns of evolution. To frame the analysis of trade in "an evolutionary context is to suggest a departure from a notion of unilineal development that would tend to see earlier economies as miniature replicas or potential versions of our own market economy" (Rotstein 1970, 117). In other words, ancient trade systems are not impoverished forms of our own market economy. They have their own logic, organization, and value systems. K. Polanyi (1957) identified nonmarket trade organizational forms in ancient societies, articulated on reciprocity and redistribution.

Trade can be partitioned into three main classes that are partially or totally applicable to different historical periods (Polanyi 1957; Rotstein 1970). (1) Gift trade; (2) Administered trade; and (3) Market trade. In the gift trade, exchange consists of high-value gifts among elite members of the involved societies. Sociological criteria are determining factors of the value of the exchange goods. There is no required strict equivalence between the exchange items. A precious jewel can be offered in exchange items for a giraffe. There are many known cases of gift exchanges between Chinese and Africans of different ranks and social positions, from emperors to special envoys. Administered trade operates within more or less explicit agreement between trading partners. The value of exchange goods is stable and set by political arrangements. The transactions conducted by Zheng He mariners probably combined gift and administered trade. China wares, porcelain, and Celadon from different workshops were ordered and loaded in ships, and/or sold to Arab, Persian, or Indian middlemen. These commodities were shipped to the west flank of the Indian Ocean and exchanged for African goods. Even if it is not explicit in the book, and as far as Arab, Persian, and Indian traders are concerned, human cargo was certainly part of the "goods" shipped from the East African coast. Slave labor was used in China, particularly in the thriving metropolis of Guangzhou. And finally, market trade applies predominantly in the present-day situations featured in contemporary flows part of the book. Laws of supply and demand operate as price-fixing mechanisms and transaction are more impersonal. Gift and administered trade still operate within the contemporary predominantly market trade, depending on social and political circumstances.

The dense transaction networks that crisscrossed the Indian Ocean and surrounding lands—the continental and the Maritime Silk Roads—from at least the first millennium BCE clearly set the stage for the first globalization. Its attraction was plain and evident in the push of Europeans—Portuguese and Spaniards—to sail to India. The Spaniard with Christopher Columbus sailed West and landed in the Caribbean, at Bariay in Cuba on October 28, 1492, convinced to have reached China. The Portuguese sailed south, with Vasco da Gama reaching Calicut in India on May 20, 1498, firing cannons at Mombasa and making a stop at Malindi to hire a skilled local mariner. The circumnavigation of Africa connected the Indian Ocean sphere of interaction to the Atlantic World, stroke a deadly blow to East African coastal Swahili city-states, and paved the way for centuries of European domination. It is a crucial part of the ancient history of East Africa as the west shore of the Indian Ocean global world that is brought back to life in this volume.

## REFERENCES

Beaujard, P. 2007. East Africa, the Comoros Islands and Madagascar before the Sixteenth Century. *Azania: Archaeological Research in Africa* 42(1):15–35.

Dalton, G. editor. 1968. *Primitive, Archaic and Modern Economies: Essays of Karl Polanyi*. Garden City: Anchor Books

Deng, Gang. 2005. *Chinese Maritime Activities and Socioeconomic Development, c. 2100 BC 1900 AD*. London: Greenwood Press.

Denham, T. P., S. G. Haberle, C. Lentfer, R. Fullagar, J. Field, M. Therin, N. Porch, and B. Winsborough. 2003. Origins of Agriculture at Kuk Swamp in the Highlands of New Guinea. *Science* 301: 189–193.

Dreyer, E. L. 2006. *Zheng He: China and the Oceans in the Early Ming, 1405–1433*. London: Longman.

Ferrand, G. 1919. Les K'ouen-Louen et les anciennes navigations inter-oceaniques dans les mers du sud. *Journal Asiatique* 13: 239–333, 431–492, 14: 5–68, 201–241.

Ferrand, G. 1922. L'Empire Sumatranais de Srivijaya. *Journal Asiatique* 20: 1–104.

Filesi, T. 1970 *China and Africa in the Middle Ages*. London: Frank Cass.

Holl, A. F. C. 2018. Diffusion de l'Agriculture et de l'elevage en Afrique. In J. P. Demoule, D. Garcia and A. Schnapp (eds.), *Une Histoire des Civilisations*, pp. 213–218. Paris: La Decouverte / Inrap.

Ibn, Battûta.1982. *Voyages III. Inde, Extrême-Orient, Espagne and Soudan*. Paris Librairie François Maspero : Collection FM/La Découverte.

Kristof, N. D. 1999. 1492: The Prequel. *The New York Times*, June 6, 1999.

Levathes, L. 1997 *When China Ruled the Seas: The Treasure Fleet of the Dragon Throne, 1405 1433*. Oxford: Oxford University Press.

Li, Anshan. 2005. African Studies in China in the Twentieth Century: A Historical Survey. *African Studies Review* 48(1): 59–87.

Li, Anshan. 2015. Contact Between China and Africa Before Vasco da Gama: Archaeology, Document, and Historiography. *World History Studies* 2(1): 34–59.

Lubec, G., J. Holaubek, C. Feld, B. Lubek, and E. Strouhal. 1993. Use of Silk in Ancient Egypt. *Nature* 362(6415): 25.

*People's Daily*, April 2, 1993.

*People's Daily Online*, August 26, 2007.

Perrier, X., E. De Langhe, M. Donohue, C. Lentfer, L. Vrydaghs, F. Bakry, F. Carreel, I. Hippolyte, J.-P. Horry, C. Jenny, V. Lebot, A.-M. Risterucci, K. Tomekpe, H. Doutrelepont, T. Ball, J. Manwaring, and P. de Maret. 2011. Multidisciplinary Perspectives on Banana (*Musa spp*) Domestication. *Proceedings of the National Academy of Sciences* 108(28): 11311–11318.

Polanyi, K., C. M. Arensburg, and H. W. Pearson, editors. 1957. *Trade and Market in Early Empires: Economies in History and Theory*. Glencoe: Free Press and Falcon Wing Press.

Prinsloo, L. C., N. Wood, M. Loubser, S. M. C. Verryn, and S. Tiley. 2005. Re-Dating of Celadon Shards Excavated on Mapungubwe Hill, a 13th Century Iron Age Site in South Africa, Using Raman spectroscopy, XRF and XRD. *Journal of Raman Spectroscopy* 36 (8): 806 - 816, August.

Renfrew, C. A. 1975. Trade as Action at a Distance: Questions of Integration and Communication. In J.A. Sabloff and C.C. Lamberg-Karlovsky (eds.), *Ancient Civilizations and Trade*, pp. 3–59. Albuquerque: University of New Mexico Press.

Rotstein, A. 1970. Karl Polanyi's Concept of Non-Market Trade. *The Journal of Economic History* 30(1):117–126.

Sabloff, J. A. and C.C. Lamberg-Karlovsky, editors. 1975. *Ancient Civilizations and Trade*. School of American Research Book. Albuquerque. University of New Mexico Press.

Talib, Y. and F. Samir 1988 The African Diaspora in Asia. In M. El Fasi and I. Hrbek (eds.), *General History of Africa III: Africa from the Seventh to the Eleventh Century*, pp. 704–733. Berkeley: University Press.

Viviano, F. 2005. China's Great Armada. *National Geographic* 208 1): 28–53, July.

Wheatley, P. 1961. Geographical Notes on Some Commodities Involved in the Sung Maritime Trade. *Journal of the Malayan Branch of the Royal Asiatic Society* 32(2): 54.

# Index

Abdul Majid Hassan, 174–75
academic scholarships, 193, 211
Africa Economic Zones, 190
African Development Bank, 190, 195, 209
Albaury descendants, 92; Omani Arabs, 92, 241
Ancient Kingdom Mala, 170
Antsiraka Boira, 154
Austronesian, languages, 259
Avic International, 190–91

Bajuni, 91
beads, xi, 27, 36, 40, 41–42, 45, 90–91, 96, 106, 109. 111, 113, 115, 135, 147, 151, 158, 238; carnelian, 41; cowrie shell, 27; glass, xvi, 97–98, 106–8, 113, 115–16, 147–60, 237, 264; jewelry, xi–xii, 36, 40, 42, 45, 51, 130, 191
Beijing Jiaotong University, 193
Belt and Road Initiative, 203–5
Bila kingdom, 169
black-on-yellow, 97
blue and white, 50, 88–84, 97, 126, 260
Borneo king, 173–76
Brava, 109, 169–70, 175, 237
bribes and kickbacks, 198
Bumbuweli, 92

Bungule, 154

Central Bank of Kenya, 189
Chang Rong Light Centre, 192
Chaul, xi, 42, 55, 136, 142, 154, 160
children and juveniles, 67, 70
China-Africa Development Fund, 190, 205
China-Africa Research Initiative, 188
China Development Bank, 190, 205
China Electric Power Equipment and Technology, 189
China House, 199
China Information and Culture Communication Limited, 191
China Road and Bridge Corporation, 187–88
Chinese: admiral Zheng He, xv, 53, 79, 80, 83, 86, 92, 109, 136, 167–84, 237, 239, 261–62, 264, 266; ceramic industry, 127; ceramics, xi–xii, 45–56, 79, 81, 83–85; Chairman Mao Zedong, 178; character, 42, 217; coins (age), xii, 42, 109, 260; colonialism, 207; communist party, CCP, 204; companies, 191; construction firms, 207; debt, 206; descendants, 100; diplomats, 173; documents, 80; domination, 128;

269

exports, 190; families, 216; fleet, 168; geopolitical influence, 195; glass beads, 159; goods, 80, 261; government, 193–94, 201, 204, 216, 218; government scholarships, 193; Guangdong New South Group, 190; imperial courts, 262; imports (ters), 190, 202; influence, 199–200; invaders, 106; investments, 204; language, Mandarin, 192; leadership, 206; Longquan celadon, 135–43; Mandarin, 191–92; market, 191, 203; materials culture, 263; medical systems, 40; middlemen, 202; missions, 237; nationals, 196, 206; naval power, 261; neocolonialism, 181; News Agency, Xinhua, 190; people, 172, 200; porcelain, xvi, 36, 81, 83, 111, 122–24, 130, 264; President Hu Jintao, 171, 179, 182, 205; President Xi Jinping, 203–4; private equity, 205; private sector, 205; racism, 198; recycling, 221; sailors, 173; scholars, 204; shipwreck, 92; sites, 84; society, 215, 222; sources, 42, 85, 236; stoneware, 36; technology, 197; television, CCTV, 194; textile companies, 216; tourists, 193; traders, merchants, businessmen, xvii, 80, 83, 224–26, 230–31; used clothes, xvii, 226, 233; wholesalers, xvii, 229; workmanship, 197–98; Yuan, 216, 220
Chinese porcelain: blue on white ware, 41, 260; Celadon, 48–50, 82–83, 125, 127–29, 134–43, 184, 260, 264, 266; Changsha ware, xvi, 44, 46–47, 82–83, 109, 135–36, 260; copper red ware, 83, 260; Qingbai ware, xii, 44, 48, 55, 83, 142, 260
chronology, 147, 149, 154, 237
chrysanthemum floral, 97
cloth[hing], xi–xii, xvii, 40, 42, 45, 90–91, 135, 142, 215–33, 237, 264–65
cobalt, 49, 127, 155–57, 194

Communication Construction Company, 192
Confucius Institute, 192, 194, 206
copper, 41, 44, 83, 96, 106, 112, 155, 194, 239, 242, 260, 270
corruption, xii, 199, 201, 207
cottage industry, 90–91, 150, 152
cultural exchanges, 180, 260
currency, 82–83, 150, 189, 229
curvilinear, 97

Dadaab, 194
Dapu kiln, 137–41
daub, 71, 95–96, 98, 113–15
diplomatic missions, 168, 194
Djubo, 169–70
dog meat, 200
Dondo, 91–92
Dongguto, 4, 6, 11, 12, 13, 14
donkey, 27, 188–202; domestication and adoption, 27–28; ejiao, 202–3; meat, 202–3; population, 202; shortage, 202; skins, 202; slaughterhouse, 202
Dynasty: Five dynasty, 48, 80; Han dynasty, 260; Ming dynasty, xii, 49, 52, 79–80, 237, 239, 261, 264; North-Song dynasty, 260; Qing dynasty, 44, 46, 50; Song dynasty, 79–80, 260–61; South-Song dynasty, 260; Sui dynasty, 44; Tang dynasty, xv, xvii, 40, 43, 47, 54, 80, 237, 261; Twenty-first dynasty, 81, 260; Yuan dynasty, 46, 49, 53, 80

Early Iron Age, 26, 41, 115
Early Stone Age, 3, 4, 6, 9, 12, 14, 15
Eight principles for economic aid and technical aid to other countries, 177
emperor: Ming emperors, 261; Song Emperor Lizong, 260; Song Emperor Ningzong, 260; Song Emperor Shengzong, 260; Sung dynasty, 261; Tang Emperor Hsien Tsung, 261; The Yongle Emperor [Zhu Di], 53, 174, 176, 180, 261

exchange, ix, xii, xiv, 23, 42, 92, 97–98, 143, 156, 159–60, 172, 190, 221–23, 232, 253–54, 260–61, 266; accounts, 27; commodity, 43, 54, 91, 109, 172, 190; cultural, 180–81; gift, 40, 43, 51, 176; ideas, 86; intertwined, 89; long-distance, 39, 122; networks, 23, 25–30, 79, 39–90, 93–94, 99–100, 263; products, 45; rate, 229; systems, 38, 93, 99, 101, 265; tribute, 174; value, 228
Export-Import Bank of China, 187, 190

Faza, 90, 91, 98–99, 241
Fei Xin, 80, 170
Fejej, 5, 8, 9
Fleet ships, 170
foreigners, 176, 178, 236, 253
Fort Jesus, 50, 81, 101, 154, 240–43, 269
Forum on China-Africa Cooperation, 188, 205

Gedi (Gede), 44, 49, 53, 81, 83, 152, 154, 240, 260
Genocide, 207
Giraffe, 53, 81, 109, 237, 261, 266
Giribawa, 155
giving-more-for-less, 173–75, 177
glass, 29, 36, 41–42, 91, 96, 106; beads, 97–98, 107, 113, 116, 147–60; glass composition, 153; lead glass, 159; M-Na-Al glass, 153–56; v-Na-Al glass, 156–57; v-Na-Ca glass, 157–59; ware, 96, 109, 124
globalization, vii, xii–xiii, 13, 17, 30, 79, 84–86, 110, 121, 141, 215, 233, 263, 266
Global Trade Center, 190
gold, 37, 42, 45, 50, 53–54, 106, 112, 142, 174, 194, 202, 270; coinage, 42, 82
golden era, 53
Gona, 5
Green Linear Motif, 97

Hadar, 5, 8
Hadrami, 92
*Homo*: *Homo erectus*, 259; *Homo sapiens*, 259
Hou Wang Bo Lai, 173
human rights, 195–96, 208
Hyksos, period, 260

imported pottery, 96–98, 100, 108, 241
incense, 44, 49, 91, 237
Indian: coins, xii, 55, 142; commerce, 128; mariners, 42; markets, 27; merchants, 27, 43, 46, 98; middlemen, 266; networks, 113, 142, 156, 159; Ocean, xi, 15, 17, 23, 25–26, 28, 35, 38, 39–40, 42, 45–46, 53, 55, 73, 79–80, 83–87, 89–91, 100, 105–7, 115–16, 122, 160, 170, 204, 228, 235, 236–39, 142, 240–41, 259, 261, 263, 266; patrons, 197; porcelain, 239; potters, 50; pottery, 41, 43, 45, 97, 136; South India, 155; subcontinent, 238; trade, 51; traders, 266
instrumental neutron activation analysis, 147
interactions, 13–14, 17, 26, 28, 30, 36–37, 42, 79, 80, 93, 105, 107–9, 113, 121, 141, 191, 235, 237, 259, 261–62
international crime syndicates, 201
International Criminal Court, 209
internationalism, 177, 181, 183
Islam[ic], xv, 35–36, 38–41, 43, 45–46, 48, 51–52, 66, 81–82, 92–93, 100, 107, 112, 115, 124, 136, 149, 239
ivory, 26, 37, 39, 44, 54, 86, 91, 94–95, 100, 106, 109, 112, 122, 125, 129, 142, 194, 200–201, 238–40, 242

Jumba la Mtwana, 53, 152

Kakuma refugee camps, 194
Kanjera, 5, 7, 8
Kenya Tourist Board, 193
Khambat, xi, 55

Khanfur kilns, 97
kiln (s), xvi, 12, 44, 46–49, 51, 81–84, 99, 123, 125–28, 135–36, 139, 141
Kilwa, 37, 45, 55, 84, 106–10, 112, 115, 142, 147, 240, 260
King Abdul Majid Hassan, 174
Kingdom of Malindi, 168
King Ganlayiyidengben, 171
King Walaidunben, 171
Kizingitini, 91
Koobi Fora, 5, 7, 8

Lamu, 15, 55, 79, 81–84, 90–92, 106, 148, 159, 190, 198, 236–42, 259
laser ablation–inductively coupled plasma–mass spectrometry, LA-ICP-MS, 137–39, 147
littoral, 23, 26, 105
local pottery, 93, 95–96, 99, 100, 114
Lokalalei, 5, 7, 8
Longgupo, 3, 4, 6, 9, 10, 12, 14
Longquan celadon, 127, 135–41, 184, 270

Mafia, 105, 109, 115, 147, 154, 260
Ma Huan, 53, 80, 170, 176
Malin, 169, 171
Malindi, 37, 53, 81, 84, 98, 109, 168, 236–45, 261, 266
Manda, xv, 10, 16, 37, 42, 44–45, 47–48, 53, 55, 65–70, 72–73, 81–82, 89, 97–98, 106, 110, 124, 137–38, 140–60, 242, 260
mangrove, xv, 37, 89–93, 98–99, 109
Maritime Silk Road, 25, 28, 85, 135, 266
Masharifu, 92
masonry, 91, 93
Mbaraki, 152
Mbui, 90, 97, 99
Mbwajumwali, 91
Mcedo Beijing School, 192
metal, 96, 109
Mijikenda, 74, 91

Minor Kollam, 169
Mitumba, 215, 223–33
Mnarani, 44, 49, 53, 152
mode 1, 6, 8
Mogadiscio [Mogadishu, Muqdishu], 37, 42, 44–45, 53, 82, 84, 105, 109, 169, 170, 175, 237, 260–61
mosque [s], 35, 39, 46, 51, 94–95, 110–12, 148–49
Mtwapa, ix, xv, 16, 44, 55, 65, 66–70, 72–73, 123–30, 136–37, 142, 154, 269
Muasya, 154, 197

natural resources, 113, 116, 168, 170, 181, 194, 205
Ndau, 91
NEPAD, 190
Nihewan Basin, 4, 6, 11, 12, 13, 15
Nile Valley, 35

oils, 135
Oldowan, 5, 6, 7, 8, 9, 11, 14
Olduvai, 5, 7, 8, 9, 14
Omani Arabs, 91–92
Omo, 5
Oromo, 91–92, 149

Pate [Pate Island], xv, 37, 54, 82, 89–92, 98–99, 148–49, 237, 239, 241, 245, 261
People's Bank of China, 190
Persian: ceramics, 45; Gulf, xi, 37, 40–41, 48, 55, 80, 82, 86, 109, 142, 204; jewelry, 45; merchants, 42, 46, 137; middlemen, 266; people, 92; potters, 50; traders, 42, 266
poaching, 188, 200–203
Pokomo, 91
polychrome, 50, 97, 153, 155
porcelain, xvi, 27, 36, 40–42, 44–54, 81–82, 97, 109, 111, 121–30, 135–39, 159, 238–40, 260, 264
Portuguese, 37, 43, 81, 83–84, 92, 112, 122, 168, 170, 238–41, 266

potters, 50, 125–27; ancient, 126; Arab, 50; Chinese, 49; European, 49, 50; Indian, 50; Japanese, 50; Persian, 50; Thai, 50
pottery: wheel-drawn, 97
provenance, xvi, 122–23, 130, 138, 156, 264

Rare earth elements (REE), 141
reciprocal communication, 171
Renzidong, 4, 6, 10, 11
rhino [ceros] horn, 37, 44, 54, 84–85, 91, 106, 109, 142, 174, 188, 200

Sanje ya Kati, 109, 147
Saqqaf, 92
Sassanian-Islamic pottery, 93
Sgraffiato pottery, 41, 44, 82, 93, 97, 115–16, 124
Shanga, 47–48, 54, 65–66, 81, 92, 97, 99–100, 142, 149, 159, 237, 239, 260
Shungwaya, 91
Silk, 135, 142, 174, 175
silk fabrics, 170
Silk Road, 260, 266
Silk Road Economic Belt, 203–4
Sino-Africa Centre of Excellence, 199
Sino-African cooperation, 190
Siyu, xi, xv, 54–55, 89–101, 241
Somali refugees, 194
Songo Mnara, 44, 55, 109, 147, 154, 159
spindle whorl, 95
Sri Lanka, xi, 39–40, 47, 55, 122, 142, 155, 240
Standard Gauge Railway, SGR, 187–88
Suna kingdom, 169
survey, 94, 98–100, 112, 170, 199, 237, 244; geophysical, 107–8
Swahili, xv, 14, 173; ancestry, 68–69; burial practices, 66; city-state (s), xv, 25, 84, 89, 100, 262, 266; coast, xv, 72–73, 83–85, 92, 105–6, 108–15, 235–40, 264; complex, 72; culture, 43, 45, 107; dialects, 92; elite homes, 51–52; families, 92; legend, 54; matrilocal, 51; oral traditions, 89–90; origins, 65; peoples, 65–66, 173, 264; polity (ies), 89, 100; residents, 54; settlement (s), 92; ships, 84; sites, 45, 50, 96; social structure, 43; states, 30; tombs, 52; towns, 37, 110, 124; traditions, 115; urbanism, 25; urban residents, xv; word, 223; world, 73, 105, 149

Takwa, 55, 148, 154
Tana Tradition, 97, 99
Tanzania-Zambia Railway, 173, 177
technology, 3, 6, 11
Thika Road Development, 189
Thika Superhighway, 189
timber, 37, 149, 194, 237, 242
titanium, 48, 154
tortoiseshell, 91
trace elements, 137
trade, xi, 37, 47, 79, 93, 98, 121, 142, 150, 172, 176, 190, 210, 206, 215, 265; administered, 266; agent, 225; agreements, 40; ancient, 54, 107, 142–43; bales, 223; between the coast and interior, 27, 29; bidirectional, 106; bilateral, 172, 177; bulk, 42, 45; ceramics, 26, 45–54, 95–96, 100, 107, 123, 130; coequal, 172; commercial, 172; commodities, 89; contacts, 80, 86, 107; cooperation, 172, 180; cross-cultural, 116; ejiao, 203; exchange, 28–29, 93, 97; expansion, 46; fairs, 190; foreign, 80, 135–36, 173, 261; global, 39, 43–45, 123, 236; illicit trade in antiquities, 254; [im]balance, xii, 190, 208; Indian Ocean, 239; inland, 25; interactions, 108; intercontinental, 136; internal, 89; international, xii, 28, 41, 208; interregional, 263; ivory, 210; local, 100; long-distance, 38, 46, 136; maritime, xi, 23, 42, 85, 107, 123;

maritime silk road trade, xvii, 28, 135; market, 266; missions, 40, 43; networks, 23, 29, 40, 94, 100, 115, 123, 136, 156, 172, 263; in obsidian, 26; overland, xii, 46, 123, 143; overseas, 123, 175–76; porcelain, 82–83; prehistoric, 23; premodern, 237; principle, 175; products, 237; regional, xvi, 23, 26, 142, 263; relations, 105; routes, 86; seaward, 143; Sino-African, 207; slave, 168, 262; system, 83; transnational, 223; transoceanic, 38–39, 51, 90–91, 122, 136; transregional, 25; tribute, 175, 177, 184; used cloth, 223
traders, 40, 42–43, 80, 85, 136, 160, 176–77, 202, 219, 223–24, 226, 230, 266
Travel [lers], xv, 42, 79, 80, 90, 107–9, 154, 169, 191, 194, 202, 242, 261–62
Treasure Fleet, 261, 262
Triangular Incised Ware, TIW, 96, 99, 112
Tribute [trade], 169–70, 173–78
Tundwa, 91

Ungwana, 45, 49, 53, 154–55, 239
UN Security Council, 194, 209
uranium, 154
Urdumila, 92

variability, 6, 7, 8, 9, 10, 14, 15

Waata, 91
Wafamau, 92, 100
Wang Jinghong, 172
Waungwana Ngamia, 92
Wen Jiabao, 171, 173, 180, 182
West Ocean navigation, 167–68, 171, 175, 179–81
work permits, 198
World Bank, 189, 195, 205, 207

Xiaochangliang, 4, 6, 11, 12, 13, 14, 15
X-Ray fluorescence, xvi, 123, 125, 138, 143, 147

Zandj boys/girls, 261
Zanzibar, 29, 35, 37, 82–83, 92, 98, 105, 260, 264

# About the Editors and Contributors

**Khalfan Bini Ahmed** is a graduate student of Archaeology and Museology in the School of Sociology and Anthropology at Sun Yat-Sen University. His main research interest is on Chinese ancient ceramics unearthed in East Africa Coast archaeological sites. Mr. Bini's current master's thesis is aimed at determining the provenance of Chinese style ceramics excavated from the archaeological sites of Manda and Mtwapa, in Kenyan Coast.

**Caesar Bita** is the Head, Coastal Archaeology, Fort Jesus Museum, National Museums of Kenya, Mombasa, Kenya. He is an underwater archaeologist and currently codirects underwater and maritime archaeological research in Kenya.

**Zhan Changfa** is a senior researcher at the Chinese Academy of Cultural Heritage and Secretary General of the Cultural Heritage. His area of research is conservation of archaeological monuments. Changfa was the first Chinese citizen to be awarded the Italian Star Knight medal for his contributions in conservation science and cultural heritage.

**Louis De Weyer** teaches Prehistory in Paris Nanterre University and has ongoing research at Lézignan-la-Cèbe, the earliest hominin site in France dated around 1.1 million years ago. His research focuses on the earliest stone tool technologies in the world. He carried out his doctoral research on stone tool technologies in Western Africa, Eastern Africa, Europe, and China.

**Augustin F. C. Holl** is a distinguished university professor and director of the Africa Research center at Xiamen University, Fujian, P. R. China. He has over three decades of research in late Holocene human dynamics in West

Africa including the origins of pastoralism, settled life, and urbanism. His current project at Sine Ngayene in Senegal combines mortuary archaeology, settlement patterns analyses, craft specialization, and bioarchaeology.

**Elgidius B. Ichumbaki** is an archaeologist and Lecturer in Archaeology and Heritage Studies at the University of Dar es Salaam (UDSM), Tanzania. He completed his doctoral degree in 2015, at University of Dar es Salaam Tanzania and Roskilde University, Denmark. His research in archaeology and heritage studies has appeared in numerous journals.

**Angela Kabiru** is a researcher with the National Museums of Kenya where she has worked in the Archaeology Section for twenty years. Her research interests are in the recent archaeology of East Africa, notably during the Holocene. Other research interests include GIS Applications in Archaeology, Landscape Archaeology and Cultural tourism. She has worked in several archaeological sites on the coast of Kenya.

**Chapurukha M. Kusimba** is a professor of Anthropology at American University and Fellow of the American Academy of Arts and Sciences. He has more than two decades of extensive research in anthropological archaeology in East Africa and has published extensively on the archaeology, history, and anthropology of East Africa and the Indian Ocean.

**Wang Min** is a postdoctoral research associate in School of Sociology and Anthropology, Sun Yat-san University. She received her PhD in geochemistry from Guangzhou Institute of Geochemistry, Chinese Academy of Sciences in 2015. Her main research interest is on ancient ceramics with special focus determination of the provenance of Longquan celadon and the uses of cobalt blue pigment in Qinghua produced in Jingdezhen.

**Janet M. Monge** is a curator of skeletal biology at the Penn Museum. She has carried out fieldwork in many locations in Europe, Kenya, and Australia. Her primary interest is in the development of methodologies to study developmental processes in the formation of the human dentition. She has worked on the Swahili skeletal biology since 1997.

**Alan G. Morris** is Professor Emeritus in the Department of Human Biology at the University of Cape Town. He is an elected member of the Academy of Science of South Africa and council member of the Van Riebeeck Society for the Publication of Southern African Historical Documents. He has published extensively on the origin of anatomically modern humans, and the Later Stone Age, Iron Age and Historic populations of Kenya, Malawi, Namibia and South Africa, as well as forensic anthropology. His current research is on ancient DNA in African populations and the history of physical anthropology in South Africa.

**Ibrahim B. Namunaba** is an assistant lecturer of Archaeology at Pwani University, Kenya. His research interest include palaeo-environments, early settlements and urbanism, ancient economies, exchange systems, and subsistence. He regularly publishes his research in regional and international venues on ancient economies and subsistence.

**Emmanuel K Ndiema** is a senior research scientist at the National Museums of Kenya. His research investigates human cultural responses to climatic variability responses during the last 10,000 years. Specifically, the causes and processes of animal domestication, and the spread of managed food production in Eastern Africa. He is involved in different research projects across Africa and works on cultural heritage impact assessment and mitigation and community outreach.

**Sloan Williams** is an associate professor of Anthropology and Department Chair at the University of Illinois at Chicago. She has carried out fieldwork in many locations in South America, the United States, and Kenya. Her primary interest is in the archaeogenetics. She has worked on the Swahili coast and in the hinterland since 2003.

**Xinfeng Li** PhD, is a research fellow and director general of West Asia and Africa Research Institute of the Chinese Academy of Social Sciences, and executive vice-president of China-Africa Institute. As Africa correspondent for the People's Daily, he traveled extensively across Africa and wrote multiple major stories about it. He has published two monographs and dozens of papers on China-Africa relations.

**Tiequan Zhu** (Sun Yat-Sen University, Guangzhou, China) is a professor of Scientific Archaeology specializing in the compositional analysis of Chinese ceramics, which he uses to look at production technology and innovation as a means for understanding local, regional, and global productions histories in ancient China and the global world.

www.ingramcontent.com/pod-product-compliance
Lightning Source LLC
Chambersburg PA
CBHW020111010526
44115CB00008B/782